W9-ACD-224

www.wadsworth.com

wadsworth.com is the World Wide Web site for Wadsworth and is your direct source to dozens of online resources.

At *wadsworth.com* you can find out about supplements, demonstration software, and student resources. You can also send e-mail to many of our authors and preview new publications and exciting new technologies.

wadsworth.com
Changing the way the world learns®

From the Wadsworth Series in Speech Communication

Babbie *The Basics of Social Research*

Babbie *The Practice of Social Research*, Ninth Edition

Barranger *Theatre: A Way of Seeing*, Fourth Edition

Braithwaite/Wood *Cases in Interpersonal Communication: Processes and Problems*

Campbell *The Rhetorical Act*, Second Edition

Campbell/Burkholder *Critiques of Contemporary Rhetoric*, Second Edition

Cragan/Wright *Communication in Small Groups: Theory, Process, Skills*, Fifth Edition

Crannell *Voice and Articulation*, Third Edition

Freeley/Steinberg *Argumentation and Debate: Critical Thinking for Reasoned Decision Making*, Tenth Edition

Govier *A Practical Study of Argument*, Fourth Edition

Hamilton *Essentials of Public Speaking*

Hamilton/Parker *Communicating for Results: A Guide for Business and the Professions*, Sixth Edition

Jaffe *Public Speaking: Concepts and Skills for a Diverse Society*, Third Edition

Kahane/Cavender *Logic and Contemporary Rhetoric: The Use of Reason in Everyday Life*, Eighth Edition

Larson *Persuasion: Reception and Responsibility*, Ninth Edition

Littlejohn *Theories of Human Communication*, Sixth Edition

Lumsden/Lumsden *Communicating with Credibility and Confidence*

Lumsden/Lumsden *Communicating in Groups and Teams: Sharing Leadership*, Third Edition

Miller *Organizational Communication: Approaches and Processes*, Second Edition

Morreale/Spitzberg/Barge *Human Communication: Motivation, Knowledge, and Skills*

Orbe/Harris *Interracial Communication: Theory Into Practice*

Peterson/Stephan/White *The Complete Speaker: An Introduction to Public Speaking*, Third Edition

Rubin/Rubin/Piele *Communication Research: Strategies and Sources*, Fifth Edition

Rybacki/Rybacki *Communication Criticism: Approaches and Genres*

Samovar/Porter *Intercultural Communication: A Reader*, Ninth Edition

Samovar/Porter *Communication Between Cultures*, Fourth Edition

Trenholm/Jensen *Interpersonal Communication*, Fourth Edition

Ulloth/Alderfer *Public Speaking: An Experiential Approach*

Verderber *The Challenge of Effective Speaking*, Eleventh Edition

Verderber *Communicate!*, Ninth Edition

Verderber/Verderber *Inter-Act: Interpersonal Communication Concepts, Skills, and Contexts*, Ninth Edition

Wood *Communication Mosaics: An Introduction to the Field of Communication*, Second Edition

Wood *Communication in Our Lives*, Second Edition

Wood *Communication Theories in Action: An Introduction*, Second Edition

Wood *Gendered Lives: Communication, Gender, and Culture*, Fourth Edition

Wood *Interpersonal Communication: Everyday Encounters*, Second Edition

Wood *Relational Communication: Continuity and Change in Personal Relationships*, Second Edition

Interracial Communication

THEORY INTO PRACTICE

MARK P. ORBE
Western Michigan University

TINA M. HARRIS
University of Georgia

Wadsworth
Thomson Learning™

Australia • Canada • Mexico • Singapore • Spain • United Kingdom • United States

Executive Editor: Deirdre Cavanaugh
Publisher: Clark Baxter
Marketing Manager: Stacey Purviance
Marketing Assistant: Kenneth Baird
Signing Representative: April Lemons
Project Editor: Cathy Linberg
Print Buyer: Mary Noel
Permissions Editor: Susan Walters

Production Service: Delgado Design, Inc.
Copy Editor: Anne Lesser
Cover Designer: Delgado Design, Inc.
Compositor: Delgado Design, Inc.
Printer: Webcom, Ltd.

Printed in Canada

1 2 3 4 5 6 7 04 03 02 01 00

For permission to use material from this text, contact us by
Web: http//www.thomsonrights.com
Fax: 1-800-730-2215 **Phone:** 1-800-730-2214

For more information, contact
Wadsworth/Thomson Learning
10 Davis Drive
Belmont, CA 94002-3098
USA
http://www.wadsworth.com

International Headquarters
Thomson Learning
International Division
290 Harbor Drive, 2nd Floor
Stamford, CT 06902-7477
USA

UK/Europe/Middle East/
South Africa
Thomson Learning
Berkshire House
168-173 High Holborn
London, WC1V 7AA
United Kingdom

Asia
Thomson Learning
60 Albert Street, #15-01
Albert Complex
Singapore 189969

Canada
Nelson Thomson Learning
1120 Birchmount Road
Toronto, Ontario MIK 5G4
Canada

Library of Congress Cataloging-in-Publication Data

Orbe, Mark P.
   Interracial communication : theory into practice / Mark P. Orbe, Tina M. Harris.
      p. cm.
   Includes bibliographical references and index.
   ISBN 0-534-52850-3 (alk. paper)
   1. Pluralism (Social Sciences)—United States.   2. Intercultural communication.
   3. United States—Race relations.   4. United States—Ethnic relations.
   I. Harris, Tina M.   II.Title.

E184.A1 O68 2000

303.48'2—dc21   00-026686

Table of Contents

Part Two

INTERRACIAL COMMUNICATION IN SPECIFIC CONTEXTS   143

Chapter 7

Interracial Friendships   144

Chapter 8

Interracial Romantic Relationships   165

Chapter 9

Interracial Communication in the Context of Organizations   *189*

Chapter 10

Public/Small Group Communication   *215*

Chapter 11

Race/Ethnicity, Interracial Communication, and the Mass Media   *235*

Chapter 12

Moving From the Theoretical to the Practical   263

Preface

The closer we got to completing this book, the more important it became. The saliency of race in our personal and professional lives—either at or below surface level—is undeniable. One single day did not go by where race was not featured in one or more media outlets *and* discussed with family, friends, or colleagues. "Race still defining factor in United States society" read one newspaper headline in October, 1999. Around the same time, national polls indicated that as U.S. Americans anticipated the challenges of the 21st century, race relations were seen as the number one issue that needed to be addressed. President Clinton's "Initiative on Race" increased attention to the importance of (and difficulties in) promoting open, honest dialogue among diverse racial/ethnic group members.

The 1970s witnessed a surge of books on the topic of communication and race: *Transracial Communication* by Arthur Smith (1973), *Interracial Communication* by Andrea Rich (1974), and *Crossing Difference . . . Interracial Communication* (1976) by Jon Blubaugh and Dorthy Pennington. We draw our inspiration from these authors who worked to set a valuable foundation for current work in interracial communication. *Interracial Communication: Theory Into Practice* uses this scholarship, as well as that of countless other scholars and practitioners to provide you with a textbook that focuses on Communication and the Dynamics of Race.

The primary objective of this book is to provide a current, extensive textbook on interracial communication that promotes moving from the theoretical to the practical. We provide a resource to professors teaching an undergraduate course on interracial communication, by focusing our efforts on the ways that existing literature can be applied to everyday interactions. For those teaching a related course (i.e., intercultural communication, race relations, communication and racism, etc,), we provide a substantial component dedicated to the interactions of diverse racial/ethnic groups. We also hope that persons outside of academia will find the book a valuable resource for facilitating interracial dialogue in their respective communities. As clearly demonstrated through current and projected demographic trends, the ability to communicate across racial and ethnic groups will be crucial to personal, social, and professional success in the 21st century.

OVERVIEW

Interracial Communication: Theory Into Practice emphasizes the valuable contribution that communication theory and research can make to improve the existing state of race relations in the United States. The first section of the book provides a foundation for studying interracial communication. Chapter 1 offers an introduction to the subject area and the book. Chapter 2 presents a history of race, an important beginning to understand current race relations. Chapter 3 focuses on the critical role that language plays in interracial communication. In this chapter we highlight the role that power dynamics play in why and how one gets labeled. Chapter 4 features information on how racial/ethnic identity is developed and maintained and how we perceive ourselves and others. In Chapter 5, we discuss how other elements of culture (such as gender, age, socio-economic, and spirituality) also play an important role during interracial interactions. The final chapter in Part One is Chapter 6. This chapter introduces nine different theories that can help you understand interracial communication from a variety of different perspectives. As you will see, each chapter draws heavily from existing scholarship in and outside the field of communication. To complement this information, personal reflections from the authors, case studies, and other opportunities for extended learning are provided in each chapter.

In Part Two, the conceptual foundation provided in Part One is used to understand how interracial communication is played out in a number of contexts. In other words, each chapter presents a specific context where the ideas from Part One can be applied. Chapter 7 focuses on the challenges and rewards of friendships that transcend race. Chapter 8 looks specifically at interracial romantic relationships and offers insight to facilitate a productive discussion on this sometimes "touchy" subject. In the next two chapters, we turn to the situational contexts that are somewhat more formal. In Chapter 9, we discuss the interracial communication that occurs in various organizations. Chapter 10 continues this direction by focusing particularly on public speaking and small group communication. Chapter 11 provides insight to the important role that the mass media play in terms of perceptions of interracial communication. In addition to *Personal Reflections*, *Case Studies* and *Opportunities for Extended Learning* (which feature integrated InfoTrac College Edition exercises), each of these chapters also contains *TIP*

(*Theory Into Practice*) boxes to guide you toward more effective interracial communication. Chapter 12 highlights the primary objective of the book: to make the connection between theory and practice for you explicitly clear and concrete. It also features insight to the importance of facilitating dialogue among diverse racial/ethnic group members.

Note to Our Readers

This book truly represents a labor of love for us. We have attempted to author a book that simultaneously reflects our professional and personal interests in interracial communication. As you read the book, we hope that you come to see our sense of passion for this subject area. Both of us have spent considerable time thinking about race/ethnicity issues, and "doing race" during our daily interactions. We also have spent our academic careers engaging in scholarship that promotes greater understanding of the inextricable relationships between race, culture, and communication. Yet, we hesitate when others identify us as "experts" in this area. While our achievements signify some level of competency, there is so much more to learn that such a label seems hardly appropriate. So, as we begin the 21st century, we invite you to join us in a life journey that promises to be full of challenges AND rewards.

Authoring a book on a topic such as interracial communication is not an easy task. Trying to reach a consensus between all concerned parties (colleagues, editors, authors, reviewers, students, practitioners) was fruitless. Some agreed on *what* topics should be covered, but disagreements arose in terms of *how* they should be treated and *where* they should appear. As you read through the text, you may find yourself agreeing and/or disagreeing with different approaches that we have taken. In fact, we don't believe that there will be any one person who will agree with everything that is included. What we do believe, however, is that the book provides a comprehensive foundation from which dialogue on interracial communication can emerge. In other words, we don't claim to provide "the" answers to effective interracial communication. Instead, we have designed a resource that provides a framework for multiple answers. As the reader, then, you are very much an active participant in this process!

It was our intention to create a book that is "user-friendly" to educators who bring a diverse set of experiences to teaching interracial communication. We have completed this task with specific attention to student feedback from past interracial and intercultural communication classes, most of which indicated a greater need for opportunities for extended learning. Students wished to become more actively engaged in the topics of discussion. In light of this recommendation, and others collected from professors, students, and diversity consultants, we have written a book that is both theoretical and practical. Before you begin reading, there are a couple of things that we would like to draw your attention to:

- Existing research and discussions of interracial communication has given a hypervisibility to European American/African American relations (see Frankenberg, 1993). We have attempted to extend our discussion beyond this particular type of interracial interaction to include insights on Latino/as, Asian Americans, and Native Americans. However, this was not easy because existing research has largely ignored these groups. As scholars broaden their research agendas, we hope that a more balanced coverage of all racial/ethnic groups can be achieved with each edition.

- Different racial/ethnic group members will come to discussions about race and communication with different levels of awareness. They will also come with different levels of power and privilege (see Chapter 3). Regardless of these differences, however, we believe that ALL individuals must be included in discussions on race (see Chapter 1 for guidelines). Throughout the book, we have attempted to strike a tone that is direct and candid, but not "preachy." Our goal is to provide a resource that prepares individuals for a dialogue about race openly and honestly (see Chapter 12). This is not an easy task, but we hope that we were able to negotiate these tensions effectively.

- We have worked hard to address issues that were raised by scholars who reviewed the manuscript in various stages of development. In this regard, we attempted to include some discussion on a large number of topics and focused our attention to those that seemed to be most important. However, we see this first edition of *Interracial Communication: Theory Into Practice* as an ongoing process of discovery. We invite you to contact us with your suggestions, criticisms, and insights.

Mark P. Orbe
Tina M. Harris
http://communication.wadsworth.com

Acknowledgments

Together we have several people to acknowledge for providing crucial support. We are especially indebted to Deirdre Cavanaugh, the executive editor for communication titles at Wadsworth. Although we have expressed our deep appreciation to Deirdre privately, it is important to give voice to our gratitude in more public spaces as well. Forgive us for making this personal—the entire Wadsworth publishing team was fantastic throughout this entire process. However, Deirdre is a special woman who deserves a great deal of credit for our success. Thank you, Deirdre, for sharing our vision from the very start. Thank you for listening to us, and encouraging us to not abandon our voices. Thank you for embracing us as part of the Wadsworth family and highlighting the importance of this book with others. More specifically, we want to thank you for the enthusiasm, sensitivity, respect, love, candor, concern, encouragement, and friendship that marked the cultivation of our relationship. You are truly a blessing to us.

Additionally, we would like to thank the countless number of reviewers who committed their expertise, time, and experience to provide invaluable feedback to us. They are:

Brenda Allen, University of Colorado-Boulder
Harry Amana, University of North Carolina-Chapel Hill
Cecil Blake, Indiana University Northwest
Guo-Ming Chen, University of Rhode Island
Joyce Chen, University of Northern Iowa
Melbourne Cummings, Howard University
Stanley O. Gaines, Jr., Pomona College
Gail A. Hankins, North Carolina State University
Michael Hecht, Pennsylvania State University
Felicia Jordan, Florida State University

Venita Kelley, University of Nebraska-Lincoln
Robert L. Krizek, Saint Louis University
Marilyn J. Matelski, Boston College
Mark Lawrence McPhail, University of Utah
Betty Morris, Holy Names College
Dorthy Pennington, University of Kansas
Laura Perkins, Southern Illinois University-Edwardsville
Pravin Rodrigues, Carroll College
Jim Schnell, Ohio Dominican College
William J. Starosta, Howard University
Nancy Street, Bridgewater State College
Angharad Valdivia, University of Illinois at Urbana-Champaign
Jennifer L. Willis-Rivera, Southern Illinois University; and
Julia T. Wood, University of North Carolina-Chapel Hill

At each stage of production, we were able to benefit from their insights. This book is a much stronger one due to the efforts of many scholars and practitioners across the United States.

Individually, additional acknowledgments should also be made.

Mark: Writing this book was both a professional and personal journey for me. In very real ways, I could not have co-produced such a book without the support, inspiration, and love of lots of folks. In addition to the rewards of working with an anointed co-author, the never-ending blessings that come from my wife, Natalie, played a pivotal role in this process. While many can see her outer beauty, fewer individuals understand just how beautiful she really is . . . and I'm the luckiest one of them all because I get to experience it up close and personal every day of my life! Although they may not understand it, other friends/family members also helped me with this project. Talking on the phone with my brother, Philip, and chatting on-line with my sisters, Laurie and Dawn, helped me stay grounded and avoid "intellectualizing" things. In addition, my best friends, Michele, Damon, and Rex, also helped me to keep it real . . . you will never know how much the laughter we share means to me!

Tina: The process of writing this book has been a phenomenal experience for me. By the grace of God, Mark and I were yoked up to do an awesome work that has been very rewarding in numerous ways. There are several people who supported and encouraged me throughout this endeavor who deserve special thanks. Mom, I continue to thank God for you. Your unwavering love and support let me know you have faith in my work and me. Dad, you have been with me in spirit, and I thank you for our conversations about race that continue to echo in my mind ("How sweet it is!!"). I am thankful for my siblings, Greg, Sonya, and Ken. Each of you encouraged me in your own special way, and for that I am grateful. To Andrea, your support, friendship, and laughter helped me to achieve a goal I often thought was impossible. Your friendship has been a constant source of strength and "comic relief" for me. Thanks for your unwavering confidence in me. To Jennifer, your friendship is invaluable to me. Thank you for your advice and support over this year. You are truly a godsend. Thanks to all the other family members and friends who have supported me on this journey. I love you and thank God for blessing me with such wonderful family.

—Professors Mark P. Orbe and Tina M. Harris

FOUNDATIONS FOR INTERRACIAL COMMUNICATION: THEORY AND PRACTICE

STUDYING INTERRACIAL COMMUNICATION

INTRODUCTION

In 1902, African American historian W. E. B. Du Bois predicted that the primary issue of the 20th century in the United States would be related to the "problem of the color line" (1982, p. xi). From where we stand today his words—written approximately 100 years ago—appear hauntingly accurate. Without question, race relations in the United States continue to be an important issue. But do you think that W. E. B. Du Bois could have anticipated all of the changes that have occurred in the last century? Take a minute to reflect on some of these events and how they have changed the nature of the United States: Land expansion and population shifts westward. The Great Depression. World wars. The Cold War. Civil rights movements. Race riots. Immigrant and migration patterns. Technological advances. A competitive global economy. This list is hardly conclusive, but it does highlight some of the major events and developments that the United States experienced during the 20th century. Clearly, the world that existed in 1902 when W. E. B. Du Bois wrote his now famous prediction is drastically different. Yet "the problem of the color line" (or, in other words, racial/ethnic divisions) still remains a difficult issue in the United States.

The basic premise of this book is that the field of communication, as well as other related disciplines, has much to offer us in working through the racial and ethnic differences that hinder effective communication. Although it is difficult to predict what the 21st century will hold for the future of the United States, in order to live up to the ideals on which it was founded, the nation must confront the various issues related to race. U.S. Americans from all racial and ethnic groups must learn how to communicate effectively with one another. During the early to mid-1970s, several books emerged that dealt specifically with the subject of interracial communication (Blubaugh & Pennington, 1976; Rich, 1974; Smith, 1973). These resources were valuable in setting a foundation for the study of interracial communication (see Chapter 6). Given the significant societal changes and scholarly advances in the communication discipline, however, their usefulness for addressing race relations in the 21st century is somewhat limited. Our intention is to honor these scholars, as well as countless others, by creating an up-to-date interracial communication resource guide that provides theoretical understanding and clear direction for application.

Toward this objective, the book is divided into two parts. Part One focuses on providing a foundation for studying interracial communication and includes chapters on the history of race and racial categories, the importance of language, the development of racial and cultural identities, and various theoretical approaches. In Part Two, we use this foundation of information to understand how interracial communication is played out in a number of contexts (friendship and romantic relationships, organizations, public and group settings, and the mass media). The final chapter in Part Two (Chapter 12) makes the connection between theory and practice explicit, especially as it relates to the future of race relations in the United States.

In this opening chapter, we provide a general introduction to the topic of interracial communication. First, we offer a specific definition of interracial communication, followed by a clear rationale of why studying this area is important. Next, we explain the concept of racial standpoints and encourage you to acknowledge how social positioning affects perceptions of self and others. Finally, we provide some practical insight into how instructors and students can create a positive, productive climate for discussions on issues related to race. Specifically, we advocate for cultivating a sense of community among discussion participants and suggest several possible guidelines toward this objective.

Two important points should be made before you read any further. First, we initially authored this book to be used in intercultural and interracial communication classes at the undergraduate level. As our vision for the book developed, we realized it could be a valuable resource in any number of courses including those in sociology, psychology, ethnic studies, and education (both undergraduate and graduate). In addition, we hope *Interracial Communication: Theory Into Practice* will be useful for individuals and groups outside the university setting who are interested in promoting more effective race relations in the United States. Much of our focus in highlighting how communication theory and research is applicable to everyday life interactions occurs within the context of a classroom setting. However, in our minds, *a classroom is any place where continued learning/teaching can occur.* In this regard, the principles shared in this book can apply to community-based groups, formal study circles, as well as long-distance learning and other types of learning that occur through the cyberspace community. In a very real sense, the world is a classroom, and we hope this book is a valuable resource for those committed to using effective communication practices to improve the relationships between and within different racial/ethnic groups.

Second, we acknowledge the power of language, and therefore we have been careful about using specific terms and labels. Chapter 3 focuses on the importance of language in interracial communication and discusses why we use certain racial and ethnic labels over other alternatives. We think it is vital that you can understand why labels are important beyond issues of so-called political correctness. Both scholarly and personal evidence clearly shows that in most cases one universally accepted label for any specific racial or ethnic group does not exist. So, in these cases, we have chosen labels that are parallel across racial and ethnic groups (e.g., Asian American, African American, European American, Latino/a American, and Native American). In addition, we have decided to use both racial and ethnic markers (instead of focusing on race alone). This decision may initially seem odd, given that this is a book on interracial, not interethnic, communication. But according to most scientific information on race—including how the U.S. government currently defines it—Latino/a Americans (Hispanics) represent an ethnic group with members that cut across different racial groups. Thus, in order to include "interracial" communication that involves Latino/a Americans and other "racial" groups, we consciously use descriptors such as "race/ethnicity" or "race and ethnicity."

DEFINING INTERRACIAL COMMUNICATION

Early writings on *interracial communication* defined it specifically as communication between Whites and non-Whites (Rich, 1974) or more generally as communication between people of different racial groups within the same nation-state (Blubaugh & Pennington, 1976). Interracial communication was distinguished from other types of communication. *Interpersonal communication* traditionally refers to interactions between two regardless of similarities or differences in race people; the term is often synonymous with *intraracial communication*. *International communication* refers to communication between nations, frequently engaged through representatives of those nations (Rich, 1974). *Intercultural communication* was used specifically to refer to situations in which people of different cultures (nations) communicated. *Interethnic communication*, sometimes used interchangeably with interracial communication, referred to communication between two people from different ethnic groups. Some scholars use this term to expose the myths of racial categories (Orbe, 1995a) (see Chapter 2). Others use interethnic communication to illustrate the differences between race and ethnicity and highlight how interethnic communication could also be interracial communication (e.g., interactions between a Japanese American and Filipino American or between a German American and French American).

Over time, the study of *intercultural communication* has gained a prominent place within the communication discipline. It also has emerged as an umbrella term to include all aspects of communication that involve cultural differences. Currently, this includes researching interactions affected by age, race/ethnicity, abilities, sex, national origin, and/or religion. Interracial communication, then, is typically seen as one subset of many forms of intercultural communication. We believe this framework has been a mixed blessing for interracial communication study. On one hand, scholars interested in studying how communication is experienced across racial lines are able to draw from a significant body of existing intercultural research and theory. Because of this, we have a "home" in the discipline complete with various frameworks to use in our research. On the other hand, such a positioning appears to have had a marginalizing effect on interracial communication study. Because intercultural theoretical frameworks are designed to apply generally to a variety of contexts, they do little to reveal the unique dynamics of any one type of intercultural communication. In addition, intercultural communication study has become so broad that minimal attention is devoted to any one particular aspect. Teaching a class on intercultural communication is challenging, because most instructors attempt to include materials from various areas of intergroup relations. Thus issues of race are often times covered in insubstantial ways. One of the major points of this book is that interracial communication is such a complex process—similar to, yet different from, intercultural communication—that existing treatment of it as a form of intercultural communication are not adequate.

For our purposes here, we are operating from the following definition of interracial communication: *the transactional process of message exchange between individuals in a situational context where racial difference is perceived as a salient factor by at least one person.* This working definition, like those of other communication scholars (e.g., Giles, Mulac, Bradac, & Johnson, 1987; Tajfel, 1974, 1978), acknowledges that interracial communication can be seen as situated along an inter-personal/intergroup continuum. For instance, can you think of examples of communication that have occurred between two individuals that may be from different racial groups, but whose relationship seems to transcend these differ-ences? If racial differences are not central to the interaction, these individuals' communication may be more interpersonal than interracial. As you will see in Chapter 6, the idea of *transracial communication* (interactions in which members are able to transcend their racial differences) was first generated by Molefi Kete Asante (Smith, 1973). However, the more central role that perceived racial differ-ences play within an interaction-from the perspective of at least one participant-the more intergroup the interaction becomes.

1.1   *Defining Important Concepts*

Because of your interest in the topic, we assume you are familiar with many of the basic ideas central to understanding the interracial communication processes. But we acknowledge the importance of not assuming that everyone is operating from the same definition for certain terms. Therefore, we have defined some basic concepts related to interracial communication as a way to provide a common foundation. Throughout the text, we have included defini-tions whenever we introduce concepts that you may not be familiar with (e.g., discussions of privilege in Chapter 4). As you read each description, think about how it compares to your personal definition. Is it comparable or drasti-cally different? We recognize that differences may occur, but want to make sure you understood how we are conceptualizing these terms. These defini-tions draw from a great body of interdisciplinary work (e.g., Allport, 1958; Hecht, Collier, & Ribeau, 1993; Jones, 1972; Rothenberg, 1992), but not necessarily any one in particular.

Culture: learned and shared values, beliefs, and behaviors common to a particular group of people; culture forges a group's identity and assists in its survival. Race is culture, but a person's culture is more than her or his race.

Race: a largely social—yet powerful—construction of human difference that has been used to classify human beings into separate value-based categories.

Defining Important Concepts (*continued*)

Chapter 2 describes the four groups that make up a dominant racial hierarchy.

Ethnicity: a cultural marker that indicates shared traditions, heritage, and ancestral origins; ethnicity is defined psychologically and historically. Ethnicity is different than race. For instance, your race may be Asian American and your ethnic makeup might be Korean.

Ethnocentrism: belief in the normalcy or rightness of one culture; consciously or unconsciously evaluating other aspects of other cultures by using your own as a standard. All of us operate from within certain levels of ethnocentrism.

Microculture: term used to describe groups (in our case racial/ethnic groups) that are culturally different than those of the majority group (macro-culture). We generally use this term to refer to African, Asian, Latino/a, and Native American cultures instead of *minorities*.

Racial prejudice: inaccurate and/or negative beliefs that espouse or support the superiority of one racial group.

Racial discrimination: acting upon your racial prejudice when communicating with others; all people can have racial prejudice and practice racial discrimination.

Racism: Racial prejudice + societal power = racism. In other words, racism is the systematic subordination of certain racial groups by those groups in power. In the United States, European Americans traditionally have maintained societal power and therefore can practice racism. Because of their relatively lack of institutional power, people of color can practice racial discrimination but not racism.

WHY STUDY INTERRACIAL COMMUNICATION?

For the past couple of decades, several basic arguments have emerged to justify attention to cultural diversity when studying various aspects of human communication. Most of these have related more directly to intercultural communication than interracial communication (e.g., Martin & Nakayama, 1997). Although some of these arguments appear equally applicable to interracial communication, others do not seem to fit the unique dynamics of race relations. Therefore, within the context of these general arguments and more specific ones related to the cultural diversity in the United States (e.g., Chism & Border, 1992), we offer four reasons why the study of interracial communication is important.

First, race continues to be one of the most important issues in the United States. From its inception, U.S. culture has reflected its multiracial population (even though political, legal, and social practices have valued certain racial groups over others). Because the contradiction of the realities of racism and democratic ideals (e.g., equal opportunity), the United States has often downplayed the issue of race. We believe that in order to fulfill the democratic principles on which it is based, the United States must work through the issues related to racial differences. Racial and ethnic diversity is the primary strength of the United States. However, it can also be the country's biggest weakness if we are unwilling to talk honestly and openly. Although calls for advocating a "color-blind society"—one in where racial and ethnic differences are downplayed or ignored—are admirable, they are largely premature for a society that still has unresolved issues with race. Like Rev. Dr. Martin Luther King, Jr., we hope for the day when we will all be judged for the "content of our character" and not the "color of our skin." This ideal, however, can not be realized until we acknowledge and come to understand the significant role that race plays in our interactions with others. Studying interracial communication is a key component in this process.

Second, changing shifts in the racial and ethnic composition of the United States will increase the need for effective interracial communication. For years, we have heard about what the country will look like in the 21st century. Estimates predict that by the year 2025 people of color (that is, African, Latino/a, Asian, and Native Americans) will outnumber European Americans. In addition, non-White Latino/a Americans will pass African Americans as the largest ethnic minority group. Table 1.1 summarizes some "midrange" predictions offered by the U.S. Census Bureau. We can use these numbers as a guide, but note that some have criticized the U.S. government for utilizing practices which underrepresent the size of ethnic minority populations. As the census 2000 numbers become public, more "exact" counts will be known. Nevertheless, the stark reality is that changing shifts in racial and ethnic composition will make interracial communication more likely in every aspect of society (schools, neighborhoods, work, etc.) (Fitch, 1992).

Third, the past, present, and futures of all racial and ethnic groups are interconnected. In tangible and not so tangible ways, our successes (and failures) are inextricably linked. To paraphrase an African proverb, "I am because we are, and we are because I am." Long gone is the general belief that the country is a big melting pot where citizens shed their racial, ethnic, and cultural pasts and become [simply] an "American." Instead, metaphors of a big salad or bowl of gumbo are offered. Within this vision of the United States, cultural groups maintain their racial and ethnic identities, and in doing so, contribute unique aspects of their culture to the larger society. Learning about different racial and ethnic groups is simultaneously exciting, intimidating, interesting, anxiety provoking, and transformative. It can also

TABLE 1.1	CHANGING DEMOGRAPHICS

Statistics From the U.S. Census Bureau		
Racial/Ethnic Group	**Population in 1990**	**Estimated Population in 2050***
European Americans (non-Hispanic)	170.3 million (75%)	202.5 million (53%)
African Americans	30.5 million (12.3%)	62.2 million (16%)
Hispanic/Latino/a Americans	22.4 million (9%)	81 million (21%)
Asian Americans	7.5 million (3%)	41.1 million (11%)
Native Americans	2 million (1%)	5 million (1%)

*Government demographers associated with the U.S. Census Bureau estimate population in 2050 based on the continuance of current trends (fairly low birthrate, slightly increased life expectancy, and similar immigration patterns). The estimates provided represent mid range predictions. In the year 2050, it is projected the United States will have 382 million people (see Parrillo, 1996).

trigger a healthy self-examination of the values, norms, and practices associated with our own racial/ethnic groups. Remember, without this process we can not take advantage of all the benefits that come with being a racially diverse society. To paraphrase Rev. Dr. Martin Luther King, Jr., we can either learn to work together collaboratively or perish individually.

Fourth, and finally, productive race relations are only feasible through effective communication practices. Look to past examples of successful interracial collaboration. We would surmise that at the base of each example lies varying aspects of a productive, positive communication process. This book seeks to highlight the central role that effective communication plays in the future of race relations. We recognize that race relations are an important aspect of study for all nations, not simply the United States. Yet we believe that attempting to discuss interracial communication in a larger (international) context would be counterproductive. Although some similarities obviously exist, each country has a relatively unique history in terms of race. We have chosen to focus on the importance of interracial communication within the United States because that is what we know and where we believe we can have the greatest impact. In short, this book represents a scholarly, social, and personal mission to contribute to interracial understanding. We are not simply reporting on abstract ideas related to communication. We are, in essence, talking about our lived experiences and those of our family, friends, colleagues, and neighbors. Communication theory and research has much to offer in terms of the everyday interactions of racially/ethnically diverse people. Our explicit goal is to advocate for using this body of knowledge to improve race relations in the United States. In other words, we want to practice what we preach and give others a resource so they can do the same.

One last comment about the importance of bringing the issue of race to the forefront of human communication: Given the history of race relations in the United States (see Chapter 2), most people appear more willing to discuss "culture" than "race." Simply put, studying intercultural communication is safer than studying interracial communication. And it is this very point that makes centralizing the issue of race so important for all of us. Race can not be separated from interpersonal or intercultural communication processes. Scholars who study race as part of research in these areas have provided some valuable insights. Nevertheless, we argue that research which does not centralize issues of race can not get at the unique ways that race affects (to some extent) all communication in the United States. Starting here, and continuing throughout the entire book, we hope to increase your awareness as to the various ways that race influences how individuals communicate.

ACKNOWLEDGING RACIAL STANDPOINTS

Despite the historic significance of President Clinton's impeachment trial, many still regard the O.J. Simpson trial as the "trial of the century." One of the major social effects of this trial was that it provided a national spotlight on racial divisions in the United States. Throughout the trial, and subsequent not guilty verdict (criminal trial), media attention focused on the opposing viewpoints of two groups: African Americans (who overwhelmingly believed in Simpson's innocence) and European Americans (who overwhelmingly believed in his guilt). Based on the public polls, the perceptions of these two racial groups could not have been more different. For many U.S. Americans, this phenomenon was shocking. For others, however, it came as little surprise. Similar patterns could be found when public polls compared racial group responses to any number of national issues (e.g., Morganthau, 1995). So how is interracial understanding possible in a society where perceptual differences are seemingly defined through racial group membership? As we illustrate throughout this book, theory offers a valuable foundation from which to foster effective practical skills.

An important starting point for effective interracial communication is to acknowledge that individuals have similar and different vantage points from which they see the world. These vantage points, or standpoints, are the result of a person's field of experience as defined by social group membership (Collins, 1990). Standpoint theories are based on one simple idea: The world looks different depending on your social standing (Allen, 1998). Standpoint theories have largely been used by scholars to understand how women and men come to see the world differently (Harding, 1987, 1991; Hartsock, 1983; Smith, 1987; Wood, 1992). Additionally, standpoint theories have been instrumental in promoting a deeper understanding of

1.2   *Personal Reflections*

As described earlier, one of the important keys to promoting effective interracial communication is the recognition that each of us experiences life from a particular racial standpoint. Because we have asked you to identify your racial standpoint, it is only fair that we also publicly acknowledge our own. This is important because it helps identifies us, the authors of this book. Clearly, our racial standpoints inform our understanding of interracial communication. Therefore, throughout the book, we share our personal experiences through a series of personal reflections. This first reflection serves as an introduction to how I give consciousness to my racial standpoint (see the other personal reflection in this chapter for TMH's racial standpoint).

A central component of my racial standpoint revolves around the fact that I don't fit neatly into any one racial category. My grandfather came to the United States from the Philippines in the early 1900s; the Spanish lineage is clear given our family names (Orbe, Ortega). Some of my mother's relatives reportedly came over on the *Mayflower*. Like many European Americans, her lineage is a mixture of many different European cultures (Swiss, French, English). So, my racial standpoint is informed by the fact that I am biracial and multiethnic. However, it is not that simple. Other factors complicate the particular perspective I bring to discussions of interracial communication.

I am a thirtysomething-old man who was raised in a diverse low-income housing project (predominately African American with significant number of Puerto Ricans) in the Northeast. In this regard, other cultural factors—age, region, socioeconomic status—also inform my racial standpoint. Except what I've seen reproduced through the media, I don't have any specific memory of the civil rights movement. I've always attended predominately African American churches (initially Baptist, but more recently, nondenominational ones) and have always felt apart of different African American communities. For instance, in college, I pledged a predominately Black Greek affiliate organization; these brothers remain my closest friends. My wife also comes from a multiracial lineage (African, European, and Native American); however, she identifies most closely with her Blackness. We have three children who are being raised to embrace strongly all aspects of their racial and ethnic heritage. Over time, they will develop their own unique racial standpoints.

Through these descriptions it should be apparent that my racial standpoint (like yours) is closely tied to age, gender, spirituality, family, sexual

Personal Reflections (*continued*)

orientation, and region. So, what's your story? How are our racial standpoints similar yet different? As we explained earlier, acknowledging and coming to understand self and other racial standpoints are important steps toward effective interracial communication.—MPO

1.3   *Personal Reflections*

In the first section of this textbook, we discussed the importance of history and multiple identities in understanding interracial/interethnic communication. As my coauthor has indicated in his personal reflection, it is important for you, the reader, to understand our racial/cultural standpoints. Here, I will share with you my journey for self-understanding.

By all appearances, I am African American; however, my family history will tell you otherwise. I am in my thirties, and for many years have wondered about the details of my heritage. My father (who passed away in 1996) was in the navy. After I was born in Detroit, Michigan, my family and I lived there for 2 1/2 years until we were stationed in Rota, Spain. For 4 1/2 years, I was immersed in Spanish culture. During the day, both my father and mother worked, and my older brother and sister were in school. Our maid, Milagros (no, we were not rich), kept me during the day, and she taught me how to speak Spanish fluently and all about the rituals of the Spanish people. I felt as if I were a part of the culture.

After living in Spain, we moved from Pensacola, Florida, to Atlanta, Georgia, to be closer to my parents' families. As we moved across the world, it was my age, family status, and interpersonal interactions that shaped who I was. It was not until I was around family and peers with southern dialects, different life experiences, and few interracial/interethnic interactions that I became aware of my racial standpoint. I was accused of "not being Black enough" because I spoke "proper" English. One vivid memory involves being left out of the "best friend game" by my Jewish friend and a Pentecostal European American friend. They both decided that they were each other's friend because they knew each other longer than they knew me. I was the odd person out: Everyone had a best friend except me. I knew immediately that the reason I was not chosen was because of my race/ethnicity.

Variations of the Race Question (*continued*)

My quest for learning about my family's history and realization of how we are socialized to view racial/ethnic groups has challenged me to explore the significance of racial/ethnic identity in a society that values a racial hierarchy. Although we do not have a family tree that shows us where we came from, I do find some peace in knowing a few pieces of the puzzle have been completed. I am aware that both of my grandmothers are of Native American and European descent. However, there is a big puzzle piece that does not complete the picture of who my family and I are. For this very reason I am committed to becoming continually aware of the importance of our multiple identities in an increasingly diverse society.—TMH

how women and men perceive life issues, such as sexual harassment, differently (Doughtery, 1999). The connection between standpoint theories and effective practice is clear (e.g., Swigonski, 1994). Given the assumption that societal groups with varying access to institutional power bases have different standpoints, standpoint theories appear to offer a productive framework to link existing interracial communication theory and research to everyday life applications. In fact, the value of using standpoint theories as a framework for studying race relations has not gone unnoticed by scholars (Smith, 1987; Swigonski, 1994; Wood, 1992).

Standpoint theory is based on the premise that our perceptions of the world around us are largely influenced by social group membership. In other words, our set of life experiences shape—and are shaped by—our membership with different cultural groups like those based on sex, race/ethnicity, sexual orientation, and so on. According to standpoint theorists (Collins, 1986; Haraway, 1988; Hartsock, 1983), life is not experienced the same for all members of any given culture. In explicit and implicit ways, our standpoints affect how we communicate as well as how we perceive the communication of others. Acknowledging the standpoints of different social groups, then, is an important step in effective communication. Part of acknowledging diverse standpoints involves recognizing that different U.S. racial and ethnic group members perceive the world differently based on their experiences living in a largely segregated society. Simply put, racial and ethnic groups share common worldviews based on shared cultural histories and present-day life conditions. The largest differences in racial standpoints, it is reasoned, are between those racial and ethnic groups that have the most and least societal power (Collins, 1990). In the United States, this means Native Americans, African Americans, and Latino/a Americans have more similar racial standpoints. European Americans, in comparison, have had greater access to societal power, which has resulted in dominant group status. Based on the arguments of standpoint theorists (Swigonski, 1994), European Americans and U.S. Americans of color have different—even possibly oppositional—understandings of the world. In other words, they see life drastically differently based on the social standing of their racial/ethnic group membership.

Take, for example, the different perceptions of African Americans and European Americans in terms of O.J. Simpson's innocence. For many African Americans, the trial was being played out within a racist system (police, courts, media) that historically presumes the guilt of African American men despite any real evidence. Their perceptions were grounded in a personal/cultural awareness of countless examples of innocent African American men being arrested and ultimately found guilty (especially those whose alleged offenses involve European American women). Most European Americans, in comparison, do not have these negative perceptions of the police or court systems. Standpoint theory, as explained by Wood (1997), provides a framework for understanding the connection between cultural group membership and interpretations of reality:

> Standpoint logic would suggest that whites are less likely than people of color to recognize the continuing legacy of racism and discrimination and to support affirmative action and other programs to equalize opportunities in education, politics, and business and industry. Because minorities in many societies have suffered historical injustices and persisting consequences of these, they are more likely to perceive and denounce inequities and to see the need for and the justice of programs designed to reduce or eliminate inequality. (p.255)

Understanding how racial standpoints create different worldviews, in this regard, assists in beginning the process toward more effective interracial understanding.

In the past, some scholars have criticized standpoint theories because they focused on the common standpoint of a particular social group while minimizing the diversity within that particular group. For instance, traditionally standpoint theorists have written extensively about the social positioning of women with little attention to how race/ethnicity further complicates group membership (Bell, Orbe, Drummond, & Camara, in press; Collins, 1998). The challenge for us is to use standpoint theories in ways that encourage identifying the commonalities among a particular racial, ethnic group while simultaneously acknowledging internal differences (Wood, 1992). Balancing these two—seeing a person as an individual and seeing him or her as a member of a particular racial/ethnic group—is difficult, but necessary to achieve effective interracial communication. This point is extremely important because it helps us avoid mass generalizations that stereotype all racial and ethnic group members as the same. But, in the same light, standpoint theories give attention to the common aspects generally shared by particular racial and ethnic groups (language systems, perceptions, dress, and so on). As you will see, this point will be invaluable as you learn about the existing interracial communication research that has focused on general communication styles for different groups (e.g., Carbaugh's {1998} finding that Native Americans use silence differently than European Americans when communicating with elders). Although this information is useful in providing a framework for understanding, it can also be counterproductive when assumed to be true for racial group members. Standpoint theories remind us to see the great diversity within racial and ethnic groups based on individual and other cultural elements (e.g., age, education, gender, sexual orientation, socioeconomic status).

According to most standpoint theorists (e.g., Harding, 1991), the marginalized position of U.S. racial/ethnic minorities forces the development of a "double vision" in terms of seeing both sides of interracial communication. Because of this, they can come to understand multiple racial standpoints. How and why do they do this? According to Collins (1986) and others (e.g., Orbe, 1998c), people of color are relative outsiders within the power structures of the United States. In addition to their own racial standpoint, they must develop the ability to see the world from European American standpoints in order to function in dominant societal structures (e.g., a predominately White college or university). Learning the ropes from an outsider's position, some argue, creates a better grasp of that racial standpoint than even insiders can obtain (Frankenberg, 1993). Although this has typically been required for the "mainstream" success of people of color, it can also be true for European Americans who are motivated to understand the perceptions of different racial/ethnic groups. However, standpoint theorists remind us that given the existing power and privilege structures, the levels of reciprocal understanding are hardly equal (Wood, 1997).

Through this brief overview of standpoint theories, you can see why identifying your racial standpoint is an important ingredient for effective interracial communication. Such a move is invaluable because it helps you acknowledge a specific life perspective and recognize its influence on how you perceive the world. In addition, it promotes an understanding that different racial standpoints potentially generate contrasting perceptions of reality. Nevertheless, remember that standpoint theories also require a conscious effort to pay attention to the various standpoints within any one particular racial or ethnic group. In other words, this approach to interracial communication hinges on your abilities to understand the possible commonalties of people who share a common racial group while simultaneously recognizing intra-group differences. Focusing on how racial identity is just one aspect of our multicultural selves, Chapter 5 discusses the cultural diversity *within* different racial and ethnic groups.

1.4   *The Problem With Stereotypes*

According to the literature (e.g., Leonard & Locke, 1993; Waters, 1992) as well as our personal experiences, stereotyping is a major barrier to effective communication. Stereotypes are generally defined as overgeneralizations of group characteristics or behaviors that are applied universally to individuals of those groups (e.g., Allport, 1958). Despite the negative impact that racial stereotypes have on interracial communication (Leonard & Locke, 1993), research suggests that greater exposure to racial group members has positive effects in dispelling stereotypes (Sigelman & Welch, 1993). This line of logic matches what our personal experiences tell us.

It is fairly easy to stereotype racial and ethnic members who belong to groups to which you have little exposure. The greater the number of Mexican Americans you know, for instance, the more difficult it will be for you to accept mass generalizations about this diverse group. However, here is the catch. The way to move beyond stereotyping is to increase authentic communication between racial groups; however, the existence of stereotypes is a significant barrier to authentic communication. Stereotyping others based on race/ethnicity discourages the recognition of the great diversity *within* racial and ethnic groups. Therefore, one key element for effective interracial communication is clear. We must come to terms with the overt and covert stereotypes we have of other racial and ethnic groups, and then continue to seek out opportunities to increase our exposure to different facets of other cultures. It appears that the most effective guideline is to create a balance where people are seen simultaneously both as individuals and as members of larger cultural groups.

SETTING THE STAGE FOR DISCUSSIONS OF RACE

In many interracial contexts—social, professional, family—the issue of race and racism continues to be a taboo topic. Lack of opportunity and high levels of anxiety and uncertainty decrease the likelihood that honest discussions on racial issues will take place. Ironically, such discussions are typically the primary way that anxiety and uncertainty are reduced. Thus a vicious cycle is created. People generally do not have sufficient opportunities to discuss issues related to race outside their largely intraracial network. This leads to unproductive levels of anxiety and uncertainty when any such interracial communication opportunities do arise. And what do these elements typically lead to? Either avoidance of interracial communication altogether or participation in interracial interactions in superficial ways. One of the theories discussed in Chapter 6, anxiety/uncertainty management theory, provides additional insight into the central role that these elements play in interracial communication.

We turn next to the importance of classroom climate in promoting effective interracial communication. Race can be an emotional and personal topic for both students and instructors. A positive, productive classroom climate is therefore, essential to maximizing discussions related to race, racism, and interracial communication. Consider the reflections of Navita Cummings James, a University of South Florida professor who has extensive teaching experiences in the areas of race, racism, and communication:

> Perhaps the most critical step for me is creating a classroom climate where students can learn from each other, develop their critical thinking skills by agreeing and disagreeing with each other, with assigned readings, and even the professor; where students can live with each others' anger, pain, and other emotions and not personally be threatened by it; where they can "let down" their own defenses and begin to explore and better understand other people's lived experiences . . . and where at least some can move away from the stereotypical "us against them" mentality and begin to see potential allies across the racial divide. (James, 1997b, p. 200)

Based on our own teaching philosophies and past experiences teaching about race and racism in our classes, we agree wholeheartedly with these sentiments. Interracial discussions, in and outside of the classroom, that are attempted without a supportive communicative climate can actually do more harm than good. Thus we encourage cultivating a sense of community in the interracial communication classroom.

Building Community in the Classroom

Under ordinary circumstances, there is no such thing as "instant community" (Peck, 1992). We tend to use the label *community* to describe any number of settings (e.g., neighborhoods, colleges, churches). In most instances, these characterizations involve a false use of the word (Orbe & Knox, 1994). A single working definition of community is difficult to pinpoint (Gudykunst & Kim, 1992). Nevertheless, Peck's (1987) writings on what he calls "true community" appear to offer the most productive approach, especially in terms of the interracial communication classroom. He restricts the use of *community* to a "group of individuals who have learned how to communicate honestly with each other" (Peck, 1987, p. 50). Those who are part of a true community have relationships that go deeper than typical interactions that only involve "masks of composure." They also involve a significant level of commitment to "rejoice together, mourn together" and "to delight in each other, make others' conditions our own" (Peck, 1987, p. 50).

Building a sense of community in any classroom is ideal. It appears essential for courses that involve topics related to issues of culture, race, and oppression (Orbe, 1995b). Sometimes it can seem like an impossible task, especially given the time and commitment it takes. Because race continues to be a volatile issue in the United States, studying interracial communication typically involves some tension. The most productive instances of interracial communication, at least initially, work to sustain rather than resolve this tension (Wood, 1993). This involves probing the awkwardness that sometimes comes with learning new perspectives, especially those that appear to conflict a person's existing views. It also includes dealing with a range of emotions—anger, fear, pride, guilt, joy, shame—associated with under- standing your own racial standpoint. Negotiating the tensions that accompany such strong emotions can encourage classroom participants (including both instructors and students) to recognize racial/ethnic differences while also seeing the common- alities among different cultural groups. Julia T. Wood (1993) explains how her philosophy supports this approach:

> Realizing that humans are both alike and different—simultaneously diverse and common—allows us to honor and learn from the complexity of human life . . . I hope to create a productive discomfort that provokes more holistic, inclusive, and ultimately accurate understandings of human communication and human nature. (p. 378)

Cultivating a sense of community in the classroom is facilitated by the instructor, but is the responsibility of each member of the class (Orbe, 1995b). A major aspect of building classroom community involves establishing relationships. According to Palmer (1993), "real learning does not happen until students are brought into relationship with the teacher, with each other, and with the subject" (p. 5). So, how do we go about cultivating a sense of community in interracial communication classes? Peck (1987, 1992) identifies six characteristics of "true community": inclusiveness, commitment, consensus, contemplation, vulnerability, and graceful fighting. As will you see, each of these elements of community contributes to maximizing the potential for interracial communication interactions.

Inclusiveness refers to a general acceptance and appreciation of differences, not as necessarily positive or negative but just as different (Crawley, 1995). First and foremost, "community is and must be inclusive" (Peck, 1992, p. 436). Maintaining ingroup/outgroup status within the interracial communication classroom is counter- productive to cultivating a sense of community (Gudykunst & Kim, 1992). Community members must establish and maintain a sense of inclusiveness.

Commitment involves a strong willingness to coexist and work through any barriers that hinder community development (Peck, 1992). Part of your commitment to community is a faithfulness to work through both the positive and negative experiences associated with the tensions of racial interactions. In other words, being committed to community involves "hang[ing] in there when the going gets rough" (Peck, 1987, p. 62). Typically, it is exactly this sense of commitment that allows people to absorb any differences in racialized standpoints as a healthy means of community development and preservation (Peck, 1987).

Consensus is another important aspect of community. Interracial communities, in the true sense of the word, work through differences in opinions and seek a general agreement or accord among their members. Racial and ethnic differences are not "ignored, denied, hidden, or changed; instead they are celebrated as gifts" (Peck, 1987, p. 62). In every situation, developing a consensus requires acknowledging and processing cultural differences. In the interracial communication classroom, reaching a consensus does not imply forced adherence to majority beliefs. Instead, it involves collaborative efforts to obtain a win-win situation or possibly "agreeing to disagree."

Contemplation is crucial to this process. Individuals are consciously aware of their particular racial standpoint as well as their collective standing as a community. This awareness involves an increased realization of self, others, and how these two interact with the larger external surroundings. Becoming more aware of your multicultural selves is an important component of this process, and Chapters 4 and 5 are designed to facilitate greater self-discovery in this area. Note that the "spirit of community" is not something forever obtained; instead it is repeatedly lost (Peck, 1992, p. 439). Constant reflection of the process toward community is necessary.

For community to develop, individuals must also be willing to discard their "masks of composure" (Gudykunst & Kim, 1992, p. 262) and expose their inner selves to others (Peck, 1987). In other words, a certain degree of *vulnerability* must be assumed. For interracial communication instructors, this means creating a relatively safe place where students are accepted for who they are (Orbe & Knox, 1994). It also involves assuming the risks associated with sharing personal stories related to culture, race/ethnicity, and social oppressions. Vulnerability is contagious (Peck, 1992). Students are more willing to take risks and make themselves vulnerable when they perceive the instructor as personally engaged in the process of building community.

The final characteristic of community, according to Peck (1987, 1992) is *graceful fighting*. As described earlier, tension in the interracial communication classroom is to be expected. Conflict is a natural process inherent to any intergroup setting and should not be avoided, minimized, or disregarded (Hocker & Wilmont, 1995). The notion that "if we can resolve our conflicts then someday we will be able to live together in community" (Peck, 1987, p. 72) is an illusion. A community is built *through* the negotiation (not avoidance) of conflict. But how do we participate in graceful fighting? The next section explores this important question.

Ground Rules for Classroom Discussions

We do not particularly like the term *graceful fighting*, to describe the type of communication that we want to promote during interracial interactions. The word *fighting* has such a negative connotation because it triggers images of nasty disagreements, physical confrontations, or screaming matches. Nevertheless, we do believe that our ideas of a positive, productive interracial communication classroom climate is consistent with what Peck's writings on graceful fighting. In short, we see it as referring to an expectation that agreements and disagreements to be articulated, negotiated, and possibly resolved, productively. One point needs to be raised before outlining the process of creating ground rules for discussion: Some general differences in how different racial/ethnic groups engage in conflict.

A number of general ground rules exist that commonly are adopted to guide effective group discussions. Chances are, based on your experiences with working with different types of groups, you could generate an elaborate list of conversational guidelines. Be open minded. Be an active listener. Use "I" statements when articulating thoughts, emotions, and ideas. Act responsibly and explain why certain things people say are offensive to you. Assume that people are inherently good and always do the best they can with what information they have. Over the years, we have come across a number of lists of ground rules, many of which overlap significantly. In terms of discussion specifically involving issues of race and racism, the best basic list of ground rules comes from James (1997b). As you read each of the following items, think about how it contributes to a productive communication climate. We hope you will see the importance of each ground rule in overcoming some of the potential barriers associated with interracial communication.

1. Remember that reasonable people can and do disagree.
2. Each person deserves respect and deserves to be heard.
3. Tolerance and patience are required of all.
4. Expect to offend and be offended. (Forgive yourself and your classmates in advance.)
5. Respect the courage of some who share things we may find highly objectionable. We may learn the most from their comments.
6. Understand the rules for civil discourse may need to be negotiated on individual, group, and class levels (e.g., gender-linked and race-linked styles of communication may need to be considered explicitly).
7. Acknowledge that all racial/ethnic groups have accomplishments their members can be proud of and misdeeds they should not be proud of (i.e., no racial/ethnic group walks in absolute historical perfection or wickedness).

8. Each person can only be held accountable for what he or she has done. She or he cannot be held accountably for what ancestors or relatives have done.

9. Each person should understand the privileges that he or she has in the United States based on skin color (e.g., Whites and lighter skin people of color) and other social assets such as social class, gender, level of education, and so on.

10. "Equality" between and among discussants should be the relational norm. (Adapted from James, 1997b, pp. 197–198)

Do you agree with each of these ground rules? Why or why not? Consistent with the characteristics of cultivating a sense of community, it is important to recognize that a consensus of all participants must be gained in terms of classroom discussion ground rules. If just one person does not agree with a ground rule, it should not be adopted. Of course, some members may provide convincing arguments that persuade others to adopt certain guidelines. This, however, should not translate into peer pressure or intimidation. Again, after some extended discussion on each ground rule, a consensus needs to be reached or the ground rule is not adopted by the classroom community. Because the dynamics of each community are different, ground rules are likely to be different from group to group. We must also take into consideration the specific situational context (dyadic, small group, open discussion) and communication channel used by the group. For instance, think about the interracial communication occurring on the Internet. Individuals sitting at computer terminals all over the world are interacting via chat rooms and other means without ever seeing the other people and their voices. Given this type of cyberspace interaction, do you think the ground rules for discussions would be the same? Or would they be different because of the absence of face-to-face interaction? One of the Opportunities for Extended Learning at the end of this chapter allows you to explore this idea further.

Another factor that should be recognized when creating ground rules for class discussions is the readiness levels of the participants of the group (including the instructor). In this regard, it is important not to simply adopt the various ground rules that we have generated here. Each community must create a set of communication norms that meet the expectations and competencies for their particular members. In some instances, different groups will be willing and able to incorporate additional guidelines that reflect their deeper understanding of race, racism, and race relations in the United States. For instance, some interracial communication classes may decide to adopt one or more of the following guidelines:

1. Communicate with the assumption that racism, and other forms of oppression, exist in the United States.

2. Agree not to blame ourselves or others for misinformation that we have learned in the past; instead assume a responsibility for not repeating it once we have learned otherwise.

3. Avoid making sweeping generalizations of individuals based solely on their racial/ethnic group membership (e.g., I can't understand why Asian Americans always . . .).
4. Acknowledge the powerful role of the media on the socialization of each community member.
5. Resist placing the extra burden of "racial spokesperson" or "expert" on anyone.
6. Respect, patience, and an appreciation of diverse perspectives is required (Note: Can you see how this guideline is at a different level than number 3 in the more basic list?).

Each of these six examples represents another guideline that your classroom community may want to adopt as they engage in meaningful interracial communication. What other ground rules, relatively unique to your situation, might you also adopt? Once a consensus has been reached on a workable set of guidelines, post them in the class so members have access to them. Over the course of the life of the community, review, reemphasize, challenge, and/or revise your ground rules. As the relational immediacy of the students and instructors increases, so might the need for additional guidelines for classroom discussions. Other rules may no longer seem relevant. The key is to create and maintain a set of communication ground rules that serve to guide your discussions on race and racism.

CONCLUSION

Chapter 1 was designed to introduce you to the study of interracial communication in the United States and outline the importance of cultivating a sense of community to maximize the potential for productive dialogue on topics related to race. Interwoven throughout this chapter are several important assumptions that are central to effective interracial understanding. We summarize them here to facilitate your navigation of future chapters.

The first assumption deals with the history of race. Although race is largely a socially constructed concept, it must be studied because, it is such an important external cue in communication interactions. Race matters in the United States. Ethnic differences may be a more credible marker (scientifically), but people see and react to race differences. Second, relying on racial and ethnic stereotypes when communicating with individual group members is counterproductive. Seeing others as individuals, while maintaining an awareness of general cultural norms, promotes effective interracial communication. The third assumption has to do with honest self-reflection in terms of the social positioning that your particular racial/ethnic group occupies. Acknowledging, and coming to understand, self and other racial standpoints is crucial to effective interracial communication. Fourth, research and theory within the field of communication has significant contributions to make in terms of advocating for productive communication within and across different racial and ethnic groups. And while we do not assume that communication is a cure-all, it does appear to be the primary means to advance race relations in the United States.

OPPORTUNITIES FOR EXTENDED LEARNING

1. Can you think of real-life or hypothetical examples of racist acts? Independently generate a list of three different examples of racism. Then break into groups and share examples. Take special note of those examples that you would not consider racist and explain why. See if the group can ultimately, come to a consensus as to what is, and what is not, racist behavior. It may be helpful, for instance, to differentiate behaviors that reflect prejudice, discrimination, and racism.

2. Some suggest that the key to effective race relations in the 21st century is to become colorblind. Break into intraracial and interracial groups and discuss that feasibility and effectiveness of this guideline. As a whole, does the group believe that transracial communication is possible? Or is race such a prominent feature of identity that it always serves as a central marker during human communication?

3. In an attempt to understand your particular racial standpoint, create a list of statements in response to the question, What does it mean to be _____ (insert racial/ethnic group) in the United States? Once you have compiled your list, share it with others within and outside your racial/ethnic group. What similarities and differences exist? Learning about others' racial standpoints is an excellent way to generate an increased level of understanding your own racial standpoint.

4. In 1997, President Clinton established the President's Advisory Board on Race to coordinate the President's Initiative on Race. One of the major aspects of his efforts was to "promote a national dialogue to confront and work through challenging issues that surround race." By using your *InfoTrac College Edition*, search for different articles that cover how different discussion groups were created in various communities across the United States (Keyword: *Dialogue on race*). Once you have located one or more sources for these real-life examples, use them as a means to understand further how important cultivating a sense of community is to positive, productive interracial dialogue.

5. As indicated within the chapter, guidelines for classroom discussions should reflect the specific dynamics of a particular group. Think about what guidelines might be necessary for computer chat rooms or classes conducted via the

Internet. How might these be similar to, yet different from, more traditional classrooms?

6. One strategy for facilitating discussions relate to race, racism, and communication is to generate a list of propositions and see if the class can reach a consensus in terms of their agreement or disagreement (James, 1997b). First break the class into groups. Then give each group one of the following statements (or create your own), and instruct them to reach a consensus if at all possible.

   a. In the contemporary United States, people of color cannot be racist.

   b. Racism can be unconscious and unintentional.

   c. Many European American men in the United States are currently the victims of reverse discrimination.

   d. All European Americans, because of the privilege in the United States, are inherently racist.

   e. Asian Americans can be racist against other people of color, like African and Latino/a Americans.

History of Race

The presence of race in the United States is like the presence of the air we breathe: something always around us that we use constantly, sometimes without much thought. Have you ever thought about the racial categories that you and others are placed in? Chances are some of you have and others have not. This chapter is designed to give you a brief overview of the concept of race. Tracing the history of the evolution of race and racial classifications is important in identifying the various ways that current designations affect our everyday communication.

The concept of race is a highly complex one, reflected in the great body of literature that deals with issues associated with race. In fact, some might suggest the issue of race is central to nearly every aspect of the national agenda of the United States. Thus we acknowledge that this text is simply an introduction to the various perspectives on race. We have included a number of references that will give you a more in-depth treatment of the issues discussed here. Our hope is that you will take the initiative to do further reading (see Opportunities for Extended Learning at the end of each chapter for some direction).

As evidenced throughout this book, the United States is a country where, in the words of Cornell West (1993), *race matters*. Attempts to promote a deeper understanding of the complexities inherent in interracial communication must begin with an exploration of the idea of race and racial designations.

HISTORY OF RACIAL CLASSIFICATION

The concept of race as we know it did not exist in the ancient world (Snowden, 1970). Over the years, many scholars have examined the emergence of the idea of race and attempted to document the developmental history of racial classifications. Some suggest (e.g., Gosset, 1963) that a French physician, Francois Bernier, was the first to write about the idea of race in 1684. Bernier created a racial categorization scheme that separated groups of people based on two elements: skin color and facial features. The result was the formulation of four racial groups: Europeans, Africans, Orientals, and Lapps (people from northern Scandinavia). Other scholars (e.g., West, 1982) point to the work of Arthur de Gobineau (1816–1882), whose work divided the human race into three types (White, Black, and Yellow), with the White race described as the most superior of the three. But the most influential of all racial classifications, especially as they relate to the ideas of race in contemporary times, was established by Johann Friedrich Blumenbach in the late 1700s. When tracing the history of race, nearly all scholars point to Blumenbach's typology, first created in 1775 and then revised in 1795, as a central force in the creation of racial divisions (Lasker & Tyzzer, 1982; Montagu, 1964, 1997; Spickard, 1992). Because his ideas served as a foundation for much of the subsequent work on race, our coverage of the history of race begins with a focus on his work.

Blumenbach (1752–1840) was a German anatomist and naturalist who had studied under Carolus Linnaeus. In 1758, Linnaeus constructed a system of classification of all living things (Gould, 1994). According to the Linnaean system, all human beings are members of a certain kingdom (Animalia), phylum (Chordata), class (Mammalia), order (Primates), family (*Homihidae*), genus (*Homo*), and species (*sapiens*) (Spickard, 1992). Each level of this pyramidlike typology contains a number of specific subdivisions of the level above. Blumenbach's (1973/1865) work was based on the premise, supplied by Linnaeus, that all human beings belonged to a species known as *Homo sapiens*. His work focused on extending this system down one more level to human *races*, primarily based on geography and observed physical differences. His identification of five distinct races, as well as other fundamental work on race, appeared in the third edition of his book *De Generis Humani Variatate Nativa* (On the Natural Variety of Mankind).

It is important to note that Blumenbach's original text (made available in 1775) recorded only four races based primarily on the "perceived superior beauty" of people from the region of the Caucasus Mountains. Interestingly, these four groups were defined primarily by geography and not presented in the rank order favored by most Europeans (Gould, 1994). Instead the Americanus, describing the native populations of the New World, were listed first. Second were the Europaeus (Caucasians), who included the light-skinned people of Europe and adjacent parts of Asia and Africa. The Asiaticus, or Monogolian variety, were listed third. This grouping included most of the other inhabitants of Asia not covered in the Europaeus category. Finally listed were the Afer (Ethiopian) group, who represented the dark-skinned people of Africa. This initial taxonomy, like the earlier work of Linnaeus, did not imply any inherent form of social hierarchy. Blumenbach is cited as the founder of racial classification, because unlike his predecessors, he purportedly advanced the earlier work by rearranging races along a hierarchical order with Caucasians occupying the most superior position.

In the most simple terms, Blumenbach's 1795 work incorporated an additional ordering mechanism into his classification of race. This one addition would set in motion a series of developments that led to our current state of racial relations. In essence, "he radically changed the geometry of human order from a geographically based model without explicit ranking to a hierarchy of worth . . . [based on] a Caucasian ideal" (Gould, 1994, p. 69). He accomplished this by recognizing one particular group as closest to the created ideal and then characterizing the remaining groups as progressive derivations from this standard. In order to create a symmetrical pyramid, Blumenbach added the Malay classification in 1795. This grouping included the Polynesians and Melanesians of the Pacific, as well as the aborigines of Australia. In his own words, Blumenbach (1973/1865) describes the process of creating a social hierarchy:

> I have allotted the first place to the Caucasian . . . which makes me esteem it the primeval one. This diverges in both directions into two, most remote and very different from each other; on the one side, namely into the Ethiopian, and on the other the Mongolian. The remaining two occupy the intermediate positions between the primeval one and these two extreme varieties; that is the American between the Caucasian and Mongolian; the Malay between the same Caucasian and Ethiopian. (p. 131)

The result was an implied racist ranking of Europeans first, Africans and Asians last, and Malays and Americans between them (see Figure 2.1). Over the years, the implied worth of human races—as indicated by the conventional hierarchy created by Blumenbach—has permeated the various attempts at racial classification. Most systems of classification divide humankind up into at least four groups based primarily on skin color and physical features: Red, Yellow, Black, and White (Native Americans, Asians, Africans, and Europeans respectively). Whether or not brown-skinned peoples are considered a separate race depends on who is doing the categorizing (Lasker & Tyzzer, 1982; Spickard, 1992). Subsequent sections in this chapter explore the biological and social nature of racial classifications, as well as

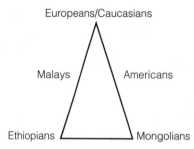

FIGURE 2.1

Blumenbach's Geometry of Human Order (1795)

how these perspectives inform our current perceptions of race and interracial communication. However, before doing so, we need to explore the ways that earlier racial classifications were used in terms of world, national, and local events.

ECONOMIC AND POLITICAL EXPANSION AND RACE

The history of race is intertwined with one of the major themes of the past five centuries of world history: economic and political expansion of European countries (Lasker & Tyzzer, 1982; Tolbert, 1989). As a way to justify their domination of Native populations of land they deemed desirable, Europeans developed and maintained ideologies and belief systems that supported their policies. (At this juncture, it is not productive to label these endeavors as intentionally oppressive or not. The bottom line is that such systems were created and maintained.) In addition, existing racial classifications, and the inherent cultural values associated within a hierarchy of race, served to fuel certain behaviors. Promoting a greater understanding of how race has been used by some as a means of economic and political expansion is an important aspect of the history of race. According to Tolbert (1989), three specific ideologies warrant attention: (1) the idea of a "chosen people," (2) racism, and (3) colonialism.

A Chosen People

The first ideology that helps us understand the role of race in international affairs is a version of the Judeo-Christian concept of a chosen people. This idea appears both in the Hebrew Scriptures and the New Testament. Within this interpretation (Jackson & Tolbert, 1989), Europeans were the race chosen by God. It was their responsibility, therefore, to reclaim the world in his name. One movement related to this idea became known as Manifest Destiny.

It was in the name of Manifest Destiny that Europeans proceeded with their expansion in North America. Although initially embracing Europeans as potential traders, Native peoples faced grave adjustments in the face of a relentless encroachment by these strangers. The principles inherent in a Manifest Destiny clearly clashed with the nearly universal Native American belief that the land was a living entity the Creator had entrusted to them for preservation and protection (Jackson & Tolbert, 1989). Years of wars, disease, and negotiations, including the 1830s national "removal policy," which called for the resettlement to Oklahoma, of all Native Americans living east of the Mississippi, had a devastating impact on America's Native populations. By 1850, for instance, the estimated 12 million Native people in North America at the time of Columbus's arrival had been reduced to 250,000 (Tolbert, 1989). By 1914, the 138 million acres that Native peoples "oversaw" had been reduced to 56 million acres.

Native Americans were not the only people who were engulfed by the Europeans' expansion of the Americas. The U.S. annexation of Texas from Mexico, the U.S. war with Mexico, and the subsequent acquisition of the New Mexico and California territories all were completed under a general charge of Manifest Destiny (Parrillo, 1996). Although Mexicanos were guaranteed, as new U.S. citizens, the protection of basic rights, discrimination and racism were commonplace. During prosperous times, with an urgent need for workers in agriculture, railways, and industry, Mexicans were welcomed by employers. In times of scarcity, however, they have been dismissed as "disposable field hands"—oftentimes without hearings or confirmation of their U.S. citizenship (West, 1982).

Racism

According to Hodge (1989), racism is "the belief in, and practice of, the domination of one social group, identified as a 'race,' over another social group, identified as of another 'race'" (p. 28). To justify their economic and political expansion in the New World, European Americans relied on the perpetuation of racist thinking. This frame of reference had three basic components.

First, they maintained that humankind consists of well-defined races. This basic belief was evident in the ways that diverse ethnic and cultural groups, like those included in the larger groupings known as Native Americans and African Americans, were regarded as similar when contrasted to European American norms. Second was a belief that some races are inherently superior to others. In order to support the idea of a chosen people—one that is superior over other groups—they attempted to prove the inferiority of other racial groups by ignoring the achieved levels of learning, wealth, community, and established spirituality of Native American and African civilizations (see, for example, the work by Toynbee,

1939). Instead, they created and maintained stereotypes that generalized non-Europeans as inherently lazy, evil, savagelike, and irresponsible (Fredrickson, 1971; Jordan, 1969). Third was the belief that the superior race should rule over inferior races, which was viewed as good for both European Americans (who were fulfilling their responsibilities as the so-called chosen people) and other racial groups (who would benefit from the European influences). For example, European Americans believed that Africans had a natural defect which made it nearly impossible for them to function as free women and men. Using this reasoning, slavery was deemed productive in partially civilizing these "savages" and introducing them to a faith by which they could achieve salvation (Tolbert, 1989).

Colonialism

Colonialism is a formal system of domination that removes the power of self-determination from one group and gives it to another. Given the examples provided in earlier sections, it should be relatively clear how colonialism was central to European economic and political expansion. Comments from Paul R. Spickard, an expert on issues of race and ethnicity, offers a nice point of summary for how this works:

> From the point of view of the dominant group, racial distinctions are a necessary tool of dominance. They serve to separate the subordinate people as Other. Putting simple, neat racial labels on dominated peoples—and creating negative myths about the moral qualities of those people-makes it easier for the dominators to ignore individual humanity of their victims. (p. 19)

> Calling various African peoples all one racial group, and associating that group with evil, sin, laziness, bestiality, sexuality, and irresponsibility, made it easier for White slave owners to rationalize holding their fellow humans in bondage, whipping them, selling them, separating their families, and working them to death. (p. 19)

With this foundation in place, the remainder of this chapter discusses race as a biological and/or social construct, and the role of racial classifications in the contemporary Americas.

THE BIOLOGICAL FOUNDATIONS OF RACE

By definition, a race is a "subdivision of a species; it consists of a population that has a different combination of gene frequencies from other populations of the species" (Lasker & Tyzzer, 1982, p. 458). In the 19th century, the popularity of Darwinian theory served as a catalyst for scientists who were attempting to prove the existence of racial differences. Throughout history, the so-called commonsense view of race was based in the idea that at one time a handful of supposedly pure races existed. These subgroups had physical features, blood, gene pools, and character qualities that diverged entirely from one another (Spickard, 1992). Over the years, some racial group members mixed with others outside their racial group, which resulted in some overlapping in racial characteristics. Clear distinctions remain in the identifying markers of each group, however. For instance, popular thought is that most observers can still distinguish a Caucasian type by his or her light skin, blue eyes, fine sandy or light brown hair, high-bridged nose, and thin lips. In contrast, a Negroid type is identified by dark brown skin, brown or black eyes, tightly coiled dark hair, broad flat nose, and thick lips (Diamond, 1994). Similar prototypical classifications could be generated for the Mongoloid and other races.

Over time, the increased number of interracial unions has contributed to a blurring of the distinct boundaries between "pure" races. However, additional problems arise within this commonsense approach when we look at specific examples within each racial category. For instance, Europeans who reside near the Mediterranean have dark, curly hair. The Khoisan peoples of southern Africa have facial features that closely resemble the people in northern Europe (Diamond, 1994). The !Kung San (Bushmen) have epicanthic eye folds, similar to Japanese and Chinese people (Begley, 1995).

Various scientists have engaged in countless studies searching for proof for the biological differences that exist in different racial groups. Some researchers, for example, conducted extensive analyses of geographical differences, only to come away with inconclusive findings. Once blood was ruled out as a possible distinguishing trait, some researchers began to study genetic composition (Spickard, 1992). Others measured body parts—brains, calf muscles, jaws, lips, and noses—in attempts to link the more "inferior" races with apes (Valentine, 1995). In 1965, researchers studied gene clusters and proposed the formulation of hundreds, even thousands, of racial groups (Wright, 1994). Alternative bases for designating racial groups (e.g., by resistance to disease or fingerprints) have also generated a wide variety of equally trivial divisions (Diamond, 1994). Regardless of what was being measured and how, scientists were not able to come up with consistent evidence or proof of biological differences between racial groups (Begley, 1995).

In fact, extensive research indicates that pure races never existed (Lasker & Tyzzer, 1982; Montagu, 1997; Spickard, 1992), and all humankind belongs to the same species, *Homo sapiens*. National, religious, geographic, linguistic, and cultural groups do not necessarily coincide with racial groups. The cultural traits of such groups have no demonstrated genetic connection with racial traits (Montagu, 1972).

According to King (1981), the "genetic variability within populations is greater than the variability between them" (p. 158). In other words, the biggest differences are *within* racial groups, not *between* them. This is not to say that physical features have no connection to geographical and genetic factors (the two primary factors in Blumenbach's work). But it is now understood that the few physical characteristics used to define races account for only a very tiny fraction of a person's total physical being (Tolbert, 1989). The differences that are apparent in different racial groups—but not exclusive to any one racial group—are better understood by considering environmental influences and migrations, as well as genetic factors.

Ashley Montagu (1964, 1997) was one of the first, and clearly the most successful, researcher to make use of scientifically established facts in debunking what he referred to as "man's most dangerous myth." His work has revealed how existing "racial mythologies" have supported countless attempts of "superior races" to prevail over more "inferior" ones. For example, think about the basic premises for slavery, manifest destiny and cheap labor, discussed earlier. In the 20th century, Adolf Hitler and others who believed in the notion of white supremacy have accounted for millions of deaths. A review of current events or even a quick search on the Internet indicates that such beliefs still exist across the United States. All of these ideologies have one characteristic in common: They reflect attempts to foster the advancement of a superior race. In fact, the power of *eugenics* (the idea that intergroup breeding is a desirable mechanism to ensure the existence of superior races) has been used to explain the brilliance of African Americans such as Booker T. Washington, Frederick Douglass, and George Washington Carver. Each man's highly regarded accomplishments, it has been argued, were achieved through the genes inherited from the "white bloodlines" of a European American parent (Spickard, 1992).

As much as existing research has revealed the illogical notion of racial classifications as a means of self-and other identity, most people in the United States continue to use race as a way to distinguish human qualities, potential, and behaviors. Despite a lack of scientific evidence, race continues to be a largely accepted means of categorization. Instead of seeing race as a biological determinant, a more productive way to identify the power of race is to understand it as a sociopolitical construct.

THE SOCIOPOLITICAL CONSTRUCTION OF RACE

In the most basic sense, race cannot be considered a scientific construct if its categories are constantly being changed depending on laws, history, emotions, and politics (Nakashima, 1992; Wilson, 1992). Instead, race is best understood as a product of social, political, and economic dynamics (rather than as a phenomenon based on biology). Through identifying and discussing the various ways that different social, political, national, and regional groups define racial classifications, exactly how political these decisions are becomes readily apparent. We present two primary areas: (1) how racial classifications charged over time (and location) within the Americas, and (2) the varying ways in which biracial or multiracial persons have been classified.

2.1   *Personal Reflections*

For most of us, challenging existing ideologies about race is not easy. Such a process involves letting go of some basic ideas that have been commonly accepted as fact by the larger society. I vividly remember the first time that someone confronted me with the idea that there was only one human race and what we have come to recognize as different racial groups were not, in fact, different races at all. It occurred in the early 1990s during a graduate seminar that I participated in as part of my doctoral program in interpersonal/intercultural communication. I remember publicly nodding in agreement to my fellow classmate's comments, but privately thinking that she was playing around with the semantics of the word race, or trying to intellectualize our conversation by using abstract academic jargon that had no relevance to everyday living.

But, somehow, that brief encounter planted a seed that would be nurtured as I continued to explore the complex dynamics of culture, race, and communication. In various places, I found other scholars and practitioners who embraced the idea of one human race. "Race, an idea whose time has passed," was a phrase I saw on T-shirts, bumper stickers, and posters. Upon greater exploration of this issue, I found more and more evidence that indicated the concept of race was a social construction, with little or no biological foundation. Trying to communicate this idea to others was not easy, nor always well received. During discussions with family, friends, and colleagues, I got a chance to see a wide variety of reactions, including those that mirrored my own initial response.

Not to be deterred from embracing this newly founded idea, I consciously avoided using the term *race* and instead used *ethnicity*. I subsequently found out that this substitution was first suggested in 1950 (Montagu, 1972)—was I behind the times! Nevertheless, I began to use *interethnic* to describe the communication between African Americans and European Americans,

Personal Reflections (*continued*)

biethnic to describe my cultural identity, and *multiethnic* to describe my family. Recently, I have shifted back to using racial terminology, especially in my teaching and research (or adopting a combination of the two: *race/ethnicity*). Race is a powerful concept in the United States, and whether a scientific or social phenomenon, it is one that must be acknowledged when exploring the relationships between culture and communication. Not to use the term would be ineffective and unrepresentative in describing the type of research that I do.

What has your personal journey been like, in terms of understanding your own and others' racial/ethnic identity? What role has this book played in the process?—MPO

Comparing and Contrasting American Systems

Roughly speaking, race has become a way to describe human variation created by the interplay of geography, migration, and inheritance (Lasker & Tyzzer, 1982). Racial designations, however, vary in different social networks. Historically, they have been defined with regard to geographical, cultural, economic, and political factors. In many cases, social distinctions based on race develop when two or more groups of people come together in a situation of economic, political, or status competition (Spickard, 1992). Through a competition for perceived limited resources, a sense of us-versus-them is created and maintained. Depending on the introduction of additional players into the competition, these distinctions may change. People indigenous to the New World, for instance, did not experience themselves as Native Americans prior to the arrival of Europeans. Instead, they were Pequot, Osage, Mohegan, Sioux, or Oneida, for example.

This underlying principle is also evident in how various countries and states officially define and designate their population in terms of race. Given the world's attention on its recent fight against apartheid, South Africa has probably one of the best known systems of racial classification. Four racial groups are commonly designated there: Whites, Coloureds, Asians, and Blacks. Within this system, two groups—the racially mixed Coloureds and the Asians—act as buffers between the historically dominant Whites and native Blacks (Davis, 1991). Although this type of racial classification may seem remote to most people living in the United States, several examples closer to home also illustrate the inconsistencies of racial designations. The following examples from North, Central, and South America may seem strange, alien, or confusing. Such reactions are natural, especially for those of you who have always accepted the rigid racial designations (Black/White) of the United States (see Box 2.1).

- In the United States any degree of African ancestry has historically made a person Black. Such is not the case in Latin America or the Caribbean. In some societies, any degree of non-African ancestry means that a person is not Black (Winn, 1995).
- The same person defined as Black in the U.S. may be considered Coloured in Jamaica or Martinique and White in the Dominican Republic (Hoetink, 1967).
- In Brazil, a survey of Blacks generated 40 different words to describe their race/color (Page, 1994). The possibilities between Black and White are many: *preto, cabra, escuro, mulato escuro, mulato claro, pardo, sarara, moreno,* and *branco de terra* (Degler, 1971). Some "Blacks" in Brazil change their designations as they move to different social classes.
- Three fifths of Puerto Ricans who come to the mainland and are identified as Black were defined differently in their homeland. Most were considered *blanco* (white), *mulato* (mulatto), *trigueño* (wheat colored, olive skinned), or any of a number of color designations other than Black (Davis, 1991).
- To a West Indian, black is a literal description: You are Black if your skin is black. If you are lighter—like the coloring of Gen. Colin Powell—you would describe yourself as "middle-class brown" or "a light chocolate." (Gladwell, 1996)

These examples *represent* clearly illustrate the ambiguous ways that race has been defined in various American societies. How race is designated in each culture is best understood within its national, political, and economic history (for a comprehensive treatment, see Davis, 1991).

Race Designations in the United States

Another means of critically examining the sociopolitical construction of race in the United States is to trace the ways that different racial group members, including multiracial persons, have been designated. The first census, supervised by Thomas Jefferson in 1790, had three categories: "free White males," "free White females," and "other persons." This last category included free Blacks and "taxable Indians," referring to those Native Americans living in, or in close proximity to, European settlements (Wright, 1994). For most of the 19th century, distinctions were made between gradations of enslaved Blacks, including mulattos (one-half Black), quadroons (one-quarter Black), and octoroons (one-eighth Black) (Davis, 1991). After 1920, such distinctions were eliminated with the estimation that nearly three quarters of all Blacks in the United States were racially mixed and that "pure" Blacks would soon disappear. This assumption, coupled with the socially accepted principles of hypodescent and the "one-drop rule," resulted in more exclusively rigid categories of White and Black persons.

Unlike many other countries, the United States has historically embraced a *one-drop rule,* whereby a single drop of Black blood makes a person Black. This idea was grounded in the ideal of a pure "white race," one that would be forever tainted by even the most minuscule addition of Black blood. The rules of *hypodescent* were based on a similar assumption. According to Root (1996), this principle occurs in a "social system that maintains the fiction of monoracial identification of individuals by assigning a racially mixed person to the racial group in their heritage that has the least social status" (p. x). Both of these commonly accepted practices led to the continued social separation between Black and White worlds, despite the blurring of these distinctions (Davis, 1991; Root, 1992). For instance, some scholars (Degler, 1971; Jackson & Tolbert, 1989; Spickard, 1992) believe that attempts to cling to these sociopolitical distinctions, in addition to clear economic reasons, led many White slave owners to regard some of their children (born to female slaves) as slaves. Recent DNA evidence suggests this was the case with the children of President Thomas Jefferson and Sally Hemmings (who was one of Jefferson's slaves).

Given the idea that racial designations are socially constructed, it is important to understand that different states had varying legal specifications as to the degree of Black ancestry which qualified residents as "officially Black" (see Spickard, 1989). Many states, especially those in the Northeast, did not have such legal definitions. Others were quite specific in their statutes. For instance, a person with one "Negro or Mulatto" great-great-grandparent was defined as "Negro" in North Carolina or Louisiana. However, this same person could be "White" in several states where racial lineage was only traced to great-grandparents (e.g., Indiana, Tennessee, Maryland, and Florida) or grandparents (e.g., Oregon). All of these state laws, to varying degrees, attempted to legalize the one-drop rule. Many of us would like to believe that such statutes are relics of an embarrassing past. However, many of these state laws remained on the books—if not in practice—until the late 20th century. Consider the following case: In 1986, the U.S. Supreme Court refused to review a ruling from a lower court in Louisiana. In this case, a woman, whose great-great-great-great-grandmother was a Black slave, sued over the right to change her race legally from Black to White (Wright, 1994). Although she could trace her lineage to the point where she could conclude that no more than three thirty-seconds of her genetic heritage was Black, the state court's decision that she was legally Black in Louisiana was upheld.

In the absence of such supposedly clear definitions for other racial groups, the process of racial designation was even more inconsistent. Even with these state laws regarding African Americans, most designations historically were completed by what was commonly known as the *eyeball test* ("No Place for Mankind," 1989). This nonscientific, random measure involved various untrained laypersons (e.g., census takers, hospital staff, educational administrators) making decisions about others' racial makeup based on their own perceptions of race-based physical characteristics (see Orbe, M. 1999). Without question, such common practices resulted in numerous classifications that are largely ambiguous, illogical, and inconsistent.

This point is best illustrated through the example of three brothers who lived in Dulac, Louisiana, in 1969. Part of the Houma nation, the brothers shared the same father and mother. Each man was given a racial designation by the hospital staff who had assisted with his birth. The oldest brother was born with the help of a midwife at home. Because the state of Louisiana did not recognize the Houma as an official Native American nation prior to 1950, he was classified as a Negro. Born in a local hospital after 1950, the second brother was designated as an Indian. The third brother was assigned to the White category. Born in a New Orleans hospital 80 miles away, his designation was primarily based on the French family name (Stanton, 1971). Do such designations make sense to you? Or do they seem absurd? Much has changed in the past 50 years; however, many U.S. Americans still operate from such dated ideologies (see, for example, Orbe, M. 1999).

As we saw earlier, an analysis of the ways that individual states treated racial classification provides some insight into the unscientific nature of these designations. The examples described thus far have focused on the experiences of African American, Native American, and biracial people. But note that certain states needed ways to name and define groups of people that were relatively unique to their geographical location, for example the Creole of Louisiana and the Mestizo of Texas and New Mexico. The state of Hawaii, added to U.S. territories at the end of the 19th century, also provides an interesting insight into the social construction of race (Tolbert, 1989). Unlike the remainder of the United States which traditionally embraced the one-drop rule with little question, Hawaii has a long tradition of treating race designations more fluidly and inclusively because of the multiracial background of its native population.

The original Hawaiian settlers can be traced back some 1,500 years. The first inhabitants came initially from the Marquesas Islands and then from Tahiti (Howard, 1980). Hawaii's earliest residents were Polynesians, whose racial/ethnic composition represented a blend of Southeast Asia, Indonesia, and possibly the Middle East (Davis, 1991). After the arrival of several Spanish ships in the late 18th century, the Hawaiian Islands have been the adopted home for a number of other racial groups, including those from China, Japan, the Philippines, Puerto Rico, and Portugal (Day, 1960). Unlike other parts of the United States, Hawaii has a history of greater acceptance of ethnic and racial intermarriages, which has resulted in an affirmed melting pot of cultures. Steeped in a strong tradition opposing rigid racial categories, residents have long used a variety of ways to describe themselves including the creation of multiple ethnic and racial configurations. Despite this localized sociopolitical system, official racial designations changed when Hawaii became the 50th state in 1959. At that time, the U.S. Census Bureau imposed its monoracial categories on a population that up until then had had little use for such categories (Lind, 1980). The strong tradition of affirming multiracial heritages continues in Hawaii despite the attempts of the government agencies. This was demonstrated in the 1980 census when close to 70% of Hawaiian residents, not satisfied with the unrepresentative sampling of separate race categories, defined themselves as "Other" (Davis, 1991).

THE SIGNIFICANCE OF RACE TODAY

At various times in its history, the U.S. Census Bureau has used a wide variety of racial categories to classify its citizens. In addition, different definitions historically have been used to designate who should belong to which group. For instance, some individuals who share a common national origin, such as Mexicans and Filipinos, have been counted as racial groups. Such peoples represent cultural groups whose descendants originate from two or more of the traditionally accepted races (Cordova, 1973; Fernandez, 1992). Over the years, changes have ranged from ones largely expected to others that appear illogical. For instance, did you realize the following?

- From 1920 to 1940 some Asian Indians were counted as members of a "Hindu" race?
- In the 1960 U.S. census, Latin Americans were counted as White?
- The U.S. census has stopped asking about race in their count of the residents of Puerto Rico because of the contrasting definitions of racial designations?
- Prior to 1977 Asian Indians were considered White, but are now designated as Asian/Pacific Islanders?
- Current categories consider persons with origins traced to North Africa and the Middle East to be White?

- Latino/Hispanic people (from Mexican, Puerto Rican, Cuban, Central or South American, or other Spanish culture or origins) can be of any race?

In 1950, the United Nations Educational, Scientific, and Cultural Organization (UNESCO) spoke about the constantly changing ideas related to classifications of race: "These divisions," they concluded, "were not the same in the past as they are at present, and there is every reason to believe that they will change in the future" (Montagu, 1972, p. 72). Historically, the maintenance of racial categories has been similar to a game of musical chairs: Each round always seems to be a little different from the first, and someone inevitably is left out! Concurrently, traditional racial categories have experienced problems with the millions of U.S. citizens who identify their heritage as multiracial (Root, 1996). As we begin the 21st century, the inherent problems of attempting to classify a multiracial, multiethnic population along rigid racial categories continues.

Responsibility for determining the standard classifications of racial and ethnic data is maintained by a federal agency, the Office of Management and Budget (OMB.). In 1977, racial categories were made official through OMB Statistical Directive 15, the policy that established the categories to be used for all federal forms and statistics (Wright, 1994). At that time, four general racial groups were acknowledged: (1) American Indian/Alaskan Native, (2) Asian/ Pacific Islander, (3) Black, and (4) White. This directive also included ethnicity to be recorded as "Of Hispanic Origin" or "*Not* of Hispanic Origin." According to federal guidelines all U.S. citizens were required to fit themselves into one racial and one ethnic category.

2.2   *Variations of the Race Question*

The 1977 OMB Statistical Directive 15 established the minimum designations for recording race (American Indian/Alaskan Native, Asian/Pacific Islander, Black, or White) and ethnicity (Hispanic Origin or Not of Hispanic Origin). According to the directive, these were established to collect data for a number of purposes including civil rights compliance reporting, general program administration, grant reporting, and statistical reporting. However, the document made it clear that these categories were not the only means by which to collect such demographic data; other configurations could be used except they had to be aggregated back to the original categories when filing federal reports.

Consequently, some individual states, agencies, and institutions collect racial and ethnic data along guidelines different from the federal categories. In some states, like North Carolina and California, the options are not consistent from city to city. (Remember, the only stipulation is that administrators ultimately reorganize the data according to the federal categories when submitting required reporting.) Many cities and states have adopted legislation that requires the addition of alternate categories such as "Other" or "Multiracial." A brief description of Michigan's legislation provides some interesting insights into just how complex this process can be.

Variations of the Race Question (*continued*)

Shortly after the 1977 OMB directive, Michigan adopted the use of an "Other" category. However, concerns arose from two fronts. One, the increasing number of persons choosing this category created problems when the responses had to be converted for federal reports. Two, the "Other" category was not viewed as an acceptable alternative for those persons whose ancestors came from more than one racial group. (The original OMB directive instructs these persons to choose the category with which they most identify, another policy that has come under fire in preparation for the 2000 census.) In 1995, Michigan Public Acts 88 and 89 were enacted with the intent of updating how racial and ethnic data were collected. The major focus of this legislation was the provision for collecting data on multiracial persons. Specifically, these acts (1) required a question, separate from the one about race, that asked if a person was multiracial, and (2) prohibited the use of an "Other" classification when collecting racial/ethnic data. Although this move has resulted in an affirmation of the growing number of multiracial persons, it also still forces them to choose one racial category that they "most identify with" (something not easily done for some).

How is this information collected on the forms that you must fill out? How do you typically respond to such questions? Have your responses changed over time or remained relatively consistent?

Note that, despite this national policy, several individual states enacted their own procedures to collect information concerning race and ethnicity (see Box 2.2).

A great deal of debate accompanied the planning of the 2000 U.S. census. Government officials, academicians, social service and community agencies, education officials, politicians, and everyday citizens were active participants in discussions about how racial and ethnic groups should be counted (Eddings, 1997; Marable, 1997; Morganthau, 1995; Root, 1996; Shreeve, 1994; Wright, 1994). We might ask why so much debate-often times passionate, confrontational, or hostile-about seemingly meaningless government categories occurs. Why were these racial/ethnic designations so important? Was it not more important how individual persons identified themselves, regardless of which box they chose for the census?

What many national, state, and local leaders understood was that these numbers do count in various decisions that affect the livelihood of their communities. The ways that racial and ethnic designations are defined are used on a multitude of forms that seek to collect demographic information. As you have probably seen personally, identifying your race and/or ethnicity is a part of school enrollment forms, job applications, loan and mortgage applications, hospital and insurance forms, and countless other documents. Information gathered through these means is used to record, monitor, and enforce civil rights legislation and a multitude of other programs that protect against racial/ethnic discrimination (e.g., affirmative action and funding for other entitlement programs).

In short, the answer to the ways in which racial and ethnic groups are designated as important is quite simple. More than an issue of personal identity or cultural pride, racial and ethnic numbers drive dollars and political leverage (Marable, 1997; Wright, 1994). In the past, census numbers were used to create formulas that distribute federal aid to various minority groups, recreate minority districts for congressional elections, and maintain records for affirmative action purposes (Morganthau, 1995). Thus large shifts in the population of certain racial/ethnic groups have a direct impact on the relative power of the group in terms of their political and economic leverage.

As our examples have illustrated, the racial classification in the United States is arbitrary, confused, and illogical. Thomas C. Sawyer, chair of the House Subcommittee on Census, Statistics, and Postal Personnel, which reviewed the ways in which racial and ethnic groups should be officially recognized by the United States in its 2000 census, called the present system "an absurd counting game. Part of the difficulty is that we are dealing with the illusion of precision. We wind up with precise counts of everybody in the country, and they are precisely wrong" (quoted in Wright, 1994, p. 55). The nature of these illogical race designations is made readily clear on most forms. For instance, on close reading, the instructions of most federal forms clearly state that the categories should not be interpreted as scientific or anthropological. The stated purpose of race and ethnic questions is for the collection and use of compatible, nonduplicated, exchangeable racial and ethnic data by federal agencies. In this regard, race and ethnic demographic data (however imperfect) allow for government bodies to monitor and enforce antidiscrimination laws. In the words of one political leader, "We need these categories essentially to get rid of them" (Robert A. Hahn, quoted in Wright, 1994, p. 53).

After collecting input from a number of individuals and groups and debating a number of complex issues, the OMB decided on several changes to be implemented for the 2000 Census Dress Rehearsal in Spring 1998 as well as the actual 2000 census (Schmid, 1997; U.S. Office of Management and Budget, 1997). Specific changes include allowing individuals who identify themselves as multiracial to check more than one racial box, changing the "Black" category to "Black or African American," and using "Latino" (instead of "Hispanic") in areas where that label is preferred. The OMB rejected proposals to change "American Indian" to "Native American" as well as to include Native Hawaiians in this category or to create a separate category for them. In addition, proposals for several new categories, such as "Creole", "Middle Easterner-Arab," and "Cape Verdean", were also rejected (Schmid, 1997).

Race continues to be a significant sociopolitical maker in the United States because, in most people's minds, race is a fundamental way to understand human diversity. Regardless of its unscientific and illogical foundation, thinking along long-established racial categories dominates national discussions. And although racial categories have served as a means of discrimination throughout U.S. history, they have also facilitated a sense of identity and common experiences for many racial groups (Spickard, 1992). In the face of historical uses of racial classification systems, many African Americans, for instance, have embraced their Blackness as a source of pride, unity, sense of belonging, and strength. Similar renewed expressions of cultural pride have emerged in recent years from those of Native American descent, both "mixed bloods" and "full bloods" (Wilson, 1992). In this regard, the one-drop rule—used to maintain the myth of superior and inferior races—has been used by microcultural groups in the United States to create a unified front against White supremacy. It has also cultivated a sense of distinct cultural values and traditions (Thomas, 1993).

From all accounts, it appears that the idea of race as a way to understand cultural differences will remain an important fixture in the United States. Despite their history, racial categories currently are accepted by individuals who otherwise reject traditional thinking about race. It appears that the concept of race is nearly impossible to shake—even for those persons who reject the existence of separate races. Consider the words that many of these individuals (e.g., Root, 1996; Spickard, 1992) use as they promote the commonality of one human race. Many describe themselves or their children as "biracial" or "multiracial." Others study "racially mixed people." Think about how this language, although attempting to get past existing racial categories, continues to reinforce the idea of separate races. One thing remains true: The United States has had a long history that remains inextricably linked to a great variety of racial and ethnic groups. Its future, at least far into the 21st century, will also be tied to the ways that the different racial/ethnic groups can work together.

CONCLUSION

One central task of the study of interracial communication is to describe what we mean when we discuss race and racial categories. This chapter was designed to give you a historical perspective on these concepts. Specifically, we provided insight into the complex ways that designations based on race and ethnicity have been tied to social, political, and economic events. In addition, we focused on how the progression of race categories is tied to interracial communication in the 21st century.

Distinctions attributed to racial differences were initially used by Europeans in the 18th century to justify political and economic expansion. This continued well into the 20th century as the political and economic systems in the New World continued to take shape. Despite a lack of scientific evidence, race continues to be a largely accepted means of categorization in the United States. Various attempts to prove the existence of racial differences have only resulted in revealing the myth of "pure" races. In fact, it is commonly accepted that the greatest variability of human differences occurs within traditional racial categories, not between them. The most compelling evidence indicates that race is a sociopolitical construction, one that is actively maintained by our communication in various contexts including interpersonal, small group, organizational, and mass media (to be highlighted in Part Two). The reality remains, however, that most people continue to utilize this framework as a marker to distinguish human qualities, potential, and behaviors.

This foundation is important in setting the stage for our understanding of the complexities inherent in interracial communication. First, it allows us to debunk the myths of superior and inferior racial groups. Second, it helps us affirm the existence of some differences when comparing different racial/ethnic groups while at the same time recognizing the similarities of all people belonging to one human race.

OPPORTUNITIES FOR EXTENDED LEARNING

1. Request a copy (if you do not already have one) of a form that your college or university currently uses to collect racial/ethnic information. What directions or guidelines are provided for this section? What categories are included? How are they defined? Inquire about whether these forms strictly follow federal guidelines or incorporate changes specific to state legislation. If you can, compare different forms from past years. How have questions pertaining to race and ethnic designations changed?

 2. While on the *Oprah Winfrey Show* in the spring of 1997, champion golfer Tiger Woods explained that as a youngster he coined the term *Cablinasian* to capture the essence of his multiracial heritage (Caucasian, Black, American Indian, and Asian ancestry). His comment seemed to raise the consciousness level of the nation in terms of embracing the idea of a multiracial identity. Through your *InfoTrac College Edition*, attempt to understand the various responses to such a movement. (Using the keyword, *Cablinasian* will only result in one or two hits. Instead use keyword *biracial*.) What impacts might a new multiracial identity have on our society? How do traditional civil rights groups feel about such a move?

3. Are you familiar with the fairly recent work of Leonard Jeffries? Jeffries, a professor of Black studies at the City University of New York, made the argument that the key determinant of personality is the skin pigment melanin (Adler, 1991). Using this guide, he divided humanity into "Ice People" (the greedy warlike inhabitants of the North) and "Sun People" (the generous, communal natives of the South). What is your reaction to his basic ideas? How are they similar, (yet different), from the basic ideas of such groups as the Ku Klux Klan and the Aryan Nation?

4. Use your *InfoTrac College Edition* to do a keyword search for *2000 Census*. Based on the list of citations generated, what are some of the key issues that were debated over this monumental process? How do politics affect the ongoing discussions of who and what is counted, as well as how the counting is done?

5. Take the role of the director of the Office of Management and Budget, the federal agency given the task of determining how racial and ethnic groups will be defined. (If you are working in a small group, assume you are a member of the OMB committee given the same task.) Given your increased knowledge of the history of race, how would you construct categories (if at all) for the 2010 U.S. Census? Spend some time discussing the rationale for your resolution, because this decision has direct consequences for the country. In addition, be sure to identify what values, if any, are to be served by your suggestions for designating race. Share your ideas with your professor and classmates.

The Power of Language, Labels, and Naming

While reading Chapters 1 and 2, how conscious were you of the terms used to describe different racial/ethnic groups? Did some labels offend you? Confuse you? Enlighten you? One of the challenges in writing a book on interracial communication involves the various decisions that must be made in terms of language, labels, and naming. Such decisions are difficult because racial/ethnic groups are not static entities (Gonzalez, Houston, & Chen, 1997; Nakayama, 1997). Instead, the ways in which ingroup (as well as outgroup) members identify and label themselves change and evolve over time (Larkey, Hecht, & Martin, 1993). Throughout the book, we have attempted to determine and utilize those terms and labels that are most currently used by the particular racial/ethnic group we are discussing.

We have also maintained a high level of consciousness in our labeling and naming choices. As you will undoubtedly come to realize, if you have not done so already, language is a powerful element in communication processes. Unlike the popular old adage, we do believe "sticks and stones may break your bones *and* that names can and will hurt you." Historically, the process by which racial/ethnic groups—as well as those cultural elements central to their standpoints—were labeled has in fact had a tremendous effect on self and other perceptions. For example, did you notice in Chapters 1 and 2 we avoided using the terms *America* or *American* to describe the land or people of the United States? Instead we used phrases like North, Central, and/or South America or American to help specify the particular people/land to which we were referring. The term *Americas* is used to alert you that we are describing more than simply the United States. Is all this simply splitting hairs, lingering examples of the destructive legacy of political correctness? As you will see in this chapter, our response to this question is "No, not necessarily." Using the term *America* to describe the United States—or using *American* to describe U.S. citizens-is egocentric and reduces the visibility, attention, and importance given to other diverse countries in the Americas (Canada, Mexico, Argentina, Brazil, and so on). In a historical sense, it is also important to recognize that "America" was the home to civilizations of people years prior to the arrival of Europeans. What became known as the New World to European settlers was, in the experiences of the indigenous people of the land, not "new" at all. Many knew it as Turtle Island (Gonzalez, 1998).

Our objective here is not to provide a laundry list of politically correct language for you to use when interacting with individuals who are racially/ethnically different. Given the complexity of interracial communication processes, such a list would be limited, ungeneralizable, and possibly counterproductive. Nor is it to report the general differences in language use among racial and ethnic groups (see Chapter 6). Instead, we want you to recognize the inherent power of language choices in determining levels of communication effectiveness. Specifically, this chapter discusses the importance of language in interracial communication, and how societal power is directly related to issues of labeling and naming specific cultural groups. Before offering some general guidelines, we discuss the centrality of other communication elements, such as nonverbal cues and situational context, in making language choices. Our treatment of the power of language, labels, and naming begins with exposing some of the myths surrounding the phenomenon that has become known as political correctness.

THE MYTHS OF POLITICAL CORRECTNESS

The furor over political correctness (PC) has died down some in recent years. However, it is still common to hear references to the concept as it has become associated with a specific set of ideologies and, in turn, a collection of socially accepted terms. For instance, students commonly begin their comments in class by stating, "I know this isn't PC, but . . ." Other students use certain terms, and following the nonverbal reactions of others, immediately add—"Oops, I guess that's not the polit-

---

Personal Reflections

One of the most difficult aspects of coauthoring a book on interracial communication involves the careful ways in which many topics must be handled. Our goal is to provide sufficient knowledge, theories, and experiential application that promote a greater understanding of the complexities of culture, race/ethnicity, and communication. When it comes to verbal and nonverbal cues, much of the existing literature focuses on highlighting the various differences that were found in cross-group comparative studies. Based on these findings, a significant amount of literature offers generalizations on how African/Asian/Latino/a/Native Americans communicate both verbally and nonverbally. In almost all cases, European Americans are used as the point of comparison. For instance, Blacks (as compared to Whites) have been found to use forms of highly rhythmical rappin' (Ribeau, Baldwin, & Hecht, 1997). Although this type of information may be helpful in the creation of a general body of knowledge, it offers little practical value for everyday interactions. In fact, I believe the result of such studies has contributed to a well-documented characterization of a "stereotypical African American" (see Orbe, 1995a). Such generalizations, communicated in "black-and-white" terms (pun intended!), do not encourage persons to recognize the great diversity *within* particular ethnic groups based on other salient issues such as gender, class, or age. Instead, the focus is on generalized differences *between* racial/ethnic groups.

In light of this unproductive trend, this chapter avoids giving significant attention to such research. Instead, we focus on the central role that social power plays in the usage and effects of language choices. Through the discussion presented, we hope you will achieve an increased awareness. In terms of generalized differences across ethnic groups, we believe the ultimate means for determining their value is through actual interracial communication!— (MPO)

---

ically correct term nowadays. Sorry, but you know what I meant!" During the early 1990s, discussions of political correctness took place mainly on college and universities campuses (Ethridge, 1991; Taylor, 1991). However, the issue of "being PC" soon spread to other aspects of society, such as corporate organizations, which were also experiencing an increased number of traditionally underrepresented group members entering their ranks (Aamidor, 1994). So, exactly what *is* politically correct language? In its most basic form, it refers to the elimination of speech that often-times works to exclude, oppress, demean, or harass certain groups (Remar, 1991). However, being PC developed into a media phenomenon that clearly expanded beyond its original intentions.

In the early 1990s, media attention to what was described as the "political correctness movement" on college and university campuses made it into a national issue. PC referred to recent challenges to institutions of higher education to trans-form their campuses in order to reflect their changing demographics. It also included challenges to the existing curriculum and group labels that were seen as oppressive to or unrepresentative of certain segments of society. As described in the major national outlets, political correctness was "an umbrella term that describes what is deemed acceptable by an eclectic group of radical feminists, homosexuals, Marxists, and 'multiculturalists'" (Taylor, 1991, p. 100). Right-wing radio talk show host, Rush Limbaugh for example, spent considerable time—and as a result, received increased attention—defending the rights and legitimacy of traditional language, thought, and college curriculum. Media attention specifically was drawn to those campus community members labeled as "PC police" (Adler, 1990) or "thought police" (Taylor, 1991). Examples of more sensitive language were repre-sented, not by some of the more productive and central proposed label changes, but by more extreme and seemingly absurd labels.

Advocating language choices that reflected a sensitivity to the historical power dynamics that informed such labels was reduced to a parody in major media outlets: national magazines (Taylor, 1991), PC dictionaries (Moody, 1993), and feature films such as *PCU: Politically Correct University* (Leff & Penn, 1994). On December 24, 1990, for example, *Newsweek*'s cover story debated the value of political correct-ness. Some time was spent discussing the rationale behind advocating for changes in the ways that colleges and universities currently marginalize groups. However, the series of articles presented this information using extreme examples of "PC language." Nine-year-old females should not be called girls, according to one article (Adler, 1991). Instead, they should be referred to as "pre-women" (p. 49). "No one has suggested renaming the sexes," the article also states, "only the way they're spelled. Womyn takes the 'men' out of 'women.' That still leaves the 'son' in person" (p. 52). The ways in which these phrases are presented, and subsequently treated, result in the positioning of *all* suggested language changes as absurd. The impor-tance of language, then, was reduced to one of simple "semantics" or "the search for euphemisms" as seen within this excerpt:

> It sometimes appears that the search for euphemisms has become the great intellectual challenge of American university life. Lest anyone take offense at being called "old," he

or she becomes a "non-traditional-age student." Non-Caucasians generally are "people of color." This should never be confused with "colored people." Dennis Williams, who teaches writing at Cornell, recently wrote an article on affirmative action in which he tweaked the PC with the phrase, "colored students." "'Students of color' sounds stupid," reasoned Williams, who is black. (quoted in Adler, 1991, p. 50)

Within this context, political correctness was seen as "a breed of left-wing academic intolerance and exclusion that ends up shackling not only free speech but free-flowing intellectual inquiry" (Gitlin, 1991, p. 54). Through new campus policies, PC imposed a conformity on how those on college campuses thought and spoke (Mackenzie, 1991). The commonly accepted idea that higher education represented a free marketplace of ideas was no longer accurate. Instead students, faculty, and staff were forced to become PC. The result was often self-censorship, especially for those who were well intentioned but cautious to speak because they might offend others. The comments of one European American man capture the sense of frustration felt by many: "I don't know how to talk to African Americans. I'm scared of saying the wrong thing to women. . . . There are times when I want to be very cautious about offending a feminist colleague, but I can't seem to find the right terms" (Adler, 1991, p. 54).

Thus PC became popularized as a satirized response to addressing the increased cultural diversity (including race/ethnicity) in higher education. From another perspective, it can also be interpreted as a debate between the First Amendment rights to free speech and the Fourteenth Amendment rights that guarantee all students equal opportunity to obtain an education (Cornwell, Orbe, & Warren, 1999). For many advocates of an increased tolerance/respect for campus cultural diversity, the creation of the label "political correctness" was nothing more than an attempt to reduce the credibility and legitimacy of their efforts. From this perspective, the furor over PC was seen as an organized conservative campaign to turn back gains made by people of color, and other underrepresented groups, in higher education amid anxious economic times (Heller, 1991). The phrase, some argue, was created by the media to denigrate, exaggerate, and misrepresent the underlying principles of new policies that protect students' rights to a quality education (Ethridge, 1991). In this regard, the media construction of PC can be seen as a response to the increased presence and activism on college campuses. According to some (e.g., Aamidor, 1994), the myth of political correctness is that it stifles conservative and independent thinking. In reality, labeling terms that are sensitive to the power that language holds as nothing more than "being PC" has just the opposite effect. It squelches the challenges to traditional language and thought and works to maintain the status quo.

At this point, we want to be explicit about why we are including a chapter on language. Embracing one or the other interpretations of what it means to be PC is not important. Regardless of your particular perceptions of political correctness, we hope you will recognize the importance of language choices (terms, labels, names) on communication effectiveness in general, and interracial communication effectiveness specifically. Teaching others how to be politically correct is not our objective. Instead, we hope to increase your awareness and sensitivity to the power of language when communicating with others. In addition, we will help you understand why certain racial/ethnic groups prefer some terms over others. Through the insights shared throughout the remainder of the chapter, you will be able to make informed decisions about what language choices you incorporate into your everyday interactions. One important aspect of the idea of making an informed choice includes an awareness of the history of racial/ethnic terms and insight into how others might interpret contemporary use of specific labels.

THE POWER OF LANGUAGE

Language is central to human communication processes. Although certainly it is incorrect to equate language with communication itself, the important role of language in communicative effectiveness can not be denied. For most individuals, however, their native language is a ubiquitous entity, one that is constantly in use but seldom critiqued or questioned consciously. Their language—their words, gestures, phrases, and styles—is natural and effortless when used with others who share a common speech community (see Chapter 6). In this regard, language is an abundant public resource that many utilize with little attention to its powerful nature. In terms of interracial communication, the power of language can be seen in the ways it has been used to label, and subsequently define, some *groups* of people while leaving others—the dominant or "standard" group—unlabeled. Prior to our discussion of the power of labels and naming, some background information is needed. Specifically, we want you to see the important role that language plays in human communication processes. This is best achieved by describing language as (1) a tool, (2) a prism, and (3) a display.

Language as a Tool

In its most basic form, language is a tool that humans have utilized, sometimes effectively, sometimes not so effectively, to communicate their ideas, thoughts, and feelings to others. Language systems include semantic, syntactic, pragmatic, and phonetic patterns and are accessed either through written or spoken channels. Language is the means by which our internal cognitions (beliefs, values, attitudes, emotions, and so on) can be shared with others. As described earlier, this process is central to human communication as seen in the word's origin. Communication comes from the Latin *communicare*, which means "to make common." Without any common experiences, human communication would be impossible. The ability to share even our most basic internal cognitions with others as a means to establish and locate common experiences is central to the human experience. Without these common experiences to draw from (some use the term *homophily* to describe the common experiences you share with others), communication would be impossible.

The analogy used here can be productive in understanding how a language system is similar to a tool box. Language systems are comprised of a set of tools used to communicate in different settings. No limitations are put on the number of tools that a person is capable of acquiring, nor is any one person restricted from learning how to use any one set of tools. In fact, we would guess that many U.S. Americans find themselves using different languages systems (tool boxes) for achieving different objectives in various communities of which they are a member. For instance, a student may draw from one set of tools when interacting with family members and another when discussing his or her chemistry test with a professor. In order to communicate effectively, the same or different tools might be necessary when in the company of friends, professional colleagues, or those with a common interest or hobby. In essence, a well-stocked tool box (language system) is essential to getting the job done (communicating effectively). Trying to complete a job without the proper tools is possible, but increasingly more complex and time consuming. And even when all of the right tools are available, most jobs are more difficult than they initially appear to be, in part because of the imperfection of the tools. It also can be the result of a person's lack of ability to use the tools properly. In similar ways, these tool issues impact language and interracial communication effectiveness.

One aspect of language that sometimes hinders effective interracial communication is the arbitrary nature of words. As is commonly discussed, words do not have any inherent meaning. Instead, they are abstractions of the things they represent and, subsequently, are always incomplete representations. In other words, a person uses a word or phrase in an attempt to capture the essence of an idea or thing. Assuming a phrase exists that comes close to representing one's ideas, the key for effective communication lies within the other person's ability to decode the phrase in a manner consistent to that which it was encoded. Meaning is created not by the words themselves, but how the words are interpreted by *both parties*. Some responsibility for specific language, therefore, must be assumed by both the senders and the receivers. The ability to communicate effectively with others depends on our language capabilities as well as the commonality of experiences (homophily), which lends to the increased likelihood of shared meaning. Generally speaking, the wider and more divergent the language communities from which we normally reside, the more difficult mutual understanding becomes.

Language as a Prism

Language is more than simply a passive, neutral tool that we use to communicate their internal cognitions to others (Hymes, 1974). In addition to serving as an "instrument for voicing ideas," it also provides a guide for an individual's mental activity (Hoijer, 1994, p. 194). In other words, language serves a central role in providing linguistic, semantic, and verbal categories that have a direct relationship to how we come to understand abstract ideas. Within this perspective, language can be regarded as a prism in the way it helps shape the ways in which we perceive reality. One of the central ideas associated with this interpretation of language is the Sapir-Whorf hypothesis (sometimes referred to as simply the Whorfian hypothesis).

The Sapir-Whorf hypothesis, a major proponent of linguistic relativity suggests that language structure is necessary in order to produce thought (Fong, 1997). Within this perspective, language is a guide to social reality. Although it helps articulate our experiences, it also plays a central role in defining them. In its most extreme form, this approach to language suggests that the particular elements of a language system predispose us to think in particular ways and not in others. Edward Sapir explained that "Human beings do not live in the objective world alone, nor alone in the world of social activity as ordinarily understood, but are very much at the mercy of the particular language which has become the medium for their society" (Sapir quoted in Mandelbaum, 1949, p. 162).

You may need a set of examples to help you understand this abstract concept. A significant amount of research has been completed on color terms and perceptions (e.g., Kay & Kempton, 1984) and provides support for the Sapir-Whorf hypothesis. An easy experiment serves as a great illustration of how a person's language capabilities in terms of color act as a prism for his or her reality. Select a piece of clothing that is a really unusual color. Ask several of your friends, both women and men, to identify its color. Inevitably a variety of different terms will be generated to describe one item. For instance, you may hear the same item called blue, green, blueish green, teal, turquoise, seafoam green, or malachite. Depending on the particular person's set of life experiences (e.g., working as a salesperson for J. Crew clothing), perceptions of the item probably differed greatly. According to the Sapir-Whorf hypothesis, varying perceptions of reality are due to the differences in language abilities (color terms) of specific people. In other words, the ways in which a person thinks about a particular thought, object, or emotion is confined by the terms to which she or he has access. If one of your friends does not have the term *seafoam green* in her repertoire of color terms, she will not be able see something as seafoam green (even if others do). In this regard, her reality is shaped by her language structures.

Along this same line of inquiry, other research (e.g., Wong, 1997) has revealed how varying elements (semantics or syntax, for example) of different language systems (English, Spanish, Japanese, and so on) impact the specific worldviews of those who were raised using a particular language. But the Sapir-Whorf hypothesis also has its critics. Other scholars have found it difficult to test the strength of the relationship between structure of language and perceptions of reality. Carroll (1992), for example, concluded that "[i]n general, the Sapir-Whorf hypothesis has come to be regarded as either unconfirmable or incorrect. . . . If the hypothesis can be sustained at all, it implies only a weak influence of language structure on thought" (p. 45). Given the varying reports about the relationship between language structure and thought processes, a precise understanding of the exact impact of language structure on thought processes is inconclusive. However, what is not in question is that our language capabilities do have *some* tangible effect on how we come to understand reality.

Language as a Display

As you can see, the importance of language in the communication process can be seen through the many roles it plays. In addition to its use as a tool and a prism, language also serves as a display for our internal thoughts. Humans utilize their language capabilities to communicate their thoughts. In this regard, language is a tool. However, the language choices we make as a means to communicate certain ideas do more than simply articulate those ideas. Although oftentimes unintentional, they provide additional information—beyond the presentation of our ideas—about internal cognitions regarding a particular subject. It has often been said that language is an index to, or reflection of, our internal thought patterns (Hymes, 1974). Consider the following example to help you understand how individuals' language choices sometimes communicate more about them than they always recognize.

In the English language, several words (synonyms) can be used to communicate any one idea. The unconscious or conscious choice of words can provide a great deal of insight in terms of how one feels about the idea—in some cases, even more than is directly communicated. Take the case of Geoffrey Fieger, the 1998 democratic candidate for governor in Michigan. Positioned in the race as an antipolitician fighting for the rights of everyday people, Fieger's unorthodox approach to politics resulted in several fellow Democrats denouncing some of his ideas as illogical or unfeasible. Such was the case with Jennifer Granholm, the Democratic candidate for attorney general. When she publicly disagreed with Fieger's stance on handling those persons convicted of drug crimes, Fieger labeled her response as "hysterical." Many saw his choice of words as less reflective of his views on her ideas and more of a public display of his perceptions of women in general. By choosing the word *hysterical* instead of *passionate*, Fieger tapped into long-standing stereotypes concerning women and their communication styles. Although the conclusions drawn about Fieger may or may not have been completely accurate, this incident provides a vivid illustration of how a person's language choice serves as a public display of perceptions of his or her internal cognitions.

The phrase "semantics of prejudice" can be used to describe how language choices can unintentionally reveal information about individuals' internal thoughts (regardless of other unconscious attempts to shield them in public). For those persons who have spent considerable amounts of time involved in varying forms of interracial communication (like the authors of this book), language choices often serve as a way to understand the perspectives of others (see, for example, Houston, 1997). When you hear a new acquaintance refer to a third party as "Oriental" (as opposed to Asian, Korean, or Laotian), do you draw any about how she regards people of Asian descent? How about if a person commented on the "savagelike behaviors of some Blacks" or how he thought that "mulatto women are beautiful"? Would these language choices impact your perceptions of this person's views on race, ethnicity, and interracial communication? It is safe to say that for those experienced in interracial communication-including both authors of this text—such a display of language choices would certainly send up red flags!

This is not to say the use of certain phrases are a direct reflection of certain thoughts, beliefs, and/or values. Nor is it accurate to conclude that everyone who uses a specific term has similar internal cognitions regarding any one particular topic. Remember, however, what the Sapir-Whorf hypothesis suggests: Our language structures predispose us to think in certain ways. For those persons interested in becoming effective communicators within racially and ethnically diverse settings, a clear consciousness of language choices must be maintained. Although some terms may be used with no malice or intention to offend, it is important to recognize that others' perceptions of your internal cognitions may be largely informed by the words you use. We recognize that some of you may counter this argument by suggesting the particular terms you use to describe yourselves and others may or may not accurately reflect your personal views. However, our argument is that, generally speaking, an advanced understanding of the complexities of race/ethnicity is reflected through a highly evolved language system in which racial/ethnic labels are consciously chosen for specific reasons (rather than out of habit, ignorance, or tradition). Part of this advanced understanding is a recognition of the inherent power of those who label others.

THE POWER OF LABELS

Part of human nature is to use labels to refer to other people and ourselves. Systems of classifications are a natural means by which we make sense out of a complex world. But we must critically examine the genesis and development of labels for particular categories. Labels communicate on many levels of meaning. They also implicitly work to establish, maintain, or challenge specific kinds of relationships between individuals and/or groups of individuals. Labels, as a form of language, can be used strategically to communicate closeness or distance among individuals depending on the intentions and effects of the speech act. In the context of our discussion revolving around the power of language, it is important to recognize that the labels designated for specific racial/ethnic groups in the United States reflect this reality.

As illustrated in Chapter 2, the contextualization of language is itself very much a political act. Asante (1998b) explains that whenever categories and labels are created in an effort to make certain concepts functional, certain choices are made from many different possibilities. Typically the categories ultimately chosen can create mechanisms that benefit some groups to the disadvantage of others. Some suggest that persons with political, social, and economic power occupy positions that allow them to label less powerful groups of people. In many instances this is completed in ways that maintain or increase the power bases of those already in the most powerful societal positions. Take, for example, the situation of multiracial persons in the United States during the 19th century. During this time period, these individuals were labeled in different ways (mulatto, octoroon, colored, and so on). However, each label was still considered a part of the general category of Negros, which equated these persons as slaves or second-rate citizens.

Over the course of U.S. history, European American men have held most of the social, economic, and political power. From this position of privilege, they have consistently created and used labels to define other ethnic groups in ways that have benefited their own existence. Chapter 2 described how Africans, Asians, Latinos, and those indigenous to North America never defined themselves as such until coming in contact with Europeans. Prior to European influences, the labels that were used reflected the diversity of particular groups of people based on ethnicity and culture. Think about how one label based on race (e.g., Oriental or Asian) has come to represent a multitude of diverse ethnic and cultural groups (e.g., Chinese, Filipino, Hmong, and Indonesians). Each label created a category that served the purpose of defining these groups from a European perspective. Within different perspectives, varying sets of labels existed previous to those created by Europeans. However, the differences in political and economic power have made some sets of labels (those created and used by European Americans) more utilized than others.

This critical line of thinking provides a vivid illustration of Asante's argument that the choice of certain labels (over others) is situated in a political context, one in which dominant power bases are maintained or increased. Why didn't Europeans recognize and account for the diversity within different racial groups? Some scholars, focusing on the ideas of linguistic relativity (i.e., Wong, 1997), would point to the effect of their relative ignorance in terms of these differences. It is apparent that European perspectives were informed by the language that was created and maintained in terms of pure, distinct races. Can you understand how their language systems included racial terms that had a direct influence on the ways individuals come to understand others who are different? Other scholars (e.g., Frankenberg, 1993), taking a more critical perspective, might conclude that Europeans' positions of privilege worked to render this labeling process "natural" and "logical" while *unintentionally* reaping the benefits of such a language system.

The idea of societal privilege is an important concept in terms of the ways that certain groups have the power to label others while remaining unlabeled. Based on the work of Peggy McIntosh (McIntosh, 1995a, 1995b), a greater understanding of how societal privilege operates within specific contexts has been advanced in terms of its effect on perceptions of "reality." McIntosh has written extensively on male privilege. However, her recognition of white privilege (McIntosh, 1989) is especially relevant to discussions on interracial communication. Societal privilege, in this vein, refers to a general favored state, one that has been earned or conferred by birth or luck. Unlike that which is earned, power from unearned privilege can look like strength but what it typically represents is an *unearned entitlement*. According to McIntosh, part of white privilege is seeing racism in terms of individual acts and not as largely invisible systems that confer dominance on European Americans (McIntosh, 1989). In terms of the power of labeling, a position of privilege is a position that remains largely unnamed. This is the case because this position is situated as the unevaluated standard from which all other positions are contrasted.

In no uncertain terms, the power to categorize and label others inherently includes a privilege to refrain from being labeled. Countless examples of this phenomenon exist within the United States. Have you ever given thought to how the term *homosexual*, was created and used to label others prior to the creation of *heterosexual*? The same could be argued for the process that saw *handicapped/disabled* (describing persons with disabilities) come into use prior to *able-bodied*. These examples reveal how social privilege based on sexual orientation and abilities is maintained. Additional evidence, highlighted later, is apparent in the ways in which self-identity labels for persons of European descent remain vague and largely undetermined (Martin, Krizek, Nakayama, & Bradford, 1996). In order to promote effective interracial communication, we must recognize how the issues of power and privilege are presented in the labels we choose to describe self and others. Any attempt to improve the existing state of U.S. race relations must occur through an understanding of the history of racial/ethnic labels. This includes, as articulated by McIntosh (1989), breaking the silence that accompanies privilege:

> The silences and denials surrounding privilege are the key political tool here. They keep
> the thinking about equality and equity incomplete, protecting unearned advantage and

conferred dominance by making these taboo subjects. Most talk by whites about equal opportunity seems to me now to be about equal opportunity to try to get a position of dominance while denying that systems of dominance exist. (p. 12)

The remainder of this section presents an overview of the labels that have been used to describe the major racial/ethnic groups in the United States. Recognize that such groups are not merely static entities. As you will see, racial/ethnic groups—as we have come to understand them—are products of a lengthy process of labeling and identification. Our primary objective in including this material is to create awareness of how labels have evolved over time. Through exposure to this information, you will obtain some additional insight about our rationale for the language choices in this book. Ultimately, these insights will contribute to your increased awareness and understanding of the complexity of labels help each of you make informed choices about the language you use.

African Americans

Research on the evolution of labels to describe persons of African descent is well documented (Davis, 1997; Fairchild, 1985; Holloway, 1990; Larkey, Hecht, & Martin, 1993). Variations have included African, Colored, Negro, Black, Afro-American, and African American. According to Holloway (1990), the different labels reflect changes in how persons of African descent negotiated their identity in the United States. This ranges from strong African identification to nationalism, integration, and attempts at assimilation to a renewed sense of cultural identification. Larkey et al. (1993) see recent shifts of African American self-identification as connected to issues of self-determination, strength, progress, and control. One major issue in labeling, for all racial/ethnic groups generally and people of African descent specifically, is the general preference for labels that have been generated from within the community (as opposed to those imposed by others). For many African Americans, language preferences reflect personal choice.

Given the variety of choices, which term—Black or African American—is correct? Because of the diversity of thought within this heterogeneous group, one term is not necessarily more correct than the other. Much has to do with the specific personal choices of the individual. Recent polls indicate that African American is more commonly preferred over Black (Vox Pop, 1994). The majority of people see either term as appropriate. Other literature indicates that reactions to labels may differ somewhat across age groups. For instance, younger people of African descent (18–29 years of age) are much more likely than their older counterparts (over 50 years of age) to be offended with others' use of labels to describe them that are not consistent with self-defining ones.

Davis (1997) argues that African Diasporans anywhere in the world need to be designated with great clarity. He believes that an all-inclusive term like *African*

American is not appropriate. First, it does not differentiate between White and Black people descending from Africa. Second, it often is used exclusively to refer to U.S. citizens while ignoring the existence of Caribbean-born Blacks such as West Indians. Davis argues that people of African descent born in the United States should be labeled as Black Americans; those born in Africa and gaining U.S. citizenship are best described as African Americans. However, we argue that in order to be consistent with other racial/ethnic labels, African American should be used to refer to all persons of African descent, regardless of place of birth. It might be important, however, to acknowledge ingroup differences and use U.S. African American when exclusively referring to those persons currently residing in the United States.

Asian Americans

From a historical perspective, the term Oriental to describe people of Asian descent can be traced to European travelers who identified Asia from a self-focal point. Hence Asia became the East or the Orient. Although some Asian Americans, particularly those from older generations, still refer to themselves as Orientals, most persons active in or familiar with the Asian American community take offense to the term (Sing, 1989). However, describing objects, such as food or artifacts, as oriental is still acceptable. Like the terms Colored or Negro in the African American community, using Oriental to describe persons of Asian descent has a negative and outdated ring to it. It also, like the other terms, represents an objectionable term that has been imposed on the community by non-Asians.

The label *Asian American* is an umbrella term used to describe people from several culturally diverse countries including Chinese, Japanese, Koreans, Vietnamese, Cambodians, Laotioans, Thai, Hmong, Indonesians, Malaysians, Burmese, and Filipinos. Because of the great diversity represented within this commonly used label, it is often helpful to use more specific identifiers when possible (see, for example, *Publication Manual of the American Psychological Association*, [APA, 1996, p. 53]). This practice recognizes and distinguishes Asian Americans from Asian nationals, and it also helps differentiate among different Asian nationalities. Such distinctions are important given the wide variety of cultures and experiences of those commonly referred to as a single entity. For instance, recognizing a person as a Korean American, rather than more generally as an Asian American, allows greater insight into that individual's cultural heritage (Sing, 1989).

European Americans

As we discussed earlier, Europeans American have historically remained unnamed because of their positions of privilege in the United States. In fact, this privileged social positioning results in little conscious awareness of the racial/ethnic identity for most persons of European descent (Frankenberg, 1993). Unlike other racial/ethnic groups, the identity of this dominant group is not seen as central to everyday life interactions. Hence, when faced with the question of self-identification (e.g., "What are you?" or "What race do you consider yourself?"), a common response from many European Americans is simply to label themselves as "Americans." Although this label can be seen as focusing on their current standing in the United States, it indicates how their self-identity is void of any consciousness of their particular racial/ethnic identity.

Recently, communication scholars have begun exploring "Whiteness" with the same scrutiny of past research that has examined the identity labels embraced by U.S. racial/ethnic minorities. However, it is important to recognize that labels for European Americans, like the other labels discussed in this section, have evolved over time. For instance, many groups that were not initially considered White (e.g., Catholic Irish immigrants or persons from eastern Europe) over time have "achieved" status as White/European American (Roedieger, 1994). Researchers (Martin, Krizek, Nakayama, & Bradford, 1996) have done some significant work in the area of exploring how people of European descent describe themselves. Specifically, they examined which terms (Anglo, Caucasian, Euro-American, European Americans, WASP, White, or White American) were most commonly used in self-identification. Based on extensive research conducted throughout the United States, they found that when forced to use a racial/ethnic marker, people of European descent most often chose "White," followed by "Caucasian." Labels that were least reported were "WASP" (White Anglo Saxon Protestant) and "Anglo." Are you surprised by these results? For European American readers, do they coincide with the labels you use?

As noted by Martin et al, (1996), the labels most commonly used by persons of European descent reflect terms that are significantly vague and general (as compared to those that are more historically and geographically based). You have probably noticed that we have opted primarily to use *European American* in attaching a label to this group. This is done in attempts to use parallel terms that are geographically based, as reflected in the headings of this section. Although this rationale is strong, it—along with other language choices in terms of interracial communication—is not invoked without some concerns. For instance, some scholars, such as Frankenberg (1993), warn that using parallel terms "falsely equalizes communities, who are, in terms of current reality, unequally positioned in the racial order" (p. 231).

Latino/a Americans

As we illustrated and discussed earlier, naming is not a neutral act. In many cases, we have seen how racial/ethnic labels have been used to downplay micro-level differences in order to maximize the distance between certain groups and European

Americans. Such is the case for the term *Hispanic*, a label first sanctioned for official and generalized use in the United States in 1968 (Melville, 1988). *Hispanic American* is a term that has come to represent persons with a similar use of the Spanish language and other aspects of Spanish culture, regardless of the distinct differences of the many groups that it includes. For instance, the label refers to those U.S. citizens from Mexico, Cuba, Spain, Chile, Dominican Republic, and many other countries (Pino, 1980; Spielberg, 1980). In this regard, both of the designations—Hispanic and Latino/a—group people of Spanish-speaking descent into a single category and thereby erases any designations based on national origin.

In order to remain parallel in terminology and consistent in linking people to a specific geographical area, we have adopted the use of Latino/a Americans throughout the text. *Latino*/a is more often used today by people themselves, rather than by governmental agencies. Note, however, that specific differences in preferred labels exist in different regions of the United States. An Hispanic label is generally more accepted in the East and Midwest; Latino/a is more common in the West. In addition, the specific terminology used in self-identity labels reflects the concentrations of Spanish-speaking communities in that particular geographical area. In New Mexico, for example, the accepted term has always been *Hispanos*. In Miami, most people would label themselves as *Cubanos* (Melville, 1988).

Another label oftentimes used to describe people of Mexican descent in the United States is *Chicano/a*. This term emerged from the civil rights movement in the 1960s and early 1970s to emphasize the working-class status of Mexican American activists (Tanno, 1997). Regarded by some as the only term that emerged directly from within its community, Chicano/a has come to connote a political standpoint along the lines of a nationalist position (Mirandei, Enriquez, 1979). With the variations of terms to describe this fastest growing segment within the United States, Tanno (1997) reminds us of the "worth of multiple names." She argues that in our personal lives we simultaneously embrace various labels like student, child, friend, employee, and sibling. Such can also be the case with racial and ethnic labels:

> In my case, I resort to being Spanish and all that implies whenever I return to my birthplace, in much the same way that we often resort to being children again in the presence of our parents. But I am also Mexican American when I balance the two important cultures that define me; Latina, when I wish to emphasize cultural and historical connectedness with others; and Chicana, whenever opportunities arise to promote political empowerment and assert cultural pride. (p. 31)

When individuals use these terms to describe themselves, different meanings can be attached to the very same label (Delgado, 1998). Take the term Chicano/a, for instance. Some Latino/a Americans use La Raza to signify political unity among diverse cultural groups (Delgado, 1998). For many, La Raza encourages different Latino/a communities to recognize the power of "one race," something advocated by the Chicano movement.

Native Americans

The story of how the indigenous people of what is now regarded as North America were labeled as "Indians" is common knowledge. Prior to the arrival of European explorers/settlers, diverse nations of native people—Oneida, Sage, Pequot, Mohegans, Blackfeet, Sioux, Cherokee, Potawatomi, and so on—lived off the land. Christopher Columbus, thinking he had reached India via a quicker route, incorrectly labeled these Native persons as Indians (a label that has been maintained). Currently, a general lack of agreement exists among Native people in the United States on the most preferred group name (Shaver, 1998). Among the many terms that are currently used are American Indian, Native American, Native People, Natives, Indigenous People, and Indians.

Pratt (1998) found that the term *Indian* (and not *Native American*) is the label almost always used by tribal elders and the indigenous people of North America. Currently, the U.S. government recognizes close to 450 Native groups. Whenever possible, identifying individuals or groups by their specific *nation* (preferred over "tribe") is preferred by most Native Americans (*Publication Manual of the American Psychological Association* [APA, 1996]). This terminology allows for the recognition and appreciation of specific nations that have largely been unacknowledged by many non-Native people.

Currently, federal agencies include Alaskan Natives in the same category as American Indians; in some instances, Native Hawaiians and Samoans are also included. Although these groups are lumped together for statistical purposes, they can also be quite culturally diverse (as can particular nations). When describing Alaskan Natives, for example, little attention is given to the diversity of people comprising this group. Not all are Eskimos, an offensive term applied by non-Natives that literally means "raw meat eaters." Indigenous people of Alaska, as well as their descendants from northern Canada, eastern Siberia and Greenland, prefer Inuk (plural form, Inuit) over Eskimo. Like many of the other racial/ethnic groups discussed in this section, preferences for labeling Native Americans call for naming their specific nation whenever possible.

NONVERBAL COMMUNICATION

In his book *The Silent Language*, Edward T. Hall (1959) first discussed the great importance of recognizing verbal and nonverbal behaviors in intercultural communication contexts. We can easily talk about verbal and nonverbal language in similar terms, although some key differences exist (e.g., the punctuation of verbal exchanges as compared to the continuity of nonverbal cues). However, can you see

---

<table>
<tr><td>3.2</td><td>*Case Study*</td></tr>
</table>

Throughout this book, we introduce several case studies for you to use as specific avenues to apply different concepts. We also hope that—through class discussions, journals, and other means—you will use past and current experiences to describe your own case studies. Many times, these real-life experiences serve as a better way to apply different concepts since that are understood in a specific (localized) context that can be explained more fully.

Think about some of the things that you learned after reading the sections on labels for different racial and ethnic groups. We hope that you gained some valuable insights into the complexities of language in terms of interracial communication. However, we recognize that several questions may remain unanswered. Why not describe the specific situations (case studies) that still cause unproductive levels of anxiety and uncertainty? The more specificity you provide for each situation, the deeper the analysis can be.

Here's a suggestion: Why not use notecards and have each person in the group/class provide some questions that they have in terms of "appropriate" language use in a specific instance of interracial communication? These should be anonymous. Then, as a class or in small groups, try and use the resources in this chapter as well as the *human* resources in your class to generate additional insight to particular questions. You may be surprised at how thought provoking these case studies can be!

---

how our earlier metaphors (language as a tool, prism, and display) also apply to nonverbal language systems? Given the focus of this chapter, some specific attention to the crucial role that nonverbal cues play alongside specific forms of language is warranted. In fact, according to some scholars (e.g., Mehrabian, 1982), the actual meaning of the message carried through the verbal portion of the message is quite low—only 7%. Others (Birdwhistell, 1970) suggest that the majority of the meaning comes through vocal qualities (38%) and facial expressions (55%). The exact science behind attempting to identify precise formulas by which meaning is created are, at best, inconclusive. However, the point of these studies is clear: The role that nonverbal cues plays in interracial communication processes is crucial.

In the simplest of terms, nonverbal and verbal communication can be differentiated from each other based on one element: the presence or absence of messages coded through words. Nonverbal research has included studies based on proxemics (space), kinesics (body gestures), haptics (touch),vocalics/paralanguage, and chronemics (time). Hall's (1959) initial work has stimulated a large body of cross-cultural communication research that examines the nonverbal differences within different cultures, including differences among various racial/ethnic groups. For instance, research has reported the following:

- Puerto Ricans use touch communication much more frequently than North Americans and the British (Knapp, 1973).
- African American speech has more vocal range, inflection, and tonal quality than European American speech (Garner, 1994).
- Native Americans' use of silence is much different than European Americans in that it can reflect respect, active listening, or possibly a response to ambiguity (Braithwaite, 1990; Carbaugh, 1998).
- U.S. Americans are much more likely to use public displays of affection than their Japanese counterparts (Nakane, 1984).

The generalizable conclusions of these few studies are offered here as representative of the hundreds of studies that have explored the nonverbal differences among diverse cultures.

Our objective here is explicitly not to summarize existing studies in interracial nonverbal communication. We align ourselves with Collins (1990), who encourages a critical thinking approach to social scientific research whose "aim is to create scientific descriptions of reality by producing objective generalizations" (p. 205). Because of the great diversity within each group, such "objective, statistically significant" generalizations typically provide little direction in actual face-to-face interactions with persons who are racially/ethnically different (Orbe, 1995a). In most circumstances, generalizations focus on racial/ethnic differences with little attention to other cultural variables such as sex, socioeconomic status, or age. These elements, in fact, may play a more salient role in one's communication in some situational contexts. For instance, research reports that sex differences within and between groups are often lost in cross-cultural comparisons (e.g., see Waldron & Di Mare's 1998 work on the impact of sex differences on Japanese/U.S. American communication differences). Sex and/or gender differences, then, are erased within a focus on race/ethnicity. What is ultimately concluded in these studies applies to the so-called typical racial/ethnic group member, an entity that is largely a creation of social science. For instance, do you think you could find a Japanese American who displays all of the verbal and nonverbal qualities generalized to her cultural group? In his early work, Edward T. Hall (1966) made the problematic nature of generalizations apparent when he stated, "It should be emphasized that these generalizations are not representative of human behavior in general—or even of American behavior in general—but only of the group included in the sample" (p. 116).

Problems of generalization notwithstanding, the information generated on patterns of nonverbal behaviors among different racial/ethnic groups can provide an important backdrop to effective interracial communication. Such insight can increase awareness of the possible perceptions of specific behaviors (see Table 3.1). Next we briefly discuss several nonverbal elements that should be acknowledged when choosing appropriate/effective language.

The Context of Language Choices

Oftentimes, people with little experience in intergroup relations desire a quick and easy fool proof list of the "do's and don'ts" for communicating with others who are racially or ethnically different. We have made a conscious attempt to avoid such a simplistic treatment of the complex issues related to interracial communication. We are often approached by colleagues and students who are seeking insight into an interracial communication problem. Typically, they offer a brief summary of a problematic interracial case scenario and then ask the supposedly simple question, "What should I do?" We have found that, in almost all cases, there is never a simple answer to these types of inquiries. Most of the time, the best response we can come up with is "It depends. . . . ." Past experiences reveal that the most productive way to help someone deal with interracial conflict is to provide some applied research guidelines. Then we can help others gain a more complete understanding of what they perceive as relatively simple problem.

One of the most important considerations in choosing appropriate/effective language centers around the specific relationship between the parties involved, as well as the particular situational context. Where did the interaction take place? Who was present during the interaction? How well do you know the individuals? What past experiences do you share with one another? What do you (they) know about their (your) lived experiences? Within what relationship is the interaction enacted (classmates, co-workers, friends, acquaintances, strangers)? One basic axiom states that communication has both a content and relationship dimension. Within our discussion here, this axiom can be used to understand that certain verbal cues (content) will have varying meanings and effects depending on the status (relationship) of the parties involved. Effective interracial communicators must come to understand the appropriate nonverbal language for the particular interaction *as negotiated by all parties involved.* In this regard, the same relationship can be perceived quite differently from each person's perspective. For instance, research has indicated that African American women often take offense when European American women assume a position of familiarity with their language cues (i.e.,

TABLE 3.1 **GUIDE TO PERCEPTIONS OF INTERRACIAL VERBAL AND NONVERBAL BEHAVIORS**

The information included in this table highlights some specific examples of how verbal and nonverbal cues can generate various meanings depending on ingroup and outgroup perceptions. They are offered here not as generalizations applicable to all ethnic group members in any one group, but as information to assist in you recognizing potential sources of miscommunication.

Specific Behavior	Possible Ingroup Perception	Possible Outgroup Perception
Avoidance of direct eye contact by Latino/as	Used to communicate attentiveness or respect	A sign of inattentiveness; direct eye is preferred
An African American who aggressively challenges a point to which she or he disagrees	Acceptable means of dialogue; not regarded as verbal abuse, nor a precursor to violence.	Arguments are viewed as inappropriate and a sign of potential immediate violence.
Asian American use of finger gestures to beckon others	Appropriate if used by adults for children, but highly offensive if used to call adults.	Appropriate gesture to use with both children and adults.
Interruptions used by African Americans	Tolerated in individual/group discussions; attention is given to most assertive voice.	Perceived as rude or aggressive; clear rules for turn taking must be maintained.
Silence used by Native Americans	A sign of respect, thoughtfulness, and/or uncertainty/ambiguity.	Silence indicates boredom, disagreement, or a refusal to participate/respond.
The use of touch by Latino/as	Perceived as normal and appropriate for interpersonal interactions.	Deemed as appropriate for some intimate or friendly interactions; otherwise perceived as a violation of personal space.
Public displays of intense emotions by African Americans	Personal expressiveness is valued and regarded as appropriate in most settings	Violates U.S. societal expectations for self-controlled public behaviors; inappropriate for most public settings.
Asian Americans touching or holding hands of same-sex friends	Seen as acceptable behavior that signifies closeness of platonic relationships.	Perceived as inappropriate, especially for male friends
Latino/as use of lengthy greetings or the exchange of pleasantries prior to business meetings	Regarded as an important element of establishing rapport with colleagues.	Seen as a waste of time; getting to the business at hand is valued.

"Hey, girl, how are you?") in their interactions, which they perceive as premature (Orbe, Drummond, & Camara, 1998).

This line of reasoning is also useful in offering insight into the importance of recognizing cultural ownership of certain verbal cues. Because of shared cultural experiences and an acknowledged relationship status, two members of a particular racial/ethnic group may use language that is appropriate between them but highly inappropriate when others (ingroup and especially outgroup) use it. One example is when Filipino American men use the term "Pinoy" (pee-noy) to describe one another, but regard the term as derogatory when used by non-Filipinos (Sing, 1989). The use of "niggah" among African Americans (not to be confused with outgroup uses of "nigger") also helps illustrate the idea of cultural ownership. Some argue that, among African Americans, the term reflects the positivity and unity of ingroup relations: "I have heard the word "niggah" (note the spelling, dig the sound) all of my life. Many of my elders and friends use it with phenomenal eloquence. They say it to express amusement, incredulity, disgust, or affection. These people are very much being themselves—proudly, intensely, sometimes loudly." (Brown, 1993, p. 138). Other African Americans argue that any forms of the word, given its negative history, should be not used. Regardless of where individuals fall within the debate of ingroup use, clearly it represents a word extremely offensive when used by non-African Americans.

The Context of Nonverbal Cues

Growing up, it was not uncommon for children to be reminded by their parents that, "It's not *what* you said, but *how* you said it." This childhood lesson is a valuable one in terms of the importance of verbal and nonverbal cues in the context of inter-racial communication. Language choices, and subsequently the meaning they generate among interaction participants, can not be understood outside of their context. This crucial idea is oftentimes ignored by communicators who focus on the specific language used, with little recognition of the importance of the context. The following real-life example illustrates this point:

> Recently, an African American woman filed charges of racial/sexual harassment against a European American male supervisor. Her major complaint was that he consistently referred to her as a "little African princess." When confronted about his specific language, he could not understand how this phrase could be offensive to someone who identified with her cultural roots as strongly as the accuser.

What is your initial reaction to this case scenario? Were the man's continued remarks the basis for a racial/sexual harassment suit or was the woman being overly sensitive? (This specific example might serve as an excellent resource to explore perceptual differences based on a number of cultural elements, including race/ethnicity, sex, and age.) Gut reactions aside, it is extremely difficult to evaluate this case without the contextualizing power of nonverbal cues. Given the focus of our discussion, a number of questions should have arisen. For instance, think of the value of potential insight gained from the following questions: What vocal qualities were used by the man? Was his tone condescending, sarcastic, or complimentary? What specific context did the phrase occur in? One-on-one interaction? In front of a large group? In a business meeting? Or at the annual holiday party that celebrates Christmas, Hanukkah, and Kwanzaa? What type of eye contact (if any) was maintained during these interactions? Was the man standing over the woman, walking past her, or in her face? As you can undoubtedly see, obtaining answers to these questions helps develop a fuller understanding of meaning associated with specific language choices.

Remember the important point that, despite particular language choices, scholars believe a majority of the meaning of a message is communicated nonverbally. This crucial element of interracial communication does not cancel the importance of making good language choices. However, it does assist us in recognizing the key role that nonverbal cues play within the negotiation of meaning between racially/ethnically diverse persons. An increased consciousness of the meanings that others attach to your nonverbal behaviors—especially given that nonverbal cues are used more unconsciously than verbal ones—is crucial to effective interracial communication.

The most effective communicators, particularly those who are committed to maintaining and strengthening intergroup relations, acknowledge *intentionality* as a key issue in their response to certain language they regard as inappropriate or offensive. The most effective responses for the same language clue may be drastically different for those individuals who are identified as "unconscious incompetents" (naive offenders) as opposed to those whose language choices are more consciously offensive (Howell, 1982). For instance, would your response to a child's use of the word, *Chink*, to describe a person of Chinese descent, be the same if one of your professors used it? This is not to say that intentionality is necessarily more important than the effects that certain language choices have on interactions. However, it does take the motive (or lack thereof) behind using certain terms into consideration. As we discussed earlier, language can be regarded as a tool, prism, and display of internal cognitions. Persons who come to understand how the language, consciously and/or unconsciously, serves multiple roles are at the best vantage point to manage an effective communication interaction.

CONCLUSION

After reading this chapter, you should have an increased consciousness of the importance of verbal and nonverbal messages within the context of interracial communication. Language is a powerful resource that serves multiple functions in our everyday lives. Throughout this chapter, as well as in the remainder of the text, we have made a conscious attempt to avoid what might result in a definitive laundry list regarding interracial language use. Instead, our discussion revolves around the understanding of the crucial role that language systems play in our everyday lives.

Several general guidelines, however, may help summarize the central points of this chapter. Although these bits of advice offer quick points of reference for everyday interactions, they are best understood within the context of the information provided within this chapter. To summarize, effective interracial communicators do the following:

- Recognize the role that power plays within language, labels, and issues of naming (including ingroup cultural ownership of certain terms and phrases).

- Make informed choices about the verbal/nonverbal cues they use in particular situational contexts *and* assume responsibility for their effects.

- Develop a deep understanding of the similarities and differences of verbal and nonverbal language systems within and between different groups.

- Seek out additional information when needed! If an appropriate relationship has been established, this may mean asking specific people of color their perceptions of particular verbal cues. It may also include using other means, such as books, videos, and/or other educational resources.

OPPORTUNITIES FOR EXTENDED LEARNING

1. In order to gain a more personal understanding of the associative power of labels and names, take the Implicit Association Test developed by Yale University. You can find it at http://www.yale.edu/implicit/. Follow the instructions to the "Black-White IAT." After taking the test (it will take approximately 5 minutes), discuss your impressions of the test with your friends, family, and classmates.

2. Sometimes recognizing one's own position of privilege is difficult. Try to create a list of specific "privileges" that European Americans have in the United States. These are benefits that, because of their dominant group status, European Americans take for granted (e.g., "flesh-colored" bandages matching their skin color). If you need some prompting, check out the work of Peggy McIntosh (1995b). In order to understand how all persons have some positions of relative privilege, it may be helpful to generate different lists of privilege based on gender, abilities, sexual orientation, or socioeconomic status.

3. Use your *InfoTrac College Edition* and complete a search on recent examples of interracial miscommunication (key word: *U.S. race relations*). Select one or two case scenarios and attempt to locate specific sources that might have served as barriers to effective communication. If you conclude that the article does not include enough information for you to render an evaluation, what type of additional facts-in terms of verbal and nonverbal cues—are needed? Create a list of questions for the participants.

4. Generate a list of responses to the following sentence: "I find it offensive when I hear (*name of specific group*) using terms and phrases like (*name specific language*), because . . ." Then share your responses with others. Is there a general agreement among both people racially like, and not like, you? Why or why not?

5. Based on what you have learned from this chapter, create a list of language guidelines to be used in classroom discussion. First, think about certain rules individually. Second, discuss your list with others in groups. Finally, see if all of the groups can come together with a consensus of general (or possibly specific) guidelines. You might also want to reflect back to the guidelines for discussions that were created as you attempted to build community (see Chapter 1). Remember, the value of this exercise is more in the process than the actual results of these discussions!

THE DEVELOPMENT OF RACIAL IDENTITY AND RACIAL PERCEPTIONS

Some have described the United States as having a general preoccupation with identity issues (Field & Travisano, 1984). According to other scholars, cultural identities are bound to get more, rather than less, complex as we move into the 21st century (Tanno & Gonzalez, 1998). A good place to begin any discussion on racial/ethnic/cultural identity (topic of both Chapters 4 and 5) is with some honest, straightforward self-assessment. Before reading any further, take a few minutes to reflect on how you would describe your cultural identity. (Box 4.1 can be used specifically for this purpose.) What aspects of "who you are" quickly come to mind? How do these characteristics and/or roles reflect how you have come to define "culture"? Is your response to this line of inquiry relatively easy, extremely difficult, or somewhere between the two? Have there been particular events in your life that have triggered a search for a deeper understanding of your cultural identity? How comfortable do you feel identifying one specific aspect of your cultural identity as most central to who you are?

This chapter will provide you with some detailed descriptions of theoretical frameworks that explain how racial/ethnic identities, as well as perceptions of racially/ethnically diverse others, are formed. Although the information will not directly answer any of the questions just listed for any particular person, it will help you understand your own particular cultural standpoint more easily. The first portion of this chapter presents general information concerning identity formation. The remainder of the chapter details the stages that specific racial/ethnic group members (European Americans, U.S. ethnic minorities, and biracial U.S. Americans) experience as they form their particular race/ethnic identities.

APPROACHES TO STUDYING IDENTITY

The concept of identity is universal. Nevertheless, the ways in which personal/cultural identities are played out in different cultures varies (Geertz, 1976).

4.1   *Who Am I?*

A common exercise used to help people self-assess their identity is known as the "Who Am I?" exercise (e.g., Kuhn & McPartland, 1954). Before reading any further, take a few minutes to reflect on how you define yourself. Take a piece of paper and jot down "I am" 20 times down the left side of the paper. Then take a few minutes and complete each statement. Do this with the assumption that no one but you will see the list. The key is not to take a lot of time on this exercise. Just write down what pops into your mind in the order it occurs to you. Do not continue reading until you have completed this exercise.

Take a minute to read through your list and reflect on the descriptors that you provided to the question, "Who am I?" Pay attention to the types of responses you used to complete the sentence. How many of your items represent specific roles that you play in life (e.g., student, friend, mother/father, daughter/son)? Do others refer to aspects of cultural groups to which you belong (e.g., women, Asian American, Generation X, gay/lesbian/bisexual) and/or personal characteristics (e.g., handsome, intelligent, caring, aggressive)? Scholars suggest that the ordering of statements may also be significant in identifying a hierarchy of the most important aspects of your personal/cultural identity (Kuhn & McPartland, 1954). For instance, are the responses at the top of your list the most central to who you are? How might your list have changed given a different time, location, and set of consequences? If prompted, could you articulate why you listed the particular characteristics in the order they appear?

Research on how individuals come to establish their identities has generated a significant amount of information regarding what has been established as a complex, intricate, lifelong process. Much of the work in the area of identity development has focused on how young children and adolescents engage in the process of formulating personal/cultural identities.

Most notable in the existing literature is the work and influence of Erik Erikson (1963,1968). According to Erikson (1963), the major task of adolescence is establishing an independent identity. Central to his ideas about identity formation is the recognition that individuals move through a series of interrelated stages in their psychosocial development. Each stage, according to Erikson (1968), involves a particular aspect of identity crisis. Individuals are able to move to another stage by resolving issues related to current stages. Social science theorists, representing a number of fields including psychology, sociology, and communication, have applied the fundamental works of Erikson to a number of contexts.

Consistent with the dominant worldview of the United States and most other Western cultures, much of this work has tended to view identity as an individual entity (Carbaugh, 1987; Geertz, 1976). Within this perspective, self is regarded as a unique, separated whole. This underlying cultural assumption is clear in most of Erikson's (1963) work. He stresses that the formation of a personal identity coincides with establishing autonomy and independence. More recent perspectives have recognized that this work is based on the individualistic notions of Western cultures. In doing so, they have worked to embrace a more collectivistic approach to studying identity, one in which the self is defined in relation to others (Shotter & Gergen, 1989).

For the purposes of this chapter, we identify ourselves as scholars who see the important role that both the individual and relational serve in identity formation. Like Rosenthal (1987), we believe a person's cultural identity develops through interaction with others. Additionally, identity formation is a function of the individual and his or her relations to a particular cultural reference group and that group's place in larger society. Therefore, we suggest viewing identity as both an individual entity (representative of traditional psychological perspectives) *and* as a relational one (representative of social communication theory). Like Hecht, Collier, and Ribeau (1993), we believe the most productive way to approach identity formation is to avoid accepting the false dichotomy that sees the location of identity within the self or the interaction. In other words, we argue that identity development simultaneously involves personal and individual characteristics (e.g., personality characteristics) *and* cultural identities associated with particular roles, reference groups, and cultural categories. Attempting to isolate one or the other is impossible. Instead, we use a dual approach to identity formation that views cultural identities as co-created between individuals and the communities.

The Co-Creation of Identity

One of the most influential works in identity development scholarship is *Mind, Self, and Society* (Mead, 1934). In this book, George Herbert Mead described the concept of self in terms of its direct relationship to various segments of social life. His work marks a shift from a focus on the self to one on the communication (symbolic interaction) between self and others. Although some communication scholars have identified problems associated with Mead's work (e.g., Tanno & Gonzalez, 1998), his attention to the important relationship between self-identity and society highlights the central role that communication plays in identity formation. In this regard, Mead's contributions inform the current perspectives of cultural identity development, especially those that appear in the literature associated with the field of communication. For instance, his approach to identity development is well represented in Goffman's (1967) proposition that identities are both negotiated and enacted through communication and relationships. Mead's work is also fundamental to the current work in symbolic interactionism, both the Chicago and Iowa schools (Meltzer & Petras, 1970). The framework provided in this section draws from these schools of thought, in addition to more current scholarship on racial/ethnic identity development (e.g., Hecht et al., 1993) that sees identity formation as a co-created entity.

Simply put, cultural identities are co-created and re-created in everyday interactions (Yep, 1998). This general idea is grounded in Mead's work and subsequently strengthened by the advances of his students. For instance, Blumer (1969) has championed the idea that the sense of self emerges from a process of definition/redefinition that occurs through social interaction. In other words, identity is negotiated—formed, maintained, and modified—through our interactions with others. Identity also simultaneously influences these very interactions through our expectations and perceptions of others' behaviors (Hecht et al., 1993). In essence, a person's sense of self can be seen as an integral part of that person's social behavior (and vice versa). Part of a person's social behavior includes finding appropriate names and labels (remember the discussion on the importance of language in Chapter 3) that locate the self in socially recognizable categories (Burke & Reitzes, 1981). Most often, we gain our self-identities through a process of contrasting ingroup and outgroup characteristics (Brewer & Campbell, 1976; DeVos, 1982; Turner, 1987). In other words, we come to understand who we are as we compare and contrast ourselves with others. Helms (1994) suggests, for instance, that most European Americans largely define their "Whiteness" in terms of the opposite or lack of "Blackness" (see, for example, Morrison, 1991). Through socialization, we learn and adopt social categories that allow us to make sense out of complex environments (Tajfel, 1974).

The self, within this perspective, is best understood as an organized system of meanings created through interaction (Burke & Tully, 1977). In order to understand this idea, you must recognize the fundamental role that both interactants play in the process of identity creation (Yep, 1998). Therefore, the individual herself or himself is not the only—or the major—source of identity creation. Forming your identity comes from multiple interactions over the course of your life (Hegde, 1998).

Think about how others—especially those that play an important role in your life—interact with you. What messages do they send you about their perceptions of you through both their verbal and nonverbal cues (both directly and indirectly)? Do you accept, reject, or ignore their perceptions of you? Symbolic interactionists would suggest that the images others communicate to you are a central aspect of identity formation. Another central element is your reaction to their communication. Gradually, some of these meanings generated through this interaction are generalized over time and become established as core elements of your identity (Hecht et al., 1993).

FOCUS ON RACIAL/ETHNIC IDENTITY

So far, we have summarized some existing research on identity and identity formation to help you understand how persons come to define themselves culturally. Toward this objective, we have combined research on personal identity and cultural identity issues. This section continues to use these cultural identity perspectives, but we focus our attention more narrowly on racial/ethnic identity development. Specifically, we discuss three fundamental contributors to the co-creation of racial/ethnic identity (family and friends, dominant societal institutions/organizations, and media) to illustrate the process by which perceptions of racialized self and others are formed. One of the premises of this text is that race and ethnicity represent social categories that develop during early socialization and maintain a central place in self, culture, and communication processes (Gordon, 1978). In the next few sections, we discuss how individual racial/ethnic identity is co-created through interactions with family and friends, societal organizations, and the mass media.

Family and Friends

One of the central aspects of Mead's (1934) framework is the idea of a generalized other, a concept he uses to refer to the collective body from which the individual sees the self. In other words, it is an individual's perception of the general way that others see him or her. Throughout your life, you have learned these perceptions from years of socialization and interaction with others. Each person has a number of significant others who have been particularly influential in her or his identity development. Hecht et al. (1993) refer to these individuals as orientational others. For most individuals, orientational others are family members (not restricted only to blood relations) and friends.

How do family and friends help co-create our racial/ethnic identity? The answer to this question is complicated. Racial/ethnic identity is developed in a number of ways, including direct communication about race/ethnic issues, role modeling, and general socialization (see, for example, Orbe, 1994). An extremely powerful component of the co-creation of race/ethnic identity is reflected in the labels that family and friends use. Taylor (1992) notes that "People do not acquire the languages needed for self-definition on their own. Rather, we are introduced to them through interaction with others who matter to us" (p. 32). Think back—as far as your memory allows—to the terms and labels that friends and family members have used to describe you as well as themselves. How does your self-identity reflect some level of conscious or unconscious acceptance of these labels? Can you think of instances when you felt uncomfortable with the racial/ethnic labels used by or about family and friends? Such experiences reflect one aspect of the powerful role that family and friends play in the co-creation of identity (Dodd & Baldwin, 1998). Pratt (1998), in his work on American Indian identity, also recognizes the central role of these orientational others in terms of peer group influence.

As described by a number of communication scholars (e.g., Gangotena, 1997; James, 1997a; McKay, 1997; Stone, 1996), one of the primary ways that racial/ethnic identity is created for people is through family stories. Most often, but not always, family stories are passed down orally from generation to generation and represent some truth or life lesson. In terms of those particular family stories that focus on race/ethnicity, many provide pertinent information used to develop perceptions of the racial/ethnic identities of self and others. Navita Cummings James (1997a) describes how significant stories from her youth (e.g., stories of lynching, murder, slavery) represented a specific set of beliefs and stereotypes about European Americans and African Americans, including the following:

- Black people are "just as good" as White people—and in some ways
  (e.g., morally) better . . .
- Black people have to be twice as good as Whites to be considered half as good . . .
- White people probably have some kind of inferiority complex which drives them to continually "put down" Blacks and anyone else who is not White . . .
- White men are usually arrogant. White women are usually lazy.
- There are some good White people, but they are the exceptions. (pp. 49–50)

These perceptions were gained through the communication of both European and African American sides of James's family. In addition, she is quick to point out that these childhood beliefs and stereotypes did not immediately become part of her self-identity (p. 50). Instead, her work on family stories, culture, and identity suggests that family stories represent one source of cultural information used in the co-creation of racial/ethnic identity.

Dominant Societal Institutions/Organizations

As we saw in the descriptions in the previous section, our family and friends typically (but certainly not always) serve an important role in providing information concerning our racial/ethnic identity (Dodd & Baldwin, 1998). For many parents with children of color, cultivating a positive racial/ethnic self-identity in their children is seen as important (Hale-Benson, 1986), especially for those who believe children from racial/ethnic microcultures who lack a strong, positive identity are prone to fail in dominant societal institutions/organizations. What do we mean by "dominant societal institutions/organizations"? This is a phrase that best represents various predominately European American organizations that reflect the dominant cultural values of the United States (e.g., hospitals, schools, government agencies, police, etc.). Oftentimes the messages that individuals receive from these institutions concerning their racial/ethnic identity either explicitly or implicitly contradict those from friends and family. In other words, certain institutions serve as the "recognition, nonrecognition, or misrecognition" of racial/ethnic identities (Taylor, 1992, p. 32). Think about how certain persons in authority—teachers, police officers, doctors, social workers, —have interacted with you over the course of your life. How has their communication, both verbally and nonverbally, contained messages concerning their own as well your racial/ethnic identity? Consciously or unconsciously you have dealt with these messages as part of an ongoing process of identity development.

The lived experiences of biracial and multiracial persons in the United States offer a vivid example of how the co-creation of racial/ethnic identity involves ingroup and outgroup perceptions. Autoethnographical research indicates that multiracial families talk about race and ethnicity issues among themselves differently depending on a variety of interrelated factors. These include the influence/presence of parents, racial/ethnic makeup of neighborhoods, and personal philosophies of race/racism (Orbe, 1999). A growing number of parents are raising their children to resist pressure to choose one racial/ethnic identity. Instead they embrace a multiracial identity that allows them to express all aspects of who they are (Wardle, 1987). Problems occur when orientational others (e.g., a teacher or a social worker) fail to recognize this identity and continue to see them in traditional racial categories that follow a one-drop rule. What happens, then, when a child must deal with conflicting messages in terms of her or his racial/ethnic identity? Take the case of a young girl whose racial lineage consists of African, European, Asian, and Native descent (in that approximate order) whose experiences were described by Orbe, (1999). At birth, her parents believed the hospital records should indicate her "race/ethnicity" as multiracial and list all of her racial heritage (as was done with their first child). The assisting records nurse, based on her perceptions of the baby's mother, listed her race/ethnicity as "Black." The family's pediatrician, despite knowing the multiracial family for over a year, recorded "White" in the appropriate box on another hospital form. Her designation was based on the girl's physical features (blond hair, blue eyes, and peach complexion). Despite some conflicting perceptions, the little girl has been raised to see herself as multiracial. Nevertheless, distinct differences in how outgroup members describe and perceive her continue to contradict this racial/ethnic identity.

This case study helps us understand the complex ways that interactions with authority figures must be negotiated within the context of family and friends' communication about racial/ethnic identities. Only time will tell how her co-created self-identity will ultimately be formed in the context of interactions with family, friends, and members of the larger macroculture. We would suggest that all people experience some conflicting messages about their identities (although at various levels of intensity). This process is aptly described by Hegde (1998) as "identity emergence." It refers to the multiple, sometimes contradicting, interactions that characterize the experiences of human life. One societal institution that plays a significant role in this process of identity emergence is the mass media. Because of the growing interest in the power of mass-mediated images, we separate it from other dominant societal organizations/institutions.

| 4.2 | *Personal Reflections* |

While I was lecturing at another university recently, an African American woman described me as a "cultural enigma." Her comment was part of a question she was asking about the presentation that I had just given about my research. Although I probably shouldn't be, I am surprised at the level of intensity that often accompanies people's need to know my racial/ethnic/cultural identity. Within the context of this woman's comments, she seemed to accept the difficulty that occurs when people try to classify my cultural identities in terms of "either/or" categories (see MPO's personal reflection in Chapter 1). However, this is not typically the case. More often

Personal Reflections (*continued*)

than not, people exhibit an intense need to know "what I am." In the past few years, I've experienced acquaintances and colleagues who do the following:

- use direct questions ("What *are* you?," "Are you Black?," "What's your cultural background?—You have *something* in you, but I can't figure it out!"),
- touch the back of my head in an attempt to measure how "nappy/kinky" my hair is (I had just met this African American woman at a conference; this was her way of trying to figure out my racial background),
- tell me that "everyone is dying to figure out what you are" and that "some people don't feel comfortable interacting with you until they know".
- assume they know my race/ethnicity and then try to argue with others (including some of my good friends) when they are corrected!

Part of me wants to respond to these types of inquiries by saying, "What difference does it make?" But of course I realize that race and ethnicity do make a difference in the United States (as well as other countries).

Writing this book has increased my consciousness of how these experiences work in the cocreation of my racial/ethnic identity, especially in terms of how others see me. It's interesting because more often than not people of color typically recognize that "I've got something in me" whereas many European Americans are quicker to designate me as a "White male." When I correct them (which is often, but not always), reactions include shock, apologies, embarrassment, and aggression. "You can say what you want, but I see you as a White man and that's how I'm going to interact with you!," responded one person. Although each of these interactions is both symbolic and significant to me, I imagine that most of these individuals are relatively unaware of the power of their verbal and nonverbal cues. Part of their uncertainty and anxiety is probably fueled by a recognition that their self-identities are tied to how they identify me. As James Baldwin (1990) put it, "If I'm not who you say I am, then you're not who you think you are." So how do these interactions affect my racial/ethnic identity? I'm not exactly sure, but I do recognize that they definitely do have some impact—if they didn't, why would I remember them so vividly?—MPO

Mass Media

Considerable research exists on the impact of mass media representations on an individual's perceptions of race, ethnicity, and culture, both in terms of self and others (e.g., Stroman, 1991). In light of this research, Chapter 11 discusses how mass-mediated communication comes to represent—and ultimately affect—inter-racial communication in a variety of contexts. Several theoretical frameworks have been created to assess the impacts of the mass media on perceptions of self and others. These include, but are not limited to, cultivation theory, agenda setting theory, critical theory, uses and gratification approach to media, social learning theory, and the theory of a spiral of silence. Each of these theoretical frameworks suggests different levels of mass media influence. However, one consistent idea is common across this diverse set of media theories: Mass media representations do have some impact on societal perceptions of self, culture, and society. According to Kellner (1995), media culture "provides the materials out of which many people construct their sense of class, of ethnicity and race, of nationality, of sexuality, or us and them. Media culture helps shape the prevalent view of the world and deepest values. . . . Media culture provides the materials to create identities" (p. 1).

Much of the research on mass media representations and effects has focused on television images and their impact on viewers who watch large amounts of television programming (Stroman, 1991). However, of equal or possibly greater importance, are the mass-mediated representations found in mainstream books, films, maga-zines, newspapers, and music—all of which seem to reinforce those racial/ethnic images found on television. For children of color, these forms of mass media serve as a relentless source of dominant cultural values, beliefs, and attitudes (Miller & Rotheram-Borus, 1994). Mainstream mass media forms have been largely criticized for simply perpetuating negative racial/ethnic stereotypes (Harris & Hill, 1998). According to bell hooks, exposure to negative images is unavoidable for African Americans, given the pervasive nature of the mass media. "Opening a magazine or book, turning on the television set, watching a film, or looking at photographs in public spaces, we are most likely to see images of black people that reinforce and reinscribe white supremacy" (hooks, 1992, p. 1).

Clearly, the messages contained in the mass media serve as another source of information concerning racial and ethnic groups that all persons, regardless of cultural background, must deal with. Halualani (1998) describes this process as a "struggle of culture"—the clash between cultural identities produced for us and by us (p. 265). In terms of Mead's (1934) focus on symbolic interactionism, we can see how mass-mediated images might contribute to how an individual understands her or his own "generalized other."

Thus far, we have focused primarily on the co-creation of racial/ethnic self-iden-tity. However, during this time, we also gain perceptions of others who are racially/ethnically different. When opportunities for substantial interracial interac-tion are limited because of personal, social, or physical distance, mass media representations have a greater impact on outgroup perceptions. The following excerpt illustrates the power of mass-mediated forms of communication. As you will see, this is not only in terms of how an individual perceives himself or herself, but also how others come to perceive and interact with those who are racially/ethnically different from themselves.

> A white woman acquaintance at my university pulled me aside and in a serious voice announced that she understood what I had been talking about all of these months about my ethnicity and race. "I saw the movie THE JOY LUCK CLUB with my husband over the weekend. I feel so close to you now, like I understand you so much better! Chinese women are so lucky to have relationships with their mothers with such deep emotions!" I felt confused and speechless and didn't know where to begin. In addition to the fact that I am not Chinese American, I wondered what in the world this woman and her husband have fantasized about my life and family relations based on this Hollywood movie. (Wong, 1998, p. 131)

Within this example, a clear connection is made between media influences and personal perceptions of others (see Chapter 11).

Our discussion of the co-creation of cultural identities has provided a framework to gain insight into a highly complex process. Individuals come to understand racialized perceptions of self and others through many different mechanisms. This information provides an important backdrop for the next section on cultural identity development models. As you read the descriptions of the various stages in each model, think about the crucial role that these and other information sources play in this dynamic, ongoing process.

CULTURAL IDENTITY DEVELOPMENT MODELS

According to Phinney (1993), the formation of cultural identity generally involves three phases: (1) unexamined cultural identity, (2) cultural identity search, and (3) cultural identity achievement. Following a description of each of these identity formation components, we turn to the specific ways that scholars have described how macrocultural and microcultural group members (including those persons identifying as biracial) form their racial identities. As you will see, all of the existing racial identity development models (e.g., Banks, 1976; Hardiman, 1994; Helms, 1994; Jackson & Hardiman, 1983; Ponterotto & Pedersen, 1993) reflect Phinney's (1993) three general phases.

During the first stage of cultural identity formation, we function in society with an *unexamined cultural identity*. We take our cultural values, norms, beliefs, customs, and other characteristics for granted. Our culture is experienced as "natural" and generates little interest. Microcultural group members to tend to become aware of racial differences and identities earlier than persons of European descent (Ferguson, Gever, Trinh, & West, 1990; Nance & Foeman, 1998). Even so, many children experience their early years from an unexamined cultural identity standpoint. Typically, young people lack an awareness of cultural differences and the central role that culture plays in everyday encounters. At some point, however, something triggers a move into the next stage (*cultural identity search*). Typically this shift can be caused by conflicting messages from family, friends, social organizations, or the media about race and ethnicity issues. Searching for our cultural identity involves an ongoing process of exploration, reflection, and evaluation. In other words, it involves thinking about our self-identity and how we fit into any number of different cultural groups. For some of us, this is completed in our young adult years. For others, it takes longer. The final stage, according to Phinney (1993), is *cultural identity achievement*. Within this final stage, we develop a clear, confident understanding and acceptance of ourselves. Subsequently, we internalize a strong cultural identity. Although this element is apparent in each of the racial identity development models we describe later in this chapter, one crucial element must be acknowledged: Our cultural identities are not static, fixed, or enduring. Instead, our identities are dynamic and subject to change as our field of lived experiences increases.

Identity formation, along these lines, is best seen as "becoming" rather than "being" (Sarup, 1996). The racial identity development models discussed here take on a linear, unidimensional form (Miller & Rotheram-Borus, 1994). Still, we must not oversimplify the complex ways that cultural identity is developed. Seldom does it occur in a neat, orderly fashion. Although some of us experience a straightforward progression of identity formation—moving from an unexamined state, to an identity search, and concluding with a clear sense of identity achievement—most eventually experience a "recycling" of stages based on new experiences (Helms, 1994). Because of this, the process of identity formation is more like a spiraling loop than a straight line.

As we alluded to earlier, Phinney's (1993) three general stages of cultural identity formation apply generically to all persons. Given the history of race in the United States (see Chapter 2), it should come as no surprise that the process racial/ethnic microcultural and macrocultural group members use to form their identities is similar, yet different. U.S. Americans of European descent create their identities within a dominant society that affirms the value of their culture. Persons of color within the United States, in contrast, must deal with social norms that define their life experiences as "sub-cultural." Because of this reality, macrocultural and microcultural group identity formation processes differ. People of color must form their racial identities within a larger society that does not necessarily value the same things. For example, think about how our society defines standards of beauty. Traditionally, beauty has been defined through European American standards in terms of skin color, hair texture, body shape, and facial features. How do you think identities are formed for individuals who do not match these standards? Without question, all persons are affected by these standards. However, you can see how the effects are different for people of color whose cultural standards contradict those present in the larger society.

Understanding Whiteness

The color of a person's skin holds social significance in the United States (Wander, Martin, & Nakayama, 1999). Historically, much of the research and self-reflection related to race and racism has focused on experiences of racial/ethnic microcultures. Because European Americans were in the majority, their culture was less visible than others (Hayman & Levit, 1997) who seemed deviant and in the minority. Being "White" was a sign of normalcy, importance, or privilege (in that it is viewed as the standard by which other racial categories are compared). This idea is not limited to race and ethnicity, though. Other macrocultures have also benefited from their majority status. Their experiences (e.g., heterosexuality, able-bodied, masculinity) have also remained unnamed and uninvestigated compared to those of specific microcultures.

Studies that explore Whiteness have increased tremendously in the past 10 years (Johnson, 1999). The interest in talking about Whiteness has been seen in academic fields such as sociology, English, education, women's studies, and communication. One of the major areas in which Whiteness has been placed at the center of analyses is in the work done by critical race theorists (see Chapter 6). Discussions of Whiteness have also appeared in the popular press (Stowe, 1996). We think it is important to address Whiteness here before our discussions on racial/ethnic identity development. Based on our experiences and those of our colleagues across the United States, we have come to realize that many European Americans do not see themselves as cultural beings. Because of their relative privilege, they are more likely to focus on the cultures of other racial/ethnic groups. Therefore, when asked about their cultural identity most European Americans struggle with understanding their Whiteness as a cultural entity. Some students even felt silly or embarrassed identifying themselves as "White people." Some European Americans feel they are unaffected by racism and/or have nothing to contribute to discussions on racial issues. Thus studies on Whiteness encourage European Americans to identify and understand a cultural/racial specificity that previously has gone unexplored.

By naming and exploring European American culture, Whiteness studies play an important part in effective interracial communication research and practice. First, studying Whiteness fosters an increased awareness of how race and racism shapes the lives of European Americans (Frankenburg, 1993). It helps all of us to view communication as a racialized process—meaning that our communication is structured by larger societal racial dynamics. Second, understanding Whiteness sharpens our awareness of how racial categorization is used to reinforce old hierarchies in which some races are more superior than others (see Chapter 2). It also helps us recognize how Whiteness signals dominance, normalcy, and privilege (rather than subordination, deviancy, and disadvantage) in the United States (Frankenberg, 1993). Finally, Whiteness studies also assign each person a role in race relations. No longer can European Americans sit by the sidelines in discussions of race and racism. Naming and understanding their Whiteness means they, as much as people of color, have a stake in issues related to race. In this regard, the increased attention to Whiteness is part of a larger attempt to better inform race relations.

In short, Whiteness studies enable us to advance our understanding of European American culture beyond that of a normalized and raceless category. Understanding Whiteness helps us recognize how race shapes European Americans' lives. As this growing body of research continues to develop, other important insights are also gained. For instance, Nakayama and Martin (1999) advance studies on Whiteness in innovative ways. In particular they study the role that communication plays in forming of this aspect of social identity. Their edited book also points to an important aspect of this line of research: Understanding Whiteness requires us to see how it relates to other aspects of a person's cultural identity. In other words, Whiteness is not the only—or necessarily the most important—cultural marker we need to recognize. Instead, we must increase our understanding of how Whiteness intersects with other cultural elements (socioeconomic status, gender, sexual orientation, etc.) to inform a person's lived experiences (Frankenburg, 1993) (see Chapter 5). Next, we focus our attention on how the social identity of Whiteness has developed.

Macrocultural Identity Development Model

Ever since the work of Erik Erikson (1963), scholars have been interested in the concept of identity development. Earlier theoretical models did not focus explicitly on the experiences and processes of macrocultural group members. However, they were based on the lived experiences of being a European American in the United States. More recently, the focus of identity development models has moved from more generic stages to those specific to particular macrocultural and microcultural group experiences (see Table 4.1). Several majority identity development models (e.g., Hardiman, 1994; Helms, 1994) contain conceptually similar stages. For the purposes of a specific focus, we offer a detailed account of Janet Helms's (1990, 1994) model. We chose her model because it is one of the most comprehensive.

Helms's (1994) book begins with an insightful statement on interracial communication: "In this country, Whites seem to be the only racial group that spends more time and effort wondering about the implications of race for other groups than it

TABLE
1.1   A SAMPLING OF RACIAL IDENTITY DEVELOPMENT MODELS

Microcultural Group Members

Banks, 1976	Jackson and Hardiman, 1983	Phinney, 1993	Ponterotto and Pedersen, 1993
Psychological captivity	Acceptance	Unexamined identity	Conformity
Encapsulation	Resistance	Conformity	Dissonance
Identity clarification	Redefinition	Resistance/separation	Resistance/denial
Biethnicity	Internalization	Integration	Introspection
Multiethnicity			Synergetic articulation

Macrocultural Group Members

Hardiman, 1994	Helms, 1994
Unexamined identity	Contact
Acceptance	Disintegration
Resistance	Reintegration
Redefinition	Pseudo-independent
Immersion/emersion	Integration
Autonomy	

Biracial Persons

Kich, 1992	Poston, 1990	Jacobs, 1992
Awareness of differentness	Personal identity	Pre-color constancy
Struggle for acceptance	Choice of group categorization	Racial ambivalence
Self-acceptance and assertion	Enmeshment/denial	Biracial identity
	Appreciation	
	Integration	

does for itself" (p. i). In order to increase our awareness of how European Americans formulate their racial/ethnic identities, Helms outlines six specific stages: contact, disintegration, reintegration, pseudo-independence, immersion/emersion, and autonomy.

The first stage in Helms's model is *contact*. Within this stage, European Americans' self-perception does not include any element of being a member of the "White race." Instead, they assume that racial/ethnic differences are best understood as differences in individuals' personalities (as opposed to related to cultural norms). When questioned about their race, persons at this stage might respond simply that they are "Americans" (Helms, 1994). Contact with people of color is limited and highly insubstantial. European American perceptions are guided by minimal knowledge of other racial/ethnic groups, which may result in behaviors that are naive, timid, and/or potentially offensive (Helms, 1990). Comments that reflect an existence at stage 1 include, "When I talk to you, I don't think of you as Puerto Rican" or (to an African American) "I've never owned slaves and you've never been a slave, so why can't we be equals?"

Once European Americans maintain a certain level of contact, two options are presented. One option involves avoiding any real interracial contact and continuing to believe that individuals are equal and should be color blind (and ignore the racial identities of others). A second option is to make a conscious effort to learn more about the lived experiences (historically, socially, politically, economically, etc.) of people of color. According to Helms (1994), "the person who chooses the first option can remain in contact as long as her or his safe-haven is not violated by undeniable contradictory information" (p. 38). The person who opts for the second choice, sooner or later, discovers that macrocultures and microcultures have rules about interracial communication.

Disintegration is the second stage of Helms's model. Within this stage, European Americans first begin to understand their position of privilege in society (see Chapter 3). In other words, Europeans Americans acknowledge that prejudice, discrimination, and racism exist and are forced to view themselves as dominant group members. Typical reactions at this stage include experiencing overwhelming feelings of guilt and confusion, seeing oneself as less prejudiced than other European Americans, or proudly protecting microcultural group members from negative interactions with "White bigots." For some, recognizing their privilege is too overwhelming. Their reaction to an increased racial/ethnic awareness is to reenter the contact stage with a distorted perception that if Europeans Americans are advantaged, it is because they have earned it (Helms, 1994). An alternative reaction is to enter the third stage of majority identity development.

Reintegration, according to Helms, represents the last stage of the abandonment of racism phase of majority identity development. In this stage, European

Americans tend to focus less on themselves in comparison to microcultural group members and more on themselves as a member of the "White race." They may deny any responsibility for the social problems experienced by people of color. In addition, European Americans in this stage may idealize "White culture," oftentimes at the expense of other racial/ethnic cultures. Some comments about affirmative action help illustrate this level of racial identity development. These include statements such as "quotas that give preference to minority groups are wrong" or "the most oppressed group of the 21st century are White males." Although such ideas explicitly support a general belief in fairness and equality, they implicitly deny the historical politics that have resulted in European American privilege.

The fourth stage of majority group identity development is characterized by that of a *pseudo-independent*, a European American who unintentionally believes his or her culture is more advanced and civilized than others. Within this stage, individuals accept people of color as a whole and become interested in helping them become successful in society. Consciously or unconsciously, however, the underlying assumption is that "successful" means becoming more like European Americans (Helms, 1990). One of the most common communication strategies utilized by pseudo-independents is to minimize the effects of racism and discrimination by providing parallel examples from their own life histories (Dace, 1994). This may include sympathetic European Americans who can identify with the problems of people of color because of past experiences of being an outsider. Helms (1994) offers the following example, provided by a European American corporate executive who reflects the power of "pulling yourself up by your bootstraps": "When my great-grandfather came to this country, he had no money, he couldn't speak a word of English, and he was fleeing religious persecution. So, I understand how you people feel. But my family made it and so can you" (pp. 66-67).

Distinguishing the fifth stage of Helms's model, *immersion/emersion*, from the fourth stage (pseudo-independence) can sometimes be difficult. In fact, movement from one stage to the next can be quite subtle. The basic difference is that European Americans in the pseudo-independence stage continue to blame racial/ethnic group members for their own problems. In comparison, those at the immersion/emersion stage recognize the contributions of European Americans in such matters. Most individuals, according to Helms (1994), do not advance to this stage of majority identity development. Operating at this stage requires European Americans to assume personal responsibility for racism and to understand the subtle ways that their actions (or lack thereof) perpetuate it. In short, it involves a dual process of identifying racism and discovering one's own "Whiteness" (Helms, 1994, p. 75). This stage can evoke intense feelings of anger and embarrassment on the part of particular European Americans. It can also result in isolation and abandonment from others whose identity formation is at earlier stages.

The final stage of European American identity development is *autonomy*. According to Helms (1994), this is the "stage in which the person attempts to interact with the world and commune with himself or herself from a positive, White, non-racist perspective" (p. 87). European Americans at this sixth stage are committed to working toward what they see as an nonracist position. Many continually are involved in life experiences that will move them to this ideal. Within this framework, we must recognize autonomy as a lifelong process of discovery, recommitment, and social activism. Operating at this level of consciousness is reflected in the ideas articulated by European Americans (e.g., "I see myself as a recovering racist" or "Discrimination against any group has a negative effect on us all").

Microcultural Identity Development Model

As indicated by Table 4.1, various models describe the process of how microcultures (African Americans, Native Americans, Asian Americans, and Latino/a Americans) form their racial/ethnic identities (see also Cross, 1971; 1983). Each of these models overlaps considerably with other existing frameworks. In addition, some commonalties with macrocultural identity development models exists. Instead of describing each of these models, we focus on the model presented by Phinney (1993). Do not confuse this model with the more general one discussed earlier in this chapter. In order to provide sufficient detail, we include additional research associated with other models (e.g., Banks, 1976; Jackson & Hardiman, 1983; Ponterotto & Pedersen, 1993).

According to Phinney (1993), the identity development process for U.S. racial/ethnic microcultural group members involves four stages: unexamined identity, conformity, resistance/separation, and integration. Note that a person does not typically arrive at the final stage and remain at that level for the rest of his or her life. Instead, people experience a recycling of stages as they engage in the process of dealing with life changes within their current sense of identity (Jackson & Hardiman, 1983). Because of this, the experience of identity formation is best understood as a series of continuous loops rather than a straight line. Phinney (1993) describes the first stage in this process as *unexamined identity*, a period of a microcultural group member's life with little or no exploration of racial/ethnic background. During this stage, individuals may have an extremely low awareness of their cultural heritage, often because of a lack of interest in particular cultural values, norms, language, and other elements. One likely outcome of this phase is the unconscious acceptance of macrocultural group values, norms, and attitudes—including particular negative assumptions about one's own cultural system.

The second stage (conformity) involves accepting and internalizing these dominant group perspectives. For some people of color, this stage may include accepting negative group stereotypes (Jackson & Hardiman, 1983), which results in an intense desire to try and adopt the values of European American culture (Phinney, 1993). Each racial/ethnic group has ingroup terms that describe those in the conformity stage (e.g., an African American who is labeled as an "oreo"). Banks (1976), in his research on minority identity development, uses a particular phrase to grasp this concept: "ethnic psychological captivity" (p. 191). He relates the process of internalizing negative beliefs about one's own racial/ethnic group to self-rejection and low self-esteem. Can you think of ways in which people of color in this stage of identity development may try to alter their appearance to be more like European Americans? Can you see how many efforts to assimilate into the dominant culture are part of stage 2 (conformity)? These issues are explored further in chapters that deal with theory (Chapter 6) and organizations (Chapter 9).

Stage 3, *resistance and separation*, typically begins when individuals experience some tension when trying to understand themselves in the midst of ingroup and outgroup cultural perceptions. It is difficult to determine exactly when stage 2 dissolves and stage 3 begins. Much of this process depends on when (if) a person of color begins to think critically about macrocultural values and his or her own cultural standpoint. Once this process has started, however, the sense of resistance to Eurocentric perspectives appears to grow more intense. Oftentimes this leads a person to search for an increased understanding of racial/ethnic group histories. The result is the development of an extreme sense of pride based on the significant accomplishments of other racial/ethnic group members—oftentimes despite great obstacles. It also involves more open challenges of discriminatory and racist acts against self and other group members (Jackson & Hardiman, 1983). Another outgrowth of this stage involves a conscious attempt to separate oneself from European Americans. Instead, multiple opportunities to share community with others who also identify in similar racial/ethnic terms are sought out. *Ethnic encapsulation* is the term used by Banks (1976, p. 191) to describe attempts at voluntary separatism in various settings. Think about how much attention is given to different racial groups, for example, African Americans, who typically separate themselves in some settings (e.g., campus cafeterias and Greek organizations). (It is interesting that when European American students eat together no one pays much attention.) Nevertheless, this behavior can be better understood as part of what goes on at this stage.

Another important aspect of stage 3 is the initial transition that occurs between old identities (informed by outgroup cultural perspectives) and new ones (encouraged by a greater awareness of racial/ethnic pride). This process of identity transformation is continued in the fourth stage of microcultural identity development, *integration* (Phinney, 1993). The basic issue involves achieving a public racial/ethnic identity that is consistent with one's inner sense of self (Jackson &

Hardiman, 1983). The ultimate outcome of this final stage of microcultural identity development is internalizing a confident and secure racial/ethnic identity. This newly found sense of self understands the central role of racial/ethnic cultural norms in everyday interactions. In addition, the integration stage promotes a greater understanding of how other cultural identities (e.g., those based on gender, age, sexual orientation, etc.) emerge differently in different settings.

Think back to reading through the descriptions for each of these stages of microcultural identity development. Did specific examples of behaviors and comments from your own personal experiences (self or others) jump out at you? If so, be sure to make note of these, because connecting personal examples to theoretical models is a great way to understand these models! The next section deals specifically with how persons with more than one racial/ethnic heritage formulate their identities. Based on the descriptions provided earlier, you will be able to understand how biracial identity development models are similar to, yet different from, Phinney's (1993) minority identity development model.

Biracial Identity Development Model

For many years, biracial identity development was understood via frameworks developed for U.S. ethnic minorities. This makes sense, given the societal one-drop rule described in Chapter 2. However, we can now understand why using existing majority and minority identity development models to understand biracial identity development is less than ideal. First, unlike microcultural and macrocultural based models, biracial identity has no clear-cut ultimate outcome (Miller & Rotheram-Borus, 1994). Because their identities do not fit into simple categories, the last stage in identity formation may be ambiguous and tentative. For many biracial persons, identity development has no single end state (Root, 1992). Second, existing models do not allow for several racial/ethnic identities. Biracial individuals typically have been forced to "choose" one over the other (Poston, 1990). In reality, these persons may identify with one group, both groups, an emergent group (multiracial community), or all three simultaneously (Orbe, 1999). For some biracial persons, self-identities may even change depending on the specific situational context (Harris, 1997b). Third, research indicates that biracial identity development takes on even a greater spiraling process when compared to the creation of monoracial identities (Alexander, 1994; Herring, 1994). Evidence shows that many biracial individuals repeat earlier stages as they mature (Nance & Foeman, 1998). This ongoing process is typically experienced with great intensity, awareness, and a sense of purpose (Herring, 1994). In short, earlier research on the identity formation of biracial persons was flawed because existing frameworks—for both macrocultural and microcultural groups—were inadequate to speak to their unique racial/ethnic standpoints.

Stonequist (1937) created one of the earliest identity formation models that focused on biracial persons. His work has become known as the marginal person model, because it focused on how biracial persons are typically marginalized by both groups, without belonging completely to either one. In general, this model reflected the existing social myth that individuals with biracial heritage, based on their marginality, cannot establish enduring identities (Poston, 1990). This marginal person model became the foundation for other work on biracial identity formation, influencing the work of Gibbs (1987) and others. In short, these frameworks "suggest that mixed ethnic heritage serves to exacerbate problems associated with the normal process of identity development by creating uncertainty and ambiguity in individual identification with parents, group identification with peers, and social identification with a specific ethnic or racial group" (Poston, 1990, p. 153). As Poston notes, these models see biracial identity as causing additional problems in an individual's identity formation. More recently, additional models have emerged from existing social scientific scholarship (Jacobs, 1992; Kich, 1992; Poston, 1990). These frameworks, unlike Stonequist's (1937), describe a process in which biracial identity formation is seen in more positive terms. Table 4.1 summarizes a representative sample of existing models (see also Gibbs, 1987). The remaining portion of this section focuses on a detailed description of one of these models, that associated with the work of W. S. Carlos Poston (1990).

Poston's "new and positive model" (1990, p. 153) of biracial identity development is based on earlier models of African American identity development, namely the work of Cross (1971) and Parham and Helms (1985). His model for the formation of biracial identity mirrors some of the programmatic issues associated with African American identity formation. Poston also extends these existing frameworks in terms of applying specifically to those persons with more than one racial/ethnic heritage.

The first stage, according to Poston, is *personal identity*. Individuals at this initial stage are relatively young. Membership in any particular racial/ethnic group is secondary to the sense of self that is somewhat independent of his or her racial/ethnic heritage. In other words, children do not see themselves in racially specific terms. Consistent with the work of Phinney and Rotherham (1987), Poston suggests that children's earliest understanding of race/ethnicity is superficial, personal, and largely inconsistent. Their affiliation with a larger cultural reference group has yet to be established. Because of this, their identity is informed more by personality elements, than cultural ones (Cross, 1978). In most instances, biracial individuals at this stage demonstrate no awareness of race/ethnic similarities and differences.

Choice of *group categorization*, according to Poston, is the second stage in biracial identity development. At this stage, individuals gain an increased awareness of their race/ethnic heritage and are pushed to choose an identity. Typically, two likely choices are available at this stage: Identify with one group or the other. Research on the lived experiences of biracial persons clearly indicates an external pressure for them to make a specific racial/ethnic choice (Funderburg, 1994). This is oftentimes seen as necessary in order to achieve a sense of belonging with peers, family, and/or social groups (Hall, 1980). The choice made at this stage involves a number of inter-related factors, including demographics of home neighborhood, parental presence/style/influence, physical appearance, influence of peer groups, and support of social groups (family, school, church/temple/synagogue, etc.).

The third stage is *enmeshment/denial*. Following the choices made in the previous phase, this stage is characterized by an emotional tension (e.g., confusion, guilt, or self-hatred) because claiming one identity does not fully express who they are. In many cases, a biracial person feels that his or her identity choice makes it difficult to identify with both parents. This conflict can result in feelings of disloyalty, abandonment, and/or guilt (Sebring, 1985). For example, a biracial adolescent at this stage may be ashamed and scared to have friends meet his or her parent whose racial background is different than the norm in the neighborhood or school. The adolescent may also feel guilty and angry about feeling this way. Eventually the child must resolve the anger and guilt and learn to appreciate both parental cultures, or stay at this level (Poston, 1990, p. 154).

A sense of *appreciation* for one's multiple racial/ethnic background occurs at the fourth stage of biracial identity development. Poston describes individuals at this stage as attempting to learn more about all of the racial/ethnic cultures that make up who they are. But, although an appreciation of diverse cultures exists, biracial persons still primarily identify with one racial/ethnic group (as determined in stage 2: choice of group categorization). Developing a sense of appreciation in terms of one's diverse cultural heritages does enable biracial persons to begin the process of embracing each aspect of their family's culture at the core of their identity. However, it does not typically occur until they are ready to move to the fifth and final stage.

The final stage of biracial identity formation is *integration*. According to Hall (1980), integration is crucial to identity development because it is closely tied to positive mental health. Within this stage, biracial persons recognize and value each aspect of their racial/ethnic identity (Poston, 1990). Through integration, individuals are able to carve out an identity that reflects their complete selves. This was not the case in earlier stages where their identities were necessarily more fragmented and incomplete. Here you can see how Poston's biracial identity development model is helpful in emphasizing the unique challenges that biracial people face, and outlines the process of how most persons formulate their identities in a healthy, productive fashion.

CONCLUSION

This chapter described how individuals come to understand racial/ethnic perceptions of self and others. Much of the discussion focused on how a person comes to co-create his or her individual racial and/or ethnic identity. Specifically, we described in some detail the commonalties and differences of macrocultural, microcultural, and biracial identity development models. Within these descriptions, we discussed how our own identities are inextricably linked with the ways that we perceive others.

We began this chapter with a statement from Tanno & Gonzalez (1998) that suggested the more attention the concept of cultural identity receives, the more complex it becomes. The information provided here is substantial in illustrating the importance of race/ethnicity in matters of identity formation. It is also largely incomplete, given that identity, and subsequently interracial communication, is informed by other elements of social categories. Chapter 5 will complete our coverage of the multifaceted, complex process of identity cocreation.

OPPORTUNITIES FOR EXTENDED LEARNING

1. Create a chapter outline for a book that describes your racial/ethnic identity development. Create a title for each chapter that captures a significant event or time in your life which symbolizes an increased degree of awareness in terms of race/ethnicity. Chapter 1 should contain details of your first memories, and your last chapter should describe your current perceptions (the chapters in between will describe the process by which you got from there to here). Share and explain your outlines with the class.

2. The media contains a number of excellent examples of individuals at different stages of racial/ethnic identity development. Think about your favorite television show, movie, cartoon strip, or book. Who are the main characters? Think about what you have learned about them. Based on their communication about self and others, can you make an educated guess at which stage of racial identity development they are? Do you have any evidence that this has changed over time? Are there characters at different stages? How is their communication similar and/or different? If time permits, compare your judgments with others.

3. Using the frameworks presented here for macrocultural, microcultural, and biracial identity development, create a list of advantages and disadvantages for

each stage. Although you might suspect that more disadvantages exist within earlier stages and more advantages in the latter ones, this is not necessarily the case. (For instance, European Americans in the early stages of identity development are oftentimes optimistic about the future of race relations and believe these problems *can* be solved.) Break into groups for a brainstorming session (e.g., advantages for microcultural development stages, disadvantages for microcultural development stages, etc.). Following group work, share with the entire class.

4. Spend some time exploring how Whiteness is experienced in different areas of the United States. For instance, do some research on how some European American groups in the Northeast (e.g., New York, Philadelphia, and Boston) emphasize their ethnic identities through celebrations (St. Patrick's Day parade) or other means ("Little Italy"). Do similar displays of ethnic pride occur for European Americans in other regions?

5. Go to the following Web site: http://intrace/articles.html. This URL is home for Interrace Magazine, a national magazine for and about interracial couples, families, singles, and multiracial people. Look through the different resources provided on this Web site (articles, research studies, media reviews, personal essays, and so on) to gain additional insights. Pay particular attention to the various ways in which personal and social identities are expressed. How do these resources illustrate—and possibly extend—the model of biracial identity formation discussed in this chapter?

RECOGNIZING MULTIPLE SELF-IDENTITIES AND OTHER IDENTITIES

Although each of us identifies with one or more racial/ethnic groups, we also belong to a variety of other cultural groups that share common attitudes, values, and norms of relating to one another. Refer back to the "Who Am I?" exercise that you completed in Chapter 4. Can you see how some of your responses are directly linked to your membership in one or more cultural groups? Some of these aspects of cultural identity receive a great deal of attention; others are less apparent but not necessarily less influential. Furthermore, some of these aspects remain relatively stable over time (race/ethnicity, gender), but others may change (age, socioeconomic status). The important thing to remember is that, like the authors of this text, you are a member of many different cultural groups that influence who you are, what you think and feel, as well as how you communicate with others. Recognizing the multiple aspects of your cultural identity promotes a deeper understanding of the complexities of interracial communication beyond simple racial/ethnic designations. Chapter 5 will to give you a conceptual framework to enhance your understanding of how other elements of cultural identity (abilities, age, gender, nationality, sexual orientation, spirituality, and socioeconomic status) affect interracial communication. Throughout this chapter, continue the self-reflective process initiated in Chapter 4 and you will begin to discern how race and ethnicity—and other cultural elements—become more or less significant in different contexts.

ACKNOWLEDGING MULTIPLE CULTURAL IDENTITIES

Cultural identities are central, dynamic, and multifaceted components of our understanding of self and others. Once formed (at least if we could freeze time for that particular moment, before future points of negotiation), they provide an essential framework for organizing and interpreting our interactions with others. In addition, each aspect of our identity serves as a marker of who we are and, when acknowledged by others, affects how we are defined culturally.

Mary Jane Collier and others have advanced a cultural identity theory (CIT) that provides a productive framework for acknowledging the existence and impact of complexities of cultural identity and interracial communication. The main ideas of the theory revolve around the central premise that each individual has multiple cultural identities that are formed through discourse with others (Collier, 1997, 1998; Collier & Thomas, 1988; Hecht et al., 1993). Consistent with most of the scholars whose work was referenced in Chapter 4, CIT is based within the perspective that "cultural identities are negotiated, co-created, reinforced, and challenged through communication" (Collier, 1997, p. 39). CIT also helps shed light on the various ways our cultural identities are defined in relation to one another. Recognizing the multiple types of identities that make up a person's self-concept avoids defining self and/or others as unidimensional beings. This process also assists in recognizing the diversity within cultural groups (Orbe, 1995a). In this regard, the theoretical framework serves as an excellent point of transition between the basic ideas presented in Chapter 4 and the focus here.

Two of the major ideas associated with CIT are avowal and ascription. *Avowal*, according to Collier (1998), refers to the perceived identity that a person or group enacts in a particular context. It consists of a more subjective identity, one that is typically viewed from the point of a specific individual (Collier, Thompson, & Weber, 1996). *Ascription*, in comparison, is framed more from a collective position. It consists of an individual's perception of how others see his or her cultural identity. Although these two identity components can be described independently, they function together in inextricable ways. For instance, our self-identity is informed largely by our interactions with others including our perceptions of how others perceive us. Others' perception of us—or at least our perceptions of their perceptions (ascription)—has a direct impact on how we come to see ourselves (avowal). In fact, membership within a cultural group typically occurs when a person self-identifies as a group member and then has that status confirmed by other members of the group (Carbaugh, 1990).

Another major aspect of CIT involves understanding the enduring/changing quality of cultural identity. Typically passed down from one generation of group members to another, cultural identities are enduring in that historical group orientations inform present and future reality. Although certain aspects of a person's cultural knowledge can be readily attributed to the enduring quality of group membership (e.g., that which is based on religion), others are not so clear. Think for a moment about how you have accumulated other information about what it means to be a woman/man, member of a particular national/regional group, or specific group based on sexual orientation. Although possibly less apparent, most of us can remember specific aspects of cultural identities based on sex, national/regional origin, and sexual orientation that were directly or indirectly communicated to us from older members of these respective groups. But although our cultural identities possess an enduring quality, they simultaneously are also apt to change over time. Our cultural identities are dynamic and subject to constant examination, reexamination, and possibly alteration based on our interactions with others. This involves all aspects of our identity, including those more permanent (race/ethnicity and gender) as well as those more fluid (socioeconomic status and age). Most of us—especially students who have invested significant amounts of time, money, and energy in obtaining a college degree—foresee how this accomplishment might alter our self-identity in a number of ways (definitely age, possibly regional/geographical location, and hopefully socioeconomic!). However, even with a stable cultural marker such as race, our identities may also change over time. Just think about how an increased knowledge of self and others changes—if not your particular race/ethnicity—the ways you label, understand, and identify with that particular set of racial/ethnic lived experiences.

Furthermore, cultural identities comprise both context and relational levels of interpretation (Collier, 1998). This aspect of CIT recognizes that the meanings within interracial interactions are created not only by the content shared between interactants but also their relationship. Although much of communication effectiveness typically focuses on language usage (see Chapter 3), such an analysis can not be removed from the relational context of the interaction. For instance, the mere adoption of ingroup or outgroup language creates meaning, as do efforts to emphasize one position over the other (Collier, 1998). Various aspects of *content* (language, jokes, self- and other labels) must be understood with in the *context* of the participant's relationship (see Chapter 7). Take, for example, the use of *girl*. Among African American women, this term is used to refer to one another in a positive, affirming, and celebratory manner (Scott, 1996). In an interracial communication context, the use of *girl* by a European American woman to refer to an African American woman (e.g., "Hey, girl, how are you?") may generate a set of different meanings. The European American woman might perceive it as a way to establish rapport. The African American woman might perceive it as presumptuous, offensive, and insulting in lieu of the sociohistorical context of the United States and absence of an established relationship (Orbe, Drummond, & Camara, 1998). In the context of an established, close relationship *girl* may be used by both African American and European American women as a sign that racial differences may be transcended (Allen, 1997). Again, an effective interpretation of meaning involves both the content and relationship dimensions of the message.

A final aspect of CIT relates to the salience and intensity of particular cultural elements in any given interracial communication context. Saliency, along these lines, "refers to the relative importance of one or two identities to others" (Collier, 1998, p. 374). Intensity is used as a marker that indicates the level of involvement and investment that a person has in a particular aspect of her or his identity (Collier, 1997). Both of these concepts are important because, as we described at the beginning of this chapter, people communicate within multiple cultural identities. CIT brings this issue to the forefront by generating attention to the roles that saliency and intensity serve in interracial communication. Within this framework, we can begin to understand that the salience and intensity of various cultural identities changes contextually and relationally (Burke & Franzoi, 1988; Harris, 1997b). For instance, imagine seeing two female friends—one Mexican American and the other European American—involved in a fairly intimate conversation. Some may question that such high levels of interracial communication can even exist (Leonard & Locke, 1993). However, what they may be failing to recognize is that the saliency and intensity of the friends' racial/ethnic identities at that particular time and place are not as strong as others (e.g., age, gender, socioeconomic status, spirituality). Given another context, this might change dramatically. The Mexican American woman, for instance, might barely acknowledge her friend while with a group of Latinas. Within this setting, the increased saliency and intensity of her avowed and ascribed ethnic identity has directly informed her communication.

Have you ever heard (or been a part) of a similar scenario when a person is friendly in one interracial context and then has acted drastically different when with other racial/ethnic group members? CIT, through its attention to several properties related to multiple cultural identities, assists in understanding this type of scenario more productively. In this regard, CIT provides a framework to advance our knowledge of the various ways that different (interrelated) cultural identities are seen in interracial communication contexts. The intersections of race/ethnicity, class, gender, and so on involve a highly complex process, one which we return to later. Before tackling this topic, however, let's look at the cultural influences of particular aspects of identity and their effects on human communication.

POTENTIALLY SALIENT ASPECTS OF CULTURAL IDENTITY

Because our focus here is on interracial communication, it is not feasible to offer a detailed description of each cultural variable that has the potential to impact any

5.1   *Case Study*

Consider the case scenario described here. Given this chapter's focus on acknowledging multiple cultural identities, what do you make of Professor Smith's efforts to make Michele more comfortable in her class? How might some of the insights provided throughout this chapter promote more effective interracial communication and understanding?

Professor Smith teaches a number of undergraduate communication classes at a small liberal arts college whose student population is very "traditional"—largely European American students, 18 to 24 years of age. In one of the introductory communication classes she teaches, Professor Smith has noticed that one student, a thirtysomething African American woman (Michele), seems isolated—both physically and psychologically—from the rest of the class. As the only person of color in class, she typically sits in the front corner of the room and keeps on her Sony Walkman until class starts. Although she is doing well in the course, Professor Smith is concerned because she does not speak at all in class and other students appear to ignore her presence (even though the class is highly interactive).

One day during office hours, Michele stops by to ask Professor Smith a question about an upcoming paper. Seizing the opportunity to interact with Michele on a one-to-one basis for the first time, Professor Smith is surprised to see how personable and energetic she is in this more intimate setting. Thinking would be good for her to meet other students in a more casual atmosphere, Professor Smith makes a suggestion:

> PROF. SMITH: Have you been over to the student organization area yet?
> MICHELE: No, I haven't . . . I have been real busy with school, and . . .
> PROF. SMITH: Well, why don't we take a walk over there right now? It will only take a couple of minutes and I want to introduce you to some of my other students.
> MICHELE: I really need to leave campus, and start . . .
> PROF. SMITH: Oh, come on! It will just take a moment!

On the walk over, Professor Smith is proud of herself for taking the initiative to make Michele feel more at home on campus. When she brings Michele to the Multicultural Student Union's office, she is relieved to see some familiar faces. After introducing everyone, Professor Smith is surprised to see Michele become quiet and clearly ready to leave. Following an awkward silence, they

Case Study (*continued*)

leave and start walking past other student organization offices, including the Non-Traditional Student Union. Professor Smith tries to get Michele to attend a meeting, but Michele appears disinterested and somewhat annoyed.

Driving home that night, Professor Smith is troubled about Michele's lack of interest in getting to know other students, especially students with similar cultural backgrounds. In fact, she spends much of the weekend mentally replaying her interactions with Michele. Imagine her surprise (and relief) on Monday morning, when she finds the following e-mail message from Michele:

> Prof. Smith: Thanks for taking the time to introduce me around on Friday afternoon. I have been feeling a little uncomfortable on campus because it seems like all the students do is talk about partying, drinking, and having sex. This definitely is not my cup of tea; in fact, some of their attitudes are quite shocking! But guess what? At church on Sunday, I met two other people who just started taking classes on campus and we intend to start a Christian Student Union soon. Having an opportunity for fellowship with other Christians on campus is just what I needed to feel more comfortable. Thanks again for your help. Michele (Communication 101)

particular instance of interracial contact. Such a task appears especially difficult given the broad ways in which culture has been defined by most communication scholars. Instead, we have identified several specific elements of cultural identity that seem especially relevant to interracial communication in the United States. This conclusion, although not definitive, is the result of a thorough review of existing literature as well as our own research and lived experiences. Nevertheless, we acknowledge that additional elements of cultural identity may represent significant factors during interracial interactions (see Opportunities for Extended Learning, number 3). As a means to illustrate the process by which multiple cultural identities are enacted, we focus on seven specific elements: abilities, age, gender, nationality, sexual orientation, spirituality, and socioeconomic status.

In the sections to follow, each cultural aspect is described specifically in terms of its influence on communication processes. These descriptions: (1) distinguish how each variable represents a cultural identity marker, (2) generate an understanding of its relationship to perceptions of communication, and (3) highlight the ways it intersects with racial/ethnic identity in the context of intraracial and interracial communication. As you read, reflect on how multiple cultural identities are negotiated in different contexts. Specifically, ask yourself the following questions: What is the saliency and intensity of this cultural marker within my self-concept? How is this directly related to particular situational contexts and relationships with others? Are there any cultural elements that are enacted with more salience and intensity than those marked by race/ethnicity? If so, within what contexts and/or relationships?

Abilities

Research that conceptualizes persons with disabilities as a cultural group has resulted in a growing body of literature in and outside of the field of communication (Braithwaite, 1990, 1991; Emry & Wiseman, 1987; Padden & Humphries, 1988). The basic argument is that because people with disabilities are treated so differently in the United States, a set of distinctive rules, speech habits, and norms have been developed that serve to reinforce cultural differences between those persons with disabilities and those who are able-bodied (Braithwaite & Braithwaite, 1997). When discussing persons with disabilities as a cultural group, two points must be acknowledged. First, a person with a disability may identify with a community of other persons with disabilities generally or those with a particular disability (e.g., blind, deaf, or mobility-related disabilities) (Braithwaite & Braithwaite, 1997). Second, like any other cultural group, differences in experiences (e.g., being born with a disability or having lived as a TAB—temporarily able-bodied person) affects the phases of identity development (Padden & Humphries, 1988). These clarifying issues notwithstanding, much of the existing research in this area has been referred to as "interability communication" (Fox & Giles, 1997). This term represents a growing field of study that examines communicative processes of persons with disabilities and able-bodied persons; Braithwaite and Thompson's (in press) *Handbook of Communication and People With Disabilities: Research and Application* marks a contribution of a major volume of work dedicated to ability and communication issues.

Persons with disabilities recognize that more often than not, able-bodied persons primarily see them as disabled first, and a person with other personality and cultural traits second (Braithwaite & Braithwaite, 1997; Chan, 1989). In most instances, a disability invokes a number of widely accepted stereotypes for people including being "dependent, socially introverted, emotionally unstable, depressed, hypersensitive, and easily offended, especially with regard to their disability. In addition, disabled people are often presumed to differ from able-bodied people in moral character, social skills, and political orientation." (Coleman & DePaulo, 1991, p. 69). Based on these stereotypical images of persons with disabilities, many able-bodied persons' communication is characterized by one of two approaches (Chan, 1989). First, they try to ignore that any disability exists. This oftentimes results in ignoring people with disabilities completely. Second, able-bodied persons may become oversensitive to the disability and treat a person with a disability in an overly protective and/or patronizing manner. The result of such treatment is the development of a distinctive cultural perspective for persons with disabilities, one that is different from that associated with able-bodied persons (Braithwaite & Braithwaite, 1997).

Some existing research indicates that co-cultural perspectives of people with disabilities are similar to those of U.S. ethnic microcultures (Orbe, 1996). So, does this result in an increased saliency and intensity of a person's disability during inter-racial interactions? Although no specific research could be found to answer this question, our personal experiences prompt us to say, "Yes sometimes, but not always." This is based on the idea that personal experiences with oppression lend themselves to reaching out and connecting with other oppressed people. The inter-section of abilities and racial/ethnic identity does provide some interesting case scenarios of interracial communication. Take, for example, the experiences of Sucheng Chan (1989), a person with a disability who is of Asian descent. Her expe-riences are especially interesting because in many East Asian cultures a strong folk belief exists that sees a person's physical state in this life as a reflection of how morally or sinfully she or he lived in previous lives. Reactions to her decision to marry an able-bodied man outside her racial/ethnic group provide an insightful illustration of how race was more of an important factor for some (her father-in-law), and her disability was for others (mother-in-law, parents' friends). As you read the following excerpt, see if you can also notice how other cultural elements (national/regional origin and religion) are inextricably linked to those based on race/ethnicity and disability:

> Different cultural attitudes toward handicapped persons came out clearly during my wedding. My father-in-law, as a solid representative of middle America as could be found, had no qualms about objecting to the marriage on racial grounds, but he could bring himself to comment on my handicap only indirectly. He wondered why his son, who dated numerous high school and beauty queens, couldn't marry one of them instead of me? My mother-in-law, a devout Christian, did not share her husband's preju-dices, but she worried aloud about whether I could have children. Some Chinese friends of my parents, on the other hand, said that I was lucky to have found such a noble man, one who would marry me despite my handicap. (Chan, 1989, p. 268)

Age

Senior citizens. Generation X. Baby boomers. Teenagers. What images do you typi-cally associate with each of these terms? How natural was it to characterize each group with little attention to the diversity of those who identify with each group? A significant amount of research has been done by communication scholars on the cultural aspects of different age groups (Ayers, 1994; Baxter & Goldsmith, 1990; Hummert, Wiemann, & Nussbaum, 1994). Most of this work is based on the idea that the shared life histories of generations of U.S. Americans have resulted in a common culture of sorts, including common values, norms, language, dress, and so on. "Drawing boundaries around various life stages and making them special and distinct also tends to overemphasize life stages as distinct from each other with chronological age marking out who belongs in which age groups" (Williams & Giles, 1998, p. 155).

Take the case of *Generation X*. This term, used generally to describe those persons born between 1961 and 1981, reflects the facelessness and aimlessness of a group of U.S. Americans who have been criticized for having no distinct identity, cause, or ambition (Williams & Giles, 1998). Generation Xers are often regarded as losers, whiners, and/or slackers who are overly dependent on their parents. This group of young people feel patronized by older generation members who do not take them seriously, disapprove of their lifestyle choices, and force their values on them. Contrast the stereotypical characterizations of Generation Xers with those associated with senior citizens. Research (e.g., Radford, 1987) indicates that most perceptions of the elderly revolve around negative stereotypes: "greedy, lonely, afraid, incompetent, senile, sexless, inarticulate, forgetful, depressed, stubborn" (McKay, 1997, p. 176). Most of the images are reinforced by the media (Coombes & Holladay, 1995) and communicated through the large array of negative labels used in everyday talk to describe senior citizens (crone, old-timer, geezer, old fogey, hag, old fart) (Nuessel, 1982). The elderly are also the recipients of patronizing talk from young adults including simpler, slower, and more childlike talk (Cohen & Faulkner, 1986). Given the focus of this text, it is important to recognize that "elders" in different racial/ethnic groups are regarded different levels of status.

How does age intersect with race/ethnicity during instances of intraracial and interracial communication? No definitive answer to that question exists; much depends on the particular individuals and the specific situational context of the interaction. Nevertheless, we must recognize that the age of the participants may be a central issue in some interactions. Older U.S. Americans, for example, have experienced (albeit somewhat differently, depending on their particular set of lived experiences) a culmination of events and occurrences that younger generations have only learned about indirectly: World wars, the Great Depression, Cold War, civil rights movements. These common experiences are bound to have an effect on life perspectives, values, normative behaviors—all of which, in turn, have substantial potential to influence communication in various ways. Probably one of the most obvious of these involves perceptions of language and appropriate speech codes (Collier, 1998). This was made apparent in our discussion of how age serves as a strong indicator of label preference (Black, African American, or Afro-American) for people of African descent (see Chapter 3).

Another issue is the role that ageism plays in interracial communication.

Ageism, according to Williams and Giles (1998), is a life-span issue. However, it clearly is more pertinent at some life stages than others. Traditionally, ageism has referred to personal, social, and institutional discrimination against older persons. However, other types of ageism exist including "gerontophobia" (extremely negative perceptions of older persons) and "new ageism" (elderly people are seen as weak and needy but also worthy and deserving) (Kalish, 1979; Levin & Levin, 1980). Some evidence indicates that senior citizen collectives which rally against discrimination, stereotypes, and oppressive practices may transcend racial and ethnic differences. More simply put, a common age may become more important than racial/ethnic differences in certain situations. These include informal friendship networks among the elderly that represent a crucial source of support (McKay, 1997) as well as more formal organizations like the Older Women's League (OWL) that represent women from diverse sets of lived experiences (Kautzer, 1986).

Gender

Of all of the aspects of cultural identity we have chosen to describe here, gender is the one most extensively researched by communication scholars. Julia T. Wood (1996, 1997a) is probably one of the most influential communication researchers who has approached gender communication studies using a cross-cultural perspective (Wood & Dindia, 1998). Scholars have achieved significant progress in identifying communication differences based on biological sex and psychological gender (Andersen, 1998; Pearson & Davilla, 1993). More recently, research has focused on both the communication similarities and differences of men and women (e.g., Canary & Dindia, 1998). The attention that scholars have paid to sex differences in communication is substantial, yet nothing compared to the central focus of the mass media on female/male communication issues. Every aspect of the mass media—television, music, magazines, radio, newspapers, and so on—includes images of (heterosexual) sex, sex roles, and sexual relationships. Deborah Tannen (1990), John Gray (1992), and others have written best-sellers on the subject. In light of the extensive research on sex and gender communication differences, we do not attempt to summarize it here, especially because a growing number of books focus on this subject area. Instead, we look at specific ways in which sex communication differences and similarities play out during intraracial and interracial interactions.

Typically a person's sex and race/ethnicity are central to her or his cultural identity. In many instances, the interlocking nature of these two aspects of identity are so powerful that both are simultaneously enacted with high degrees of saliency and intensity. Attempting to describe the impact of sex and race on interracial communication, in this regard, is not feasible unless we also pay attention to other elements of identity in specific interactions. Nevertheless, in some situational contexts, the commonality established through one aspect—let's focus on sex—may serve as a strong foundation for effective interracial communication. Traditionally, sports represent a context where men from different racial and ethnic groups come together for a common purpose (winning). Following the advances made possible through programs that promote equal resources for women and men (e.g., Title IX programs), more women have also recently experienced the synergy, collective energies, and close relationships that come with competitive sports (e.g., WNBA, 1999 World Cup). Although criticized by some as simply another societal mechanism where the "politics of inequality" are played out (Messner, 1989), research does indicate that positive, long-lasting interracial relationships are initiated through participation in various sports.

Given the existing research in the field of communication, competitive sports may be atypical in their ability to generate opportunities for effective interracial communication. Other organizational contexts appear to contain barriers to effective interracial communication (e.g., Botan & Smitherman, 1991). Women of color, for instance, must deal with a double burden of oppression in terms of sexism and racism. Frustrated by issues of sexism within their own communities, some of these women turn to women's coalitions in order to fight various oppressions (Allen, 1986). The goal of many of these organizations is to focus on the common experiences of all women, transcending barriers based on racial/ethnic, class, and sexual orientation differences. However, according to women of color, addressing commonalties based on sex while ignoring differences of race between women represents a threat to the mobilization of women's collective power (Anzaldua, 1987; Cole, 1995; Horno-Delgado, Ortega, Scott, & Stembach, 1989). According to Lorde (1984), "By and large within the women's movement, white women focus on their oppression as women and ignore differences of race, sexual preference, class, and age. There is a pretense to a homogeneity of experience covered by the word sisterhood that does not in fact exist" (p. 115). African American women report that their interpersonal interactions with European American women (even those perceived as well intentioned) reflect this focus on common experiences while ignoring salient racial differences. Attempts at solidarity, according to Marsha Houston (1997), come in phrases like "I never even notice that you're Black," "You're different than other Blacks," and "I understand your experiences as a Black Woman because sexism is just as bad as racism" (pp. 191–192).

Chicana feminists is a cultural identity marker that helps Latina women distinguish their experiences as different than Chicanos and other feminists (Flores, 1996). In recent years, Chicana feminist scholarship has featured voices that describe the challenges of crossing cultural borders (e.g., Anzaldua, 1987). The lessons of this literature, as well as those associated with Black feminism/womanism, is clear. Although rallying around issues central to women can create a unified front, it should not be done by ignoring differences based on race/ethnicity. Effective interracial female relationships recognize the negative impacts of trying to downplay the importance of race. Instead, they consider the crucial role that racialized lived experiences play in how all individuals perceive self and others (Frankenberg, 1993).

Nationality

Traditionally, nationality has been used to refer to the nation in which one is born and holds citizenship. This simplistic definition, however, has grown increasingly complex given the large numbers of people who change their citizenship, have dual citizenships, or affiliate with multiple national cultures (Collier, 1998). For example, consider the lived experiences of Gust Yep (1998), who describes his "multicultural self" as follows:

> I am Asianlatinoamerican. Although I have never been to China, I am racially what my parents describe as "100% pure Chinese." During my formative years, we lived in Peru, South America, and later moved to the United States. . . . I am trilingual (English, Spanish, and Chinese). . . . I "look Asian American," yet at times my Latino culture is most prominent in some communication settings. I strongly identify with all three cultures, and they are more or less integrated into this complex entity that I label as 'multicultural self.' (p. 79)

Clearly, this example serves as a vivid illustration of the complexity that sometimes accompanies a person's nationality.

Some clarification may be necessary to distinguish nationality from other cultural identity elements such as race and ethnicity. Paying attention to these differences should shed some light on how complex cultural identity perceptions can be. Literature on the cultural experiences of one racial group, that of Asian/Pacific Islanders, serves as an excellent point of analysis. Designations of drastically diverse cultural groups into one label based on race is problematic because it ignores other cultural differences such as language and religion (Sodowsky, Kway, & Pannu, 1995). For many non-Asian Americans, *race* serves as a primary cultural marker and *ethnic* differences remain less visible. Consider for a moment that Asian Americans can be Chinese, Japanese, Filipino, Korean, Indian, Cambodian, or Laotian (among other groups). Looking at *nationality* brings additional complexities into the negotiation of multiple cultural identities. Take, for instance, a Chinese person whose nationality may be closest defined with the People's Republic of China, Taiwan, Hong Kong, or the United States. *Regional* differences (urban/rural, east/west/north/south) also come into play here. Imagine the differences of two Chinese Americans who were born and raised in different regions of the United

States: one in Mississippi and the other in San Francisco's Chinatown (see Gong, 1997). The importance of regional identity markers can also been seen in other ethnic groups, like persons of Mexican descent. For instance, individuals in New Mexico are more likely to perceive their national origins with Spain as more important than those with Mexico. In Oregon, however, national ties are more closely affiliated with Mexico (Collier, 1998; see also Delgado, 1998).

Nationality identity issues also intersect with other issues such as age. Some Asian Americans, for instance, have struggled with issues of identity that involve balancing centuries of traditional Asian values against the individualistic values of U.S. Americanism (Orbe, Seymour, & Kang, 1998; Wong [Lau], 1998). Identity formation for many Asian Americans can be best represented as a both/and (as opposed to an either/or) process of negotiation in that multiple racial, ethnic, and national identities are simultaneously balanced (Chen, 1997). In some situational contexts, one aspect may emerge as more important than others. Still, many Asian Americans describe that others most often pay greater attention to racial markers than any other—even for those persons who were born and raised in the United States. In this context, racial distinctions have played a larger role in interracial communication than nationality, so much so that Asian Americans are constantly asking themselves, "What does it mean to be a 'perpetual foreigner' in one's native country?" (Nakayama, 1997, p. 15).

Unfortunately, most instances of interracial contact do not reflect a clear understanding of differences based on nationality. Typically, identity elements related to nation of origin, as well as ethnicity, are ignored or downplayed in light of the more visible issue of race. We hope that our use of Asian/Pacific Islander Americans has increased your understanding of the important issue of nationality. But recognize that any racial/ethnic group could have been used as a point of illustration. Just think about the great diversity of nations/countries that are assumed within groups of European Americans (Irish, German, Italian, etc.), African Americans (South African, Ethiopian, Nigerian, etc.), Latino/a Americans (Guatemalan, Cuban, Brazilian, etc.), and Native Americans (Mohegan, Osage, Cherokee, etc.)!

Sexual Orientation

Homosexuality has long been regarded as a taboo topic in Western society—"the sin that cannot be named"/"the love that dare not speak its name" (Boswell, 1994, p. xxiii). However, recent research on gay/lesbian culture and communication has established the value of investigating sexual orientation as a cultural phenomenon (Byers & Hart, 1996; Roberts & Orbe, 1996; Spradlin, 1995; Woods, 1993). Studies have provided descriptions of various cultural aspects of gay communities that strongly indicate sexual identity is about more than simply being attracted to members of the same sex. More recent self-generated labels reflect this idea: "affectional orientation," "transgendered," or "omnisexual" (Bawer, 1994; Moore, 1993/94). Each of these terms resists dominant perceptions that label gay, lesbian, and bisexuals exclusively in terms of sexual activities (Nakayama, 1998).

One of the central aspects of gay culture is dealing with dominant (heterosexual) beliefs that see gay and lesbian love as deviant, sinful, and unnatural. A strong component of the messages that society generates concerning homosexuality are negative stereotypes of gay men and lesbian women. These stereotypes (gay men as effeminate/promiscuous/weak/pedophiles and lesbians as masculine/butch/man haters) affect both how society views gays and lesbians, as well as how they perceive themselves whether "closeted" or "out" (Cooper, 1990; Duckitt & du Toit, 1989; Krupansky, 1995). Fighting off these societal stereotypes, as well as other incidents of verbal and physical intimidation/abuse, creates a sense of a "cultural family" (Roberts & Orbe, 1996) for gays and lesbians: "I honestly felt like the gay people I met were a part of my 'chosen family.' We try to support each other. If we don't support our brothers and sisters, who will? This feeling follows you wherever you go . . . people make you feel like you are welcome and like you belong" (Byers & Hart, 1996, p. 13).

Living the life of a cultural outsider in the United States provides gays and lesbians with a perspective shared with many other microcultures. For many individuals a basic assumption exists: A person who experiences oppression is more likely to identify with others who are also oppressed, regardless of the source of their oppression. Based on this idea, we can conclude that the ability to transcend racial and ethnic differences might appear more feasible between two women—one of whom is African American, and the other who is a European American lesbian. Can the sting of confronting isms (racism, sexism, heterosexism) on a daily basis work toward creating a bond for these two racially diverse people? According to Brenda J. Allen (1997), it can and did in her close relationship with one of her colleagues, Anna. Both women have a great deal in common: baby boomers from the Midwest, raised with a similar socioeconomic status, and strong religious backgrounds. However, Allen (1997) attributes their strong friendship to sharing a similar marginalized position in society and concludes that "despite our similarities in personal style and background, Anna and I would probably not have become such good friends if she were straight" (p. 147).

Luna (1989), however, provides strong evidence that the discrimination gay communities face does not naturally lead to a greater vision of racial understanding and harmony. In fact, what appears prevalent in the gay male culture is a level of "gay racism" (Luna, 1989, p. 440) that parallels that which exists in the larger society. Although the racism that men of color face within certain gay communities is not a total surprise, it does seem to hurt a little more given the common bond shared with other gay men. In many instances, the racism in gay establishments appears to be fueled by racial and sexual stereotypes that European American men have of Asian, African, and Latino American men. When interracial contact is initiated, stereotyping affects the quality of the interaction. Consider the perceptions of an African American gay man who described his interactions with European American gay men in the following way:

> There is a situation that's happened to me every time I've gone out. White men will approach me. They assume I don't know anything. They assume that I'm uneducated and stupid. . . . They don't expect me to be able to carry on a conversation. But, when they find that I can converse and I do know something, then they're not interested. They walk away. They want THEIR images. (Luna, 1989, p. 440)

Race appears to emerge as a key issue in some areas of gay culture. Gays and lesbians of color also often find that their affectional/sexual orientation (if known by others) takes center spotlight within their respective racial/ethnic communities as well (Nero, 1997).

Spirituality

Spirituality generally refers to an individual's identification with and belief in a higher power. We prefer using the term, spirituality rather than religion as a way to be more inclusive in our treatment of this aspect of cultural identity (Collier, 1997). Although religious and spiritual communities have not been studied extensively as cultural entities per se, group membership does represent an important aspect of cultural identity for many U.S. Americans. As evidenced by recent polls (Woodward, 1993), a resurgence in spirituality has caused an increased awareness of the central role of religion in the cultural values of many individuals. Examining various levels of spirituality in the context of interracial communication appears especially relevant, given that many people's perceptions of different racial/ethnic groups (as well as other cultural groups, such as women and gays and lesbians) are informed by such belief systems. Throughout this section, we explain the potential influences of spirituality on communication among different racial and ethnic groups. In addition, we explore how this aspect of cultural identity may serve as a more salient and intense variable for certain interracial communication participants.

U.S. history demonstrates the central role of spiritual beliefs in the ways that different racial and ethnic groups have interacted. The call for a Manifest Destiny (see Chapter 2) was regarded as a "spiritual endeavor" and set the tone for how European Americans interacted with the people of color they found in North America. Select biblical scriptures were often presented as evidence for the necessity and value of slavery and other oppressive measures against African Americans and other microcultures. The Ku Klux Klan, a self-defined religious organization, uses traditional Christian symbols like the cross as a means to illustrate their "spiritually inspired" actions (Ezekiel, 1997). Fighting back the advances and influences of groups that promised to kill the legacy of what it means to be a "real American" (by African Americans, Jews, Catholics, and so on), the KKK's ideology of white supremacy is grounded in "good old-fashioned Christian values." A similar sense of spirituality was intertwined with the messages of the nation of Islam, guided by the Honorable Elijah Muhammed, Malcom X, and minister Louis Farrakhan. For many Black Muslims, defining all European Americans as "White devils"—along with other teachings from the nation of Islam—were regarded as spiritual Truths. These religious beliefs, and the various ways in which they maintain tremendous barriers to effective interracial communication, are still apparent today. For members of these religious communities, their beliefs are overtly discussed. For others, the indications of such beliefs are less obvious and extreme, yet still highly influential in terms of how the individuals perceive interracial communication.

Interestingly enough, many individuals indicate it is their spirituality that promotes interracial understanding which transcends racial and ethnic differences (see, for example, Clark & Diggs, in press). Historical accounts provide various examples of how interracial coalitions based within an overarching spiritual purpose generated positive relationships across racial and ethnic lines. The Quakers and other religious groups within the abolitionist movement and the various religious communities involved in the civil rights movement are two such examples. For many individuals, the importance of their spirituality provides them with the common faith to interact, not as different racial or ethnic group members but as extensions of the same creator. Despite such beliefs, spiritual gatherings remain one of the most segregated aspects of society. So much so that when interracial, interdenominational collectives are formed, they make big news in various media outlets. Without question, spirituality seems to hold great potential for transcending racial/ethnic differences. Yet the "baggage" that comes with particular cultural systems oftentimes includes problematic perceptions, expectations, and behaviors that ultimately interrupt ideal relationships operating on purely spiritual levels (Gonzalez, 1998).

Socioeconomic Status

In the social sciences, the examination of socioeconomic status (SES), or class, can be traced back to Karl Marx and Max Weber (Crompton, 1993). The field of communication has been slow to examine how SES impacts communication, although some significant work does exist (Houston & Wood, 1996; Moon & Rolison, 1998; Philipsen, 1975, 1976). One reason for this dearth of substantial research might be the lack of awareness and general silence about of the role of SES in a country that values equal opportunity to achieve the "American dream" (Langston, 1995). Ehrenreich (1990) explains,

> Americans are notorious for their lack of class consciousness or even class awareness. We have a much greater consciousness of race and gender issues than we do of class. Race and gender are immediate—and they are irreversible. Class is different: The American myth is that we can escape (transcend) our class. We can work our way up and out of it. (p. 46)

An important consideration when examining class differences is recognizing that SES is not equated with economic standing. Are you familiar with the term *new money*? (Think about Molly Brown in the movie Titanic.) Typically, this term refers to individuals whose economic standing has drastically improved, yet their values, interests, attitudes, and behaviors have remained fairly constant. The term has been used by the upper class to distinguish themselves from others who have more recently achieved economic success, emphasizing that how much money you have does not automatically translate into a particular "class of people." Beyond current levels of income, class also entails assumptions concerning levels of economic security, the importance of family and kinship ties, interests and leisure time activities, and specific communication styles (Houston & Wood, 1996). According to some scholars, class is all encompassing and influences every aspect of our lives. "Class is your understanding of the world and where you fit in; it's composed of ideas, behav-

---

5.2   *Personal Reflections*

I have quite a few memories about the role that socioeconomic status played in my self-concept and how I interacted with others. Growing up in a low-income housing project with subsidized rent meant that my family didn't have a lot, but neither did anyone else, so our lives seemed pretty "normal." This continued during elementary school when most of my classmates dressed like me, talked like me, and liked to do the same things as me (watching lots of TV, listening to music, and playing basketball, Kick-the-Can, Red Rover, and Cartoon Freeze Tag). Getting "free" or "reduced" lunch everyday at school was the norm, not the exception.

One of my realizations of class differences occurred in the seventh grade when I attended a citywide junior high school. During one of my first days of school, I vividly remember one of the teachers taking attendance and asking

Personal Reflections *(continued)*

each student what elementary school he or she had attended. I couldn't help but notice that she seemed to treat students differently based on that information. Such treatment seemed to strengthen the boundaries between "us" (the poor kids) and "them" (the rich kids). Although some friendships were able to cross class divisions, these were relatively few and seemed to only play out in certain circumstances (e.g., during college-prep courses where a few of *us* were able to interact with more of *them* on a more equal level). Differences in dress, speech, and interests clearly facilitated a social/class division in our school. Bringing your lunch—and looking down on those of us who ate school lunches—was the preferred norm. The few of *them who paid* for their lunch received tickets that were a different color from those tickets that were *given to us* free or at a reduced rate. Distinguishing markers based on class were everywhere.

Socioeconomic status is a way of life, and does not necessarily change with your personal or family income. Thus, while my salary today is significantly higher than that of my parents, my life perspective in terms of class remains largely the same (regardless of whether I "pass" as a middle-class person or not) (see, for example, Moon, 1998). I rarely go out to eat because it's so expensive. Several appliances at home have been repaired with duct tape (they still work fine—well, most of the time anyway!). :) I still go directly to the "reduced meat" section of the supermarket before looking at the regular-priced items. I use as many coupons and rebates as possible. In fact, I rarely buy anything not on sale. Most of my clothes are found at thrift stores, where I still barter about prices or wait for specials (fill a bag full of clothes for $5!). Last year on an interstate trip, I drove 20 minutes out of my way to save $1.50 in tolls. This list could go on and on, but I think you get the picture. Because of my early experiences growing up—something I wouldn't trade for the world!—socioeconomic status remains an important issue in most of my interactions with others. What are some of your salient cultural issues? How are they tied to specific life memories?—MPO

iors, attitudes, values, and language; class is how you think, feel, act, look, dress, talk, move, walk. (Langston, 1995, p. 101). In short, "we experience class at every level of our lives" (p. 102).

Classism is most commonly understood as a top-down practice whereby middle- and upper-class persons perpetuate discriminatory behaviors toward those of lower-class standing. One aspect of classism is the maintenance of separation, including conscious efforts of "affluent" groups to do whatever they can to avoid contact with the "less fortunate" (Ehrenreich, 1990). One result of the lack of any substantial interaction between different classes is stereotyping maintenance by all socioeconomic groups. More "enlightened" people from the middle- and upper-class segments of society stereotype the working class/underclass as ignorant, lazy, and hopelessly bigoted. It is important to recognize, though, that class prejudice (in the form of personal attitudes) functions at various levels of SES (Moon & Rolison, 1998). Wasteful, snobby, lazy, carefree, and prejudiced are some of the perceptions that members of a lower socioeconomic status have in regard to more affluent persons. Although the institutional power of individuals to enact these stereotypes into policy varies, their influence that they have on interpersonal contact remains strong for all SES groups.

Socioeconomic status remains a largely invisible issue within the United States (Houston & Wood, 1996). This is, in part, due to the reality that class standing is largely correlated with racial/ethnic identity and other cultural variables such as gender and family structure (Langston, 1995; Praeger, 1995). Therefore, many references to racial and ethnic groups are typically reflective of class distinctions more so than those solely based on racial/ethnic differences. At times, similar SES may provide common perspectives for certain members of diverse racial/ethnic groups. For others, racial and ethnic differences remain the key issue. This appears to be the case, for instance, with some African American, Latino/a American, and European Americans who have established cross-racial alliances to fight oppression based on race and class in large metropolitan areas. However, equally convincing evidence indicates that racial and ethnic boundaries along these same lines simultaneously exist amid these efforts. Looking at race and SES alone clearly, does not give us a complete enough picture to predict the quality of interracial communication. Thus any productive analysis of the potential for interracial communication effectiveness must not only account for race/ethnicity and SES, but also all of the other aspects of cultural identity described in this chapter.

INTERSECTIONS OF RACE/ETHNICITY, GENDER, AND SOCIOECONOMIC STATUS

Take a minute to reflect on the descriptions of cultural influence provided in the previous section. It should become clear that interracial communication must be understood in the context of other cultural variables besides simply race/ethnicity. In order to achieve some level of organizational clarity, we chose to discuss each of the aspects of culture (abilities, age, gender, nationality, sexual orientation, spirituality, socioeconomic status) separately. But recognize that in reality these and other cultural markers are interlocking and inseparable. No one person is simply a member of one particular group. Instead she or he simultaneously encompasses multiple cultural identities. The best vantage point to come to understand human communication is through an acknowledgment that each person experiences life as a complex individual whose cultural group identities function in concert with one another (Houston & Wood, 1996).

Gordon (1978) contends that, for many people of color, racial/ethnic identity develops during early socialization and continues to represent a core aspect of their identity throughout their lives. In the United States, this belief has often led to a narrow focus on racial identity that results in an oversimplification of how a person's cultural identity affects communication processes (Collier & Thomas, 1988). A more effective approach is to acknowledge, like Collier (1997, 1998) and her colleagues (Hecht et al., 1993) do, that cultural identities are ongoing and situational. Racial/ethnic identity may represent an enduring aspect of an individual's self-identity. Research indicates that this is more likely in situations where group identity is threatened (Bourhis & Giles, 1977), racial/ethnic comparisons are made (Tajfel, 1978), or a person is perceived as a prototype of his or her group (Gudykunst & Hammer, 1988). More than likely, race/ethnicity is not the only enduring aspect of identity in all situations. In fact, people are constantly negotiating their identities (Brown & Levinson, 1978), and in some situations normally important cultural issues (like race/ethnicity) become less central to interaction. For instance, think about a recent *intra*racial small group discussion you have had (where all participants identified with the same racial/ethnic group). Within this context, do other cultural differences—based on sex, age, sexual orientation, and/or SES—typically become more visible at some point in the interaction? Recent research on race and communication (Drummond, 1997) supports the basic idea that other aspects of cultural identity emerge as more significant (at least temporarily) during intraracial conversations.

Most communication involves multiple cultural identities, with the exceptions reflecting one single identity to overwhelm all others (Hecht et al., 1993). Think about the previous statement for a moment. Can you generate any examples of communication that are *solely* the result of one aspect of your cultural identity? More than likely, any example you can come up with reflects an intersection of various cultural elements. For example, you may have heard the statement, "It's a Black thang . . . ," a phrase illustrating how certain behaviors are directly related to a particular racial experience. (The second part of the phrase, "you wouldn't understand," highlights the difficulty of outgroup members' understanding ingroup cultural norms, values, and/or ideas.) However, how many times is something described as a "Black thang," when in essence it refers to something more than simply race? In many cases, "it's a Black thang" might be better described as "a

Black *urban* thing," "a Black *Generation X* thing," or "a Black *working-class* thing." These phrases help acknowledge that some African Americans may not share certain cultural experiences (because of regional, age, or SES) and some non–African Americans may, because of similar cultural identities other than race/ethnicity.

One way to help us understand the interconnections of multiple cultural identities (Cupach & Imahori, 1993) is by recognizing that persons typically form a "hierarchical organization of identity" (Hecht et al., 1993, p. 36). In other words, without assigning status to any one aspect of identity for all people, this idea assumes that certain sets of lived experiences result in moving specific identity elements to the core of a particular person's self-concept. Some theorists, such as McCall and Simmons (1978), see such multiple identity hierarchies as largely fluid, changing from one situation to another. Others, such as Stryker and Statham (1984), believe such organizations of key cultural identity markers are more enduring. One way to incorporate the idea hierarchical organizations of identity as both fluid and enduring—a basic property of cultural identity theory—is to envision a pyramid of sorts. Those more enduring aspects of an individual's self-identity exist at the top of the identity pyramid. Other more fluid cultural markers, those whose saliency and intensity vary depending on the particular situational context (Harris, 1997b), are positioned at the bottom. This framework is productive in that it: (1) embraces the interconnectedness of multiple cultural identities, (2) recognizes both the enduring and fluid nature of cultural markers, and (3) avoids the trap of building a rigid, definitive hierarchy of cultural identity for all U.S. Americans. This latter point is especially important given that some scholars (e.g., Smith, 1983) have criticized attempts to present a universal ordering of cultural experiences (e.g., "dealing with racism is worse than dealing with sexism, which is worse than . . .).

CONCLUSION

Cultural identity, of which racial/ethnic identity is a part, is abstract, complex, multi-dimensional, and fluid (Cupach & Imahori, 1993). Developing a consciousness of the role that racial/ethnic differences play in communication process is important. It should not be overemphasized, though, to the point of stereotyping each person based on his or her race/ethnicity. In other words, treating people as if they are solely defined by one facet of their cultural identity is problematic and arguably the best formula for *ineffective* interracial communication. Consider the following quote from Audre Lorde (1984):

> As a Black lesbian feminist comfortable with the many different ingredients of my identity, and a woman committed to racial and sexual freedom from oppression, I find I am

constantly being encouraged to pluck out one aspect of myself and present this as the meaningful whole, eclipsing or denying the other parts of self. But this is a destructive and fragmenting way to live. My fullest concentration of energy is available to me only when I integrate all the parts of who I am, opening, allowing power from particular sources of my living to flow back and forth freely through all of my different selves, without the restrictions of externally imposed definitions. Only then can I bring myself and my energies as a whole to the service of those struggles which I embrace as part of my living. (p. 120)

As Lorde points out, interacting with others based on a single aspect of their identity denies them the opportunity to participate as complete cultural beings. Race remains a salient issue in the United States. But we should recognize the role that race/ethnicity plays in the communication process *alongside* other elements of a person's multiple cultural identity. Ultimately, the ability to recognize the multiple identities of self and others—and identify key elements of cultural difference of any given interaction—appears to be a fundamental component of interracial communication competence (Collier, 1998). In addition, paying attention to the multiple cultural identities of others and the various ways they influence communicative behaviors generates opportunities for enhanced self-identity development.

OPPORTUNITIES FOR EXTENDED LEARNING

1. Create a case study that details a particular scenario in which multiple cultural identities directly influence intraracial or interracial communication. Ideally, these should be based on real-life experiences. Share your case study with the rest of the class/group and discuss the importance of recognizing multiple cultural identities in communication effectiveness.

 2. Recent predictions of future demographic trends has resulted in an increased focus on growing influences of Latino/a culture. Use your *InfoTrac College Edition* to identify sources that describe various aspects of the cultural similarities and differences of La Raza. A keyword, like Latino, will return hundreds of cites. Therefore, you may want to use *La Raza* or *Latino culture*. Pay particular attention to the different labels used within these resources. How do they reflect the complexity of multiple cultural identities?

3. Create an identity pyramid that reflects the various components of your self-identity in the context of reading this book (as a student, scholar, practitioner, etc.). Then break off into dyads and share why certain elements are more salient than others. What other cultural elements did you include that were not specifically described in this chapter (i.e., profession, organizations, etc.)?

4. Use role-play scenarios to examine the impact of identity, culture, and communication. Within small groups, select one person to be the observer. Two persons will role-play a first encounter between two individuals who share one aspect of their cultural identity (this can be real or imagined, but both people need to agree on it). Within a period of 3 to 5 minutes, engage in a typical conversation. However, be sure to include self-disclosures that point to other aspects of your cultural identity (religion, sexual orientation, class, etc.). At the end of the conversation, ask the observer to share his or her perceptions of how the conversation changed, if at all, as other cultural markers were introduced.

5. A study done in the late 1980s reported that the most important issues of identity for college students were gender, religion, and ethnicity. School major and student status were of secondary importance, followed by hobbies and athletics (Garza & Herringer, 1987). After breaking into small groups, discuss your reactions to this study. As a whole, do you think these results hold true for college students today? Why or why not? Can you obtain a group consensus of the most salient cultural issues for students today? How might these vary from context to context? Lastly, discuss how this exercise helped clarify the idea of a hierarchical organizational identity.

THEORETICAL APPROACHES TO STUDYING INTERRACIAL COMMUNICATION

Theory. For most college students, this word triggers visions of abstract, dull, unnecessary complex ideas that "academic types" use to intellectualize the world around them. Many believe that theories hold little practical value in terms of their everyday life experiences. Although these perceptions are not universally shared by all students, they do seem to hold true for significant numbers. We have collectively taught communication theories to thousands of undergraduate and graduate students at six different universities across the country, and we can also vividly remember our own perceptions as undergraduate students, being forced to study various theories that appeared to be the work of people who simply had too much time on their hands! As communication scholars (and emerging theorists), we now see theoretical frameworks differently. Theories are the mechanisms that allow us to understand communication phenomena in more complex ways. Without theories to guide our efforts, studying different aspects of interracial communication would be haphazard, disjointed, and random. Good communication theories expand our knowledge beyond superficial understanding. They also have practical value in enhancing communication effectiveness.

One of our challenges here is to help you make the connection between theory and practice. Obviously, we do not want you to see theory as abstract, confusing, and largely irrelevant to your life experiences. Instead, begin to understand theoretical frameworks as lenses that assist us in seeing the world clearly. Using this metaphor can be a useful way to embrace the importance of theory, especially those of us who share common experiences at the eye doctor's office. Do you remember eye examinations where the doctor changed the lens and then asked you if the letters on the wall were clearer or not? For those of us who have been wearing corrective lenses for some time, these memories are quite vivid. Some lenses that were tried increased our vision slightly, whereas others made our vision more blurry. The key to this process (patience is a must!) is to continue trying on different combinations of lenses until 20/20 vision is achieved and the letters on the wall can be read with great clarity and confidence. Imagine the tremendous difference that corrective lenses make for those who have been experiencing life (sometimes unknowingly) without clear vision. Without a doubt, you see things in a different light!

Theories are very much like lenses. They help us see communication phenomena in new, more vivid ways. This chapter introduces nine different theoretical frameworks that hold great promise for increasing our understanding of interracial communication. A general description of each theory or model is presented. Consistent with the lens metaphor used earlier, we acknowledge that some theories may be a better personal fit for you than others. The key is to identify and concentrate on those theories and models that facilitate the greatest understanding in terms of your life experiences. Ultimately, we hope that you are able to use multiple theories/lenses to view interracial communication. A great number of communication theories can be used to gain insight into the process of interracial communication. We have chosen nine specific frameworks that appear most relevant to how different racial/ethnic groups communicate in the United States. Before presenting these theories, however, let's look at the early work on interracial communication..

INTERRACIAL COMMUNICATION MODELS

The earliest interracial communication models can be traced to the mid-1970s and linked to the increased attention to race relations in the United States at that time. During the 1960s and 1970s, people of color—most notably African Americans and Chicanos—gained national attention as they confronted historical, political, and social practices that were discriminatory and oppressive. Although most civil rights struggles continue today to a certain extent, these historical acts of civil disobedience were instrumental in forcing a society to deal with a social ill traditionally ignored by most European Americans. As should have been the case, several communication scholars acknowledged the key role they could play in building productive relations among different racial/ethnic groups. For many scholars, interracial communication represented an area of both great academic and practical relevance beyond most traditional work that focused on culture from an international perspective. A brief overview of three models that laid the groundwork for interracial communication study is presented here: Smith's (1973) model of transracial communication, Rich's (1974) interracial communication model, and Blubaugh and Pennington's (1976) cross difference model of communication.

Transracial Communication Model

The earliest interracial communication model stemmed from the work of Molefi Kete Asante (previously known as Arthur L. Smith). His model focused on describing the process by which individuals could "cross racial lines" to communicate effectively (Smith, 1973). However, Asante avoided traditional approaches of racial differences (based on genetics) that were prevalent in most research. Instead, he focused on interactions that were impacted by *perceived* racial identity distinctions on the part of one or more individuals. Interracial communication, then, included interactions when perceived racial differences were a critical feature.

One of the important contributions of this model was increased attention to how each person's communication was reflective of a particular "ethnic perspective." For instance, the model was instrumental in illustrating the influence of individual worldviews—for both communicators—on how messages are created, articulated, and ultimately perceived. According to this model (Smith, 1973), the goal of transracial communication is the "normalization" of communication. Normalization was used to describe the process of identifying and moving toward a central threshold where both parties can find common ground to base their communication. To this end, ethnic differences could be transcended. Asante's model also included the realization that interracial communication is best understood within a "universal context." Although crossing racial lines was possible, it had to be accomplished within a recognition of the past histories of humans communicating with one another. This involved an acknowledgment of the sociopolitical history of race and racial/ethnic relations.

Interracial Communication Model

Andrea L. Rich (1974) and colleagues (Rich & Ogawa, 1972) created a model that approached interracial communication differently than Asante's model. They believed that people of color could live within their respective communities relatively uninfluenced by the dominant structures of European Americans. This model focused on the process by which different non-White racial groups leave their own cultures and enter European American–dominated social structures. Specific attention was paid to the various ways that other cultural factors (socioeconomic status, skin color, degree of cultural differences) influenced the communication between European Americans and people of color.

The interracial communication model was based on a number of assumptions. First, racial/ethnic minorities could never *totally* move within the realm of dominant European American society. Although people of color could move freely within certain areas, certain portions of White America remained off limits (e.g., certain neighborhoods, clubs, and so on). Second, the model was based on the premise that European Americans controlled the amount of accessibility that people of color had in dominant societal structures. Depending on related factors (e.g., SES or degree of cultural difference), some racial/ethnic groups were permitted access to areas where others were excluded. Third, the model assumed that European Americans could never become full-fledged members of other racial/ethnic cultures. They believed that, regardless of well-meaning intentions, European Americans could never fully understand the experiences of racial microcultures in the United States. And because racial/ethnic microcultures share a common marginalized positioning, communication between people of color (Latino/a and African Americans, for instance) has a greater chance of communication effectiveness than that which occurs between European Americans and U.S. Americans of color.

From Rich's perspective (1974), this model dealt with the realities of race relations in the 1970s. Some might suggest that much has changed since that time. Others would attest that nothing much has changed ("the more things change, the more they stay the same"). You can be the judge of the relevance of the interracial communication model to life in the 21st century. Nevertheless, it marked a significant development in attempts to theorize interracial communication.

Cross Difference Communication Model

The work of Jon A. Blubaugh and Dorthy L. Pennington (1976) differs from the interracial communication model in two distinct ways. First, their analysis of interracial communication is not limited to White–non-White communication. It can be used to understand European American–African American, interactions, as well as those involving different racial/ethnic minorities (e.g., Asian American–Latino Americans, Native American–African Americans, etc.). Second, the cross difference model of communication recognizes that all racial/ethnic groups (including European Americans) share some aspects of a "common culture" affiliated with living in the United States. Furthermore, the model acknowledges the mutual influences of different racial/ethnic cultures on one another. In this regard, no culture in the United States could escape being influenced by other co-cultures.

The cross difference model focused on the importance of transcending racial differences while simultaneously understanding how such differences remain a part of one's culture. Blubaugh and Pennington (1976) believed that while cultural influences will still be apparent during interracial interactions, they must be diminished in order for communication to be effective. And although some racialized stereotyping and attitudes may arise from time to time, they no longer serve as a primary source of difference for the individuals. According to the model, effective interracial communication is possible if each person bears responsibility for reducing the influence of racial/ethnic differences. Blubaugh and Pennington specifically discuss six features of interracial communication that need to be addressed: racism, power relations, racial assumptions, language, nonverbal cues, and core beliefs and values. In short, the cross difference communication model advocates transcending (not erasing) racial differences so that persons can communicate on a "same-race (human race) basis" (Blubaugh & Pennington, 1976, p. 17). Such an accomplishment involves a gradual process; however, the potential for such communication is immeasurable.

> When the point is reached that both parties can communicate across difference, then their options and possibilities for increasing the depth and meaningfulness of their relationships becomes a true potential. They may now agree or disagree, find pleasure or displeasure, love or hate for reasons other than race of the special differences that initially inhibited interracial communication. (Blubaugh & Pennington, 1976, p. 18)

THEORIZING INTERRACIAL COMMUNICATION

The past 25 to 30 years have yielded significant changes in terms of the political, social, legal, and economic structures that inform race relations in the United States. But a distinct voice among racial/ethnic minorities asserts that "the more things have changed, the more they have stayed the same." A quick review of some of the statistical information on race seems to support this perspective. When compared to European Americans, African Americans, Latino/a Americans, and Native Americans are significantly overrepresented in disadvantaged categories across the board (economic status, education, housing, health, and so on). Consistent with the idea represented throughout this book, we do not assume an either/or positioning on this issue. Some advancements clearly have been made (e.g., increased levels of education and a growing middle class for different racial/ethnic groups). Nevertheless, a more critical review reveals that divisions between the haves and have-nots are still largely based on race.

For this reason, we believe early interracial communication models contain elements and approaches that are still pertinent to the 21st century. Still, they do not reflect some of the changing realities of the past three decades. The field of communication generally, and the area of intercultural/interracial communication specifically, offers a broad range of theoretical frameworks that provide insight into interactions and relationships among people of diverse racial and ethnic backgrounds. We have chosen to focus on nine theories/models that appear most relevant to the study and practice of effective interracial communication. As you will see, these theoretical frameworks represent a variety of approaches. Most theories reflect a body of research that has primarily been applied to intercultural communication in international contexts. Others are situated specifically in terms of interracial communication, or other forms of co-cultural communication, in the United States. Each of the theories described in this chapter, regardless of its initial focus, has something unique to contribute to a deeper understanding of interracial communication.

In addition, each theoretical framework is based on certain ideological assumptions. Some are more humanistic than scientific and reflect a way of knowing that focuses on developing compelling interpretations from a particular subjective positioning. Humanistic perspectives are grounded in the assumption that people create their own multiple meanings of realities. Ultimately, humanistic frameworks work to enhance understanding. Other theories are more scientific in their approach to interracial communication study. A scientific perspective attempts to understand the causes of human behavior as a means to increase the prediction and control of future interactions. Based on an assumption that truth is singular, scientific theories work to discover universal laws of human behavior. Objectivity is a key element of good scientific theory.

Notice that in this discussion we are emphasizing epistemological differences (ways of knowing) on a continuum of sorts, rather than solely associated with one approach or the other. The fact is, some of the theoretical frameworks discussed in this chapter are grounded in assumptions that reflect, to a certain degree, both humanistic and scientific perspectives. The point of this discussion is not to extol one perspective over another. Both perspectives make unique contributions to interracial communication study. We did want to highlight some of these basic differences, however, in order to increase your awareness that some theoretical lenses may be grounded in seemingly contradictory approaches.

The remainder of this chapter is divided into two sections. The first section covers theories (speech community theory, critical race theory, Afrocentricity, and co-cultural theory) that help us understand the communication of different racial/ethnic groups. As you read through this section, note how each theory provides insight into how racialized standpoints (see Chapter 1) affect communication. Michael Hecht and his colleagues have produced a substantial amount of research on what we call "theorizing satisfying communication." This body of work serves as an effective transition between the first section and the second section, which highlights four theories (anxiety/uncertainty management theory, third culture building, cross-cultural adaptation theory, and communication accommodation theory) that focus on the interracial communication process itself.

UNDERSTANDING DIFFERENT FORMS OF RACIALIZED COMMUNICATION

Speech Community Theory

Speech community theory, also known as the ethnography of communication and speech codes theory, is useful in explaining the misunderstandings that surface in communication between people of different social groups (Carbaugh, 1995; Hymes, 1974; Philipsen, 1996). According to Labov (1972), a speech community exists when a group of people understands goals and styles of communication in ways not shared by people outside of the group. In terms of interracial communication, speech community theory is useful for interactions with people with different language systems (e.g., a Spanish-speaking Cuban American and a Chinese-speaking Chinese American). It is also useful for those who use the same language (e.g., English) but whose racial groups have a different set of speech codes (e.g., a Native American and European American). A speech code, according to Philipsen (1996), refers to "a system of socially constructed symbols and meanings, premises, and rules, pertaining to communicative conduct" (p. 126). In other words, speech community theory focuses on how different cultural groups (including those defined by racial/ethnic differences) instill within their members distinct styles of communicating and interpreting the communication of others. Some instances of problematic interracial communication can be traced to a misunderstanding of the other person's speech code.

Speech community theory is grounded in four assumptions (Philipsen, 1997). First, members of cultural communities create shared meaning among themselves. These communities are oftentimes defined by differences in language and geography, as well as other less visible boundaries. Whenever there is a distinctive culture, there is typically a distinctive speech code. Second, communicators in any cultural group must coordinate their actions. Even though it may not be apparent to nonmembers, each speech code is guided by some order or system. Third, meanings and actions are particular to individual groups. During interracial interactions, attempts to understand another person's communication by using your own cultural norms may be ineffective. Carbaugh (1998) provides a vivid example of this in describing how European Americans can misinterpret a Native American's use of

---

6.1   *Case Study*

In late 1996, the Oakland (CA) school board passed a resolution recognizing the important role that Ebonics (Black English) plays in the language development and academic achievement of young African Americans (Close, 1997). Their decision triggered a national debate on the value of Ebonics and its place in institutions of learning. Proponents pointed to evidence indicating that when teachers understood and respected Ebonics, they were able to use it effectively to teach standard English. Opponents to the resolution—across racial and ethnic lines—criticized it as discriminatory, misinformed, and counterproductive to longterm African American student success.

In terms of our discussion on interracial communication theoretical frameworks, the use of Ebonics serves as an excellent case study. From a communication perspective, what is Ebonics? What role does it play during interracial interactions? How does it impact ingroup and outgroup communication? How is its influence impacted by other variables? As you read through the descriptions of various theories and models contained in this chapter, think about these questions. How does each framework provide a different way of looking at this communication phenomenon? How does Afrocentricity, for instance, regard Ebonics as compared to models of third-culture building? Try to take the perspective of each theory. How can Ebonics be understood through each framework? The variety of images might surprise you!

---

silence. Fourth, each cultural community has a set of distinct resources for assigning meaning to its actions. Not only are patterns of communication different among some racial/ethnic groups, but each group may also have its own set of meanings with which to understand its own codes. In other words, every attempt possible should be made to understand speech codes within their cultural context.

Within the field of communication, this theoretical framework has proven instrumental in understanding how people from different cultural groups follow different sets of communication rules. Much of the work was based in ethnographic research that discovered how groups create shared meaning through unique cultural norms (e.g., Carbaugh, 1995; Philipsen, 1975). More recent work has extended ethnography, traditionally a humanistic methodology, to a more scientific perspective. This includes using knowledge of speech codes to predict and control the communication of others in order to facilitate more effective communication

(Philipsen, 1997). Remember, however, that understanding that speech is structured via different cultural groups is not to say it is absolutely determined (Philipsen, 1992). In other words, attempts to predict another person's communication based on knowledge of her or his speech community must recognize that a speech code represents a pattern, not an absolute. Speech community theory, then, offers a valuable perspective to understanding the communication styles of different racial/ethnic groups when we acknowledge that variations of understanding, accepting, and using speech codes exist within and across groups.

Critical Race Theory

Compared to all of the theories presented in this chapter, critical race theory represents a framework that was developed outside the field of communication (Calvert, 1997). Its origins can be traced back to the late 1970s and early 1980s (Crenshaw, Gotanda, Peller, & Thomas, 1995). Specifically, critical race theory was developed by civil rights activists who were seeing many of the gains achieved during the 1960s disappearing (Matsuda, Lawrence, Delgado, & Crenshaw, 1993). The earliest work in this area was done by scholars in critical legal studies. Their efforts generally challenged dominant values of equal opportunity and justice for all by highlighting the realities of race. Recently, communication scholars have drawn this emerging theoretical approach to inform their research on race, ethnicity, and communication (e.g., Cornwell, Orbe, & Warren, 1999; Hasian & Delgado, 1998).

The essence of critical race theory can be best captured by identifying several core elements (Matsuda et al., 1993). First, it recognizes that racism is an integral part of the United States. Instead of debating whether racism can ever be totally eliminated, critical race theorists work to challenge existing structures that reinforce racial oppression. Second, critical race theory rejects dominant legal and social claims of neutrality, objectivity, and color blindness. It embraces the subjectivity that comes with a particular field of experience. As part of the rejection of neutrality, critical race theorists describe their work as explicitly political. The third core element rejects a historical approach to studying race. Instead, this theoretical approach insists on looking at interracial communication from within a contextual/historical context. From this perspective, the current state of race relations in the United States is directly linked to earlier events. Attempting to understand interracial communication in the 21st century, then, is only possible through an awareness of the history of interracial contact in the United States (see Chapter 2).

Fourth, critical race theory recognizes the importance of experiential knowledge that comes from various microcultural standpoints. In other words, it (like Afrocentricity, discussed later) values insight grounded in the experiences of those racial and ethnic groups that have historically been marginalized. The fifth core element relates to the interdisciplinary and eclectic nature of critical race theory. The ideas of this theory are borrowed from several traditions, including Marxism, feminism, critical/cultural studies, and postmodernism. Finally, critical race theory actively works toward the elimination of racial oppression. But although the focus is on racial oppression, the ways that racism is closely tied to other forms of oppression based on gender, class, and sexual orientation is acknowledged. And although critical race theorists have focused on legal remedies, they also understand that racism cannot be solved by creating additional laws (Hasian & Delgado, 1998).

Like standpoint theory (see Chapter 1), critical race theory believes our realities are defined by our experiences, as well as the collective historical experiences of our communities of origin (Matsuda et al., 1993). Traditionally, scholarship that addresses race has not included the diverse perspectives of those it seeks to explain. Because of this, critical race theory promotes the need for frameworks that come from the experiences of traditionally disenfranchised groups (Hasian & Delgado, 1998). In addition, further attention is needed on theories that no longer ignore the diversity within different racial and ethnic groups. According to this interracial communication approach, what should be emphasized are "situated knowledges that come from detailed investigations of unique experiences of socially constructed races" (Hasian & Delgado, 1998, p. 252).

As described by Matsuda et al. (1993), the work of critical race theorists is both pragmatic and idealized. Specifically, their scholarship attempts to address the immediate needs of those who are oppressed. In doing so, they strive to work toward the ideals of equal opportunity and justice that the United States was founded on. New forms of critical race scholarship have emerged including the use of personal histories, stories, dreams, poems, and fiction (Matsuda et al., 1993). These nontraditional approaches to scholarship have been used effectively to examine the relationships among labels, knowledge, power, and reality (see Chapter 3). In addition, critical race theory has been used to gain insight into the ways that "neutral" discussions of race often implicitly reinforce existing racial/ethnic dynamics (Hasian & Delgado, 1998). In terms of interracial communication, this emerging body of work contributes to a more complex understanding of how race affects our everyday communication.

Afrocentricity

Without question, Molefi Kete Asante is the foremost scholar associated with Afrocentricity (also known as African-centered scholarship). His work has provided much of the framework for personal, social, educational, and theoretical/methodological development (Asante, 1988, 1998a), and other scholars from various disciplines have also contributed important ideas. In its most basic form, Afrocentricity places Africans and the interest of Africa at the center of research and practice. Do you see how this idea is consistent with standpoint and critical race theories? Such a move is especially important given that for many years communication research on persons of African descent was completed with European frameworks (Asante, 1998a). With this in mind, Afrocentricity has provided a powerful critique of the problems with communication research that is solely situated in traditional Western thought (McPhail, 1998). Asante (1998a) contends that critics who label the theoretical framework as anti-European and divisive are misinterpreting his positions (see also Phillips, 1983). Afrocentricity is not meant to be placed above other perspectives. Instead it should exist alongside other cultural/historical standpoints. In this regard, Afrocentric thought provides an alternative to traditional frameworks when exploring the perspectives of people of African descent. Afrocentricity is not the opposite of Eurocentrism. In fact, some scholars (e.g., McPhail, 1998) have found a complementary foundation between the two based on how both approaches implicate one another. In short, "The Afrocentric idea is one way of revealing the multicultural essence of our effort to understand the human experience" (Woodyard, 1995, p. 43). Other approaches, like an Asiacentric perspective (Wong, Manvi, & Wong, 1995), also offer valuable frameworks for studying interracial communication from non-European standpoints.

What exactly is an Afrocentric theoretical framework? First, it involves the development of a theoretical perspective that reflects African ways of knowing and interpreting the world (Ribeau, 1997). Afrocentricity assumes that people of African descent, despite some diverse lived experiences, share a common set of experiences, struggles, and origins. The African Diaspora provides a common cultural base that reflects a key set of values: harmony with nature, humaneness, rhythm, and communalism in terms of how wealth is produced, owned, and distributed. Second, Afrocentricity seeks agency and action through collective consciousness (Asante, 1988). In other words, Afrocentricity serves as a mechanism to embracing African ideals at the center of intellectual/personal life. It relies on the self-conscious actions of individuals with direct attention to the way they relate to one another. Note that being African American does not make you Afrocentric (Asante, 1998a). In fact, non–African Americans who embrace the principles of Afrocentricity can produce Afrocentric research (Asante, 1991; Brummett, 1994).

One of the major components of Afrocentricity—as it relates to interracial communication—is that it represents an intellectual framework which sees people of African descent as participants (rather than subjects/objects) in their human existence. It also recognizes that features of the human condition (feeling, knowing, and acting) are interrelated and should not be viewed as separate (i.e., viewing emotion as irrational and less valuable than reason). According to Delgado (1998), Afrocentricity is important because it embraces an "alternative set of realities, experiences, and identities" (p. 423) for research attempting to view interracial communication from a non-Western perspective. From the beginning, U.S. history has been pluralistic. Given this, interpretations of human existence (communication) from any one cultural standpoint is unproductive. Afrocentric scholars believe that to truly understand and appreciate the communication behaviors of African Americans one has to study them from within an Afrocentric perspective. Studying other racial/ethnic groups members should also be completed within a framework that is culturally relevant and situated in social, political, and historical contexts.

Take, for instance, existing research that attempts to understand African American communication apart from its cultural influences. The result largely has been interpretations that fail to completely understand the nuances of language. Afrocentric scholars have advocated for a culturally centered focus on the generative and productive power of the spoken word (*nommo*). According to Jahn (1979), nommo can be regarded as the life force, "a unity of spiritual-physical fluidity, giving life to everything, penetrating everything, causing everything" (p. 124). Seeing the power of the speech within this perspective promotes a more culturally centered analysis of racialized communication. And, in short, it is that aspect of Afrocentricity which proves most valuable to the study of interracial communication. All analyses are situated within a particular cultural standpoint, complete with ideological assumptions. Afrocentricity offers a theoretical framework that draws attention to existing problems with scholarship that solely reflects one group's cultural experiences.

Co-Cultural Theory

Co-cultural communication refers to a particular form of intercultural communication research that centers on issues of societal power and dominance within the United States (e.g., Folb, 1997). Co-cultural communication theory, as described by Orbe (1996, 1998a, 1998b, 1998c), helps us understand the ways that persons who are traditionally marginalized in society communicate in their everyday lives. Grounded in muted group (Kramarae, 1981) and standpoint theories (Smith, 1987), co-cultural theory focuses on the lived experiences of a variety of "nondominant" or co-cultural groups. Subsequently, it represents a relevant framework for studying the experiences of people of color, women, people with disabilities, and gays, lesbians, and bisexuals (Fox, Giles, Bourhis, & Orbe, 1999; Orbe, 1996, 1998d). In terms of interracial communication, it can be used (like Afrocentricity) to understand interracial communication from the perspectives of racial and ethnic microcultural group members. In its most basic form, co-cultural theory lends insight into how members of microcultures negotiate their underrepresented status with others (both a part of macrocultures and microcultures) in different situational contexts (Orbe, 1997, 1998c).

Co-cultural theory is based on the idea that, because of their marginalized societal positioning, people of color have to develop certain communication orientations in order to survive and/or succeed in the United States. However, it is important to recognize the vast diversity within and among different racial and ethnic groups. Therefore, the adoption and maintenance of certain orientations—as well as the rationale behind such decisions—varies greatly. Six interrelated factors (field of experience, perceived costs and rewards, ability, preferred outcomes, communication approach, and situational context) reportedly influence such decisions. *Field of experience* relates to the sum of lived experiences for people of color. Through a life-long series of experiences, individuals learn how to communicate with others. They also come to realize the consequences of certain forms of communication. Based on her or his unique field of experience—which is simultaneously similar to, yet different than others—an individual comes to recognize that certain *costs and rewards* are associated with different communication practices. In some instances the advantages and disadvantages are clear. However, in others, they are less straightforward and more complex.

A third factor influential to interracial communication is the *ability* to enact certain strategies that work to establish and maintain a specific communication orientation. Consistent with communication accommodation theory (discussed later), co-cultural theory understands that people of color have varying levels of success in using certain strategies (e.g., "passing" or networking with other people of color). Much depends on the specific dynamics inherent in any given *situational context*. This includes where the interaction takes place, other parties that are present, and the particular circumstances that facilitate the interaction. It should be apparent that situational context, like the other five factors, intersect in highly complex ways to influence interracial interactions.

The final two factors are *communication approach* and *preferred outcome*. Communication approach refers to the specific "voice" used by racial/ethnic microcultural group members in the United States. Is the communication approach aggressive, assertive, or more nonassertive? Preferred outcome relates to the ultimate goal that the person of color has for the interaction: (1) Is he or she aiming to fit in and not bring any unnecessary attention to racial differences (assimilation)? (2) Or is the goal to recognize racial and ethnic differences and work with others to ensure that these differences do not translate into unequal treatment (accommodation)? (3) Or still yet, is the goal to limit interaction with European Americans and create affirming communities exclusively of people of color (separation)?

Note that no one approach or preferred outcome is most (or universally) desirable. Much depends on how the other factors influence the person's perceptions. The stated objective of co-cultural theory, then, is not to predict the behaviors of people of color. Instead it is to understand the complex factors that influence how they communicate in a society that traditionally has treated them as cultural outsiders (Orbe, 1998c). Identifying how these factors are apparent in specific tactics and communicative stances (see Orbe, 1998a for a detailed description of these) is an important step in this process. The basic idea of co-cultural theory, as it directly relates to interracial interactions, can be summarized as follows:

> Situated within a particular *field of experience* that governs their perceptions of the costs and rewards associated with, as well as their *ability* to engage in, various communicative practices, U.S. racial and ethnic microcultural group members will adopt certain communication orientations—based on their *preferred outcomes* and *communication approaches*—to fit the circumstances of a specific *situation*. (Orbe, 1998a, pp. 15, 18)

THEORIZING SATISFYING COMMUNICATION

The work of Michael Hecht and colleagues has been instrumental in providing models for satisfying communication from the perspectives of U.S. racial and ethnic

---

6.2   *Personal Reflections*

In the spring of 1992, I was a graduate student in my last quarter of course work. During a graduate seminar on qualitative research methodologies, I worked with a colleague and friend, T. Ford-Ahmed, on a project about how African American graduate students deal with racial prejudice at predominately European American college campuses (Ford-Ahmed & Orbe, 1992). With the humblest of beginnings, that project launched a series of research projects that has contributed to the development of co-cultural communication theory. The theory is still very much a work in progress.

Within this personal reflection I wanted to present an idea inherent within co-cultural theory that probably was not apparent in the description included in this chapter. One of the assumptions of the theory is that co-cultural groups (e.g., people of color, women, people with disabilities, gays, lesbians, and bisexuals) deal with oppression (racism, sexism, ableism, heterosexism) in similar ways. In other words, traditionally marginalized group members draw from common communication tactics regardless of the type of oppression they are faced with. Evidence from personal experience, as well as that gained from more scholarly endeavors, indicates that the types of strategies used vary significantly within and between different co-cultural groups

Personal Reflections (*continued*)
depending on the particular standpoint of the particular person.

This idea is tied to a personal philosophy that I've adopted over the years. I believe that people who come to understand the oppression(s) they face are more likely to understand their role in oppressing others. Differences in terms of how racism, sexism, ageism, heterosexism, and so on, are played out clearly exist. However, I see them in strikingly similar terms in the way that they are tied to power, control, and dominance. Understanding the direct and indirect influences that power has in interracial communication is a crucial element of ultimate effectiveness. We all possess varying levels of power. Simultaneously recognizing the similarities and differences across life experiences can facilitate the process of naming privilege and power in productive ways. I hope that co-cultural work provides such a theoretical/practical framework.

microcultural group members (Hecht & Ribeau, 1984; Hecht, Ribeau, & Alberts, 1989). Particularly, they have engaged in ongoing research that has looked at how African Americans and Mexican Americans characterize satisfying intraracial and interracial (primarily focusing on interactions with European Americans) communication (Hecht, Collier, & Ribeau, 1993; Hecht, Ribeau, & Sedano, 1990; Ribeau, Baldwin, & Hecht, 1997). Some of the early work in this line of research focused on identifying satisfying conversational themes among African Americans and Mexican Americans. In terms of interracial communication, Hecht and his colleagues have provided great insight into specific issues that people of color find most important for effective, satisfying communication.

In research that tapped into a Mexican American perspective to interracial communication (focusing on interactions with European Americans), five specific themes were found (Hecht & Ribeau, 1984; Hecht et al., 1990). These themes are not assumed to be complete, but are offered as a contribution to workable frameworks for effective interracial communication. They capture "how things operate"— what is important/unimportant, acceptable/unacceptable, and effective/ineffective from the perspective of Mexican Americans. The first theme relates to *worldview*. Sharing common experiences and interests is seen as crucial to communication satisfaction. *Acceptance* is the second theme. Interracial interactions that were regarded as satisfying involved a perception that one's ideas and culture were accepted, confirmed, and respected. The third theme, *negative stereotyping*, is a main source for dissatisfying communication. Being categorized solely in terms of your ethnicity (as opposed to being seen as a unique person first) creates barriers between persons. *Relational solidarity*, the fourth theme, relates to the positive value attributed to developing close interracial relationships. According to Mexican Americans, the most satisfying communication was seen as part of a process of ongoing, potentially intimate relationship with a European American. *Expressiveness* is the fifth, and final, theme. Interracial communication was characterized as satisfying when a comfortable climate was developed by both parties. In other words, individuals could express themselves openly, honestly, and fully without a fear of rejection, judgment, or retaliation.

In parallel research on an African American perspective of interracial communication (again primarily with European Americans), similar themes were identified (Hecht et al., 1989; Ribeau, Baldwin, & Hecht, 1997). These included issues such as the rigid use of negative stereotyping, acceptance, emotional expressiveness, authenticity, understanding, goal attainment (achieving desired outcomes), and power dynamics (not feeling controlled or manipulated). In order to generate some practical guidelines from their research, Hecht and his colleagues used their data to identify a series of improvement strategies for enhancing effective interracial communication. Some of these are summarized here:

1. Engage in interracial communication with an open mind; do not dismiss others' points of view without sufficient consideration.
2. Identify a common threshold of language that is accessible to both parties (e.g., avoid cultural slang that might be unfamiliar to the other person).
3. Be genuine in how you present yourself and views of others.
4. Practice other orientation. In other words, attempt to involve the other person as you locate common ground. This will enhance understanding.
5. Do not be afraid to assert your point of view; discussing disagreements and confronting problematic issues can be beneficial to building long-term relationships.
6. Take advantage of teachable moments where learning about other cultures can occur naturally.

Hecht and colleagues see this work as an ongoing inquiry into what constitutes satisfying and effective interracial communication. Future research is needed to clarify some of the themes and improvement strategies that have been identified. Nevertheless, they have provided both scholars and practitioners with the foundation for a valuable framework.

UNDERSTANDING INTERRACIAL COMMUNICATION PROCESSES

We began by describing some theories that help us understand the importance of recognizing intraracial communication processes. Then we used the work by Hecht and his colleagues to gain insight into what particular racial/ethnic group members define as satisfying interracial communication. Now we move to another cluster of interracial communication theories—those that focus specifically on what happens when members of different racial and ethnic groups interact.

Anxiety/Uncertainty Management (AUM) Theory

Anxiety/uncertainty management theory largely has been used in a number of inter-cultural communication contexts (Gudykunst, 1988, 1993, 1995). It also serves as a valuable framework for interethnic and interracial interactions (Gudykunst & Hammer, 1988). AUM theory focuses on interactions between cultural ingroup members and "strangers," defined as persons who are outside their primary cultural communities. The work of Gudykunst and his colleagues is largely scientific. In this regard, it can be seen as based on one central idea: An increase in our abilities to (1) manage our anxiety about interacting with others who are from different racial/ethnic groups, and (2) accurately predict and explain their behaviors will work to increase communication effectiveness (Gudykunst, 1995). Effective communica-tion, then, refers to the process of minimizing misunderstandings and involves certain levels of self-consciousness and cultural competencies (Howell, 1982).

The central idea of AUM theory is that anxiety and uncertainty are the basic causes of communication failure in intergroup interactions. Although these two elements are closely related, they are different in a few crucial ways. *Anxiety* is an emotion triggered by anticipation of things yet to come. Gudykunst (1995) defines it as "the feeling of being uneasy, tense, worried, or apprehensive about what might happen" (p. 13). *Uncertainty*, is best understood as a cognition. It includes doubts of one's abilities to predict the outcomes of interracial interactions. All communication encounters involve varying levels of anxiety and uncertainty. AUM theory suggests that minimal levels of these two elements can be productive in that they motivate us to keep focused on being effective communicators. However, levels of anxiety and uncertainty are closely tied to the degree of perceived cultural difference among individuals. More simply put, the greater the perceived racial/ethnic differences, the more prevalent role that anxiety and uncertainty will play. As alluded to earlier, AUM theory is built on the idea that higher levels are the major cause for commu-nication ineffectiveness.

According to the AUM theory, three variables contribute to the prevalence of anxiety and uncertainty during interracial communication. One of these variables involves *motivational factors*. How important is interracial communication success in any given context? How do these efforts work toward achieving certain needs, gaining valuable information, and other desired outcomes? *Knowledge factors* represent a second variable. Examples include expectations and awareness of other racial/ethnic groups, understanding different perspectives, and information gained through shared networks. Knowledge also involves a recognition of the similarities and differences of racial/ethnic groups. The third variable, *skills*, refers to factors that allow individuals to put knowledge bases into practice. They include the ability to practice empathy (not sympathy), tolerate ambiguity, and accommodate new behaviors.

An article by Gudykunst (1995) used these three factors, and how they inform varying levels of anxiety and uncertainty, to generate a total of 94 axioms (self-evident truths) concerning intercultural communication effectiveness. We have applied these directly to the context of interracial communication and have included a sampling here. Numbers 1 and 2 deal with motivation, 3 and 4 with knowledge, and 5 and 6 with skill factors. As you can see, AUM theory focuses on increasing abilities to predict behavior to develop interracial communication competence.

1. An increase in our need to develop a sense of belonging with others who are racially/ethnically different will produce an increase in our anxiety. (motivation)
2. An increase in our shame when interacting with "racial/ethnic strangers" will produce an increase in anxiety and uncertainty and a decrease in our abilities to predict behavior. (motivation)
3. An increase in the shared interracial networks will produce a decrease in our anxiety and an increase in our confidence in predicting behavior. (knowledge)
4. An increase in the perceived similarities between racial/ethnic groups will increase the likelihood for effective management of anxiety and uncertainty. (knowledge)
5. An increase in our ability to process information about "racial strangers" in complex ways will increase our ability to predict their behaviors accurately. (skill)
6. An increase in our ability to empathize with others from different racial and ethnic groups will produce an increase in our ability to predict their behaviors accurately. (skill)

In one study of interracial interaction, AUM theory was used as a framework to examine how racial/ethnic identity impacted the development of close relationships between different groups (Gudykunst & Hammer, 1988). A number of interesting conclusions can be drawn from this work that looked at European, Mexican, and African American perceptions of interracial communication. The authors found that cultural identity involved two components central to the management of anxiety and uncertainty in intergroup relationships: ingroup identification and interracial comparisons. The stronger a person identified with her or his racial/ethnic group, the more confidence was brought into interracial interactions. In addition, racial/ethnic identity was found to play an important role in how anxiety and uncertainty are managed within interracial relationships only when racial/ethnic differences were activated as an important feature.

Third-Culture Building

The idea of third-culture building can be seen within Asante's model of transracial communication. Remember that the model included movement of two people, communicating from particular ethnic perspectives, toward a common threshold. Third-culture building represents a theoretical model that envisions common threshold as an emergent culture related to, but independent of, existing cultures (Starosta & Olorunnisola, 1995). Through the identification of common objectives, participants in an interracial interaction can achieve a cultural synergy whereby a new (third) culture develops over time (Moran & Harris, 1982). The new culture draws from—and subsequently extends—the cultural norms of each person's racial/ethnic group. Advocates of third-culture building emphasize that both parties involved in interracial communication can create a new culture that advances the strengths of each independent culture (Chen & Starosta, 1998). This approach, however, is not without its critics. Some (e.g., Casmir, 1993; Shuter, 1993) indicate that complex power dynamics, historical manipulations of racial/ethnic microcultural groups, and questionable personal motivations must be addressed when theorizing the process of third-culture building. These criticisms notwithstanding, such an approach to interracial communication is a valuable lens in that it outlines the productive outcomes when participants work to mutually accommodate cultural differences. In this context, third-culture building represents a strong prototype for effective interracial communication.

According to Starosta and Olorunnisola (1995), the process of third-culture building involves five phases that occur in a cyclical order (see also Chen & Starosta, 1998). The first phase is *intrapersonal interpersonal communication*. Beginning at a point when individuals are aware of other racial/ethnic groups, this phase is characterized by a curiosity about others. It can also involve a desire to work with others in order to maximize mutual benefits. Motivations for contact with others grows to the point of initial contact, which reflects the second phase, *interpersonal intercultural communication*. This phase begins at the stage of inquiry when the person who initiated the contact seeks out information about others in different racial/ethnic groups. Ultimately this interaction becomes more reciprocal with both parties exchanging information about self and others. This phase is characteristic of mutual adjustment, especially in terms of identifying common goals for benefits of working together.

The third phase is *rhetorical intercultural communication*. Here both persons increase their consciousness as to how the other person's culture influences current (and future) interactions. In order for third-culture building to continue through this phase, individuals must develop a conscious awareness of cultural similarities and differences, as well as a willingness to fight the negative influences of ethnocentric judgments. Through ongoing communication, the emergence of a third culture, one that draws from the best of both independent cultural worlds, occurs. Over time, the patterns of interaction associated with this new culture become integrated into everyday communication. *Metacultural communication* represents the fourth phase of third-culture development. Within this phase, individuals continue to work through the complexities of the new emergent culture, including co-created roles, norms, and mores. Through this process, third-culture practices are readjusted, reinforced, and fine-tuned. Over time, a mutual assimilation of all parties occurs that results in a unique culture that becomes more permanent. The fifth phase, *intracultural communication*, involves a movement away from one's primary culture toward identification with the newly created culture. Here the development of the third culture accompanies a newly created identity for both individuals. Following this final phase, the model begins a new cycle (returning to phase 1 again).

In addition to presenting a productive model for interracial communication, third-culture building also advances the perspective that all existing cultures can be seen as "third cultures" (Starosta & Olorunnisola, 1995). Through this framework, we can come to a general understanding that all cultures have grown out of other cultures. We can also develop specific understanding of how certain "third cultures" develop (e.g., Puerto Ricans) through long-term interaction of diverse racial/ethnic groups (e.g., Spanish, African, and Native cultures).

Cross-Cultural Adaptation Theory

Cross-cultural adaptation theory, largely based on the work of Young Yun Kim (1988, 1993), has been applied primarily to intercultural interactions stemming from international travel. According to Kim (1988), cross-cultural adaptation focuses on the process of change that occurs over time when individuals whose primary socialization is in one culture come into continuous, prolonged contact with a new and unfamiliar culture. Given Rich's (1974) conceptualization of interracial communication, it appears a valuable mechanism to understanding the adaptation process that some racial/ethnic groups members experience when communicating with others outside their communities. This is especially true for racial/ethnic group members whose early life experiences involve little contact with members outside their particular group. Think about Latino/a or African American students who are raised in predominately ethnic communities and then go to public state universities. Or European Americans who, because of humanitarian or religious convictions, decide to dedicate their lives to working within communities where they are the clear minority. How do these persons adapt to these instances of prolonged interracial contact? Cross-cultural adaptation theory represents one window into the central role that identity and communication play in answering this question.

Cross-cultural adaptation is based on the idea that humans have a natural drive to adapt and grow. While we become enculturated with specific norms, values, and beliefs early on in life, entrance into an unfamiliar culture increases our awareness of self and others. Facing new situations can trigger both stress and adaptation responses and ultimately cause us to grow as individuals. Because it is neither reasonable nor practical to expect any large population to significantly modify its own cultural habits, cultural newcomers must adapt. Part of that process involves learning and acquiring the elements of the new culture (acculturation) (Shibutani & Kwan, 1965) and possibly unlearning some of the old cultural habits (deculturation) (Kim, 1988). Because cross-cultural adaptation usually requires both acculturation and deculturation, individuals may experience varying levels of stress. This is especially true during initial encounters. According to cross-cultural adaptation theory, such experiences help individuals develop a new sense of their cultural identities.

Cross-cultural adaptation is a complex and dynamic process that occurs through communication via a number of channels (interpersonal, small group, mass media). Successfully adapting to a new culture involves an intercultural transformation of sorts that includes three specific outcomes. First, a functional fitness is achieved whereby an individual develops skills to communicate and build satisfying relationships with the host culture (Kim, 1993). Second, these communication skills have a direct impact on the psychological health of the cultural newcomer. Not being able to manage the internal responses (mental adjustment) and external demands (physical adjustment) in the new culture is directly tied to poor psychological adjustment. Third, the "self-shock" (Zaharna, 1989) of new cultural experiences generates a new emergent intercultural identity. Unlike third-culture building, however, only the identity of the cultural newcomer is transformed. She or he develops an increased self-consciousness of multiple identities that may result in feelings that come from being on the borders (margins) of both cultures.

Several factors influence the abilities of individuals to enter different racial/ethnic communities and adapt successfully to new cultures. One is the preconceived expectations that the newcomer has of the racial/ethnic communities. Another is the level of preparation that has been accomplished through attempts to learn cultural histories, norms, and values. Preparation also involves an emotional state of "motivational readiness" whereby individuals strongly desire successful adaptation. Finally, research (e.g., Kim, 1998) indicates that certain personality traits—being open, resilient, flexible, resourceful, and willing to take risks—also are connected to effective cross-cultural adaptation. In addition, attention to certain aspects of the host culture must also be taken into account. How accessible and receptive is the culture to those who are identified as racially or ethnically different? What levels of racial pride exist and how are ingroup/outgroup distinctions enforced? What is the tolerance levels for attitudes, beliefs, values, and behaviors that do not conform to cultural norms? As described earlier, cross-cultural adaptation is a dynamic and complex process, especially given the constant evolution of cultures over time (Berry & Sam, 1997). Effective moves from one culture to another reflect an increased attention to these issues.

Communication Accommodation Theory (CAT)

CAT was first presented as a "speech" accommodation theory by Howard Giles and colleagues in the early to mid-1970s (Giles, 1973, 1977; Giles, Taylor, & Bourhis, 1973). It was initially a theoretical framework that focused on language and linguistic elements, but has developed into an insightful lens through which all aspects of communication between different racial/ethnic groups can be understood. Specifically, CAT explains the ways that individuals adjust their communication during intergroup interactions (Giles, Mulac, Bradac, & Johnson, 1987). Accommodation can be seen in almost all communication behaviors, including accent, rate, loudness, vocabulary, grammar, and gestures. In addition, it has important consequences in terms of self- and other identity, ingroup/outgroup distinctions, and communication effectiveness.

Following the foundations of social identity theory (Tajfel, 1978), CAT maintains that individuals derive a significant portion of their identity from groups to which they belong. As we discussed in Chapter 5, remember that different aspects of a person's identity may be more important in different contexts (see also Giles & Hewstone, 1982). During interactions where racial/ethnic differences are significant, CAT can be used to understand how a person's communication will be used to emphasize or downplay those aspects of group identity. In other words, CAT focuses on how verbal and nonverbal communication is used to achieve the desired level of social distance (immediate or distant) between ingroup and outgroup members.

Two major aspects of CAT are how convergence and divergence are present during intergroup interactions. *Convergence* is defined as a strategy that individuals use to adapt their communication to become more like the other person. Convergence, like divergence, can be partial or complete. People may converge for different reasons including a desire to gain acceptance, social integration, or a means for effective communication (Gallois, Giles, Jones, Cargile, & Ota, 1995; Giles, 1973). In all intergroup interactions, and especially in the context of interracial communication, it is important to note that convergence may be toward a person's actual communication *or* a preconceived stereotype of how the racial/ethnic group members communicate (Hewstone & Giles, 1986). According to Tajfel and Turner

(1979), persons react to others, not necessarily as individuals, but as representatives of different racial/ethnic groups. Can you see how some attempts at convergence may be quite offensive and work to construct barriers to effective interracial communication? Clearly, convergence is not the best strategy for all case scenarios (Giles, 1977). The success of convergence in intergroup interactions depends on a number of factors, including a person's ability to converge effectively (Kelley, 1973) and how his or her efforts are perceived by the other person (Basso, 1979).

Divergence refers to the ways in which communicators stress verbal and nonverbal differences between themselves and others. Divergence is an active process that emphasizes communication differences; it is not doing nothing about different communication styles (Bourhis, 1979). Convergence is typically the result of internal scripts and occurs on a largely unconscious level. In comparison, persons are oftentimes more aware of divergence in interracial interactions. In many cases, divergence is used by racial/ethnic microcultural group members as a means to maintain their identity, cultural pride, and distinctiveness (Giles et al., 1987; Ryan, 1979). But it is important to understand that divergence (as well as convergence) can be mutual or nonmutual. In other words, one person or both persons can use divergence to emphasize the social distance between racial/ethnic groups.

In summary, Giles et al. (1987) record a number of scientific propositions that reflect the basic ideas of CAT. Read through the following statements. Do they make sense to you based on your interracial communication experiences?

People will attempt to converge communication behaviors when they desire social approval and a shared identity base.

People will attempt to diverge when they desire to communicate a contrasting self-image and define the interaction in intergroup ways.

People are more likely to evaluate convergence positively when they perceive the other person's efforts to be well intentioned and based on actual communication style (not stereotypes).

People are more likely to regard divergence as negative when they perceive it as a mismatch to their own communicative style or reflective of selfish and/or manipulative motives.

These propositions represent just a few that Giles and his colleagues have generated. In this light, general CAT research (e.g., Cargile & Giles, 1996; Giles & Noels, 1998) seems to offer some valuable practical guidelines for interracial communication effectiveness. Of course, as articulated throughout this book, much depends on the particular individuals and their cultural identities as well as the specific context of the interaction. The sociopolitical history of race relations—and the ways it continues to inform dynamics of power—in the Unites States must also be considered (Giles, Bourhis, & Taylor, 1977; Orbe, 1998a). Generally speaking, the

<table>
<tr><td>6.3</td><td>Code Switching</td></tr>
</table>

Looking at specific racial and ethnic group members who are involved in code switching is an excellent way to see the practical implications of convergence. Code switching, also described as style switching (Seymour & Seymour, 1979) or language mobility (Sachdev & Bourhis, 1990), refers to a communication strategy used by individuals who have mastered the speech codes from two different cultural communities. During interactions with others, these individuals discern which system of communication is more appropriate in the specific situation and adapt accordingly. Research (Hecht et al., 1989) reports that interracial interactions where no code switching occurs is more likely to be ineffective. According to Collier (1988), European Americans are less willing (and possibly less able) than African Americans to adopt outgroup speech codes. What is your reaction to this statement? Do you agree? Why or why not?

This research has some interesting implications for interracial communication in a variety of contexts. The following questions are provided as a means to understand the possible practical implications of intergroup convergence. Think about how they might be used to guide specific behaviors. What factors must be taken into account when using code switching during everyday interracial interaction? What are some of the consequences—positive/negative, anticipated/unanticipated, individual/group—of code switching? Are these consequences the same for all persons generally, or do they vary from group to group? Is it possible to create some practical guidelines for code switching and interracial communication?

most satisfying interracial interactions typically involve a delicate balance of convergence (as an indication of a willingness to communicate effectively) and divergence (as a means to acknowledge the importance of racial/ethnic group identity) *for both persons*.

CONCLUSION

Over 20 years ago, Pennington (1979) reported that the state of interracial communication research and theory was in its infancy. Her call for increased productivity focusing on the "deep structures" (p. 392) and different worldviews that inform interracial interactions does not appear to have gone unnoticed. More recent research and theory appears to face additional challenges , especially in terms of its application to everyday practice. According to Orbe (1995a), interracial communication research must continue to explore the value of alternative methods and theories. As illustrated within the broad range of frameworks described in this chapter, substantial options are available to theorists and practitioners who are interested in validating, critiquing, and/or extending existing research. However, other challenges still exist.

First, theoretical frameworks must create a delicate balance between providing insights into the general cultural norms of each racial/ethnic group and acknowledging the great diversity within each group. Theories and models that generalize racial and ethnic groups fall into the trap of promoting stereotypes that hinder effective interracial communication (Orbe, 1995a). In other words, seeing an Asian American person as a prototypical member of her race (and assuming that you understand how she will communicate based on this one fact) is likely to result in communication ineffectiveness. The most effective instances of interracial communication are grounded in a working knowledge of the similarities and differences within and between racial and ethnic groups.

Second, interracial communication theoretical frameworks must assume an action-sensitive approach to theory development and practical application. Lee (1993), for instance, argues that a change in research and theory priorities is needed in academia. He, like van Maanen (1990), calls for a new purpose of research where theory development is put into practice and used for the improvement of life. In a country where race relations continue to be highly adverse, communication scholars have a unique opportunity—and responsibility—to utilize theories in the discipline to improve effectiveness of everyday interracial interaction. Responding to this challenge, Part Two extends theory into practice within a number of specific interracial communication contexts.

OPPORTUNITIES FOR EXTENDED LEARNING

1. Select one theory and conduct a more thorough analysis of its usefulness to interracial communication. Start by locating and reading the references that we cite. Then reflect on the strengths and weaknesses of the theory. This will allow you to identify certain criticisms of each theory (something that we did not do because of space limitations). During your analysis, ask yourself other questions such as. What are the basic assumptions and main ideas of the theory? How does the theory help guide future research? How can it be applied to everyday interactions?

2. Think about your favorite television shows and movies. How would you characterize the portrayal of interracial communication within these media forms? What attitudes, values, and behaviors promote effective communication among different racial and ethnic groups? What about interactions that are less productive? How does the work by Hecht and others assist in identifying specific themes of satisfying and dissatisfying communication? Check your perceptions with other ingroup and outgroup members.

3. The following is a productive avenue to move theory from the conceptual to the practical. Break the class into several groups, and assign each group a particular theoretical framework. The objective of each group is to create a 3-hour cultural diversity training program that focuses on race relations. Group members must decide on the following details for the program: (1) Who is the target audience? (2) What structure will it follow? (3) What aspects of the theory will be used and how they will be incorporated into the training? and (4) What types of experiential learning will be included? Time permitting, share your race relations training modules with the class.

4. According to speech community theory, each distinctive cultural group has a distinct speech code. Select one cultural group of which you are a member, and brainstorm its communication rules, norms, and values. How easy or difficult is this process? Then break up into groups and share speech codes. During this interaction, take special note of similarities and differences across groups. Also, discuss any different rules that were recorded by others for the same cultural group.

5. Use your *InfoTrac College Edition* to do a search for articles that highlight model programs of cross-racial collaboration. These can be related to college campuses, professional organizations, different religious denominations, community-based organizations, and so on. (For a general search, use the keywords *U.S. race relations. Interracial unity* or *cross-racial alliances* will provide a more focused search.) Review the key aspects of these programs in terms of their success. How can different theoretical frameworks assist in understanding the effectiveness of these real-life success stories?

6. Gudykunst and his colleagues believe that anxiety and uncertainty are the primary sources of miscommunication for interracial interactions. Spend 10 to 15 minutes of class time brainstorming all of the different aspects of interracial communication that are likely to cause unproductive anxiety and uncertainty. Then take the time necessary to process this information. How are these things closely related? What are some possible strategies to overcome high levels of anxiety and uncertainty?

INTERRACIAL COMMUNICATION IN SPECIFIC CONTEXTS

INTERRACIAL FRIENDSHIPS

Part One explored the theoretical and conceptual issues needed to understand the evolution of race as an oppressive ideology in the United States. As Chapters 1–6 have illustrated, race has been, and continues to be, a volatile issue in society. From a political standpoint, race relations have been strained as a result of the racial/ethnic hierarchy that dictates how we develop or avoid our interracial relationships. The initial goal of racial oppression as a political agenda was to perpetuate the position of power occupied by European Americans. By limiting access to resources and opportunities that would remedy this economic, political, and occupational inequity, this racial/ethnic hierarchy has had consequences that extend beyond politics.

Part Two addresses the effects of racial oppression on interpersonal relationships, mass media, public communication, and organizational communication. This transition from theory to application is designed to illustrate how the history of race relations affects our interpersonal and interracial interactions today. This chapter discusses the significance of intraracial and interracial friendships and the factors influencing the (non)initiation, maintenance, and dissolution of interracial friendships as observed in the United States. By examining the current state and perceptions of interracial friendships, we hope to provide you with a knowledge base for understanding how critical our interpersonal relationships are in improving

144

race relations. We are often socialized to perceive interracial relationships as negative (or unnecessary) relational experiences, which has negative consequences in terms of interracial communication. Because interpersonal relationships are touted as the most effective means for improving race relations, it is important for us to understand what perceptual and communicative barriers are preventing these relationships from occurring.

THE SIGNIFICANCE OF INTERRACIAL FRIENDSHIPS

According to human communication literature, interpersonal relationships are essential for healthy emotional and intellectual development. This experience of understanding the importance of relationship begins with the family unit. Through family, we learn about the communication process and the skills that facilitate positive communicative interactions. Conversely, friendships provide a landscape for developing effective interpersonal relationships. Whereas the family is expected to provide its members with unconditional love and support, friendship relationships involve choice and voluntary commitment. Friendships can also give both friends love and support; however, each person can walk away from the relationship at any time. The friendship life lessons are distinct from family relationships because they prepare us for life in a very diverse world. How have your friendships helped you deal with people who are different from you? Have they assisted in your learning about communication and relationships? The communication and relational skills that have contributed to your growth as a person will ultimately be beneficial in future friendship, professional, and romantic relationships.

7.1   *Personal Reflections*

I remember reading the book *Divided Sisters: Bridging the Gap Between Black Women and White Women* (1996) by Midge Wilson and Kathy Russell. In reading the women's experiences with interracial friendships, I could not help but reflect on my own. One friendship in particular was a life lesson for me and I hope will be for you.

I was hanging out with a European American female friend. We were comfortable with one another and enjoyed spending time together. What was even more rewarding was that we shared the same sense of humor.

On one particular day, however, I began to reexamine our friendship and

Personal Reflections (*continued*)

what it really meant to me. Typically, I had playful relationships with my colleagues that allowed us to find humor in most situations. My friends and I engaged in mutual exchanges in which we used humor to laugh at the ignorance of societal racism. Rarely, however, did my female friends do the same.

One day, a female friend crossed the line and made an insulting comment that I found very racist. The comment was targeted at me and was meant to be humorous, but my friend's attempt at humor backfired. Instead, I began to question her motives. Although I do not think she was racist, I found her *subconsciously racist* by the mere fact that she would not have made the same comment to a European American person.

More importantly, my friend did not have the *license* (or right) to engage in ethnic humor often used among ingroup members (see Leveen, 1996). Although her intention was to adopt my style of communication to establish a relational bond between us, it only worked to widen the racial divide (which was rarely evident in our relationship). I did not approve of my friend's behavior, but shock prevented me from saying anything to her. On previous occasions, we had discussed racism and I had "educated" her about how real it is in my life. Although I am sure we both appreciated these interactions, I did not want to make her feel guilty, which might cause her to avoid interracial friendships altogether. She might begin to wonder if she must watch *everything* she says to all of her female friends of color.

Yes, I should have shared my feelings with her. After all, friendships are based on openness and trust, which becomes even more important when racial/ethnic differences exist. I do regret not taking a more active role in educating my friend about how hurtful I found her words to be. However, I have become more responsible in my interracial friendships. If an offense is committed in the relationship, we reestablish a safe emotional place that allows us to nurture our friendship and value our racial/ethnic differences. After all, that's what friends are for!—TMH

Unlike family relationships, friendships give us the opportunity to choose with whom we would like to interact and establish an emotional bond. Within this dyad, as friends we seek acceptance, support, and happiness as we experience and learn behaviors and attitudes that promote prosocial interactions (Lawhon, 1997). Emotional and psychological needs are met in this relationship that are critical to our well-being (Lawhon, 1997). If we are unable to communicate and interact effectively with our peers in early childhood, these interpersonal interactions become more complex and difficult to manage as we progress through life. Therefore, those friendships must provide a healthy environment that fosters personal competence and social skills (La Greca & Lopez, 1998) and emotional closeness and trust (Lawhon, 1997).

LeCroy (1988) defines friendship as "a mutual involvement between two people that is characterized by affection, satisfaction, enjoyment, openness, respect, and a sense of feeling important to the other" (p. 228). These criteria for friendship are created subconsciously in childhood wherein individuals are drawn to each other for very basic reasons. Whether it is because they are in the same class, live in the same neighborhood, or are a part of the same reading circle in school, friendships developed in early childhood do not possess the high levels of complexity associated with friendships established in adolescence and adulthood. In exploring the phenomenon of the friendship selection process, we have learned that friendships among children are developed primarily because they share the same sex or same race/ethnicity (Fink & Wild, 1995; Graham & Cohen, 1997; La Greca & Lopez, 1998; Lawhon, 1997; Lundy, Field, McBride, Field, & Largie, 1998). Studies exploring this phenomenon help us understand why friendships are initiated. However, little has been done to explore why avoidant behaviors are employed during the friendship selection process. In other words, limited research exists that examines how children are socialized to avoid friendships with someone of a different race or sex.

As we noted previously, friendships are relational bonds between individuals who share a liking and affection for each other. Lawhon (1997) suggests that if children are to establish healthy friendship relationships, teachers, parents, older siblings, and other adults must serve as relational role models. In turn, children become equipped to develop communication skills and behaviors that illicit affection, sensitivity, and cooperation (Lawhon, 1997). In essence, children ultimately model their friendship choices and communication behaviors after those closest to them. Thus, family members and friends must become more aware of how their own behaviors impact the types of friendships their children and siblings develop in childhood and later in life.

When we develop or initiate friendships, we are very likely to choose people who are very much like ourselves. If you were to do an inventory of the kinds of friends you have, what similarities would link you? Tastes in music? Extracurricular activities? Religious beliefs? Life goals? Personality? Whatever the qualities you deem most significant in friendships, we all have some qualities that we use to determine who will and will not be our friends.

Now that you have narrowed down your list, think about what role race/ethnicity plays in influencing how you have chosen those close intimate relationships. Although it is not presumptuous to assume that we are socialized to establish and develop relationships with someone from the same race (Fink & Wild, 1995; Graham & Cohen, 1997; Hallinan & Williams, 1987, 1989; La Greca & Lopez, 1998; Wilson & Lavelle, 1990), very little research has explored how issues of race may influence our friendship choices. How were you socialized to interact with classmates who were racially/ethnically different from you? Did your differences create uncertainty for you (or them)? Did your other classmates ostracize you because of your interracial friendship? Or was race/ethnicity never something you had to think about? Whatever the case may be, there is the belief that interracial friendships can contribute to improved race relations by dispelling racial myths and stereotypes through interpersonal encounters (Ellison & Powers, 1994; Greene, 1996). Unfortunately, little attention is given to the effect of politics and social oppression on interracial relationships. In order to understand the validity of these assumptions, we must explore what barriers prevent interracial friendships from occurring.

Barriers to Interracial Friendships

One of the primary barriers to interracial friendships, as with other interracial relationships, is stereotypes. According to Leonard and Locke (1993), stereotypes act as unhealthy assessments and judgments that hinder the development of interracial friendships. These researchers have confirmed the belief that interracial communication is a phenomenon that is complex and difficult to initiate. Because of society's preoccupation with race and racial stereotyping, racial/ethnic groups are more inclined to allow stereotypes to influence outgroup perceptions, which ultimately creates a barrier to effective, productive interracial encounters. For instance, European American and African American college students ascribed more negative than positive stereotypes to each other (Leonard & Locke, 1993). Relating their findings to the reality of stereotyping, Leonard and Locke conclude that despite increased opportunities for interracial interactions and relationships, people are resistant to developing relationships with outgroup members due to long-standing stereotypes.

In an effort to further explore the relationship between stereotyping and interracial friendship, communication scholar Marsha Houston (1997) examined these issues in her essay on dialogues between African American women and European American women. Houston (1997) posits that although all interracial friendships do not experience stress, the history of race relations has led to a long-standing mistrust and suspicion between racial/ethnic groups. Furthermore, Houston suggests that hesitation or uncertainty regarding involvement in such relationships is largely attributed to mutual negative stereotyping. In this case, both African American and European American women, as well as other racial/ethnic groups and men, have false perceptions of each other that ultimately create barriers to improved interracial communication.

Houston's (1997) essay is thought provoking in that it exposes the raw nerves underscoring the moral dilemma of interracial friendships. Newspaper headlines often report that race relations have improved, but in reality an interpersonal segregation remains between the races. In order to fully understand the complexities associated with interracial friendships, the following sections examine the role of history in discouraging interracial friendships, motivating factors for the initiation of friendships, and the current state of interracial friendships. While we acknowledge that interracial friendships do occur between all racial/ethnic groups, discussion in this chapter will focus on friendships between African American and European Americans. This emphasis also reflects the focus of scholarly research on interracial friendship and is also applicable to friendships involving people from other racial/ethnic groups as well.

HISTORY AND INTERRACIAL FRIENDSHIPS

Interracial relationships in Western society have historically been disproportionate and hostile. As we noted in Part One, a racial hierarchy was created to maintain an unequal power distribution that placed European Americans at the top of the social structure. Through colonization, slavery, and other forms of subjugation, a strong message was communicated to the masses that the existing social order should remain as is. As such, intermingling between the races was outlawed and/or strongly discouraged. After the abolition of slavery, racial segregation remained a driving force behind the racial dynamics in the United States. According to the Jim Crow laws (Wilson & Russell, 1996), European Americans and other racial groups were separated from one another both in public and private spheres. From separate bathrooms and water fountains to outlawing interracial marriages, all racial/ethnic groups were allotted certain areas that were exclusively used by them and no one else. The consequences of any violations of these political sanctions included imprisonment, physical abuse, social isolation, and even death. In any case, the political ramifications of racial segregation permeated both the public and social aspects of life in the United States.

A landmark U.S. Supreme Court case that had a tremendous effect on the existing racial hierarchy was *Brown v. Board of Education* in 1954 (Sigelman, Bledsoe, & Combs, 1996). Prior to this ruling, all educational institutions were racially segregated. Elementary schools, high schools, and colleges and universities throughout the nation were doing an intellectual disservice to children of color in the United States. Unlike their European American peers, African American students specifically were prohibited from receiving the same type of education in their schools. Instead, their textbooks and buildings were of less quality, thereby minimizing the educational experiences of the students. In an effort to rectify this disparity, the Supreme Court decision overturned Jim Crow laws and racial segregation in education. This shift in their legal rights would provide new educational and economic opportunities for African Americans, with interracial contact a by-product of this newfound "equal opportunity" (Sigelman et al, 1996). By increasing interracial communication through classroom interaction, members of a democratic society gained opportunities to develop friendships and professional relationships that cross the color line.

Can you imagine attending a monoracial school and then having the government intervene and say "no more"? How might people (students, teachers, parents, society) feel being forced to interact and live with racially/ethnically different others with whom they had not had prior contact? Would *you* feel frightened or apprehensive? These emotions contributed to the underlying current of racial tension in classrooms (Wilson & Russell, 1996). Racial hatred, mistrust, and stereotyping continued despite increased opportunities for interracial interactions among students and members of the community. By integrating classrooms, the U.S. government was attempting to make amends for the past by providing a context for improved race relations in the future. Unfortunately, the hostile racial climate continued and was manifested in interracial interactions within the classroom (Wilson & Russell, 1996). How would you feel if students and teachers alienated you because of the color of your skin? Even though they may not have hurled racial slurs at you, the behaviors of these outgroup members would probably create feelings of isolation that would make school a very unpleasant and lonely experience. The racial climate at the time was initially overt and explosive in the years following the 1954 decision, but today it has become covert. Instead of blatantly displaying their racial animosity, individuals now downplay the significance of this tension, thus distorting the reality of race relations.

A little noted attempt at racial harmony occurred in the mid-1960s in Durham, North Carolina (Greene, 1996). Civil unrest over poverty and racism was occurring throughout the United. States. In reaction to this disparity, an outbreak of riots was orchestrated to bring national attention to the issues of racism, classism, and sexism. While this sociopolitical revolution was taking place in the form of the *Brown v. Board of Education* ruling, the civil rights movement, and other similar forms of social resistance, race relations were devastatingly impaired. As a by-product of slavery and segregation, the separate but equal ideology became a mainstay in social circles across the nation.

Women-in-Action for the Prevention of Violence and Its Causes (WIA), an interracial women's organization established in Durham in 1968, was organized in the midst of this racial discord. WIA was formed to bring about meaningful social change for race and class justice. More importantly, members were working to bridge the communication gap between European American and African American women from all social strata (Greene, 1996). The organization was initiated by Edna Spaulding, a middle-class African American woman, who had attended a gathering of 200 women in New York City initiated by *McCall's* magazine that provided women with a forum to engage in dialogue about the racial unrest facing the nation. Inspired by this initiative, Spaulding rallied her community and challenged Durham women to eradicate racism and violence. These middle-class women from both racial groups were dedicated to diffusing the rampant violence resulting from racial hostilities in their community.

The women were attempting to bridge an economic divide with their "sisters" by establishing alliances with low-income African American women. Organization members shared views on domestic and maternal concerns and hoped to advance the struggle for racial justice through the initiation, development, and maintenance of interracial friendships across economic lines (Greene, 1996). There were 125 members actively involved, with an additional 400 to 500 members on a mailing list (Greene, 1996). Members were committed to addressing the causes of violence in their community, which were recognized as poverty and racism. This initiative allowed the women to form subcommittees to articulate their grievances with their community members. More importantly, the organization's role as mediator was twofold: to address the controversial issue of race being faced by Durham and to provide a solution that would benefit race relations within the organization and community (Greene, 1996).

WIA was successful in engaging its members and the community in interracial discourse. However, efforts to foster positive interracial relationships between European American and African American women proved complicated. Class and racial tensions were eating away at the interior of the organizational body (Greene, 1996). For example, when the women met to coordinate upcoming activities, their racial/ethnic and class differences were tabled and they worked together to achieve the task at hand. But when the women returned to the real world and resumed their respective roles in society, those differences dictated how they would interact with each other. Those African American female members who were domestic servants for some of the European American female members found this recreated social distance incredibly offensive given their shared membership in the organization. (Can you imagine being friends with someone and then having them ignore you in public? Or even at work?)

Although interracial contact among members was maximized, the women often experienced miscommunication and misunderstandings because of their diverse backgrounds. Attempts to work through these differences surfaced as members attempted to engage in dialogue about racial and economic problems. Issues affecting various sectors of the membership were sometimes dismissed as insignificant by other members, thus creating a gulf in the relational dynamics of the group. Some members even reported that the interracial alliances fostered within WIA were limited to the organization (Greene, 1996). Although they shared interests in religion, community, family, and social change, the women never socialized together in settings beyond their organizational meetings. According to their accounts of this social divide, many members attributed it to the racist attitudes and behaviors exhibited in their interpersonal exchanges. One African American woman shared how the European American women were somewhat friendly in their meetings; however, when she saw them on the streets, they would refuse to acknowledge her presence.

Overall, WIA was successful in increasing the number of women volunteers across racial and economic lines to eradicate racial and social injustice in their community (Greene, 1996). Although the social change resulting from this alliance had a positive impact on a small southern community, the political and social climate of the nation could be seen in terms of their interpersonal interactions. The efforts of this small group of women are to be commended, for they were using their interracial collective and shared commitment to social change to eradicate economic oppression and racism in the midst of violence. The members were able to work through their own race and class tensions in the organization as they remained focused on the greater good. Despite the lack of information regarding the guidelines that were effective in resolving these tensions, this case study illustrates how complex interracial friendships can be. Organizational members were able to acknowledge the influence of the sociopolitical climate on their relationships and how they could use this relational context as an opportunity to improve race relations on a micro and macro level.

WIA represents only a microcosm of the complexities associated with interracial communication. Despite the fact that their attempts to bring about change in the South only received regional exposure (Greene, 1996), the experiences of WIA women as an organizational body and as individuals illustrate the societal pressures that strain interracial interactions. Common ground was established between and among the women. However, they continued to find it difficult to establish relational bonds that extended beyond the organization (Greene, 1996). Essentially, they could work together as members of WIA but were not able to take those relational ties into their personal lives. It is reasonable to assume that the women were experiencing external pressures from family, friends, and society to limit interracial contact to the organization itself. Additionally, how the women were socialized to perceive and interact with people who are racially/ethnically different may have contributed to these tensions in their relationships as well.

According to Wilson and Russell (1996) and Houston (1996), it is important to examine the significance of these sources of tension if interracial communication is to occur (Leonard & Locke, 1993). For WIA, efforts to integrate political organizations were most likely a result of national attempts to desegregate society on all levels. In a very similar vein, efforts to integrate the classrooms provided students

---

7.2   *Case Study: Understanding Interracial Friendship Alliances*

Mary Jane Collier (1998) discusses three issues that past research has indicated are central to friendships involving individuals from different racial/ethnic groups. Based on interviews with women about their intercultural friendships, Collier and Bowker (1994) found that power and unearned privilege, acknowledgment of history, and orientations of affirmation are what makes these friendships successful.

Power and unearned privilege refers to unstated power, which is often possessed by European Americans. Collier and Bowker (1994) found that European American women were rarely aware of their power until their female friends of color informed them of their privileged (racial) position in society.

Similarly, the influence of history (e.g., slavery, discrimination) of racial/ethnic identity should be acknowledged in these friendships as well. Sensitivity to and awareness of how racial/ethnic groups have been oppressed can enhance the relationship in various ways. This allows the friends to understand each other's standpoint and how they are developed and maintained through their racialized and gendered experiences.

Finally, there should be orientations of affirmation, where the discourse involves each person valuing some aspect of the other person's culture (e.g., learning more about the other person's history, cultural norms). These qualities are somewhat different from those present in intraracial (same-race) friendships; however, they allow our intimate relationships to serve as learning experiences that may last a lifetime.

Have you ever had a friend from a racial/ethnic group different from your own? Did you learn something unique about them? Did your successful interracial friendships include those issues identified by Collier and her colleagues? Your interpersonal interactions with them were probably quite similar to those you had with other friends, with the primary difference being race/ethnicity. As you begin to have more interracial/interethnic encounters with people different from you, be sure to remember how open, honest communication can contribute to a quality interpersonal relationship.

and community members with increased opportunities for interracial interactions. However, social barriers were erected that labeled such relationships and communicative experiences taboo.

Currently, same-sex interracial friendships are difficult to establish and maintain. Despite the belief that these relationships provide interactants with opportunities to engage in dialogue about racial issues in a private versus a public forum, individuals still find it difficult to initiate and maintain a relationship with someone from a different racial/ethnic group (Carter, 1990; Houston, 1996; Pope-Davis & Ottavi, 1994; Wilson & Russell, 1996). In order to fully understand the degree to which race influences the initiation, maintenance, and dissolution of a friendship, we must first understand the motivating factors influencing the friendship selection process.

Friendship Selection Process

As we have already learned, friendship selection often involves people choosing friends who are either from the same sex and/or race as themselves (Graham & Cohen, 1997; La Greca & Lopez, 1998; Lundy et al, 1998). A variety of factors are reported as contributing to this decision-making process; however, no attention is given to how children are socialized to accept these relationships as "the ideal." Discussing a number of issues will challenge our thinking about how the social implications of race unnecessarily complicate our friendship experiences.

One issue that we must consider regarding interracial friendship is the emphasis placed on similarity. Yes, we would like to have relationships with people who share our attitudes, beliefs, and values, but how early in life are we socialized to think that race determines these things? Graham and Cohen (1997) found that this socialization can occur between the first and sixth grades. In providing assessments of the kinds of friendships they had with their peers, African American and European American elementary public school students were found to have a sex and race bias (Graham & Cohen, 1997). In general, children reported having friendships with peers who were of the same sex and same race as themselves. A unique, although not startling, finding was that older African American children had more same-race friendships yet were more accepting of interracial friendships than their European American peers.

We do learn that similarity remains important during the early stages of life in general, but why is there a difference between how these racial/ethnic groups perceive interracial friendships? What do you think we can attribute this to? Does this carry over into our friendships developed in high school, college, and in our adult lives? More importantly, we must ask ourselves why these differences even exist (Graham & Cohen, 1997). How were these children socialized to perceive each other? Is this selection process perceived as natural, thus gaining the status of

THEORY INTO PRACTICE

Although there are no set rules, the following are suggestions for initiating, developing, and maintaining healthy, positive interracial friendships.

- Ask yourself why you do not have interracial friendships. Identify barriers that may have prevented you from developing such relationships.
- Challenge yourself to leave your comfort zone and develop an interracial friendship.
- Compare and contrast your monoracial and your interracial friendships.
- Are you and your friend able to self-disclose with little difficulty? Do you avoid certain topics that you would otherwise discuss in your monoracial friendships? Why or why not?
- Do not use (exploit) interracial friendships for the sole purpose of understanding racial/ethnic differences. Your actions will be perceived as insincere and offensive.
- Be willing to educate each other about racial difference when learning opportunities occur.
- Be willing to look beyond, yet appreciate, racial difference in order to recognize other similarities you and a potential cross-race friend can share.
- Do not assume that you or your friend will be spokespersons for your racial/ethnic group.
- Be sensitive to the validity and reality of a friend's experiences with racism and prejudice.
- Engage in honest communication if, and when, racial differences become problematic. Choose to benefit from this conflict/learning opportunity.

normalcy in our daily lives? Or does it simply relate to the lack of abundant opportunities to form long-term interracial friendships?

Whatever the case may be, we must reexamine how we think about interracial friendships. Instead of subconsciously gravitating toward friends who are of the same race as ourselves, we should reconsider how we can benefit from interracial relationships. We must acknowledge that our racial/ethnic differences influence our communication and interaction styles; however, they should not be perceived as barriers that will hinder either party from receiving the same benefits present in same-race and same-sex friendships (e.g., support, intimacy). Although this relationship can also teach us about different racial/ethnic groups, we should not expect our friend to be a spokesperson for his or her race. For instance, your friend may share his or her experiences with racism in the classroom, but that account does not speak for *all* other people from his or her racial/ethnic group. As you rethink race, ask yourself the following question: Would you enter an interracial friendship knowing that your new friend was expecting you to represent *everyone* from your racial/ethnic group? That is a major responsibility no one is willing to carry.

Graham and Cohen (1997) suggest that social acceptability and mutual friendships have an impact on whether or not interracial friendships are even considered an option. Because racial alliances are socially constructed as negative and taboo, children are more likely to avoid these relationships because of the consequences of such behavior (e.g., stereotyping, loss of friendships, isolation, alienation). In order to avoid these negative outgrowths, children are more apt to establish relationships where certain shared attributes (e.g., sex and race) provide a common ground for friendship development to occur without external stressors.

La Greca and Lopez (1998) have also found support for the belief that external stressors are placed on children as they engage in the friendship selection process. As we explore this assumption, think about your own experiences making friends. For most people, this is not an easy process, and, as a result, it can be stressful, particularly when we get older. This high level of stress becomes critical as children attempt to establish a personal identity and independence from family.

Do you remember how you felt as you started to develop friendships with people who were not in your family? If you felt frustrated and scared by this transition, you are not alone. All of us experienced some level of anxiety as we started to develop emotional connections with people outside of the family unit. La Greca and Lopez (1998) assert that this social anxiety (SA) becomes even more pronounced when we are in high school and have a variety of friendship opportunities to choose from.

Exploring this phenomenon further, La Greca and Lopez (1998) asked high school males and females to assess their current friendships and found females to be more concerned about feelings of social inadequacy than males (La Greca & Lopez, 1998). Although both males and females experienced varying degrees of SA, females with higher SA than males had less intimacy, companionship, and support in their close friendships. La Greca and Lopez (1998) believe there is a direct relationship between females' perceptions of social acceptance and support from a person's peer group and social anxiety. It appears that females are generally socialized to be more relationship focused. Therefore, the need to develop friendship relationships with peers becomes even more important when they are entering a new environment (e.g., high school, college). This goal becomes even more complex when girls do not have the communication skills necessary for establishing those relational bonds. La Greca and Lopez (1998) found that those females who did not have effective communication skills had fewer strong same-sex friendships. Although communication is critical to all interpersonal relationships, not having those skills deprives us of those socialization experiences and positive social functioning that are critical to the success of our personal relationships.

We now see that, in general, the initiation and development of interpersonal relationships can be a very stressful experience. When a person must consider the role of race/ethnicity in this process, the friendship selection experience is made even more complicated. As we discussed earlier, some people believe we should live in a color-blind society that ignores racial/ethnic identity. However, given our history of race relations in the United States, it is important to acknowledge the roles that race/ethnicity can play in all interracial relationships. Instead of ignoring or down-playing a person's race or ethnicity, we should respect and value that aspect of their cultural identity.

Building Interracial Alliances

Although only a small amount of research has been completed about interracial friendships, what we know about monoracial friendships can help us understand how both types of relationships have more in common than we are socialized to think. Have you ever wondered why you do not typically have friendships with others from different races? Did you allow your racial/ethnic differences to prevent you from getting to know each other? Were you afraid of what your friends and family would think? Relationships in which racial/ethnic differences are present can add a great deal to our lives. Therefore, it is reasonable to assume they can also work to improve race relations by dispelling myths and stereotypes that prevent these relationships from taking place.

Collier (1998) states that it is very important for friends to value and appreciate each other's racial/ethnic and cultural identity and what they offer each other as individuals. Although this may be perceived as common sense, Collier has done extensive research with people who have direct experience with this phenomenon. Based on their experiences with interethnic friendships, women attributed their successful friendships to efforts to "value difference *and* affirm the other person as a member of a culturally different group" (Collier, 1998, p. 377). Through dialogue, friends are able to appreciate the other's culture through "requests to be taught about an aspect of the other person's culture, storytelling, historical accounts of experiences, talk about family, or in conflict" (p. 377). Collier has also found that it is up to the friends to negotiate the rules that will guide the norms of appropriate behavior in their relationships.

Very little discussion is occurring regarding the topic of interracial friendship. However, we are finding that, in general, degree of similarity is the primary determinant for friendship selection (Fink & Wild, 1995; Graham & Cohen, 1997; Lawhon, 1997; Lundy et al., 1998). Sociodemographic variables such as school, grade, sex, ethnicity, and age are common factors that foster friendship relationships. Fink and Wild (1995) explored this assumption regarding the importance of similar interests in friendship dyads and found that they are important in maintaining friendship status. When people were paired with people with whom they had very little in common, they found it difficult to develop a high level of relational intimacy in comparison to more "naturally occurring" relationships (Fink & Wild, 1995). This difficulty is attributed to the fact that potential partners participated in activities that limited opportunities for establishing intimacy (e.g., social contact, traveling, passive entertainment, attending to demanding arts, engaging in artistic activities, and game playing).

It would stand to reason that when difference is introduced as a potential friendship characteristic or quality, the relationship is perceived as less desirable or more difficult. We have also found that societal pressures and similarity have both a positive and potentially negative effect on the friendship selection process. Have you ever had friends or family discourage you from being friends with someone who is Latino American? Did you think to yourself that you *really* liked him because you were interested in the same major and really saw nothing wrong with your friendship? These external pressures place undue stress on people as they attempt to establish relationships they may feel are essential at that time in their lives. As we approach the 21st century, this becomes even more important because of the increased likelihood that we will be in closer proximity to people from diverse racial/ethnic groups. Thus we will be more apt to develop interracial friendships and romantic relationships. Although some people find such relationships undesirable (La Greca and Lopez, 1998), we must continue to examine why race is made problematic and perceived as an insurmountable barrier in our interpersonal relationships.

Thus far, we have explored the delicate nature of the friendship selection process. Outside of family, friendship relationships are most likely the first relational bond we develop based on our own interests and needs. During this process, we are vulnerable to rejection and peer evaluations, which may potentially hinder our ability to develop effective interpersonal, relational, and communication skills. Because such skills are necessary for success in adult life, it is imperative that the friendship relationships we establish during childhood and adolescence be fostered in a healthy environment.

Lawhon (1997), Lundy et al. (1998), La Greca and Lopez (1998), and Graham and Cohen (1998) do not directly address why interracial friendships remain taboo and are judged more harshly than same-race friendships. Greene (1996) suggests that race as a social construct can potentially prevent people from developing positive interpersonal relationships. As a result, the effectiveness of relationships in improving race relations on a micro level is minimized. As with the members of WIA, interracial friendships experience a different matrix of complications than same-race friendships. Although interracial friendships can potentially improve race relations in an interpersonal context, the reality is that individuals remain hesitant to develop relationships with people who are different from themselves. In order to fully understand those mitigating factors that hinder interracial relationships from occurring, we must take a close look at experiences with race within the context of interpersonal communication.

DEFINING THE ISSUES AND BOUNDARIES OF INTERRACIAL FRIENDSHIPS

The current state of race relations has been explored in social science research, and scholars have found that things are not as good as we thought them to be. The racial climate in the workplace (Lundy et al., 1996), in brief social encounters (Sigelman et al., 1996), and on college campuses (Feagin, 1992) is typically not conducive to positive interracial communication. Racial hostility, stereotypes, and miscommunication create barriers that prevent individuals from looking beyond their differences to establish good, healthy interracial friendships.

As previously noted, desegregation in education, residential areas, and the workplace was perceived as an opportunity to improve race relations vis-à-vis increased opportunities for interracial contact (Sigelman et al., 1996; Wilson & Russell, 1996). Unfortunately, the social climate in those increasingly racially integrated environments is most likely tense, thus prohibiting interracial relationships from developing. According to sociologist Joe Feagin (1992), African American college students are constantly exposed to a hostile campus climate. The students are faced with faculty, administrators, and peers who make attending predominately white institutions very difficult. Through in-depth interviews with African American students, Feagin (1992) found that discrimination is constantly reinforced in everyday unstated assumptions regarding the priority of Whiteness in Western culture. Therefore, it is not surprising that interracial relationships would be predicated on mistrust, miscommunication, and hostility (Houston, 1997).

Such factors as racist comments and racist jokes truly prevent interracial alliances between microcultural and macrocultural groups from taking place. As an extension, the difficulties of socializing on a European American campus make

African American students' experiences at their universities very unrewarding (Feagin, 1992). By being exposed to prejudiced and discriminating attitudes, it is very plausible that the students find interracial relationships unappealing and uninviting. Instead of using this relationship to meet the same needs that are met in same-race friendships, students are cheated of an invaluable experience that could change their attitudes and beliefs about race and racism.

In a similar vein, European Americans can also be recipients of mistrust when it comes to interracial relationships. Dace (and McPhail 1998) describes how she categorized her friendships with European Americans. The purpose of each relationship was to allow (1) discussion of "anything pertinent to our existence, including race and culture," and (2) the European American friend to exercise his acknowledgment of his racial privilege. A second relationship type is apologetic in nature and operates from the framework of one acknowledging his or her privilege (see Chapter 12) and taking blame for racial oppression. This relationship is problematic because European Americans who are genuinely attempting to reach some level of consciousness regarding racial privilege (McIntosh, 1995a) may fail to value their friend's racial/ethnic difference.

Tatum (1992) has also found that in spite of a move toward multicultural curricula, the interpersonal dimension of experiences in higher education continues to be ignored. Although changes in textbooks and class content have become racially and culturally inclusive, Tatum has observed her students to be resistant to discourse about race, class, and gender. In the case of race, European American students have emotional responses when class discussion and course content are race related (Tatum, 1992). Some felt guilt, shame, and despair, which prohibits them from talking and learning about race. Tatum notes the following reasons why students experience this resistance: (1) race is a taboo topic, (2) the belief that America is a just society, and (3) denial of any personal connection to racism. So, if there is such resistance to discussing race in a controlled environment, it is very likely these feelings spill over into uncontrolled social contexts as well.

As you continue to think about your own interracial friendships, what do the findings from these studies mean to you? Are you now thinking about why you do or do not have friends from racial/ethnic groups different from your own? What has contributed to their success and/or failure? It is our hope that, as you are presented with the issues that make interracial friendships unnecessarily problematic, you come to realize and acknowledge how salient race can be. Unfortunately, the importance of race becomes even more pronounced when we begin to develop interpersonal relationships with others. Instead of seeing these relationships as natural, we are socialized to perceive relational intimacy with those with whom we have more similarities as normal and socially acceptable.

Residential Desegregation and Interracial Friendship

A context that serves as an important site for exploring interracial friendships is residential neighborhoods. With post–civil rights efforts to desegregate all public institutions also came equal access to housing opportunities for people of color in the United States. Decades after this monumental political process, Sigelman et al. (1996) wanted to determine how residential desegregation has really impacted interracial communication. Detroit was the focus of the study. It is a metropolitan area with a high probability for interracial contact between African Americans and European Americans.

Sigelman et al. (1996) found that European Americans were more likely and African Americans were somewhat likely to interact with members of the other race as compared to 25 years ago. In the midst of a hypersegregated area, there were also reports of experiences with racial hostility. Because the type of interracial interactions participants shared were very formal in nature (Sigelman et al., 1996), there was relatively no relational intimacy present to qualify these relationships as being anything more than superficial. Furthermore, approximately 50% of African American participants had no European American friends, and 50% of European Americans had at least one African American friend or acquaintance. For instance, some European Americans described their friendships with African American co-workers or classmates as friendships, whereas African Americans would describe them as acquaintance relationships with little or no intimacy. This variance in friendship affiliation captures the complexity of interracial friendships. As Sigelman et al. (1996) describe, racial integration did improve the probability of interracial contact; however, it has done relatively little to promote of close interracial relationships.

Comparing Interracial and Intraracial Friendships

Thus far, we have explored studies and essays that examine our interracial and intraracial friendships. Although we have gained insight into why these relationships are initiated (or not), few efforts have been made that ask people to share why their friendship relationships with ingroup (intraracial) members and outgroup (interracial) members are successful or unsuccessful. Hallinan and Williams (1987; 1989) conducted two studies exploring true interracial friendships and relationship stability. The longitudinal studies traced intraracial and interracial friendships of high school seniors in two separate stages. The first study revealed that context or environment (i.e., integrated school) is a very important factor influencing the maintenance of interracial relationships. When a higher number of students of color enrolled in the school, their interracial friendships proved to be more stable (Hallinan & Williams, 1987). They also observed that friendships developed prior to the school year were more stable than those developed during the school year. Although the pre–school year interracial friendships lasted only several weeks and months into the school year, Hallinan and Williams (1987) observe that those relationships most likely survived because of a strong interpersonal attraction between the friends.

In their second study, Hallinan and Williams (1989) compared two data sets of friendship experiences, and found that interracial friendships were less common than intraracial friendships. Such factors as limited opportunities for interracial contact, similarity, status or academic performance, and reciprocity were observed as deterrents to the initiation and maintenance of interracial friendships. Similar to Graham and Cohen (1997) and Lundy et al. (1998), Hallinan and Williams (1989) provide further insight into the societal pressures typically associated with interracial relationships. Because individuals are socialized to interact and develop relational bonds with individuals similar to themselves, the likelihood of deviation from societal norms decreases. In short, they may be avoiding involvement because of the taboo nature of interracial friendships specifically, and interracial relationships in general.

EFFECTIVE COMMUNICATION STRATEGIES

As Dace (and McPhail 1998) describes it, we should choose interracial friendships that value both our individual and racial/ethnic identities. You may be asking yourself, "How do we achieve this goal? What communication strategies can help us break through these barriers?" Houston and Wood (1996) make the following suggestions for how we can initiate, develop, and maintain relationships with people who are from racial/ethnic groups different from our own.

We must first come to the realization that we may not completely understand the other person. Because people often have different meanings for the "same" behaviors (Houston & Wood, 1996), we should not assume our definitions for terms are going to be the same. Instead, we should perceive these communicative exchanges as opportunities to learn about communication styles that are unique to diverse racial/ethnic groups.

Another guideline for effective interracial communication is to avoid imposing our standards on other racial/ethnic groups. Houston and Wood (1996) use the media as an example of how individuals use their cultural standards to determine the value of other social groups. In the United States, we are socialized to perceive European behaviors and attitudes as the norm; therefore, when we encounter individuals from racial/ethnic and cultural groups, we impose these standards on them. For example, Lozano's (1997) research on cultural uses of space and body reveals that in the United States, people are socialized to maintain a great deal of physical space when they are in public settings. However, for Latino/a Americans, particularly in Miami, Florida, space use has "transformed cultural practices." In other words, a cultural style of body expressivity is used that may not adhere to U.S. expectations of behavioral norms.

We should also have a commitment to "respect[ing] how others interpret experience" (Houston & Wood, 1996, p. 54). If a Korean American friend comes to you and shares that he has experienced racism in one of his classes, do not invalidate his experience. Your friendship will be enhanced if you empathize with him and understand this dimension of his (racial/ethnic) identity. Additionally, we should provide support and engage in active listening that communicates respect and acknowledgment. Houston and Wood (1996) believe that friends from different races and classes should avoid silencing or denying the other's experiences from their standpoints (see Chapter 5). They also suggest that we acknowledge but not totalize our differences.

> Although acknowledging differences can be productive, we shouldn't overemphasize them. A Latina woman is of a different race than an African American woman, but each of them is more than just her race . . . . To avoid ignoring or totalizing differences, we can recognize and learn from ethnic and class diversity that is part—but only part—of who we are. (Houston & Wood, 1996, pp.53, 54)

CONCLUSION

This chapter on interracial friendship has illustrated how complex our interpersonal relationships can be when societal norms and pressures create a hierarchy that discourages interracial relationships. Although there is limited information specifically exploring the influence of race on our interracial friendships, we must reexamine how we think about the criteria we use for selecting our friends. We have also found that race relations within the context of interpersonal relations are problematized as being more complex than they actually are. In other words, we tend to focus solely on racial/ethnic differences with little attention to human similarities. We can take the issues that have been addressed in this chapter to challenge how we think about race relations and the significance of interracial friendships. This becomes even more important as we enter the 21st century. Just think about it. As you continue to experience life, you will be a citizen fully participating in a democratic society where interracial contact will be commonplace. Such contexts as the workplace, your children's schools, and your neighborhood, among others, will place people from all racial/ethnic groups in more frequent contact with each other.

As with intraracial friendships, interracial friendships fulfill a variety of relational needs deemed important to one or both relational partners. Although interracial friendships meet the most basic interpersonal needs of human interaction, they also provide us with the opportunity to develop an increased understanding of race issues and race relations. It is through this private forum that friends can develop interpersonal skills that facilitate heightened awareness of the reality of racism and its effect on all society members. By engaging in open and honest interpersonal communication, we can work toward eradicating the racist attitudes and beliefs pervading all sectors of public and private life in the United States.

OPPORTUNITIES FOR EXTENDED LEARNING

1. Use *InfoTrac College Edition* and search for journal articles relative to interracial friendship (keyword: *contact hypothesis*). From the articles, determine what factors are suggested as promoting relational intimacy. Make a list of similarities and differences these relationships have in comparison to intraracial friendships. What topics and relational issues may be discussed or avoided? Consider how this might compare to intraracial friendships.

2. Generate a list of your best/closest friends. List descriptors (e.g., honest, funny, caring) for each friend that best describes the qualities you most appreciate about them and your friendship. In examining your list, consider whether or not those relationships are racially/ethnically diverse. Explore what role family, friends, and society might play in socializing you about the relationship selection process. This activity provides you with the opportunity to be self-reflective of your friendship experiences and to further understand what qualities constitute "true friendship."

3. As a class, students should individually write down how many cross-race friendships they have and whether the friendship is of associate status (i.e., classmate), acquaintance status (i.e., hang out occasionally), or close friendship status (i.e., have frequent and regular contact). On separate index cards, provide nonidentifying statements describing how you have been socialized to have (or not) interracial friendships. For example, someone may write the following: "I don't have any friends from other races because my parents are racist." Share and discuss these index cards.

4. Think about how friendships and race are portrayed in the media. For example, the TV show *Friends* explores European American friendship among singles living in New York. Similarly, Fox's *Living Single* explored single life for four close African American females also living in New York. As a group, compare and contrast how the media represent the communication styles, content issues (e.g., being single, managing a career), styles of humor, and identity issues relative to the racial/ethnic audiences members targeted.

INTERRACIAL ROMANTIC RELATIONSHIPS

INCREASING NUMBERS OF INTERRACIAL
MARRIAGES

HISTORY OF INTERRACIAL RELATIONSHIPS

THEORIES ON INTERRACIAL RELATIONSHIPS

PREFERENCES FOR MARRIAGE CANDIDATES

SOCIAL GROUP INFLUENCE

MODEL OF INTERRACIAL RELATIONSHIP
DEVELOPMENT

CONCLUSION

OPPORTUNITIES FOR EXTENDED LEARNING

History has shown us that Europeans who colonized North America used force, power, and violence against racial/ethnic groups to maintain a racial hierarchy. At one time or another, we have all heard someone make the remark that we should forget about the past because slavery and internment camps no longer exist. In reality, however, these institutions have had far-reaching effects on the current state of interracial communication. When they were no longer declared property possessed by European Americans, it is highly unlikely that slaves and prisoners and European Americans instantly perceived each other as equals. Instead, the underlying power struggle continued to surface in their interracial interactions. Although the master–slave relationship does not typify current interracial relationships, we are still bringing the emotional baggage of our racist past into our interracial romantic relationships.

In order to heal from the wounds of racism, we must first understand the origin of racism (see Chapters 1 and 2) and then proceed to conceptualize how, over time, racism has impacted the development of interpersonal relationships between and among racial/ethnic groups in the United States. Chapter 7 described how interracial friendships are established despite barriers to interracial communication. This chapter provides a historical and contemporary overview of interracial/interethnic marriages. By exploring the causes, patterns, and trends of interracial marriage in the United States (Foeman & Nance, 1999; Kalmijn, 1998; Pascoe, 1996), we will gain insight into how a historical racial hierarchy has affected our most intimate interpersonal relationships.

For reasons to be addressed in this chapter, marriages in which diverse races/ethnicities are represented often reveal racist attitudes that are sometimes hidden from others. Consider the following example. Sheila (African American) and Bill (Asian American) have been friends for over a year. Their friends and families know each other and like each other a great deal. After spending quite a bit of time together, Sheila and Bill begin to have romantic feelings for each other. Eventually, their respective families observe this change in their relationship and voice opposition. Sheila and Bill begin to wonder, "What happened? Why don't we continue to have the support of our loved ones?"

Although both families accept that they are friends, Sheila and Bill's racial identities became salient when the relationship became romantic. Literature on race relations between African Americans and Asian Americans reveals that communication between the groups has not always been positive (Guthrie, 1995). This strain stems, in part, from the tensions surrounding the economic potential and growth present in African American communities. In many of these neighborhoods, convenience and beauty supply (e.g., hair care products) stores are owned by Asian Americans and other racial/ethnic groups, which has caused some African American consumers to resent the economic monopoly of other "privileged" groups in this market. Unfortunately, this tension has great potential to directly affect the interpersonal interactions between members of both racial/ethnic groups. This example of economic opportunity and its impact on race relations between community members (ingroup) and economic shareholders (outgroup) only touches the surface of why interracial romantic relationships are complex. In order to fully comprehend how this matrix captures the complexity of racism, we must first understand from where these tensions surrounding interracial marriage emerged.

INCREASING NUMBERS OF INTERRACIAL MARRIAGES

Romantic interracial relationships are now perceived as a "salient indicator of social assimilation" (McCaa, 1993, p. 209) whereby the social distance and animosity between racial and cultural groups has decreased (Sailer, 1997; Shea, 1997; Turner, 1990). Marriages between partners from different racial/ethnic backgrounds are claimed to exemplify improved race relations on a macro level (Holmes, 1996; Sailer, 1997); Recent public debate on various fronts demonstrates that interracial romantic relationships provide a context to discuss and engage in dialogue about the existing racial order in the United States. Census data from 1980 to 1990 (Lee & Fernandez, 1998) reveal an interesting trend in Asian American interracial/ interethnic marriage patterns. Overall, there has been a 10% decrease in outmarriage with non–Asian Americans and an increase in intraracial marriages between different Asian ethnic groups. For those choosing to outmarry (typically women and native-born Asian Americans), they marry non-Hispanic Whites, which is consistent across all Asian ethnic groups (Fujino, 1997; Lee & Fernandez, 1998). The decrease in intraracial marriages is prevalent among Koreans, Filipinos, and Vietnamese (Lee & Fernandez, 1998), which is attributed to "demographic and other social developments during the 1980's" (p. 5). This includes socioeconomic mobility and increased racial/ethnic diversity in the workplace, residential neighborhoods, and other public spaces. Further investigation also reveals a minimal increase in interracial marriages for Hispanics (3%) and African Americans (4%), and a substantial increase for Hawaiians (17%). As for those Asian Americans choosing interethnic marriages, this trend may be a strong indication of the microcultural/macrocultural boundary existing between Asian and Europeans (Lee & Fernandez, 1998).

According to the U.S. Census Bureau (1993), interracial marriages have increased significantly, from 310,000 in 1970 to 651,000 in 1980, and to 1,161,000 in 1992, and the numbers continue to grow rapidly (Heaton & Albrecht, 1996; Hout & Goldstein, 1994; Johnson, 1980; Kalmijn, 1991b; Kennedy, 1944; Lieberson, 1963). This rise is even more remarkable given the history of interracial marriages in the United States. (see Table 8.1). Marital unions between European Americans and all

TABLE 8.1 U. S. INTERRACIAL MARITAL TRENDS			
Racial Composition	**1980**	**1995**	**% Rise**
Same-race couples	48,264,000	51,733,000	7
Interracial couples	651,000	1,392,000	114
African American/European American couples	167,000	328,000	96
African American husband/ European American wife	122,000	206,000	69
European American husband/ African American wife	45,000	122,000	171
African American/other-than- European American couples	34,000	76,000	124
European American/other-than- African American couples	450,000	988,000	120

From El Nasser (1997).

other racial/ethnic groups were prohibited by law. Interracial/interethnic marriages are problematic because of the sociopolitical history of the United States. As a nation preoccupied with maintaining racial order, the United States advanced its agenda of racial purity for its European American citizens by creating a political road map for marriage.

Although marriages between people from different races/ethnicities (miscegenation) were indeed occurring, legislation was introduced that made it illegal for intermarriages to take place. For example, Arizona, California, Idaho, Mississippi, Missouri, Utah, and Wyoming (Spickard, 1989) adopted antimiscegenation laws forbidding marriages between European Americans and Mongolians; other states outlawed European Americans from marrying American Indians (Georgia, Louisiana, North Carolina), Chinese (Montana, Nevada, Oregon), Japanese (Montana, Nevada), Croatians (North Carolina), Indians, and Malayans (Nevada, South Dakota, and Wyoming) (Spickard, 1989). Despite the fact that all antimiscegenation laws became unconstitutional in 1967, interracial/interethnic marriages remain a point of contention for many U.S. citizens today.

HISTORY OF INTERRACIAL RELATIONSHIPS

As previously noted, factors that influence interracial/interethnic placement in a new country (e.g., the United States.) are (1) migration (movement from one's homeland to the United States.), and (2) (in)voluntary displacement (e.g., choice, slave trade, war, labor opportunities (Feagin & Feagin, 1996). This influx of diverse racial and ethnic groups has created a political and social tension resulting in competition for resources (e.g., food, employment, land, etc.). Although human needs were central to this complex issue of competition, the evolving hierarchical power structure replaced those needs with a political agenda of maintaining power for its European American inhabitants.

With the passage of time, the struggle for power and ultimate domination was compounded by genocide, hierarchy, and racial and ethnic subordination (Feagin & Feagin, 1996). As a result, an ingroup (cultural group) member was expected to maintain group solidarity and commitment to preserving the group culture. Therefore, any violation of that via ingroup–outgroup communication (e.g., interracial marriage, interracial dating, etc.) is perceived as a threat to group identity. In any event, social and cultural expectations place a group member in a position of aligning herself or himself with the group or denying the group and creating a new identity with the host culture.

Social indicators (e.g., race riots, prejudiced incidents) tell us that racism is still a part of the very fabric that created the United States. Literature and historical documents indicate that colonialism and other means of oppression are a part of the foundation on which this country was built. More importantly, race scholars emphasize that in order to improve future race relations we must understand our past, thus avoiding the entrapments of racism and other oppressive ideologies in the future. In contrast, however, society members who think of race as a social issue with little significance in today's world are under the false assumption that "the past should remain in the past." Unfortunately, this is not the nature of the world in which we live. The racism of yesterday (e.g., lynchings, slavery) is still a part of this "land of the free" we refer to as America.

Our interactions with racial/ethnic group members and exposure to other racialized experiences are too often clouded by racist thoughts, beliefs, and attitudes, thereby making race relations even more difficult to improve. One type of interracial relationship that contextualizes for us the pervasiveness of modern racism is interracial romances. Unlike friendships, romantic relationships involve a deeper level of relational commitment between partners. Yes, friendship does involve commitment from both friends in order for the relationship to work. However, romantic and marriage relationships are perceived as more intimate than friendships because the partners are reaching a level of vulnerability unique to this type of relationship. At one time or another, everyone has struggled with this dilemma when they are involved in a cross-sex, interracial friendship. When the two were friends, everyone saw their relationship as positive and nonthreatening, but when it looked as if the relationship was becoming romantic, it became a threat. The external pressures placed on partners by family, friends, and strangers to avoid involvement in a historically taboo relationship (Kalmijn, 1998) often hinder the development of a romantic relationship. In the end, people may be forced to choose between their families and relational partners, largely because of racism.

The rate of interracial/interethnic marriages in the United States has been increasing steadily with each passing generation (Foeman & Nance, 1999; Holmes, 1996; "Stateline," 1996), which may be indicative of (1) a decline in negative perceptions of different racial/ethnic groups, (2) an increased desire to assimilate into dominant culture, or (3) an increased acceptance of ethnic and racial diversity. In any event, the resistance to interracial relationships that remains can be traced back in history to colonialism. In the late 1400s during European global expansion, racism was acknowledged as a framework for understanding and maintaining racial order (Feagin & Feagin, 1996). Racism was exploited and redefined by European settlers to maintain superiority and inferiority over other racial/ethnic groups. This oppression was grounded in the belief that immutable, unchangeable "physical characteristics linked to *cultural* traits [were deemed by the] dominant group as undesirable or inferior" (Feagin & Feagin, 1996, p. 7).

In order to maintain physical distinctions between racial/ethnic groups, European Americans imposed slavery, internment camps, and, more recently, Jim Crow laws to separate the races in public (e.g., restaurants, rest rooms, and stores) and private contexts. This unfounded fear of racial blending came from the belief that the "influx of swarthy 'new' immigrants might breach their region's color line, producing untold horrors" (Pettigrew, Fredrickson, Knobel, Glazer, & Ueda, 1982, p. 79). Although all "race mixing" was perceived as a threat, intermixing between African Americans and European Americans was the most disturbing type of union (Porterfield, 1982). Foeman and Nance (1999) attribute this reaction to the fact that these two groups "represent what many identify as opposites along the race continuum" (p. 540). Therefore, the closer your skin color was to European American skin, the less threatening interracial marriage would be. In any event, commitment to maintaining racial purity fueled the opposition to race mixing in general.

Antimiscegenation Laws

In his book titled *The Legal Construction of Race*, Ian Lopez (1997) explains the role of law in perpetuating the social construction and maintenance of the term *race*. Lopez asserts the laws were enacted out of fear that racial mixing would disturb the "racial purity" of European Americans. This line of thinking is at the core of our "racial meaning systems," or how we think about race. Therefore, by restricting marriage choices based on physical appearance, the European race would remain pure.

Antimiscegenation laws were enacted by 41 states (Lopez, 1997; Price, 1998; Weinberger, 1966) and perpetuated a vicious cycle of social dominance and racial oppression based on the interrelationship between race and power (Lopez, 1997). It was believed that intermixture through intermarriage would blur the lines of physiological differences (e.g., eye color, hair texture, facial features) between diverse ethnic and racial groups. Therefore, legislation preventing interracial/interethnic contact through marriage would minimize the threat to the racial order (Lopez, 1997; Price, 1998). The groups affected by these laws were Americans of European, Chinese, Japanese, Filipino, African, Latino, Mongolian, Malay, Kanakan, American Indian, and Asiatic (Indian) descent (Frankenberg, 1993; Spickard, 1989). Frankenberg further illustrates that racial purity was a primary motivation for the creation of antimiscegenation laws, but maintaining the "virginal purity" of European American females was a significant factor. The virginal purity of European American women was a tool in subjugating them. What was perceived of equal importance was the need to separate the races physically so there would be even less likelihood of sexual contact, thus the "watering down" of all races.

In the 1967 landmark case of *Loving v. Virginia Supreme Court*, the tide was turned against antimiscegenation (Davidson & Schneider, 1992; Ely, 1998; McCaa,

1993; Myra, 1994; Tucker & Mitchell-Kernan, 1995; "Woman who changed laws," 1992). In 1958, Virginia residents Richard (European American) and Mildred (African American) Loving decided to marry legally in Washington, D.C., because their home state actively practiced the 1924 antimiscegenation laws. After residing in Virginia for a year, the Lovings were arrested and persecuted in 1959 and sentenced to a one-year prison sentence for violating antimiscegenation state laws. The Virginia sheriff forced the couple from their home because of their "ungodly relationship" ("Woman who changed laws," 1992). The Lovings accepted a suspended sentence that required them to not return to the state for 25 years. Four years later, the Lovings were approached by, and ultimately retained, an American Civil Liberties Union lawyer ("Why interracial marriages are increasing," 1996) to fight the unconstitutionality of their extradition from Virginia. In June 1967, the Lovings won a legal victory that would change the state of marital law in the United States forever. The Supreme Court ruled unanimously to remove antimiscegenation laws. This legal action forced Virginia and 15 other states to eradicate their laws as well, thus making interracial/interethnic marriages legal.

The landmark legal battle of the Lovings was "instrumental in tearing down one of the legal vestiges of segregation" ("Woman who changed laws," 1992, p. 14). Although most literature documenting antimiscegenation laws focus on the institution of marriage, scant mention is made of the economic issues affected by this unconstitutional act. Price (1998) notes that all marriage-based federal benefits such as Social Security spousal benefits and special immigration rights as well as automatic inheritance rights for children were lost. In any case, antimiscegenation laws were designed to control the social and political dimensions of the existing racial order and power structure (Frankenberg, 1993) while ignoring the freedom of choice (Ely, 1998; Lopez, 1997; Feagin & Feagin, 1996; Fitzpatrick & Hwang, 1992).

Until 1910, interethnic marriages among European Americans were more common than interracial marriages because of antimiscegenation laws (Davidson & Schneider, 1992; Pagnini & Morgan, 1990). Although interethnic marriages are still commonplace, it is the rise in interracial marriages that many have difficulty accepting. Prior to the *Loving v. Virginia Supreme Court* case, there were violent consequences for interracial married couples. Irrespective of race, spouses, children, family members, and friends were beaten, murdered, or run out of town because of their relationships. These brutalities sent a clear message to the world that dire consequences awaited those who chose to be "race traitors" and marry interracially. Thirty-three years have passed; however, interracial romantic relationships continue to be stereotyped as taboo. All too often, people involved in such relationships are asked why they have chosen to be emotionally committed to an outgroup member. Instead, we should be asking ourselves, "Why *not*?"

If there were a same-race couple and an interracial couple walking down the street, to whom do you think the following question would be directed: "Why are

---

8.1   *"The Wall of Shame" at Brown University*

For many college students, the issue of interracial dating may have had little importance for them prior to their arrival on campus. At Brown University, a group of African American women publicly displayed their disapproval of romantic relationships that cross the color line. In 1996, seven African American women reacted to African American men's decisions to date European American women. The women construed the men's decisions to date European American women as rejections of them as African American women. Their reaction was to create a Wall of Shame, where they listed the names of famous African American men who either date or have married European American women. They then made a second list on the door of one of the African American female perpetrators. The second list included approximately a dozen African American men on campus "who, they said, date white women."

Although this incident is isolated, it demonstrates how racial issues within the context of interracial romantic relationships are indicative of the greater social issues that affect individuals beyond the college campus. Tarricone observes that student perspectives are grounded in "notions of community. The politicization of dating choices has some basis for argument, but it is very problematic. You're taking something personal and private and making it public and political" (Tarricone, 1996, p. 1).

In some circles, interracial dating can be very political. People sometimes interpret loyalties and identities through who you date. But in reality, our relationship choices should be matters of the heart. Because the male/female ratio on campus favors African American men, "this left African American female students with even fewer dating options in the college environment and their crusade against African American-white romance" (Gose, 1996, p. A45). In order to address these tensions, the Brown Organization of Multi- and Bi-racial Students (BOMBS) was organized to engage the university community in a dialogue about race. Through a forum on interracial dating (Schupack, 1996), the men and women were challenged to ask themselves the "why nots" instead of "whys" of interracial romantic relationships.

they together?" More likely than not, the person posing this question would be questioning the authenticity of the interracial couple's relationship. What is troublesome about this scenario is that it is not too far from reality. If we look more closely, we see it is highly unlikely that the same question or scrutiny would be posed to couples in which both partners are from the same race. In contrast, we accept the relationship for what it is and respect the partners' choice to be involved in that relationship.

Given the sociopolitical history surrounding interracial marriage, you may be surprised about the rise in the number of marriages occurring between people from different racial/ethnic backgrounds (El Nasser, 1997; Holmes, 1996). As the literature and U.S. Census Bureau data indicate, most outmarriages (marriages occurring between outgroup members) are taking place rather frequently among Japanese, Native, and Latino/a Americans, whereas African Americans are least likely to marry outside of their racial/ethnic group (Besherov & Sullivan in Holmes, 1996). Society is becoming more accepting of interracial marriages; however, a great deal of resistance remains to the idea of intermixing between some racial/ethnic groups more than others.

THEORIES ON INTERRACIAL RELATIONSHIPS

Most interpersonal communication theories of relationship development and maintenance focus primarily on same-race partners, which makes it even more difficult to understand the whys of interracial/interethnic romantic relationships. For example, the social exchange theory is used to assess the costs and rewards of being involved in an interpersonal relationship (Homans, 1961).

Relational partners describe the relationship according to the activities (voluntary behaviors), social behaviors, and interactions both partners engage in together. From there, assessments of these dimensions are made based on quantity and value. The profit = reward minus cost formula enables relational partners to determine the worth of the relationship (Homans, 1961). Unfortunately, no consideration is given to social location (e.g., racial identity, racial awareness).

Acknowledging the exclusiveness of this and other exchange theories (Heaton & Albrecht, 1996; Kalmijn, 1993; Schoen & Wooldredge, 1989; Van den Berghe, 1960), social scientists have introduced three theories or concepts to explain why some interracial relationships exist. Despite limited research in general about these so-called taboo relationships, the following theories provide a solid, more inclusive foundation for understanding interracial relationships. Instead of being presented as deviant relationships that violate society's relational norms, the theories present these unions as natural relationships that evolve for various reasons. Note that the

---

8.2   *Myths About Interracial Dating*

After surveying literature and research, there are six myths associated with interracial marriages. The myths are alleged reasons why people become involved or avoid involvement in interracial romantic relationships. In general, *social and/or economic mobility*, *rebellion* (i.e., against society, family), *sexual curiosity*, and *exhibitionism* (shock value) are cited as motivating factors for involvement. Conversely, *anti-race mixing* and *religious bias* are justifications used to express opposition to interracial marriages. As this chapter demonstrates, history has played a large role in supporting these myths that prevent interracial romantic and marriages from occurring.

Instead of assuming that ulterior motivations are behind a person's interracial romantic involvement, we should ask ourselves why we even question such unions. If we *really* want to understand how (un)real these myths are, we need to listen to the voices and experiences of partners involved in these marriages. We may find that society perpetuates these myths, thus creating stress for relational partners. Instead of supporting this cycle of racism, we must recognize that love, support, respect, and companionship are the driving forces behind most stable, healthy interracial (and same-race) romantic relationships.

---

motivating factors vary from person to person and, in general, are not a means for exoticizing the other racial/ethnic group. Conversely, the relationship is the result of mutual attraction, increased interracial interactions, and geographic location, among other factors.

Structural Theory

Currently, two theories articulate why individuals might become involved in an interracial romantic relationship. Kouri and Lasswell (1993) used the structural theory and the racial motivation theory to better understand these motivations. The structural theory suggests that demographics (e.g., socioeconomic status, education, occupation, residence) and mutual attraction contribute to the initiation, development, and maintenance of an interracial marriage, whereas the racial motivation theory believes that interracial marriages occur *because* of racial difference, whereby at least one partner finds the racially different other more appealing because of her or his race.

The first approach within structural theory is *endogamy*, which occurs when people marry within their group. This approach would include a person who prefers a marital partner from the same racial/ethnic background. A slightly different approach is *homogamy*, which describes a person's preference for a mate who is close in social status. If a person is using either an *endogamous* or *homogamous* approach to relationships, he or she is practicing a form of group closure because the person prefers to marry within the group (Kalmijn, 1998). Additionally, the person prefers a marital partner who is from the same racial/ethnic background, social status, educational background, and/or religion. Another theory that supports this assumption is the *structural theory* (Kouri & Lasswell, 1993), (e.g., socioeconomic status, education). Because of their similar backgrounds and interests, relational partners are more likely to develop a romantic relationship. This theory is quite similar to homogamy in that it demonstrates how similarity across racial/ethnic lines becomes a more salient issue for people seeking mates from the same social status.

Racial Motivation Theory

In contrast, *hypergamy* describes a situation in which a person has an interest in or willingness to marry someone of a different status. These theories are distinct from traditional exchange theories because they account for partner attributes and qualities not traditionally deemed pertinent to relationship initiation, involvement, and/or satisfaction. One motivating factor that has received very little attention in social scientific research is the *racial motivation theory*. According to this perspective, a person becomes involved in an interracial marriage (or relationship) *because* of racial difference. In essence, one or both partners are dating or married because they find the racially different other more appealing because of her or his race. Currently, there is limited research on this theory; however, it is plausible that partners could potentially exoticize each other. Unfortunately, racial motivation questions the integrity of those relationships where race is only a part of what each partner perceives as an attractive partner attribute. As for motivations for involvement in interracial marriages, Spaights and Dixon (1984) propose this behavior is grounded in curiosity about myths of sexual prowess and promiscuity, rebellion against family, display of a liberal attitude, or interest in a cultural experience. They also believe that African Americans use interracial relationships to rebel against an oppressive society, for financial gain, or to attain social status. No matter how they consider the relationship, Spaights and Dixon (1984) promote the belief that all relationships between African Americans and European Americans are anomalies and doomed to fail. Although their essay does address the reality of some misperceptions of why individuals become involved in interracial romantic relationships, Spaights and Dixon (1984) fail to acknowledge the fact that interracial relationships are as likely as same-race relationships to be healthy experiences without one or both partners objectifying each other.

In any event, the racial motivation theory may reflect the true motivations of some (but not all) people involved in interracial romantic relationships. Overall, these new theories about interracial romantic relationships reflect the reality of the mate selection process. Such factors as education, interracial contact, group size, chance encounters, geographic location, and preference (Blau, Blum, & Schwartz, 1982; Heaton & Albrecht, 1996; Qian, 1998) directly influence a person's decision to adopt a hypergamous approach to dating.

In order to understand more clearly why and how interracial relationships are initiated, developed, and maintained, we must understand the social forces (Kalmijn, 1998) that lead to the decision to date or marry interracially. In general, interracial marriages (and other romantic relationships) depend on opportunities for social relationships between racial/ethnic groups (Blau, Blum, & Schwartz, 1982; Foeman & Nance, 1999; Kalmijn, 1998; Powers & Ellison, 1995). Research has reported primarily on interracial relationships between European Americans and other racial ethnic groups, which is reasonable to assume given the racial segregation of our communities. (Very little attention, however, has been given to other interracial relationships). When integration occurs, racial/ethnic group members become a part of dominant culture as they pursue degrees in higher education, jobs in corporate America, and change social (economic status). Therefore, interracial interactions become more frequent, which increases the likelihood that romantic relationships will develop between people who are racially/ethnically different.

Although we cannot say that all interracial relationships are the result of college or work-related experiences, it is reasonable to assume that a person's environment has a direct impact on his or her decision to date or marry interracially. In order to avoid making generalizations about why people become involved in interracial relationships, we must understand the variables that influence how a person might reach the decision to become involved in a socially taboo relationship. What is more important is that social scientists acknowledge how choice and socialization work together, or separately, as a person chooses to be either homogamous or hypergamous in their mate selection process.

As we mentioned earlier, the "'generic model' of interpersonal resource exchange" (Gaines, 1997, p. 353) does little to consider how a partner's racial/ethnic identity can affect the level of relationship satisfaction. According to these models, European American expectations of male/female romantic relationships are used as a standard for all romantic relationships, thereby ignoring racial/ethnic differences. Because our social positions are an integral part of our identity, it is very difficult to ignore their significance in our interpersonal relationships. Just as we accept our friends for who they are, should not the same be done in our romantic relationships?

At any rate, it is very important that we begin to rethink how we think about interracial romantic relationships. This does not mean, however, that we become involved in cross-race relationships because of a political agenda. Instead, we should view these relationships as we do same-race romantic relationships—as a natural part of the human experience.

Upon entering a romantic relationship, we look for certain qualities and characteristics in a prospective mate. Naturally we are looking for someone who can contribute to the relationship. We consider how we will benefit or grow from this emotional attachment to another human being. No matter what background we come from, we are socialized to adopt a homogamous approach to mate selection. Theorists who study trends in interracial marriage have found *three social forces* that influence marriage patterns: (1) preferences for marriage candidates, (2) social group influence on mate selection process, and (3) constraints in the marriage market (Kalmijn, 1998). In order to demonstrate the significance of these factors, we will use data that report the current dating trends of African American women to show how a person's social positions (racial identity and status) influence his or her decision of whether or not to date interracially.

Recent data on interracial marriage trends offer conflicting information regarding who is and is not marrying interracially. For example, some data conclude that African American women are less likely to marry interracially than African American men, European American women, and all other racial/ethnic groups (Kalmijn, 1991b, 1993, 1998; Merton, 1941, Monahan, 1976), but the U.S. Census Bureau data reveal just the opposite (see Oguntoyinbo, 1997). The current trend in interracial marriages for African Americans and European Americans finds this phenomenon to be more prevalent among African American women and European American men, which more than doubled between 1990 and 1995. When trends are reported in the U.S. Census Bureau data, social scientific research assists in explaining why these trends exist. Very little literature is available to explain why some African American women are choosing to marry interracially. Recent statistics indicate that the African American male population accounts for 6% of the U.S. population and 51% of the prison population, according to the Sentencing Project, which accounts for one-third of African Americans in the criminal justice system (Muwakkil, 1998; see Patton, 1998; Taifa, 1996). Because so many African American men are incarcerated, involved in interracial marriages, and attend college at a lower rate than women, endogamous African American women find themselves either unmarried or opting to marry out of their racial group. Depending on which of three social forces become more significant for these women, they are led to maintain their *homogamous* approach or become hypergamous as they pursue romantic relationships that may potentially lead to marriage.

In the following sections, we further explore specific theories that attempt to explain preferences for marriage candidates by looking more closely at the social forces just described. Specifically, we attempt to understand why a person from a certain racial/ethnic group would change her attitudes about interracial dating/marriages. For the purpose of illustration, we use African American women to explicate the following theories regarding mate selection. This does not, however, imply that other races/ethnicities are any less important to the dialogue on this topic. Although literature posits that African American women are more resistant to interracial romantic relationships than women from other marginalized groups (Paset & Taylor, 1991; Todd, McKinney, Harris, Chadderton, & Small, 1992), they are in a precarious situation that may lead them (more so than other groups) to consider other relationship alternatives (e.g., interracial dating). These findings and assumptions are also applicable to other women and men as well.

PREFERENCES FOR MARRIAGE CANDIDATES

In his extensive research on interracial relationships, Kalmijn (1998) suggests three social forces that inform our partner choices. The first social force is *preferences for marriage candidates*, which refers to the resources partners offer each other. Have you ever been set up on a blind date by a close friend? Prior to the actual date, your friend probably considered what qualities you find attractive in another person. Education, physical attractiveness, and a sense of humor are examples of qualities you may have communicated to your friend that you find most appealing. Our decision to date or marry someone is partially based on the *socioeconomic resources* he or she can bring to the relationship. Past research indicates that socioeconomic resources are primarily expectations of males held by both males and females. This includes "resources that produce economic well-being and status . . . [which] is shared by the family members" (p. 399) (see Jacobs & Furstenberg, 1986; Stevens, Owens, & Schaefer, 1990).

Cultural resources relates to how important the individual feels it is that both relational partners share similar cultural or racial/ethnic backgrounds (Byrne, 1971; Kalmijn, 1998). The underlying implications regarding the importance of shared racial/ethnic identity stress that partners should have similar values and opinions. This shared similarity will prove attractive for each partner and allow them to share conversations, activities, and mutual understanding central to and independent of their racial/ethnic differences. According to preferences and homogamy, a person's educational attainment is directly related to the qualities he or she is looking for in a mate. Therefore, interracial marriage may become an option when people have more in common with those from a different racial/ethnic group than their own. For

THEORY INTO PRACTICE

Do you want to be supportive of romantic relationships that involve people from different racial/ethnic groups? Do you wonder how you can communicate this to friends, colleagues, family members, or others who are interested in initiating or maintaining these relationships? Here are a few Tips to guide you:

- Support these couples just as you would support others in comparable relationships (initial dating stages, bonding, marriage, termination, etc.). Do not focus on their racial/ethnic differences, but don't ignore them either.
- Acknowledge the many benefits of the relationship, as well as some of the possible unique challenges the couple may face.
- Do not automatically assume that race is the defining factor for these relationships. (Other similarities/differences in age, spirituality, socioeconomic status may be more important than racial/ethnic difference.)
- Confront existing myths (about self and others) that suggest all interracial romantic relationships are based on sexual stereotypes and/or power plays.
- Do not prejudge individuals who prefer same-race or other-race partners. Instead, get to know these persons so you can better understand these preferences in the context of their life experiences.
- If possible and/or appropriate, cultivate a relationship with the couple so you come to know them as romantic partners who happen to be from different racial/ethnic groups (as opposed to simply "an interracial couple").
- Be open and honest about your support for all types of positive, affirming relationships (even when others might criticize or dehumanize interracial relationships).

example, a microcultural group member with a doctorate may desire a same-race mate with similar interests, but may have difficulty meeting someone. The racial/ethnic identity of the potential mate may have less significance because that person places emphasis on interests, similarities, and education. This does not, however, imply a lack of commitment to maintaining the importance of one's racial/ethnic identity.

Social Group Influence

The second type of social force that influences partner choice is the social group. According to this approach, third parties have an incentive to keep new generations from marrying interracially (Kalmijn, 1998; Mills, Daly, Longmore, & Kilbride, 1995). Therefore, they employ strategies that will prevent group members from marrying someone who is not a member of the ingroup. In the case of interracial marriages, a history of opposition from external forces has worked to destroy the initiation, development, and maintenance of romantic relationships between people from different racial/ethnic groups. If people believe intermixing between the races should not occur, it is quite possible they are basing this on the belief that the internal cohesion and homogeneity of the group is being threatened (e.g., "watering down of the races").

The first type of social influence is *group identification*. According to Gordon (1964), people's desire to preserve the social history of their racial/ethnic group directly influences their efforts to prevent interracial marriages from occurring. A common retort to people considering interracial marriage is, "What will people say, or think?" This statement implies that the family heritage will be threatened as a result of the interracial marriage. In her research on Vietnamese dating trends and patterns, Nguyen (1998) found that racial/ethnic identity is important to most families. Therefore, Vietnamese men and women are socialized to believe that intraracial dating (dating within one's own race) is a Vietnamese tradition. If both partners are from the same racial/ethnic group, they are likely to have a shared belief and communication system. This exploratory study found that participants' experiences with interracial and intraracial dating are influenced by Vietnamese and U.S. American values on the opinions and attitudes of participants toward interracial dating between Vietnamese and European Americans. Overall, Nguyen (1998) found that the more acculturated a Vietnamese person is, the more likely she or he is to date interracially in spite of cultural and familial expectations.

Group sanctions refers to institutions that traditionally oppose marriage between people from different racial/ethnic backgrounds. The role of these group members is to impose some sanction against those individuals who may potentially become involved in an interracial romantic relationship. The two institutions of *parents* and *state* are cited as offering such sanctions to family members. In the case of family, parents can communicate opposition to their children in a number of ways. According to Kalmijn (1998), parents can sabotage the relationship by one of the following methods:

1. Meeting with potential partners to discourage interest in the relationship.
2. Taking on the role of matchmaker and selecting mates with whom they feel their child will be better suited.

3. Offering advice and opinions to their child to discourage interest
   in the relationship and the relational partner.
4. Withdrawing emotional and relational support to the child as a form
   of punishment for involvement in an interracial relationship.

The current list of family-oriented sanctions is by no means exhaustive. Nevertheless, it illustrates the kinds of negative reactions parents, and some family members, can have when they learn a family member has decided to date and/or marry interracially. Another institution that has been cited as imposing sanctions against marriages between people from different backgrounds is the church. In their research on interfaith marriages (Jiobu, 1988; Johnson, 1980; Kennedy, 1944; Lazerwitz, 1995; McCutcheon, 1988), social scientists have found that religious worldviews often prescribe homogamous or endogamous marriages for its members, which is

---

8.3   *Personal Reflection*

I remember teaching an introductory interpersonal communication course in the summer of 1994. As we covered the day's readings, we started talking about romantic relationships, which led to an engrossing exchange on the topic of interracial dating. This was very timely because of the recent murder of Nicole Brown Simpson, which led to discussion about murder, race, and interracial dating. A young European American female shared her opinion and experiences with her current relationship with an African American male, which generated a heated, yet healthy, class discussion.

She shared that her family and friends reacted very negatively to her relationship, which was a surprise to her. Their opposition was only heightened by the negative publicity surrounding the murder, O. J. Simpson, and society's preoccupation with race. One striking comment that resounds in my mind is the reaction she said one of her European American female friends had to both the trial and her relationship: "If you keep dating him, the same thing that happened to Nicole Simpson is going to happen to you!" The student went on to say she was not too concerned with their attitudes because this man made her happy. As a recent divorcee, she was not planning to marry this man, which was her family and friends' biggest fear. Nonetheless, she was ready to weather the storm.

Approximately three weeks later, I noticed her continued absence from class and became very concerned. The end of summer semester came and went, and still no contact. It was not until fall semester that I heard from her.

Personal Reflection *(continued)*

She called me and was apologetic for not contacting me earlier because her father backed out on his promise and purposely did not pay her tuition. She attributed his negligence and dishonesty to his unhappiness with her interracial romantic relationship. However, what bothered her the most was his willingness to give up his daughter for the sake of his racism and prejudice.

Although I only vaguely recall the entire conversation or its outcome, this student's narrative has stayed with me since that day we spoke. It speaks to the seriousness of racism and how it can affect our interpersonal relationships. Although this is only one person's reality, interracial communication research indicates that romantic relationships between two people are most difficult because of factors that typically have little to do with the relationship itself. More specifically, racism, prejudice, and stereotyping from family, friends, and society contribute to the avoidance and dissolution of what could potentially be a loving and caring relationship.—TMH

similar to research findings on perceptions of interracial marriages. Literature indicates that this worldview is adopted by very few institutions. For those churches espousing this ideology, however, there was and still is the belief that interfaith marriages decrease the number of church members and the very lifeblood of that faith. By increasing its membership through marriage, that faith would become a part of the family's history whereby children and future generations would continue in that particular faith. Social scientists have also found that interfaith marriages were often perceived as potential factors contributing to the rise in interracial marriages. Although very little data is available to support this observation, there are other social groups that have directly prohibited interracial marriages from occurring.

MODEL OF INTERRACIAL RELATIONSHIP DEVELOPMENT

As the literature has demonstrated, interracial romantic relationships have experienced a great deal of resistance in the Unites States (Eddings, 1996; Gose, 1996; Lacayo, 1995; Marrow, 1995; Murstein, Merigihi, & Malloy, 1989; Norment, 1994; Turner, 1990). Interracial relationships have been subjected to various forms of discrimination. History tells us that the antimiscegenation laws were designed to maintain the existing racial hierarchy by limiting the frequency of interracial contact between all racial/ethnic groups. Fortunately, the laws were eradicated because they were obstructing the judicial system that prided itself in providing "justice for all."

As we enter the 21st century, interracial romantic relationships are going to become more commonplace. Therefore, we must be challenged to examine our own thoughts about and attitudes toward interracial dating and marriage.

Imagine the following scenario. You are in a situation where you have few professional and personal relationships with members or your own racial/ethnic group, but you are looking for a committed relationship with someone with similar life goals and values. Will interracial dating be an option for you? Or will you approach the mate selection process from an endogamous perspective? What factors lead you toward or away from interracial dating?

In order for these relationships to withstand external pressures, Foeman and Nance (1999) propose a new model for initiating, developing, and maintaining interracial romantic relationships (see Gaines, 1997; Hall, 1980; Jeter, 1982; Poston, 1990; Poussaint, 1988). The four-stage model is designed to examine the functional dimensions of an interracial relationship. More importantly, the model provides partners with a framework for creating a committed, long-term relationship in which racial/ethnic identity influences the communicative process. Note that each stage can be revisited at any time depending on the life events of the couple and each relational partner.

The first stage is *racial awareness*: Each relational partner must "become familiar with the similarities between them and develop a shared belief that a relationship is possible" (Foeman & Nance, 1999, p. 528). Because they do not have the same racial/ethnic identity, both partners must be aware of four sets of perspectives: (1) their own, (2) their partner, (3) their collective racial group, and (4) their partner's racial group(s). The partners must acknowledge that race does matter, which will affect their decision making on a variety of levels.

For example, as the couple is making plans for an evening out, one partner suggests attending a cultural activity unique to his racial/ethnic group. From her perspective, she may think the activity boring, however; if she is aware of her partner's perspective and that of his racial group, she will be willing to compromise. In turn, he will be open to similar exchanges in the future.

Foeman and Nance (1999) state that competent communication is very critical during this phase of the relationship. The couple will actively address their awareness in an effort to establish mutual trust and effective communication within the relationship. For instance, consider a relationship between Ingrid (an African American female) and Dave (a European American male). If Ingrid and Dave expect to have a healthy, long-lasting romantic relationship, they have to acknowledge the importance of racial/ethnic identity. Dave should be empathic and sensitive to Ingrid when she shares with him her experiences with racism. Similarly, Ingrid should remind herself that racism may be something new to Dave, and possibly other European Americans. And if he does not immediately understand her racialized experiences, Ingrid should not allow her frustration with Dave to influence her perception of him. Awareness of their differences and different perspectives (social locations) will hopefully allow them to work toward resolving miscommunication and misunderstandings.

After the couple has successfully completed the racial awareness stage, they can progress toward the second stage; *coping*. During this stage, the couple determines how information regarding the four perspectives will affect their commitment to a long-term relationship. The couple develops skills that protect them from external forces (people, situations, contexts) that may harm them as individuals or as a couple (Foeman & Nance, 1999). These strategies may vary according to a person's age and the generation of their parents. Although no current research has explored this phenomenon, Funderburg (1993) found that couples use a variety of coping strategies that they perceive to be most appropriate for their personal circumstances. One participant in Funderburg's study of interracial relationships shared that her Italian family was vehemently opposed to her marriage to an African American male. The climate was so hostile that her parents "excommunicated" her from the family. In other words, her family considered her dead after her wedding day. Because her family refused to have any contact with her, this woman created a way to cope with the circumstances. She and her mother coordinated secret meetings between them and the grandchildren at a neighboring aunt's home. It was not until the father died (the daughter read the obituary in the newspaper) that the adult granddaughter was able to reunite her mother with her family of origin. This situation sounds extreme, but it is very likely representative of situations that affect a number of interracial couples. In any event, the couple is responsible for determining what coping strategies are most effective in helping them deal with external pressures to dissolve the relationship.

With the reactive strategies to their relationship established, the couple enters *identity emergence*, stage 3. The couple has begun to successfully manage the preservation of the relationship. It is at this point that "the couple and individual take control over images of themselves" (Foeman & Nance, 1999, p. 518). Instead of accepting society's definition of what it means to be an interracial couple, the couple creates their own perspective and definition of the relationship. Traditionally, interracial romantic relationships have been presented as taboo. For instance, if Ingrid or Dave interacts with a friend or acquaintance who opposes interracial relationships, either of them may be provoked to question why that person believes what he or she does. Both relational partners ideally have moved beyond questioning the relationship and appreciate it for what it is—a committed, supportive, and loving connection.

In the last and final stage, *(ongoing) relationship maintenance*, the couple must reexamine the role of race in the relationship (Foeman & Nance, 1999) and provide ways to adjust to its positive and negative impact. As a couple and individuals within the relationship, they are willing to work at preserving the relationship. Because each partner has different experiences with racism, they must negotiate how those experiences will be accounted for within the relationship. For example, Ingrid has dealt with racist attitudes from strangers and colleagues throughout her personal and professional life. With the added layering of an interracial relationship, Ingrid has developed effective coping strategies to deal with the negative feedback she receives from others. In contrast, Dave is not quite handling the pressure. He loves Ingrid but does not know how to deal with his colleagues' reaction when they discover he is involved with an African American woman. Over time, Dave will develop strategies he is comfortable using that will help preserve his relationship with Ingrid. This may include using assertive communication when others make disparaging comments about the relationship. Instead of avoiding conflict, Dave may become more assertive as he confronts others about their racist attitudes. (This may also be a strategy that Ingrid would use.) In any event, the couple will determine what best works in their efforts to preserve their relationship.

Foeman and Nance (1999) emphasize that the various stages can be revisited by relational partners, and will vary from couple to couple. Additionally, if the couple chooses to have children, they will invariably have to develop increased racial awareness, new coping strategies, a new family identity, and additional strategies for maintaining (and preserving) the family and marriage relationship. Biracial or multiracial children must deal with a great deal of pressure from society and family members who have problems trying to understand their multiple racial/ethnic identities. In order to cope with the pressures, the parents must do more than develop strategies that establish positive self-esteem (for example, see Orbe, 1999). They will teach the children to have pride in themselves, their unique racial/ethnic heritage, and their family unit as a whole. In the end, it is hoped that individuals anticipating involvement or actively involved in an interracial relationship will do what is necessary to ensure that the relationship weathers the storms of racism.

CONCLUSION

Chapter 8 provided a framework for understanding the whys of interracial romantic relationships. We have traditionally been socialized to describe romantic relationships that evolve between people from different racial/ethnic backgrounds as problematic. Instead of accepting the reality that such relationships evolve out of genuine love and appreciation, we have been taught to question why someone becomes involved in an interracial romantic relationship. According to Spaights and Dixon (1984), individuals in these relationships become involved with someone of a different race because of the "exotic" mystique they represent. The partner is ultimately valued *because* of his or her race/ethnicity. Despite the bleak picture painted by researchers, interracial romantic relationships are quite natural and very similar to same-race romantic relationships. As we have explored a traditionally taboo interpersonal relationship, we have found that most cross-race relationships are not a manifestation of one or both partners exploring stereotypical myths associated with other racial/ethnic groups. Conversely, these relationships are the result of personal choices that are influenced by a desire for a committed, loving relationship.

Whether it is society, family, friends, or our own fears of cultural difference, partners in interracial relationships experience pressures that do not surface in same-race relationships (Kalmijn, 1998). Both partners must determine the degree to which they will allow these external forces to impede the development and maintenance of their romantic relationship. People often have little hope that interracial relationships can withstand these pressures; however, research indicates that they can survive as long as the partners are committed to doing so. The partners must first engage in *racial awareness*, which challenges them to face the harsh reality of racism and its potential effect on the relationship and the psychosocial health of both relational partners. As they remain committed to the relationship, the partners must also negotiate between themselves and as individuals within the relationship how they will *cope* with external pressures of the relationship. Will they allow their differences to overshadow their commitment to each other? Or will they appreciate and value their difference and work to have a relationship that is beneficial for both of them? From there, the partners are able to experience *identity emergence* where they define who they are as a relational unit independent of what others may say about them. Finally, they must be aware of and actually engage in *(ongoing) relationship maintenance*.

As history and personal experiences tell us, racism is an inherent part of U.S. history. Therefore, interracial romantic partners are not immune to the racist, prejudiced, or discriminatory behaviors and attitudes of others. In order to preserve and nurture the relationship, both parties must be committed to fostering a communication pattern that meets the needs of each individual partner.

After reading this chapter, we hope you have come to think more positively about interracial romantic relationships. Much like same race partners, interracial partners enter relationships out of a basic human need for emotional intimacy with another person. They desire a relationship with someone who has life goals, attitudes, beliefs, and values similar to their own. So the next time you see an interracial couple and you think to yourself, "Why are *they* together?" ask yourself if you would ask the same question of a same-race couple. The answer goes beyond the physical differences that seem to separate the partners from each other. We must rethink our own and others' perceptions of the cross-race mate selection process. With the increasing racial diversity we are experiencing in the United States, we should avoid asking the "whys" and understand the "why nots" of interracial romantic relationships.

OPPORTUNITIES FOR EXTENDED LEARNING

1. Using your *InfoTrac College Edition,* do a search on resources related to "interracial dating/marriage." What are current issues surrounding this topic? Does race continue to matter in the dating experience? Who seems to place race in the center of interpersonal relationships? How would you apply what you have learned in this chapter to addressing the issue of interracial dating with your future children? Did your parents discuss this with you? Why or why not?

2. In class, view one of the two films *Zebrahead* or *Jungle Fever* (on interracial romantic relationships in class). Divide the class into groups. Each group member should write down observable nonverbal and verbal behaviors of characters that communicate negative and positive attitudes and feelings toward interracial romantic relationships. In a separate class period, groups will compare and share observations as discussions center around the film's (in)ability to reflect "real" attitudes and feelings toward these relationships.

3. Read the article *Interracial Communication: Is It Possible?* by Leonard and Locke (1993). What role does history play in constructing these negative portrayals of African Americans? European Americans? Do you think interracial communication is possible? Take an informal poll and find out how many of your friends and/or classmates have friends from different racial groups. Why or why not? Is there some truth to those stereotypes? What role does communication play in perpetuating these stereotypes?

4. Using blank index cards, write down actual verbal comments you have observed others (or yourself) make regarding their opinions about interracial romantic relationships. After collecting the cards, your instructor will share the anonymous comments with the class in an effort to understand (on a small scale) current attitudes toward the topic.

5. Each group is to examine the following racial compositions and provide pros and cons for being involved in such relationships. Assign a different sex to each racial partner to determine if gender influences the pros and cons in any way. After reviewing the list, discuss the roles that family and society play in our perceptions of these relationships. Why are some relationships more (or less)

socially acceptable or problematic than others? What role does communication play in constructing these attitudes toward interracial romantic relationships?

1. European American male/Asian American female
2. Asian Americans/African Americans
3. European Americans/African Americans
4. Native Americans/African Americans
5. Latina/African American male
6. European American/Native American
7. Latinos/European Americans

6. Using the *InfoTrac College Edition,* type in the keywords *interracial* (or *multiracial) families* or close derivations of it. As you filter through the data, search for organizations or social support groups designed to meet the various needs of the interracial family. Create a list of resources that are reported as effective in providing interracial families with the support needed to withstand social forces that work against their relationships.

INTERRACIAL COMMUNICATION IN THE CONTEXT OF ORGANIZATIONS

Thus far, we have investigated interracial relationships, which involves partners actively choosing to become emotionally intimate with someone who is racially/ethnically different. But now we must consider what happens when an organization or company becomes diverse and is no longer monoracial. The organization eventually must be restructured in order to adapt to the racial/ethnic diversity that is bound to occur. Because many people have had limited interracial interactions (and contact), we must all become sensitive to how our behaviors positively and negatively impact our interracial communication. By becoming more aware of how (1) an organization functions and (2) adapts to change in its environment, we can work toward improving how we interact and communicate with people who are racially/ethnically diverse.

This chapter is a brief overview of organizational communication. More specifically, we examine what happens when we are given opportunities to develop positive interracial relationships within an organizational context. In particular, we direct our attention to how interracial interactions and relationships are managed within organizations. In order to understand the importance of interracial communication in our organizations, we explore organizational theory, organizational communication, organizational culture, and organizational context. As you are reading this chapter, we challenge you to think critically about the direction our organizations are taking in the 21st century. Instead of divorcing ourselves from the reality of racism, we must now commit to making a difference in the way we interact with co-workers and others from racial/ethnic groups other than our own.

No matter where we are in our lives, we are bound to belong to several groups or organizations. You may not be aware of this, but you are already a member of several organizations: fraternity/sorority, Residence Hall Association, student government, the pep club, the volleyball team, and so on. Even through your job as a pizza delivery person, sales clerk, or math tutor, you belong to an organization. In any event, you are working with people who are different from you in an effort to achieve a common goal. Have you been employed somewhere or been part of an organization where you were the only person, or one of a few people, from your racial/ethnic group? How did you feel? Did the others in your group help you fit in, or did you experience feelings of isolation? For many people, the feeling of isolation is a part of their organizational reality. For whatever reason we are rejected, the group experience becomes more difficult when people fail to include us in the group experience.

Those days of being excluded should be in the past; however, human beings continue to develop more sophisticated ways to discriminate against and exclude people. Race/ethnicity, gender, sexual orientation, social status, and other demarcations are examples of characteristics we use to justify treating someone unfairly. You may be thinking to yourself that this really does not include you because you treat everyone as you would like to be treated. But what happens when you begin the job of your dreams and find out your company treats its employees and customers differently based on skin color? As an organizational member, you feel like a part of the team. However, you do not understand how employees can treat your co-worker, a Native American female, so badly. If you are empathic to and understanding of your co-worker's feelings, ask yourself questions that she may face: "Will my racial/ethnic identity impact my performance or commitment to the organization?" "Has my high school or college adequately prepared me to deal with the lack of racial/ethnic diversity in the workplace?" "Will I have to continue to work twice as hard as my peers in order to be perceived as equally qualified for my position?" "Will my colleagues think I am the result of affirmative action?" These are a few real questions that racial/ethnic group members face in the workplace. As you progress through the chapter, try to extend your thinking about what an organization is and how racial/ethnic identities influence the organizational culture. This chapter presents ways to consider how our interracial interactions in the workplace can improve race relations and promote a larger organizational agenda in a healthy, productive manner.

ORGANIZATIONAL COMMUNICATION

Think back to different organizations of which you were (or are) a member. Did you have a sense of pride in being associated with the organization? Did you feel you were a central part of its purpose? In some form or fashion, we have all been a part of an organizational culture. Whether it is being a part of a Greek fraternity or sorority, IBM's human resource group, or the volunteer program at the YMCA, membership is crucial for organizational success. Commitment from each member is vital, but it is even more important to understand *what* and *why* a culture is before we explore the benefits of organizational membership and participation.

At some point in our lives, we have joined an organization with a preconceived idea of what our involvement would entail. It was not until we became actively involved that we realized the organization was not all we dreamed it would be (or possibly more than we imagined). Whether the experience is positive or negative, an interesting dynamic operates within the organization. It is our individual choice that drives our decision to become a part of an organization. However, membership constitutes some level of people trading their individuality for group conformity.

Scholars provide a number of definitions for what constitutes organizational communication. Organizational communication is an interdisciplinary area of interest (Miller, 1999; Reardon, 1996) and has its foundations in management. Organizational communication involves "exchanging messages to stimulate meaning within and between organizations and their environments" (Infante, Rancer, & Womack, 1990). Miller (1999) has identified seven concepts associated with the terms *organization* and *communication* that provide a basic understanding of organizational communication. An organization can be described as a (1) *social collectivity* (a group of people) (2) where *coordinated activities* (3) achieve both *individual and collective goals*. These activities provide a (4) *structure* that enables organizational members to deal effectively with each other (5) within the larger *organizational environment*. In terms of communication, it is a *process* that is (6) *transactional* (which involves two or more people interacting within that environment) and (7) *symbolic* (communication transactions represent or stand for other things on some level of abstraction) (Miller, 1999). As these facets demonstrate, a great deal of negotiation takes place on the part of individuals as they become part of an organization. In order to maximize our organizational experiences, we must consider how our organizational, individual, and racial/ethnic identities are affected by our membership in that organizational culture.

Let's use a fictional company to understand how these concepts facilitate our understanding of organizational communication. You are working for a small clinical trials company that has approximately 30 employees (social collectivity) who have weekly meetings (coordinated activities) to update everyone about the progress made on various medical projects (collective goals). Each member has prior medical experience and is very much interested in their organizational roles and how society benefits from these tests (individual goals). Being aware of their roles and the organizational goals allows members to acknowledge the chain of command (structure) and how this hierarchy functions. In essence, this knowledge allows the members to see the big picture of what the organization is all about (organizational environment). In order to maintain this organizational culture, the members exchange ideas and thoughts (transactional process) that relate specifically to the organization and its goals (symbolic).

An organizational member must think about the degree to which her individual identity will be influenced by the organization. For example, have you ever had a good friend change after she joined a social group? Maybe she only wanted to hang around with her new friends and found very little time for her old friends. Or, in the case of a job, a person must determine the extent to which she will allow her life as a salesperson to consume her personal life. In any event, she must learn how to balance her organizational and individual identities in order to have success within the organization and a healthy psyche. The same is also the case for racial/ethnic identity. Just as the young woman must negotiate her identities, so must an organizational member who comes from an underrepresented racial/ethnic group.

Some organizational members, may feel their racial/ethnic identities become less important as they climb the ladder of success. Let's assume an Asian American woman has become quite successful in telecommunications. Prior to her entry into the business world, Mae was committed to understanding and learning about her race/ethnicity. She attended cultural events, learned Japanese, and valued family. As she navigated her way from sales to management, Mae attempted to maintain a sense of who she was and where she came from. Unfortunately, as she began to rise in the company, her time turned from learning about her roots to learning how to advance in her career. Eventually, her family observed this change and questioned Mae's lack of commitment to her race/ethnicity. Not only did she begin to spend much of her time attending gala corporate functions, Mae began to purposely date European American men she thought would fit into her "new world." This transformation is referred to as assimilation, which involves a slow progression from one's own race/ethnicity to that of the majority group (Frankenberg, 1993). During this process, a person may begin to devalue personal racial/ethnic group membership as he or she strives to become a part of mainstream society.

UNDERSTANDING ORGANIZATIONAL THEORIES

Organizational communication is very different from interpersonal communication in its origin and intent. Most organizational scholars agree that analysis of the relationship between communication and organizational activities originated with Max Weber (1947), Henry Fayol (1916), and Frederick Taylor (1911). With the passage of time, however, theorists began to acknowledge the importance of human relations occurring in the workplace. Before we address this very important change in the critical thinking processes of scholars in this area of research, we briefly discuss several theories that illustrate the significance of human (and race) relations within the organizational context.

In the late 1800s to early 1900s, Taylor, Weber, and Fayol developed theories that investigated the relationship between organizational culture and productivity. Classical management theory includes three subtheories that reflect the divergent principles of each theorist: scientific management theory, administrative management theory, and bureaucracy (Byers, 1997). *Scientific management theory* originated with Taylor, who placed great significance on how work was accomplished. After observing workers who were shoveling iron ore in a steel mill, Taylor deduced that a prescriptive approach to the workplace is the best method for achieving the task, which in turn maximizes efficiency. Six principles guide this organizational theory:

1. There is "one best way" to perform a task or job.
2. Employees should be scientifically selected and improved (based on skills and expertise to increase productivity).
3. Workers are monetarily motivated.
4. Management plans the work and laborers follow through with the plan (cooperation vs. individuality).
5. Clearly defined rules, regulations, and roles (creates harmony within the organization).
6. Loafing should be eliminated. (Taylor, 1911)

Taylor's theory places great importance on cooperation on the part of organizational members. According to this theory, communication between worker and employer enables the employer to direct and control the worker's behaviors, thus facilitating work standardization and planning.

In 1916, Fayol created the *administrative management theory*, which "discusses the organizational hierarchy and the flow of communication within that hierarchy" (Byers, 1997). In essence, strict chains of communication among organizational members were an essential part of the organization. The style of communication within this theory is vertical in nature. If peers wanted to communicate with each other, they had to receive permission from their supervisors. Principles under the administrative management theory were somewhat similar to scientific management theory, but differed in several ways: (1) managers should use control, (2) subordinates should yield to superiors' authority to control, (3) centralization of power with administration, and (4) employee tenure is more likely when employees do their job correctly and accomplish assigned tasks (see Fayol, 1916). Although space limits our discussion of all 20 principles involved in the theory, the overarching theme is that horizontal communication (between peers) is very limited, thus doing very little to further the role of communication within organizations (Byers, 1997).

The final theory that falls under the umbrella of classical management theory is Weber's *bureaucracy theory*. Organization described as bureaucratic are viewed as very formal, inflexible, and insensitive to the needs of its workers (Weber, 1947). Eight qualities define a bureaucratic organization:

1. Formalized rules, regulations, and procedures achieve organizational tasks.
2. Role specialization simplifies workers' activities.
3. Formal hierarchy helps direct employees' interpersonal relationships toward the goal of the organizations (e.g., title, expertise).
4. Technical competence and an ability to perform his or her task is the sole basis on which an individual should be hired and maintained.
5. Organizational tasks are more important than the individuals performing them.
6. Interpersonal relationships should remain impersonal and professional in order to accomplish organizational goals.
7. Clearly defined job descriptions provide all members of the organization with a formal outline of their duties and job responsibilities.
8. Organizations should have logical, clear cut, and predictable rules and regulations to help promote order and to facilitate accomplishing organizational goals.

Byers (1997) notes that this approach to organizational communication is self-defeating. Organizations adhering to a bureaucratic approach (e.g., government, large organizations, and universities) may potentially develop a plethora of rules, regulations, policies, and procedures that stifle its growth and progress.

Overall, the classical management perspective advocates of standardization, wherein there is a "formal and rational flow of tasks and communication, structure, and social control" (Byers, 1997, p. 24). In other words, if the organization is to

THEORY INTO PRACTICE

In 1998, the President's Initiative on Race developed some criteria that were important in creating effective race relations programs and organizations (see Smith & Ahuja, 1999). If you are currently in, or thinking about creating, an organized effort to promote more effective interracial communication, ask yourself the following questions:

- Do the participants reflect the full racial/ethnic diversity of the community? If not, how can the group become more inclusive to others who are un()represented?
- Do programs encourage participants to examine conscious and unconscious attitudes about race?
- Do your efforts explicitly educate others about the importance of historical and contemporary facts regarding race, racism, and culture?
- Are opportunities for peer-to-peer collaboration created and encouraged?
- What is done to make those institutional leaders (outside the group) aware and/or supportive of your goals?
- Are unique perspectives of different groups—racial/ethnic, gender, spiritual, age, sexual orientation, and so on—also taken into account?
- Do efforts move beyond awareness raising to specific action plans that address systemic change?
- How are your efforts, both at the micro and macro level, evaluated?
- How does your organization/program adapt to the dynamic needs of the communities it is a part of?

succeed and fulfill its goals, there must be some sense of structure regarding how members communicate and how those in positions of power maintain control. Additionally, the worker is perceived as being only interested in making money, and communication is used by workers only as a means for achieving organizational goals.

In order to resolve this disregard for individual needs, organizations must become more focused on their employees' individual and social relationships, which are becoming more paramount to organizational communication research (Byers, 1997). Instead of perceiving the human experience as external to the organization, organization members and theorists alike have come to see all members as humans in need of positive interpersonal communication in the workplace. This change was introduced to preserve some classical features of organizations while providing individuals with the tools necessary for managing relationships that exist within systems based on hierarchy and authority. After conducting test after test on human relations and the workplace, researchers learned that worker productivity was positively related to additional attention from others. Reportedly, this attention made the workers feel valued and important.

Further theorizing has advanced *human relations theory* and its goal of improving all interpersonal—including interracial—relationships among employees in the workplace. Four activities can be applied specifically to positive interracial communication. *Management development activities* involve management serving as role models for employees and being committed to human relations beliefs. *Employee relations activities* are coordinated to provide employees with the information that promotes job satisfaction, motivation, and interracial cooperation. *Labor relations activities* attempt to meet the needs of labor and management while also maintaining effective two-way communication between them. The final activity involves *public or community relations*, where employees enter an organization with preexisting attitudes. As a result, it is important that the organization acknowledge the influence of an individual's environment on her job-related behaviors.

The human relations theory best lends itself to our understanding of organizational communication by taking into consideration the multiple identities of its organizational members (see Chapter 5). Although the organizational goals remain a priority, people in positions of authority are sensitized to the identities shaped by race, gender, class, occupational, and other lived experiences. This becomes even more important when we consider the importance of interracial communication within the context of organizations.

ORGANIZATIONAL CULTURE

Because our nation is becoming increasingly diverse, we must begin to think critically about how both our personal and professional relationships can benefit from such change. It is even more important that we ask ourselves questions that force us to reexamine how we think about racial/ethnic diversity and its effect on our private and public lives. In order to engage you in this thinking exercise, consider the following questions:

"What happens when interracial relationships evolve as a result of membership in an organization?"
"What can we learn from each other?"
"Will there be a difference in our communication styles across race?"

"What positive or negative effect can this relationship have on the organization?"
"How will the organization be affected if these relationships are not formed?"

These questions are ones we should be thinking about as we enter the new millennium. In our private lives, we can choose whether or not to engage in interracial relationships. In the case of our public lives (organizations), we establish relationships based on the innate needs of the organization, not the people. Because organizational members are assembled to fulfill that need (e.g., submitting a business proposal, working in small groups, doing a class project), the forced interaction inevitably fosters interpersonal relationships. Choice is not an option; therefore, individuals are *expected* to develop positive working relationships with each other. When this expectation is met with resistance, however, it affects the overall dynamic and goals of the organization.

When people come together to either create a new or become part of an existing organization, very little consideration is given to establishing a solid foundation on which to build organizational goals. Before members determine what the organization will do, they must first conceptualize what an organizational culture is. Schein (1985) provides the following definition. An organizational culture involves "a pattern of basic assumptions—invented, discovered, or developed by a given group as it learns to cope with its problems of external adaptation and internal integration—that has worked well enough to be considered valid and, therefore, to be taught to new members as the correct way to perceive, think, and feel in relation to those problems" (p. 9).

External adaptation has to do with the influence of the environment on the goals of the organization, whereas the internal integration has to do with changes made within the organization. Members are adapting their ways of thinking and behaving to those that closely resemble those of the organization. In essence, the culture reflects or represents the values, beliefs, and expectations shared by its members (Lahiry, 1994). As an extension, members are pressured to conform to shared codes and their behaviors are shaped by the culture.

Let's use as an example a Fortune 500 company. As a new employee, you are very excited about being a part of this elite organizational culture. This is your first real job and you do not want to receive a poor evaluation from your boss. You receive your handbook on policy and procedure but are still unclear about how you should complete certain tasks (e.g., requesting copies, submitting a brief, coordinating client appointments). In order to socialize you appropriately into the organization, an employee who has gone through the ranks and is held in high esteem by senior members volunteers to mentor you. Through this person's guidance, you have learned the appropriate office etiquette, protocol for conducting departmental meetings, and what your role is as junior sales representative.

Although there is no handbook informing you of appropriate and inappropriate behaviors, members have engaged in a transactional communication process that allows them to share with you what the organizational culture is like and what normative behaviors are expected of its members.

This example is an ideal one, and we would hope that would be every employee's experience. However, what happens when a person's assumptions based on race/ethnicity are in conflict with those of the organization? Literature exploring this tension acknowledges that racial/ethnic group members are sometimes conflicted when these identities are competing. Extending the previous example further, assume that you are the only European American male in the company and

---

9.1   *Personal Reflection*

Because of our *social locations* (e.g., race, class, gender, professional status), my African American friends and I are constantly faced with "isms" that our European American colleagues rarely (if ever) face. These experiences, or *defining moments*, with racism and sexism help develop our inner strength to face adversities in spite of our circumstances. Prejudiced and racist thinking is more frequently evidenced in the perpetrators' nonverbal behaviors. (Is that some subconscious way to veil their hidden racism?)

A friend of mine in a senior position at a clinical research company frequently has defining moments on her job. One in particular involved a doctor's blatant disregard for her authority and presence when she made a request of him. Although he never verbally communicated that he did not want to assist her, his nonverbal behaviors sent this message very clearly. A very condescending tone, glaring stare, and physical distance let her know her presence was not appreciated. After pulling rank and informing him who she was, the doctor begrudgingly honored her request. Although no racist comments were made, Ann's sixth sense told her it was racism. She could sense he had a problem taking directions from an African American woman.

The doctor's blatant disregard and disrespect for Ann was only one of many instances where co-workers have further marginalized her. She, many of my friends, and I have used these opportunities to educate ourselves and others about the reality of racism. Many times, racism is difficult to prove, but it is something that you immediately just know. It may be communicated through a person's glance, tone of voce, or the fact that they are ignoring your presence. These actions are hurtful, and they can potentially cause someone

> ***Personal Reflection*** (*continued*)
>
> to mistrust all outgroup members, but is that *really* what we want? How is interracial communication going to improve if we separate ourselves, verbally attack each other, or ignore the problem altogether?
>
> Although this is one example of institutional racism, racist incidents like these occur daily. Race relations training can counter these negative attitudes for some individuals, but we must also engage in direct communication that specifically addresses racist behaviors. When a co-worker offends us or other racial/ethnic groups (this includes European Americans), we must use careful judgment when we educate them about their behavior. So, the question we ask here is, "What would *you* do?" Because race is often treated as a communication barrier for many people in the workplace and other social contexts, we (microcultural members) have to pick and choose our battles. You can either address the situation now or later, in the group or one on one, or in a very assertive, nonattacking manner. After all, if *you/we* don't take a stand, then who will?—TMH

no one lends you a helping hand. Instead, you have to learn the organizational culture through trial and error. Organizational communication literature indicates that organizations are responding to this form of institutional racism by creating environments more sensitive to how identity issues in the workplace are addressed. Ultimately, this sensitivity benefits racial/ethnic individuals as well as other employees not directly affected by this internal conflict. (We must note that society as a whole and most organizational cultures are responsible for this tension.)

RACIALIZING THE ORGANIZATIONAL CONTEXT

In Chapter 5, we discussed how important it is to be aware of the multiple self- and other identities embedded in our societal structure. Race is fluid and multiple in its production of meaning within an individual (Smalls, 1998). In other words, our racial/ethnic identities become more or less salient as we go from one social context to another.

As a nation, we have traditionally thought about race within the context of our personal relationships without giving much thought to organizations. Recently, efforts have been made to sensitize corporate America, community-based organizations, and the business world to the significance of race. In essence, these efforts are made to consider the degree to which the *organizational context* influences the organizational communication. In general, communication within an organization can be complex because of the differing work habits of the employees and management. Therefore, we must pay close attention to the importance of context in managing organizational culture and identity (see Weick, 1979). Three contexts inform us of how we communicate with each other and adapt to the culture.

The *physical context* refers to the physical environment where the communication takes place (e.g., boss's office, employee lounge). *Social context* refers to the type of relationship that exists between the communicators, and *chronological context* refers to the role of time in influencing the interaction (e.g., morning versus afternoon meetings). Through our orientation to the organizational culture, we understand the rules that guide our behaviors across these contexts. For example, if a meeting of all staff is called, you know it will be in the conference room (physical context) at 7:30 a.m. (chronological context) and very formal in nature (social context). In contrast, if you are meeting with your co-worker, you may choose to have a casual (yet productive) meeting at a restaurant over lunch. In both cases, the culture and process of communication determine the appropriate behaviors.

Historically, these are some of the general concerns many monoracial organizations have been faced with. Now they must consider how these contexts will be influenced by racial/ethnic diversity. As we have noted, the U.S. population is becoming increasingly racially diverse, which will affect our relationships both in our private and public lives (see Chapter 1). In our public lives, our relationships within organizations will experience a change that some may find difficult to cope with. Individuals who have only dealt with status, power, and interpersonal differences are now faced with the impact of racial/ethnic differences on their professional relationships. In the past, they may have only worked with people who looked just like them. Now they are challenged to work alongside racial group members with whom they have had limited interactions. In any event, a degree of uncertainty is experienced as the face of the organization continues to change.

Some people were solely concerned with power and status differentials but they are now faced with racial/ethnic difference and its impact on the organizational experience. Organization members must now consider how the organization will accommodate itself and its members to the impending racial/ethnic diversity. As these issues are considered, we must remember to value racial/ethnic difference as we work toward achieving our goals. Yes, it is imperative that organizations celebrate their newfound diversity; however, it becomes even more important that they not lose sight of their own short-term and long-term goals. If organizational members are perceived and treated as having only one identity (racial/ethnic), then they are devalued as organizational citizens. For example, Mae (the telecommunications manager) is perceived by another supervisor as "the Asian" manager, which negates the fact that she is a good manager who happens to be Asian American. As a result, she feels she is not being valued for her contributions to the organization (e.g., tokenism). According to this line of thinking, organizational members of color are totalized (see Houston & Wood, 1996), thus trivializing the importance of racial/ethnic diversity in corporate America. Racial/ethnic diversity can bring new, rich ideas to an organization that has traditionally been unidimensional. Therefore, the organization and its members should not become so consumed by race that their mission and purpose fall by the wayside. Yes, it is important to acknowledge and celebrate racial/ethnic diversity. But organizations must be sure their goals and attempts to diversify the organizational body work together to improve their mission. In the following section we discuss the influence of race/ethnicity on profit and nonprofit organizations.

GENERAL ORGANIZATIONAL PRINCIPLES

Alexander (1998) applauded President Clinton for creating an organization committed to addressing the nation's state of race relations; however, he contends that the focus should be on "what pulls us together instead of what pulls us apart" (p. 1). He further states that the common set of principles (e.g., equal opportunity, individual rights, self-government) traditionally used in the United States to address social inequalities should be central to the race initiative many people have come to support. Yes, there must be some acknowledgment and discussion about "why we are the way we are" as a nation. If we fail to understand what the problem is and how to resolve it, then we will continue to have racist, sexist, and prejudiced ideologies permeating the very core of the nation's thought processes. Therefore, we must discuss how each sector of the American public is dealing with racial diversity and race relations within that specific context. This self-reflexive approach to race consciousness and organizational communication can only lead to increased knowledge and understanding of the degree to which our racial identities influence race relations on a micro and macro level.

In every facet of American society, we will in one way or another experience the increasing racial/ethnic diversity that is projected to take place in the 21st century (see Kim, 1995; Chapter 1). Corporations and communities alike are now being forced to examine what image they are going to project to society as a whole (Etzioni, 1996). Traditionally, we have all been expected to conform to the melting pot metaphor where racial/ethnic differences are removed from this collective identity. This ultimately creates a blended identity with no distinctions between, or acknowledgments of, racial/ethnic diversity. Rejecting this assimilationist approach to diversity, others have chosen the rainbow metaphor that acknowledges various people of different colors and the significance of working/living next to one another.

9.2   *Case Study: Celebrating Diversity Festival*

You've been selected by the university to be on the advertising committee for its annual "Celebrating Diversity" festival this year. Traditionally, previous festivals have had low attendance and the quality of the program events has been subpar. University officials have informed the committee that concerted efforts must be made to include more racially/ethnically diverse groups in the festivities. Unfortunately, these university and community-based groups have voiced disinterest in being involved in such a program. They reportedly feel that after the festival is over, all appreciation for racial/ethnic diversity will be lost until the following year. As a committee, think of how you would fulfill your duties.

According to Byers (1997), there are seven steps to be followed for achieving group and organizational goals:

1. Define the *problem*.
2. Determine *goals and objectives* (for advertising).
3. Analyze *target audience*.
4. Determine media to be used to reach audience.
5. *Create a message plan* (theme, slogan, keywords, and visuals).
6. Determine your *budget* (costs and extra revenue generated).
7. *Devise evaluation measures* to assess success of the plan (advertising).

In a racialized organizational context, these steps are critical to those organizations purposely making efforts to include their members from a variety of racial/ethnic backgrounds. As the steps demonstrate, the committee members must actively work toward including people who have too often been excluded from the decision-making processes that occur within organizations. As you think about your present and future involvement in organization, consider how racial/ethnic identity can positively influence the group experience. By exchanging ideas and thoughts about how to fulfill their goals, organizations and their members can establish an inclusive culture that values and appreciates racial/ethnic differences.

Etzioni (1996) offers the framed mosaic as a metaphor that best captures the tensions underlying race/ethnic relations in the 20th (and 21st) century. Instead of compartmentalizing difference, he proposes the mosaic as a mental illustration of the collective mission that should drive Western society. The mosaic empowers individuals from various racial/ethnic groups to embrace their identities as they work, play, and live in the larger, dominant society. Instead of assimilating to mainstream ideologies, these groups are able to negotiate through both sites without compromising their collective, individual, and multiple identities. Although this frame of thought is justifiable and logical, it oftentimes is not the case, particularly when we consider organizational sites where the demographic makeup has traditionally been predominately European American (Chapa, 1998).

In Chapter 5, we discussed how our multiple identities cannot be divorced from each other. Instead they work together collectively to create a unique set of lived experiences. In terms of race/ethnicity, it is an unchangeable quality (which is a good thing!) that is "fluid and multiple in its production of the individual as a site of meaning" (Smalls, 1998). In other words, a person's racial/ethnic identity has multiple meanings, depending on the context where this meaning is being negotiated. For example, your racial/ethnic identity may become more salient for you at work where you are in the minority as opposed to your home. Therefore, the context will influence how important your racial/ethnic identity is for you and/or others with whom you interact.

Karl Weick's (1979) research on sense making provides an appropriate framework for understanding the significance of racial/ethnic diversity in organizations. Weick suggests that in order for organizations to function effectively, they must reduce the amount of equivocality or ambiguity in the types of interpretations and meanings that take place within organizations. As a process, this allows organizational goal(s) to be met through effective communication among its members. Organizational members, first, create enacted environments (*enactment*) where members put forth "efforts to make sense of their activities, experiences, and environments and reduce or clarify the various possible meanings that surround them" (Seeger, 1997, p. 28). After the environment is established, members select (*selection*) what interpretations are most appropriate for explaining what the environment means. From there, members choose those interpretations that prove most effective (*retention*) in the sense-making process. Throughout this entire process, organization members are attempting to understand the big picture of what the organization is about and how they fit in. This understanding is established through continued communication among, between, and by organization members.

Weick's approach to sense making provides a foundation for understanding how organization members can adapt to change in the environment. For example, prior to hiring several Native American and Asian American employees, an advertising company was in the habit of targeting predominantly European American clients. With this diversity, organization members are now challenged to rethink many of their marketing strategies. Although the company has not traditionally marketed products to racially/ethnically diverse consumers, the new employees are presenting them with new ways and ideas of how their audience base can be expanded. After a few trials and errors, the organization has finally created an advertising template that achieves its for-profit function as well as creating an inclusive environment for its employees of color. What is most important, however, is that the organization is willing to adapt to the environmental changes occurring within and outside of the organizational context.

For-Profit Organizations

In corporate America, individuals take different approaches in attempting to understand this phenomenon. From the standpoint of traditional researchers and consultants, the goal is to observe the organizational culture "objectively" and describe the communicative exchanges between and among members. In some cases, these observations lend themselves to providing prescriptions to the organization for how they can improve the cultural climate and communicative processes. In contrast, we have organizational members, as well as critical/cultural researchers, who subjectively experience the culture and, as a result, are biased to "outsiders'" attempts to redefine or renegotiate their organizational identity. As Hawkins (1997) describes this tension, he recognizes the need for these outsiders to have access to a variety of cultural change styles and approaches that are best suited for the needs of a specific culture and its needs in the midst of change. If an organization's membership has been historically composed of primarily one racial group and is attempting to diversify itself, it is very likely that members will experience resistance and/or apprehension to this change (Van Buren, 1997). In any case, the fact remains that the organizational members must work together in order to (1) achieve its goal of change (2) without compromising the goals of the organization as they relate to productivity, morale, and teamwork. For most organizations, this involves advocating productive interracial work relationships.

A wall of resistance unnecessarily complicates this process of change. This may be attributed, in general, to uncertainty about interracial communication and, specifically, the accommodating that the organizational culture, existing members, and new members must do in order to prepare for greater diversity. Despite this discomfort, there is hope that corporate America can effectively manage its racial/ethnic diversity while maintaining individual organizational identities. The Joint Center for Political and Economic Studies (Branch, 1998) explored the progress currently being made in the workplace and found that African American professionals are guardedly optimistic about their careers. (This nationwide poll allowed professionals to share their attitudes about career prospects in predominately European American corporations.) Despite this contradictory thinking, these professionals feel that these organizations deserve credit for the recruiting, training, and promotion of African Americans by its organizational members (Branch, 1998, p. 140).

The multiple identities of professionals from racial/ethnic backgrounds who are a part of corporate America involve dealing with feelings of being alienated and isolated in the workplace. A majority of those polled (78%) believe African American executives are "tokens" who are in those positions for "appearance's sake," which ultimately limit their opportunities for career advancement (Branch, 1998). As an extension, 60% of those professionals feel senior executives in these same corporations do not think African American employees have the management potential of their European American cohorts. One participant shared the following sentiment: "There's this unfair assessment that blacks are less qualified, no matter what they bring to the table" (p. 1). A major contributing factor to this false notion that microcultural groups, recruited by predominately European American organizations, are unqualified is the continuous debate over affirmative action (see Zinsmeister, 1998). Affirmative action was initiated in an attempt to diversify institutions that traditionally prevent women and people of color from gaining entry. Many people counter this line of thinking by asserting that this political strategy is only a means to reach a "quota" occupied by individuals who do not have the skills, intellect, and/or ability to meet the requirements of that specific position (Kim, 1998). In reality, however, employers, educators, and other members of our political institutions were given a charge to diversify as well as train those individuals for the task at hand.

As we examine the saliency of race within corporate America, we must discuss how European American males are dealing with racial/ethnic diversity. Can you imagine what it is like to be qualified for job and have someone who is part of a historically disadvantaged racial/ethnic group be hired for the position instead of you? Although you are in support of diversity, you are also concerned with how this is displacing others who are equally qualified for the same positions. According to Gates (1993), European American males account for the following percentages of various sectors of our public sites: 39.2% of the population, 82.5% of the Forbes 400 (people worth $265 million+), 77% of Congress, 92% of state governors, 70% of tenured college faculty, approximately 90% of daily newspaper editors, and 77% of TV news directors (p. 49). Therefore, we can see why racial/ethnic diversity is often perceived as a threat to European American males' positions of power in the United States. Galen (1994) describes this emotional-laden issue as follows:

> But in such companies as AT&T, DuPont, and Motorola, where diversity is becoming more than a buzzword, the emotional landscape for white males is changing. There, white men must compete against people they may not have taken seriously as rivals—mainly women, blacks, Hispanics, and Asians. White males may also say that the diversity programs often make them feel threatened or attacked. (p. 51)

European American males are being forced to deal with this sobering new reality (Galen, 1994) because of the restructuring taking place in corporate America. This phenomenon is commonly referred to as "white male backlash" or reverse discrimination (Rowan, 1995). The issue taken to task is merit, or who is best qualified for the job, which becomes even more problematic when you have candidates who are of similar merit. Reverse discrimination is cited as the reason for the European American male not being hired, when in actuality this move is an effort to remedy (by law) past discriminations in the workplace (Galen, 1994).

The company and those individuals in positions of authority are faced with a moral dilemma. They are expected to diversify the work force while they are being blamed for past discriminations. One strategy that two companies have used to resolve this tension is to hire consultants to conduct seminars on how European American males can deal with their changing status in corporate America (Galen, 1994). A support group is coordinated to address the various emotions these men feel that stem from diversification and the perceived threat of job loss. More importantly, when discrimination occurs in an attempt to "preserve" the traditional culture, the tensions in the organization only become more pronounced. In general, there appears to be a need to reassure European American males about their place and role within the organization. Although there is not one solution to this problem, we must engage in open, honest discussion about the communication climates in organizations and how racial/ethnic diversity is going to affect each individual member and the organization as a whole.

The experiences of people of color in corporate America are similar to, yet different from, those of African Americans. They must deal with the corporate discrimination (e.g., glass ceiling) (Van Buren, 1997) that prevents them from assuming senior positions and with low expectations of employers and colleagues about their ability to succeed and excel within the organization. Despite these occupational and ideological roadblocks, African American professionals remain somewhat optimistic. James Sampson (Branch, 1998), who runs a recruitment firm in Oakland, California, believes that both companies (organizations) and employees are mutually responsible for making the organizational culture a racially sensitive yet productive institution. He suggests that this can be accomplished by strategically planning one's career path. By taking the initiative and "align[ing] themselves with key players in a company" (Branch, 1998, p. 143), individuals are taking advantage of opportunities to which they would otherwise not be privy.

Some members of the Latino community have found at least one solution to this organizational problem by starting a minority-owned recruitment firm (Chapa, 1998). After observing the difficulties other large recruiting firms had locating qualified Hispanics to work for their large corporations, Heddy Pena and Lisa Torres created Pena, Torres, and Associates. (In order to respect the writing style of this

---

9.3   *Case Study*

In the 21st century, it is very likely that you will be interacting with racially/ethnically different others. To be prepared for interracial and interethnic interactions, Brilhart and Galanes (1995) suggest that we use behaviors that facilitate effective interracial communication. Although these behaviors are specific to intercultural communication, they are appropriate for interracial interactions. Because our racial/ethnic identities are central to how we define ourselves, we must be sensitive to how they influence our communicative experiences.

According to their observations (Brilhart & Galances, 1995), effective interracial communication is possible if we (1) *acknowledge* that every discussion is intercultural (racial/ethnic differences are present); (2) *recognize and accept* our differences (affirmation of each other); (3) *understand* that behaviors may be attributed to culture, (4) *engage in* open dialogue about observed differences, and (5) *be willing* to adapt to difference. These suggestions are very appropriate because they challenge you to leave your comfort zone. More importantly, you are challenged to think about how you *really* interact with racially/ethnically different others. Remember, someone may be thinking about you in the same way and may be unsure how to interact with you. Communication is an interaction that involves what we say as well as who we are.

---

author, we are using *Hispanic* and *Latino* as she has referred to them in her text.) These women created their own firm in an attempt to bridge the gap between the Latino community and corporate America. Pena and Torres suggest that Hispanics take the initiative and (1) pursue sales (the most valued position in most companies); (2) master the art of networking; and (3) seek employment with small minority-owned recruiting firms before seeking mid- to top-level positions (develop diverse skills). For recruiters (firms and organizations), they also recommend offering personal service to clients, such as giving them tips that will aid potential employees as they enter the corporate world.

An approach that has been used in organizations which can be applied to a racialized organizational environment is employee empowerment (Foster-Fishman, Pennie, & Keys, 1997). Empowerment involves an individual or group having power, authority, or influence over events and outcomes important to them. Within corporate America, individuals are operating with a shared system of meaning; therefore the notion of empowerment for the benefit of the individual is subverted. The social collective is valued more so than individuality, which makes it difficult for anyone to feel valued by the organizational culture. These feelings become even stronger when a person's multiple identities inform his or her understanding in terms of organizational experiences.

Let's take the example of a Korean American woman. If she does not feel valued as a member, she could potentially feel even more unappreciated because her identities as a Korean American and a woman are often ignored. What is even worse is that she may be expected to take on the role of spokesperson for *all* Korean Americans in corporate America (what a great responsibility!). Therefore, the onus of responsibility lies with the manager, who should be responsible for engaging organizational members in open communication about work related issues (Bell, 1997) as well as racial/ethnic diversity as it affects the employees from diverse racial/ethnic groups and those in the majority. Because corporate America is being continually educated on the urgency of racial/ethnic diversity in the workplace, it is of utmost importance that managers put forth "constant effort to build employee relations and commitment to the organization" (Bell, 1997). More importantly, the interpersonal communication skills and relationships developed between racially/ethnically different organizational members must become, and remain, a top priority as we continue into the 21st Century.

Non-profit Organizations

We have noted that corporate America (for-profit organizations) has been forced to deal with racial/ethnic diversity on various levels. Fortunately, there has been increased discussion of how this change in the racial/ethnic composition of the U.S. population is to be serviced in the business world. But as Branch (1998) demonstrates, efforts of inclusion have been nominal. Feelings of tokenism resonate among racial/ethnic group members in the organizational culture, which makes this transition a painful yet necessary part of organizational growth. Too often, people have the expectation that when microcultural group members enter "mainstream" contexts where they are few in number, their racial/ethnic identities are expected to become "invisible."

One public site that has positively addressed racial/ethnic diversity within the organizational context is nonprofit organizations. In contrast, nonprofit organization members are committed to bringing about social change without monetary reward or promotion within the organization. To illustrate this point further, we limit our discussion of race, communication, and nonprofit organizations to a general discussion of the U.S. education system and one community-based organization.

Case Study: A School in Action.   From high schools (De La Torre, 1997; Giardina, 1998; Leigh, 1997) to colleges and universities (Owen, 1998), community members, administrators, and students have actively attempted to improve race relations by creating organizations designed specifically for this goal. The increasing racial/ethnic diversity is affecting our learning institutions. Therefore, efforts within schools and other public institutions have reflected this societal change.

The New Jersey School Counselor Association was recognized in 1998 (Giardina, 1998) for its "outstanding achievements in human rights" (p. 9). Janet Giardina created a six-page guide for Human Rights Week that celebrates human diversity. The pamphlet was created through the successful efforts of school counselors at New Jersey's East Brunswick High School's Tolerance and Diversity Committee. The organizational body consisted of student and staff representatives who worked to create and/or coordinate program ideas celebrating Human Rights Week every day of the year. Programs included Human Rights Week, Martin Luther King's Birthday, Black History Month, and Women in History Month. The underlying goal of this program was to place value and significance on the multiple identities of the students and faculty in that particular school system.

Instead of ignoring the differences, students and faculty worked together to celebrate human diversity. As the program titles illustrate, this year-long celebration empowered organizational members and school community to value themselves as well as others. Instead of placing more importance on the organizational identity and goals, the committee acknowledged the role racial/ethnic identities played in creating the organizational structure as they knew it. More importantly, the multiple identities of race, gender, religion, and culture were celebrated by allowing the students to be actively involved in the programming process (see Chapter 5).

The program's goal was twofold: (1) offer programs highlighting various aspects of human diversity, and (2) engage the school community in critical thinking processes relative to human diversity. The second goal occurred after the year-end celebration Critical Issues conference, which was an evening program that brought the school and surrounding community together in celebration of racial/ethnic diversity. (No information was provided by program coordinators and evaluators regarding what critical issues were discussed at the conference.) Although the conference only lasted for one day, people were encouraged to take the idea of human diversity back to their home environments and school communities.

The New Jersey model, which is nationally promoted through efforts by the American School Counselor Association, makes the following suggestions for engaging diversity via the development of future Tolerance and Diversity Committees in other school communities: (1) *assess* the unique needs of the school community (include diversity training of committee members); (2) *draft* a mission statement with shared goals and concerns (promote respect); (3) *involve* the entire school in the planning; (4) *review* written evaluations of the human rights activities and plan follow-up activities; and (5) *evaluate* the year-long program (by original committee members). By creating organizations that directly address the significance of racial/ethnic diversity, school systems throughout the United States can better equip their students, faculty, and administrators in becoming responsible citizens in a democratic society. This mission becomes even more important as we continue to experience racial/ethnic conflict among and between all racial groups (see De La Torre, 1997). Through increased interracial contact, participants were able to learn more about other racial/ethnic groups and how a community can improve race relations by celebrating and valuing that difference. We can assume that empathy and sensitivity were used by participants as they coordinated activities and programs deemed important to their mission.

On the collegiate level, Brown University has taken great strides to empower students of color living within the university's organizational culture. A variety of student organizations were developed to acknowledge the importance of racial/ethnic identity as it relates to academic and social success on a predominately European American campus. These student organizations (as of February 1999) include the Black and Latino Pre-Med Society, Latino American Students Organization, Latino Executive Board, Brown Sisters United, Asian American Students Association, Brown Chinese Students and Scholars Association, East Asian House, National Society of Black Engineers, and Students of Caribbean Ancestry. The focus of each organization is varied; however, they share the mission of valuing both the organizational and racial/ethnic identities of their members. Each organization is committed to informing its members about professional and university-related concerns affecting their present and future mobility in a racially/ethnically diverse society. Because race/ethnicity are often salient to the members individually and collectively, the organizations provide them with the emotional and social support necessary for functioning successfully in a hegemonic culture where they are in the minority.

As organizational bodies, high schools and systems of higher education are challenging students, faculty, and administrators to prepare their organizational bodies for present and future racial/ethnic diversity. Unlike most companies in corporate America, these organizations are creating environments and cultures where racial/ethnic difference is appreciated. Unfortunately, these organizations have also faced resistance from students and administrators who believe that these "special interest" organizations are not needed, especially because there are already other organizations in existence on campus. What many fail to realize is that these macrocultural organizations often treat racial/ethnic difference as insignificant to the lived experiences of some portions of the student body. We must remember that the organizations that recognize and value racial/ethnic difference meet both the goals of the individual and the organization. Through programs and specific organizational bodies, these learning institutions serve as exceptional models for other organizational cultures. By embracing and valuing the racial/ethnic identities of its members, organizations are able to achieve their collective goals while valuing the individual goals of its members (to preserve racial identity within the organizational context).

Case Study: A Church and Neighborhood in Action.   Community-based organizations are unique entities in that they are self-initiated programs that work to serve the community and its members. Typically, they are nonprofit and address concerns specific to the needs of individuals, groups, the environment, or other social issues (e.g., housing, hunger, the ozone, homelessness). In any event, formal organizations depend on volunteers (Miner & Tolnay, 1998) to meet their desired goals. Most community-based organizations have high levels of involvement from a base of individuals from the same race, age, and economic cohorts. Therefore, when organizations are racially/ethnically diverse, they are often perceived as an anomaly. This variance becomes even more important when these organizations are committed to improving race relations through racial reconciliation (Carter, 1995). Instead of just focusing on interracial communication between African Americans and European Americans, efforts should include the concerns and needs of all other racial groups as well (Carrasco, 1996; see Carter, 1995; Galen, 1994).

The church has traditionally been an organization used to bring about social and political change in the community and, in some cases, in the nation. The organizational members were brought together because of shared religious attitudes, beliefs, and values, but they were (and still are) typically separated by their racial difference (Clayton, 1995). In the case of European and African Americans, they are able to cross those racial barriers by working together and building a spiritual relationship that allows them to work toward societal and individual change. This commitment to reconciliation often became strained, particularly during the civil rights era when the racial climate was volatile for all Americans. Today, there is still a racial division in the church; however, there is a Catholic parish that has attempted to improve race relations by openly addressing this division within the religious community (see McGreevy 1996; McMahon, 1995). McGreevy specifically speaks about African American Catholicism and its role in the Catholic church's European ideologies. The old Catholic church places great importance on neighborhood life and a religiously based educational environment; the African American church also promotes the understanding that the church is to be a witness for justice and an advocate for the poor (McGreevy, 1996). Coupled together, both frameworks unite two different racial groups who share a basic religious philosophy while working toward common organizational goals. Although the Catholic church and other religious institutions have not always resolved racial tensions within their own bodies, they must be commended for their willingness to engage a problem that is facing the nation as a whole.

Noted race relations author Lise Funderburg (1998) suggests that we address the problem of race through "normalization" in our neighborhoods. She proposes that neighbors take advantage of their proximity and learn more about our racial/ethnic differences and, more importantly, our similarities. Funderburg succinctly articulates this need in the following quote:

> Just as athletes develop a muscle memory through repetitive training exercises, we who live in proximity to otherness can't help but come to associate with that otherness a familiarity, incorporating it into our concept of what is permissible, possible, normal. And so while it may seem cynical to settle for such a small piece of the integration pie, you have to start somewhere. And it might as well be next door. (p. 26)

What do you think we should do in our communities to improve our interracial communication, and ultimately the state of race relations in the United States? What kinds of community activities should be introduced to address racial/ethnic diversity? The much needed consciousness that Funderburg suggests should not only be limited to our residential neighborhoods but should include our professional worlds as well. Instead of adopting a color-blind mentality, we should challenge ourselves to reexamine how we think about our racial/ethnic differences and similarities. By valuing our differences, we continue to challenge the traditional attitudes that exist in the United States concerning race.

CONCLUSION

This chapter examined the significance of race within an organizational context. We found through case studies and research that, although efforts are being made to prepare corporate America, educational systems, and communities for racial diversity in traditionally European American contexts, people from all sides of this racial/ethnic divide have feelings of apprehension and discomfort. The good news, however, is that people are taking the initiative to improve race relations on both a micro and macro level. In corporate America, we see that administrators and employees alike are struggling with this change in the environment. Although microcultural racial/ethnic group members face barriers to advancement, administrators are actively dealing with this glass ceiling and its effect on the overall well being of its new organizational members. In our educational systems, students, faculty, and administrators are developing and creating programs and organizations that value the multiple identities of *all* students. Instead of making these students tokens, organizational members collectively celebrate racial/ethnic diversity through learning opportunities in and outside of the classroom. As an extension, some community-based organizations are working to improve race relations by establishing a common ground (e.g., religious beliefs) that can be used toward racial reconciliation.

These different types of organizations are important if we are to increase our race consciousness in the 21st century. By using diversity training programs as a method for increased racial sensitivity, we can use the organizational site (profit and nonprofit) as a context for promoting more effective interracial communication. The increasing racial/ethnic diversity facing the United States warrants initiative on the part of organizations to create an environment conducive to greater racial/ethnic diversity.

OPPORTUNITIES FOR EXTENDED LEARNING

1. Using the Internet, do a search for organizations similar to those at Brown University (either in communities or universities) that value both the racial/ethnic and organizational identities of its members. What URLs (Web sites) are there for organizations that make improving race relations a primary goal? Be prepared to describe for your class the purpose of each URL and how each organization contributes to improving interracial communication on a micro and/or macro level.

2. Using *InfoTrac College Edition,* provide the legal definition and popular definitions of affirmative action. Compare and contrast how these definitions create dissonance for people who are either in support or opposition of "leveling the playing field." According to the legal definition, does this mean that people who are less qualified for a position are to be hired? Discuss as a class how affirmative action is still needed to provide people, including women, people of color, and physically challenged people, with equal access to opportunities that have traditionally been denied to them.

3. After reading Ellis Cole's editorial titled "To the Victors, Few Spoils," (*Newsweek,* March 29, 1993, p. 54), (anonymously) write down your thoughts, feelings, and reactions to the points made in the essay. After collecting the essays, randomly select written comments to read aloud to the class. Discuss any emotional language used to describe reactions to different points made in the essay. Respond to these comments, and think about what role emotion plays in our interracial communication. As an extension, provide suggestions for how organizations can remedy these tensions as they approach the 21st century.

4. Using 10 interview questions, pair up with someone to conduct in-depth interviews with men and women of local business and organizations facing racial/ethnic diversity. Questions should gauge their attitudes toward and beliefs about diversity and its effect on the organizational culture (e.g., "How would you define diversity?" "How do you think will your organization will be affected by diversity? Do you anticipate a change in the racial composition of

the employees?") Compare the responses and share them with the class. Discuss what, if any, types of positive or negative attitudes surfaced among the participants. Address how power/status, race/ethnicity, and sex of participants may have influenced opinions about racial/ethnic diversity.

PUBLIC/SMALL GROUP COMMUNICATION

SPEECH MAKING

SMALL GROUP COMMUNICATION

CONCLUSION

OPPORTUNITIES FOR EXTENDED LEARNING

In the past, traditional public speaking courses focused on the experience of communication without giving much consideration to diversity (Kearney & Plax, 1999). Although most textbooks have addressed the importance of analyzing one's audience, this has become an even more critical issue because of the increasing racial diversity in the United States. Nance and Foeman (1993) assert that the speech-making process taught in our colleges and universities "removes all vestiges of non-White, non-European American communication styles" (p. 449). Instead of appreciating different communication styles, the traditional learning approaches in public speaking courses have been culturally exclusive (Kearney & Plax, 1999), thus creating one style of public communication. As a result, students from various racial and cultural groups enrolled in these courses have felt alienated (Nance & Foeman, 1993).

Similarly, this cookie-cutter approach to public communication leaves little room for racial and cultural sensitivity when it comes to our audiences. Although most public speaking textbooks do not address the influence of race/ethnicity on communicator style, it should be a growing area of concern for teachers and students alike. Communication scholars Kearney and Plax (1999) and Samovar and Mills (1998) have addressed the importance of cultural and racial/ethnic diversity. In their text *Oral Communication: Speaking Across Cultures*, Samovar and Mills (1998) extend the traditional approach to public communication by addressing the ethical responsibility of the speaker to be more sensitive to culture. Although applied to culture, the speaker challenges they present are inherently very appropriate for racialized environments as well.

The first challenge for you as a speaker is to learn as much as you can about the cultural and racial group members in the audience (Samovar & Mills, 1998). In doing so, you must consider how the beliefs and values of other racial groups may be impacted by your own beliefs presented in the speech. Do those racial groups value the same things that you do? In presenting your own ideas, will you offend your audience? How much accommodating should you do in your speech without compromising the integrity of your purpose? Will your purpose be lost in the process? These are questions to consider seriously as you prepare to speak before racially and ethnically diverse audiences.

Samovar and Mills (1998) also suggest that you respect diversity. If you devalue the cultural and racial differences between yourself and your audience, you are engaging in ethnocentric thinking or the belief that your culture or race is superior to all others. Instead, think of the positive aspects of diversity from a racial and/or cultural perspective. In doing so, you are establishing respect with the audience, thus increasing the perception that you are racially sensitive and accepting of others who are different from you.

The final challenge Samovar and Mills (1998) present is for the speaker to acknowledge the similarities between culturally and racially different groups, which should determine how we construct our messages. In essence, they suggest you apply an ethical code that transcends cultural and racial differences. This ethical code, often called the Golden Rule, crosses religious and philosophical tradition (Samovar & Mills, 1998). Put simply, this canon tells us that it is unethical to construct messages designed to demean or belittle another if we would not want to be on the receiving end of that same message. By acknowledging the sense of humanity that underlies difference, we are potentially more effective in our public communication with others.

Although these challenges relate to public communication, they also apply to all forms of interpersonal communication situated within a racialized environment. If we are not able to be sensitive to and appreciative of racial differences, then we are engaging in irresponsible communication. Therefore, we must examine how we must communicate with others on a variety of levels. Because we have control over the messages we choose to communicate, we must also use wisdom and empathy during this process. By becoming more active and responsible in our public communication, we become better prepared to fulfill our roles as responsible citizens functioning in a democratic society.

SPEECH MAKING

Let's first look closely at the speech-making process as a way to assess the degree to which a racialized environment will impact the final product—the speech. Every speech we give may not focus on the issue of race. It is important, however, to reexamine how we think about the speech-making process in terms of the role that race plays in perceptions of speeches.

In general, public speaking creates feelings of anxiety and communication apprehension for many people for a variety of reasons (Ayres, 1996; Ayres, Hopf, Brown, & Suck, 1994; Ayres, Keereetaweep, Chen, & Edwards, 1998; Daly, Vangelisti, & Weber, 1995; MacIntyre & MacDonald, 1998; Neuliep & Ryan, 1998).

10.1 *The Salience of Language in Race Relations*

Within the past five years, much debate has focused on the saliency of language and its importance to racial/ethnic groups. In California, there was great resistance to using Spanish and Ebonics (see Smitherman, 1995) in the classroom. Educators who valued education and linguistic diversity were committed to using these language systems as part of the classroom experience for students who were not proficient in American English. Many criticized these efforts because they appeared to further marginalize the students; however, they failed to realize the importance of preserving the students' racial/ethnic identity as they prepared to become active members of a democratic society.

For those who use dual language systems, four criteria underscore the role of language in sustaining personal identity (Giles & Coupland, 1991). Language is "(1) a critical attribute of group membership, (2) an important cue for ethnic categorization, (3) an emotional dimension of identity, and (4) a means of facilitating ingroup cohesion" (p. 96). For all of the students for whom English is a second language (ESL), their language is an integral part of who they are. When they speak Spanish, Chinese, or Ebonics, they are communicating to others their group membership and how important that membership is to them. Although they are closely identified with their racial/ethnic group, these individuals also have the communicative skills that enable them to employ the language system most appropriate for that interracial context. For example, if a Latino male is hanging out with his Latino peers, he has the choice of using

---

The Salience of Language in Race Relations (*continued*)

Spanish, English, or Spanglish (both languages combined) to communicate with his friends. However, if he was with his African American friends, he would probably use English to engage in a conversation that does not alienate either of them. In any event, he must be flexible in determining what language system is most conducive to effective interracial communication.

Research on communication accommodation indicates that race/ethnicity, class, status, and context are variables that influence language choice. For some people, certain variables are more germane than others; however, as we enter the 21st century, we will *all* be challenged to acknowledge how important racial/ethnic identity is to our language systems. Instead of evaluating diverse language systems as substandard, we must face the reality that American English will no longer be the standard for evaluating the appropriateness of verbal communication.

Yes, a common language is needed in order for people from diverse backgrounds to communicate in public, but we must appreciate the richness embodied within these diverse tongues.

Whether it is an individual attribute such as cultural difference (Neuliep & Ryan, 1998) or gender (Ayres et al., 1994) or the context of an interview (Ayres et al., 1998), a speaker can become even more resistant to the speaking experience. It is very likely that the uncertainty of a new situation creates stress for that person. For those individuals engaging in public communication, apprehension can potentially affect the speech preparation process (Ayres, 1996; Daly et al., 1995). Whether it is receiving a low grade on a speech (Ayres, 1996) or presenting a speech of low quality (Daly et al., 1995), communication apprehension can ultimately have a negative effect on the preparation and presentation of a speech (Rowan, 1995).

In contrast, communication apprehension has prompted some speakers to improve their competence and public speaking skills (MacIntyre & MacDonald, 1998). No matter what the outcome, the stress of having to speak before others can affect how the speech's message is constructed or prepared (Daly et al., 1995; Rowan, 1995). In order to minimize the frustration associated with public communication, we explore the stages of speech making next. Understanding this process will also enable you to adjust your speech to a racialized environment.

Audience Analysis

Before you give the actual speech, first consider your audience. Adapt the speech so the material you present appeals to your audience's interests, needs, attitudes, beliefs, and backgrounds (Kearney & Plax, 1999; Samovar & Mills, 1998). Audience analysis is very important because the audience will be responding to you as well as your message (Beebe & Beebe, 1991). The audience is central to the speech because it directly influences each phase of speech writing. You might be wondering, "Is that really necessary? Isn't the topic enough?" And the answers are "yes" and "no." Yes, it is essential that you as the speaker promote rapport with your audience (Samovar & Mills, 1998), and no, just presenting the topic is not enough. It is your responsibility to appeal to the audience's race, age, gender, class, occupation, attitudes, beliefs, and/or values. Because you want them to be supportive of and responsive to your message (Beebe & Beebe, 1991; Samovar & Mills, 1998), you must appeal to your audience in some way.

In a similar vein, as you are analyzing your audience, they are evaluating you at the same time. For example, if you are an Asian American female speaking to an audience of European American males about gender discrimination, certain arguments stand the chance of putting them on the defensive, thus making them resistant to your message. Consider this point from the perspective of an audience member. An Asian American female is attending a presentation with her mostly male colleagues. Does the fact that you have men in positions of power and one racial/ethnic female in your audience affect how they will receive the message? What about *your* race and gender? Did you make accommodations in your speech to account for them? Would that have made your speech more persuasive or informative? By researching your audience and designing your speech so that it meets your goal (i.e., to persuade, inform, entertain), you are engaging in positive, productive public communication.

As a speaker, remember that within a racialized environment both you and your audience bring your attitudes, beliefs, and values, which are a product of your racial identities, to the speech context. When you are presenting your ideas or opinions, it is likely that they are shaped by racial identity as well. Therefore, you must be sensitive to these racial differences yet establish a common ground with your audience. For example, you can speak about the role of autonomy in helping businesspeople become successful entrepreneurs. Because everyone has chosen to attend your presentation, they expect to receive information that will prove beneficial to their success in the business world, thus establishing common ground. However, by placing value on the saliency of racial/ethnic differences and its impact on successful entrepreneurship, you stand the chance of alienating your audience. Therefore, you must employ the strategy that is most effective in creating a public communication experience involving a positive transaction between the audience and the speaker.

Brainstorming

After you have considered the audience, begin brainstorming or listing potential speech topics (Beebe & Beebe, 1991; Zarefsky, 1998). At this stage in the speech-

| 10.2 | *Personal Reflection* |

In the fall of 1994, I was invited to speak to 1,000-plus teaching assistants (TAs) on the topic of classroom diversity. The topic was even more important for those TAs who were about to experience diversity for the first time in their lives. I discussed the importance of appreciating difference and acknowledging diversity in our teaching without sacrificing the true goal of teaching (i.e., educating others on a specific topic). As I concluded my speech, I reemphasized the importance of adapting teaching styles to make learning an enjoyable experience for students. I shared with the audience the following sentiment: "Let's take for example the subject of math. For me, learning how to do math has always been difficult. I don't care how my teacher tried to explain it, it always frustrated me. So, if I were in *your* class, I'm certain that you would have to break things down for me really well, because 'it's all Greek to me.'"

Several smiles and nods were given in response to my use of the cliché, but then my conscience kicked in. After a short pause, I used my sense of humor and made a public apology to anyone who may have been offended. The audience immediately burst into laughter! They appeared to appreciate my honesty and forthrightness in apologizing before the group. I really learned a life lesson from this experience because I was challenged to truly engage in audience analysis when I least expected to.

I promised myself from that day forward to carefully monitor what I say in my public communication. What one group finds funny, another could find very offensive and degrading. Despite this public faux pas, I received highly positive evaluations for my presentation. The audience loved my speech, thought I did an impressive job, and wanted to invite me back the next year! Although this is flattering, the most important lesson I learned was that using my humor and ability to handle an uncomfortable public communication situation, I came out better in the long run. My credibility was increased because my audience was able to observe firsthand my responsibility to them as an ethical, competent communicator.—TMH

making process, you are being very general regarding the topic you may be speaking on. It is possible that you may be asked to give a speech on a specific topic; therefore, you are limited in your topic choice. As you develop your ideas, select information relative to the topic and meet the goal of the occasion. Because many of you have taken or will be taking public speaking courses, we use this context to illustrate how critical thinking skills are important to constructing a speech within a racialized environment.

As you make a list of topics, begin to weed out or eliminate those that are not as appropriate as others for the occasion and audience to whom you will be speaking. Let's say that as the speaker you have chosen the topic of entrepreneurialism. In selecting this topic, you will be informing your audience about the process involved in starting a new business. Although the topic may be of interest to you, you must ask yourself if your audience will benefit from it as well.

If you are speaking to a racially diverse audience or to an audience that is racially different from you, think about how you might adapt the topic of entrepreneurialism to your interests from different racial perspectives. You might want to use examples of successful businesspeople who come from diverse racial backgrounds. For example, incorporating an example of Native American businesspeople would demonstrate to your audience your ability as a speaker to be racially inclusive and sincere. In doing so, your audience will be able to relate to and be more responsive to your message.

Narrowing the Topic

After brainstorming, narrow down the topic. Choose a very specific topic that fits into your time constraints (Beebe & Beebe, 1991). As the speaker, you must determine how you will explore the topic for the occasion. Let us continue with the entrepreneurship example. Now that you have chosen to speak on starting a business, you have to be sure to focus on one aspect of this process or the process in very general terms. Because you may be limited to in three to five minutes, do not cover too many subtopics, because this may overwhelm your audience with too much information.

As you are speaking to racially diverse audiences, make sure that your topic is something to which they can relate. Although you may be restricted by time, it is your responsibility as a speaker to fulfill this aspect of the public communication experience. Such strategies as choosing a topic all audience members can relate to, giving examples/applications that reflect different sets of lived experiences, connecting with your audience, and clearly articulating the primary purpose of the speech (i.e., inform, persuade, entertain) will allow you to establish a positive rapport with the audience to whom you are speaking. By narrowing down the topic, you can be more focused on your goal while simultaneously meeting the needs of the audience.

Researching

Now that you have selected a topic, you must do research to support the points presented in your speech. Through researching, you select evidence that defines, clarifies, illustrates, and supports your position. Two ways that you can research include (1) relying on personal experience with the topic, and (2) relying on the knowledge of experts (Kearney & Plax, 1999). By using both approaches, you are using evidence and support that add coherence and credibility to your message.

The types of support may include giving your audience statistics, facts, definitions, examples, explanations, descriptions, opinions, analogies, and narratives that uphold the claims you make in your speech. In order to get this type of information, you may conduct interviews, read newspapers or periodicals, use the encyclopedia, read books, search government documents, or use the Internet (Kearney & Plax, 1999). Whatever sources you use, make sure you use the most current data available. More importantly, be certain the supporting material is relevant to the position you take in your speech. Let's take a specific example. In doing your speech on campus safety, you use *The Chronicle of Higher Education*, which has an article citing the trend of crimes committed at universities and colleges across the nation. To make your topic hit home for your audience, you include a recent article from the local paper. More likely than not, your audience will be even more persuaded to believe the seriousness of campus safety because of the support you are providing and the actual source itself. If you were to use a tabloid such as the *National Enquirer*, your argument would probably not be as persuasive or credible.

As you are researching your topic, you might also want to use sources that represent racial diversity. Look for books, magazines, and other resources targeted to specific racial groups that support the points your are making in your speech. For example, you are scheduled to speak to racially diverse businesspeople about entrepreneurship. Instead of using only such sources as *Fortune 500*, include other sources like *Black Enterprise*, among others, that also address your main points and subpoints. In doing so, you are increasing the likelihood that your audience will find your presentation more persuasive and useful to them beyond the public communication context.

Organizing and Outlining the Speech

Once you have narrowed the topic and done some preliminary research, organize and outline the speech (Beebe & Beebe, 1991). It is here that you will be challenged to use your critical thinking skills actively (Samovar & Mills, 1998) on a more complex level. The most important feature of this phase of the speech-making process is your ability to organize your thoughts and ideas to (1) determine what sequence of ideas is most appropriate for your audience, (2) assist both yourself and your audience in making sense of the ideas presented in the speech, and (3) present a meaningful sequence between the main ideas and supporting ones (Samovar & Mills, 1998). The final benefit offered from an organized speech allows the audience to (4) assign greater credibility to the message and the speaker. Ultimately, it is your ability to organize your thoughts logically that will allow audience members to benefit from this public communication experience.

No matter what style of organization you use for the speech, you will be creating main points and subpoints that clarify, reinforce, or prove your core statement (Samovar & Mills, 1998). Most speeches have five main points; therefore create statements that support, provide proof, illustrate, and/or explain the core statement. The main points and subpoints are very important to the speech-making process because they provide a logical pattern of critical thinking that is easy for the audience to understand. Because future public communication will take place in racialized environments, you must consciously organize your thoughts prior to giving the speech. However, if you are speaking to a racially diverse group, you may find it appropriate to examine the points made in the speech and determine if the audience's concerns are being addressed.

If you are a Latina trying to persuade your audience of women from different racial groups to invest in your company, how might your message change? Would your points change so that you can appeal to the race and/or gender of your audience members? Similarly, if you were speaking to women from one racial group, would your message have a different tone? Because people from different races and cultures may organize their thoughts in different ways (Samovar & Mills, 1998), choose an organizational pattern that best suits the needs of your audience. Most speakers use organizational patterns that reflect Western ways of thinking; therefore, the speaker must use a style that she is comfortable with and is inclusive of the audience's ways of thinking. As Samovar and Mills (1998) describe, Eastern cultural group members (e.g., Koreans) use "configural logic" instead of linear methods when they communicate with each other. In essence, the relationship between two points is not clearly spelled out for listeners, who are left to make the connection on their own. Western cultures use linear methods wherein specific points are made, followed by supporting points. In the end, the audience is able to follow the logical pattern of reasoning presented by the speaker.

As this example illustrates, your audience can indeed influence how you organize your speech. Although race may not be the sole determining factor, the contents of your speech must be adapted to meet the needs of audience members. Yes, race is important when you are giving a speech to a racially diverse group of people; however, race should not be the only factor that influences the structure and content of a speech. Remember, as the speaker, you do not want to offend or patronize your audience. If you place too much emphasis on race and do not give enough attention to your main points, your speech will not have achieved its goal of informing, persuading, or entertaining. Therefore, maintain a delicate balance between your goals and the relevance of racial identity as you speak in a racialized environment.

Writing

Now that you have finished organizing and outlining the speech, you move to a very important part of the speech—*writing* the entire speech. This part of the speech-making process gives you the opportunity to fully develop your ideas and thoughts before presenting them to your audience. At this point you will be challenged to give even more thought to how you will present yourself and your ideas to your audience. You will also have the opportunity to monitor any language, phrases, or comments that may be perceived as stereotypical. This becomes even more important when you are speaking in a racialized environment. Failing to do so may likely offend your audience, create a hostile environment, and make you even more apprehensive about future public communication opportunities. Therefore, it is mutually beneficial to the sender and receiver of the message to engage in linguistic sensitivity in all communication contexts.

During this stage of speech-making, pay attention to the introduction, body, and conclusion of your speech. In the introduction, you will be meeting four objectives: (1) getting your audience's attention and interest, (2) revealing the speech topic, (2) establishing your credibility and goodwill as speaker, and (4) previewing the body of your speech (Lucas, 1998). By working toward each objective, you are being both speaker- and audience-centered as you develop your thoughts and ideas.

In getting your audience's attention, try to engage them by using examples or attention getters to which they can relate. Instead of starting your speech with "Today I am going to talk to you about traveling abroad," use something that will capture their interest right from the beginning. You could use the following example to achieve this first objective: "Have you ever been in a land where you were continually fascinated by everything you saw? Well, close your eyes for a moment. Imagine yourself walking down a cobblestone street in a crowded city. Wafting through the air is the delicious smell of herbs, spices, and wines permeating from homes and restaurants in the village. You hear the laughter of children and adults speaking their native language. Even though you cannot understand what is being said, you are in awe of your new surroundings. You never imagined you would be standing in the streets of Jerusalem!" Although this example may not be riveting, you have certainly gotten everyone's attention. Prior to your speech, the audience may not have toyed with the idea of traveling abroad, or even to Jerusalem. However, because of your introduction, your audience could possibly be intrigued about doing so. It is through your illustration and exercise that you have actively engaged your audience in the experience you are sharing with them.

After you have grabbed their attention, articulate for your audience your purpose by using a thesis statement and previewing the points you are going to make (Kearney & Plax, 1999; Zarefsky, 1998). As you develop these points throughout the body of the speech, you are organizing your thoughts and writing them out completely, which makes it easier for your audience to follow as you progress through your speech. This approach is very effective when you are giving a formal speech. Your audience is gathered for a specific reason or occasion and, as a result, they come with the expectation of being challenged mentally. Therefore, you must create a well-thought-out rationale prior to speaking before your audience.

The last part of the speech-writing stage is the conclusion, whose purpose is to summarize the main ideas, make one last appeal to the audience, and provide closure (Beebe & Beebe, 1991; Zarefsky, 1998). This is your final chance to fulfill the ultimate goal of public communication. Concluding the speech is just as important as the introduction and body because the audience will more than likely remember the first and the last thing they hear (i.e., primacy–recency). By reemphasizing the main points and appealing to the audience, you are reminding them of your purpose for giving the speech. As you have done throughout the speech, you want to ensure that you are not offending your audience. Writing out your speech will sensitize you to potentially offensive and exclusive language, concepts, and assumptions.

Delivery

The final aspect of public communication is the actual presentation of the entire speech. Depending on the occasion and purpose, choose the mode of speech delivery that is most appropriate: manuscript delivery, memorized delivery, impromptu delivery, or extemporaneous delivery (Kearney & Plax, 1999). The manuscript and memorized types of delivery are most fitting for the fully written speech, and the impromptu and extemporaneous delivery styles lend themselves to speeches that require little time for preplanning. In any event, as the speaker, you must still give great detail and attention to what you say in front of your audience.

Manuscript delivery involves writing out the speech and reading the paper aloud to your audience. This mode of delivery is very appealing because it allows you to be more accurate, precise, and convincing (Zarefsky, 1998). The downside of this approach is that it may keep you from sounding normal. What is more troubling is that you can lose your place if you are distracted and look away from your paper, a problem remedied by the memorized delivery.

If you have memorized your speech, you probably know it backward and forward. Additional benefits of this type of delivery style are that you are able to use gestures, look at the audience, and move around without being restricted to the podium. However, your speech may take on a rhythmic and monotonous recitation mode that can bore your audience. Or you may become so anxious to finish that you rattle off the remaining portion of the speech. Not only will you suffer but the audience members will as well. The audience will misinterpret the message you are trying to communicate to them (Petronio, Ellemers, Giles, & Gallois, 1998; Rowan, 1995). Despite these negative aspects of the memorized speech, you can benefit from this mode of delivery. Such people as politicians, evangelists, and some management consultants use the memorized mode of delivery, which allows them to concentrate on their pitch, rate, gestures, and other vocal cues that enhance the quality of the speech (Zarefsky, 1998).

In a similar vein, the extemporaneous or impromptu style of public communication is less structured yet requires some practice prior to presentation. You benefit from this type of speaking because it allows you practice your public communication skills in a variety of contexts. Whether it is speaking up in class or a business meeting or talking to a sales manager, we all have been nervous about speaking informally at some point or another. One way to get through apprehension about public communication is by taking advantage of these opportunities to talk off the cuff with people in informal settings. By being unprepared yet anxious to engage in dialogue with others, you are forced to use your critical thinking skills on your feet. Ideally, you will improve your communication and thinking skills as the opportunities for extemporaneous speaking increase.

As you can see, the delivery is very important to the speech making experience. Which style you use is greatly determined by the occasion, topic, and your racial/ethnic identity. This is where the communication accommodation theory (CAT) becomes central to our understanding of public communication. Let's use African American oratory style as an example. As Janice Hamlet (1997) describes in her essay on the oral tradition of African American culture, the communication style used by an African American preacher is very performative and interactive. The four preaching styles Hamlet discusses demonstrate how racial/ethnic identity can influence public communication. We must note, however, that although Hamlet is describing preaching as a form of public discourse, these forms of communication styles are also a part of daily communication for many African Americans.

The first style of preaching is the use of *black idiom* or language. According to Hamlet (1997), idiom "is a powerful medium used to influence, inspire, and of ten mobilize the masses" (p. 96). Not only are audience (congregation) members challenged to work toward a common good, but the speaker/preacher has decreased the social distance between herself and the congregation, thus building rapport and achieving the desired effect. Such preachers and political figures as Rev. Dr. Martin Luther King, Jr., and Rev. Jesse Jackson have used black idiom in their speeches to motivate African Americans to become actively involved in the civil rights and other social movements that benefit African Americans and other oppressed groups of color.

The next type of preaching style is *storytelling*, which involves the art of storytelling (hermeneutics). Hamlet (1997) defines hermeneutics as the process through which the Bible is read examined, interpreted, understood, translated and proclaimed (Stewart, p. 30)" (p. 96). In essence, the preacher is presenting the Bible message in the form of a story that creates a mental picture for her audience. Instead of just instructing the congregation members on how they should live, a story is told that weaves the Bible and its application to their lives.

The third preaching style involves the use of *poetic diction and rhythm*. Poetic diction uses "symbolic and presentative words and sets up a musical structure of alliterative expression . . . sentences are short, crisp, and clear . . . The voice is considered the preacher's trumpet for proclaiming the gospel. It can challenge, convince, comfort, and charm" (Hamlet, 1997, p. 97). The preacher selectively chooses the words, rhythmic pattern, and style that will be used to communicate the message. One important feature of this preaching style is that the preacher will use repetition "for emphasis, memory, impact, and effect," hopefully ensuring that the audience members will be able to recall the purpose of the message without being swept away by emotionalism.

The final preaching style is *call and response*, in which the preacher and congregation engage in a communicative exchange as he is preaching. For example, the preacher will "call out for a specific response, such as 'Can I get a witness?' or 'Somebody ought to say Amen,' thereby soliciting responses . . . [such as] 'Amen!' 'Preach! 'Tell it!'" (Hamlet, 1997, p. 98). This form of interaction has meaning for congregation members because they "believe that they are experiencing God's presence in their midst" (p. 98).

These four preaching styles are very unique to the African American community; therefore, it is reasonable to assume that an African American speaker engaging in public communication in a racialized environment will find it appropriate and necessary to use any of these styles. But we also must not assume that *because* someone is African American, he or she will be using this style. Instead, we must be respectful of and appreciate this unique style of public communication. These forms are unique styles of expression that do not conform to what mainstream society would call normal styles of public speaking. Because we are becoming an increasingly racially/ethnically diverse society, we must begin to examine how we think about public communication. Is there really *one way* of presenting our ideas to a large group of people? More importantly, shouldn't this expectation change as we enter the 21st century?

Remember, in a racialized context, delivery style will also be influenced by the racial composition of the audience as well as the racial identity of the speaker. For some cultural groups, very little value is placed on talking (Samovar & Mills, 1998); therefore, you might need to adjust your style for the audience, or vice versa. In this case, you would minimize the amount of talking you engage in so as not to lose your audience. As these illustrations indicate, you must consider diversity, racial or cultural, when choosing a delivery style most appropriate for the speaking occasion.

THEORY INTO PRACTICE

We are all familiar with this old saying: "Sticks and stones may break my bones, but words will never hurt me." This old wives' tale holds little truth in a world where words are used to marginalize and inflict pain on others. Gates (1994) describes the consequences of these behaviors when targeted at racial/ethnic group members as "psychic injuries incurred by racist speech [which] have additional costs down the road" (p. 24). The following are suggestions for improving your public and small group communication within racialized contexts.

- Think before you speak. Would you use the same language, term, or phrase to refer to yourself and others like you? How would you feel if someone used that language with you?
- Make active efforts to use racially/ethnically inclusive language in both interracial and monoracial contexts.
- Avoid using racially exclusive language that alienates others. For example, do not assume using the phrase "We are all Americans" makes Native American audience members feel included in the dialogue or speech.
- Do research on the audience to whom you are going to speak.
- Appeal to your audience's needs, interests, and concerns.
- Avoid using negative referents such as "you people," "them," and "you all."
- Offer and receive constructive criticism when racially offensive language is used.
- Confront others (and yourself) when racial slurs, racist jokes, or any other offensive terms are used. Treat this as a learning opportunity.

SMALL GROUP COMMUNICATION

Our final topic of discussion is small group communication as it relates to public and interracial communication. Small group communication can be defined as communication among 3 to 12 people engaging in face-to-face dialogue in order to meet a common goal or purpose (Beebe & Beebe, 1991; Powell, 1996; Whelan, Murphy, Tsumura, & Kline, 1998). Unlike public communication, communication in a small group is more intimate and typically provides each group member with a sense of belonging. Because they are brought together for one purpose, the group members have mutual influence over each other. Within this context, communication is somewhat informal, yet everyone is expected to present his or her ideas to the group in a coherent and logical fashion.

We must discuss the significance of race/ethnicity within this relational context. As we noted in previous chapters, "communication among people of diverse backgrounds (and hence diverse communication patterns) is challenging; it can result in an enriching experience or a disaster" (Brilhart & Galanes, 1995). Therefore, when we are working in small groups our interpersonal, linguistic, and racial/ethnic differences inevitably are going to affect our communicative experiences. In terms of race/ethnicity and culture, the worldview of these members is going to affect how the goals of the small group are achieved. For example, there are "being cultures" (Chinese and Native American cultures) who believe humans, animal life, and plant life should live harmoniously together on earth, whereas "doing cultures" (United States and other Western countries) believe the earth and nature are to be used for the benefit of humankind (Brilhart & Galanes, 1995). Therefore, when these cultural group members engage in activities, either separately or together, their worldviews shape how they interact and work toward achieving specific goals.

As you can see, each racial/ethnic and cultural group has unique features that are inextricably a part of them no matter what communicative context they are a part of. These differences can also provide learning experiences for outgroup members when the two groups must work together to achieve a common goal. Have you ever worked on a group project for a class? During that process, it is quite possible that you learned a great deal about your group members. Thinking back on that experience, were there any group members who were from a different racial/ethnic group than you? How did your racial/ethnic differences influence how the project was accomplished?

Let's use the Hopi culture to illustrate this point. The Hopi experience time as it happens (Brilhart & Galanes, 1995); therefore, its cultural group members are not restricted by time as North Americans are. Time is perceived as having no past, present, or future; instead, the Hopi "experience time as 'what happens in the present moment'" (p. 98). As a U.S. American, you are working with time in the present and are really focused on doing the project in stages or in a linear fashion. When you and the person from the Hopi culture meet with your other group members, you find the time schedule is not really working. According to the calendar, you are a few weeks behind schedule and really need to have the project finished by a specific date. In this case, most of us would be ready to blame the Hopi group member and stereotype him according to his behavior, which does not conform to our own culture. Therefore, in order to appreciate our cultural differences, we must be first acknowledge their existence. From there, we must compromise and use this project as a learning experience.

Paralanguage

In our thinking about small group communication within a racialized environment, we must also acknowledge how racial/ethnic differences in language use are going to influence the interpersonal dynamics of the group. One prominent feature of our verbal and nonverbal communication that differs across racial/ethnic groups is *paralanguage*, or the manner is which something is spoken (e.g., rate, speed, pitch, volume, pronunciation). Are you familiar with the saying, "It's not *what* you say but *how* you say it"? It demonstrates for us how important paralanguage is when we communicate with others in general; therefore, when there is racial/ethnic diversity among members in a small group, our differences may potentially create barriers to our interpersonal communication.

Two types of paralanguage that may create barriers are the use of *backchannel* and *dialect* within a racially/ethnically diverse context. Backchanneling refers to "vocalizations such as *mm-hmm, uh-huh,* and *yeah-yeah-yeah* that are uttered to another person" (Brilhart & Galanes, 1995, p. 100). This form of paralanguage is frequently used by African Americans, Latino/a Americans, and people of southern European origin to communicate interest in the speaker and indicate they are actively listening to what is being said. Although this behavior may be perceived as appropriate nonverbal communication by the user, it can create miscommunication between ingroup and outgroup members because the intended meaning may be misinterpreted. Instead of receiving the message as an affirmation, the speaker may think the other person is not listening to what he is saying or is being rude.

Another form of paralanguage influenced by race/ethnicity and culture is *dialect*, which includes "regional and social variations in pronunciation, vocabulary, and grammar of a language" (Brilhart & Galanes, 1995, p. 100). The standard dialect of a region or social class is perceived as the norm, however, when individuals deviate and use a nonstandard dialect, they may potentially be evaluated and perceived negatively by others because their language use may not be aesthetically pleasing to the listener.

Another type of paralanguage operant where racial/ethnic difference is present in small groups is *kinesics*, or how facial expressions are used to communicate feelings or meaning. In Japan, a smile has two functions: "(1) to communicate pleasure or (2) to represent the desire not to cause pain for someone else" (Brilhart & Galanes, 1995, p.101). Using the context of a funeral, a Japanese person may smile at others as they return from her mother's funeral. From a Western perspective, we may interpret the smile to mean that she is happy her mother has died. However, her use of the smile is adhering to the Japanese rules of etiquette that tells cultural members "it is extremely bad form to inflict unpleasantness on someone else, thus no matter how bad someone feels inside, a cheerful face must be presented to the world" (p. 101). In a similar vein, rules determining *eye contact* or eye behavior (oculesics), another type of kinesic, also differs from culture to culture. For U.S. Americans, there is the expectation of maintaining direct eye contact when interacting with someone. This same behavior has a different meaning for Native American cultures, who perceive direct eye contact as rude. For Latinos/as, indirect eye contact from a child is viewed as a sign of respect. Arabic cultures, however, accept intense staring as the norm. So you can imagine the kinds of miscommunication that can take place if you had a small group with people from all of the cultures just mentioned. It is very likely that there will be tension and conflict because of the different meanings of our nonverbals because of our cultural differences. Therefore, we must be aware that just because someone else communicates differently than we do it does not mean that one form of communication is better than another. Instead, we must learn to be accommodating as we interact interpersonally with people who are racially/ethnically and culturally different from us.

Small group communication can be both a positive and a negative experience. On the positive side, groups provide more knowledge and information, offer creative problem solving, allow members to learn more than if they worked by themselves, and increase member satisfaction (synergy) (Beebe & Beebe, 1991). This form of communication is good for individuals because it allows them to improve both their critical thinking and presentational skills on a very personal level. Have you ever worked on a group project and had a good group of people to work with? Did your group members communicate well with each other? Did everyone listen to each other and work together to get the job done? Whatever your experience, your hindsight of the group process will probably be indicative of what the ideal small group experience should be like.

Unfortunately, some individuals have had negative group experiences (process loss), which may be attributed to pressure to conform, one person's attempt to dominate group discussion, unequal distribution of work, and a long decision-making process. We must also acknowledge that our racial/ethnic differences may also contribute to negative group experiences. (We hope that will not always be the case.) Working in a group results in a loss because fewer contributions are made by the group when they are compared to individual contributions. In other words, the individual contributions are more valuable than those of the group. In any event, working in groups can be problematic because of the complexity of small group communication (Powell, 1996). Not only might work styles become conflictual in the group, but the interpersonal communication styles of each group member may prove problematic as well. Instead of working through their differences, group members are forced to trudge through the small group process in order to complete their goal, which may not be met.

Ideally, small group communication allows individuals to improve their interpersonal and public communication skills on a regular basis. Although some people may groan at the mere thought of having to work with two or more other people for an extended period of time, small group communication can prove to be a life lesson for others.

Let's take interracial communication and apply it to the small group context. In this small group, you have a great deal of racial diversity among the members. The group was organized to complete a group project with a deadline, and everyone is to receive the same final grade. Once the group meets and introductions are made, the entire group begins to talk about their goal and the type of project they will be doing for the class. Introductions are made and Yen, a Korean American male, begins to assume control of guiding the group through the decision-making process. Anita, a Latina, begins to make suggestions and frequently defers to her group members to see what they think. Finally, everyone is talking and Steve, an African American, begins to watch and engage in intrapersonal communication as he observes his group members. Steve thinks to himself, "Wow, I thought Asians were so quiet and passive. Boy, was I wrong, at least as far as Yen is concerned. He seems like a pretty neat guy. And Anita. I halfway expected her to take control and start telling everybody what *she* thinks *they* should be doing. I guess I'm wrong on two counts."

This example may seem a little contrived; however, it gets to the ultimate benefit of being in a small group. If Steve had not been in this group, he would continue to believe the racial stereotypes he has about Asian Americans and Latinos/as. Because he was placed in a group for a class project, Steve was given the opportunity to challenge how he thinks about people from racial groups different from his own. Although most people may not be as fortunate to have this experience, such exposure to racial diversity is inevitable. With the racial composition of U.S. citizens becoming more diverse with each passing day, it is imperative that people practice flexibility and sensitivity when communicating within small groups and with racially diverse people. It is through these face-to-face interactions that people can learn more about other racial groups. As a result, the long-standing stereotypes ascribed to racial groups that serve as barriers to interracial communication can be debunked and discounted as myths. In turn, we can learn how to adapt our communication style to a racialized environment without being offensive to others.

CONCLUSION

This chapter on public and small group communication has demonstrated how a racialized environment can influence the communication process. Whether it is making a speech or communicating in a small group, communicators must use their critical thinking skills if they are to have a positive communication experience. In the case of public communication, we as speakers are challenged to organize our thoughts logically and rationally in order to be understood by an audience. Each stage of the speech-writing process forces us to think of the speech, our audience, and the racial environment in which we are to speak. Although race may not be the primary influencing factor on public communication, we must be aware of how both our own racial identity and that of the audience can directly influence how our message is received.

Similarly, small group communication also challenges us to think about how we communicate with others on a more intimate level. With this experience comes difference, to which we must accommodate. Although we may be afraid to communicate with racially different others, we are not considering that the group members may be regarding us with the same feelings of fear or apprehension. Therefore, it is important for the group members to welcome difference into the small group context as a learning experience and opportunity for growth.

It was the goal of this chapter to challenge you to give thought (and hopefully action) to how important racial diversity is to public and small group communication. Many people would like to say that "We're all the same," or "Color doesn't matter. It's what's on the inside that counts." In an ideal world as it relates to human interaction that might be true; however, reality tells us that our identities and life experiences shape who we are and how we see others. Whether it is race, gender, class, education level, family life, or occupation, we must consider how these attributes influence out attitudes, beliefs, and values.

Although it would be presumptuous to assume that people from the same race and/or gender share the same life experiences, we must recognize the variety of attitudes, beliefs, and values people have that are different from our own. By recognizing and appreciating this diversity in our public and small group communication, we are fulfilling our commitment to being responsible citizens living in a democratic society. The next time you are to give a speech or work in a small group, be cognizant of the fact that all participants are responsible communicators in one way or another. Whether you are speaking to a large group of strangers or interfacing with a few people, it is these opportunities for exchanging ideas and thoughts that can foster positive interracial communication between the races.

OPPORTUNITIES FOR EXTENDING LEARNING

1. Recall the last time that you spoke before a group of people. Did you have to give much thought to race within that particular context? Think of how you would adapt your speech to a racialized communication context. Make a list of

the accommodating behaviors you feel are essential to your success in the workplace. On a sheet of paper, describe how you would adapt your presentation and public communication skills to a racially/ethnically diverse audience.

2. Using Janice Hamlet's chapter "Understanding Traditional African American Communication" (in Gonzalez, Chen, and Houston's [1996] *Our Voices*), discuss the principles and assumptions she presents in her essay. Discuss how race influences religious communication in the United States. As a group, be sure to address what societal norms, if any, are violated when a non–African American adopts this style of preaching in a racialized environment. Also, make a list of how we are socialized to have expectations about how people from different racial groups engage in oral communication.

3. Using your university library, locate a hard paper copy of two speeches given by President Clinton (or any other politician) that are targeted to two different groups (e.g., racially mixed vs. predominately European American). As you compare the speeches, find examples of how the politician adapted his or her language to the audience (audience analysis) and the appropriateness of this strategy in persuading the audience. How would this speech change if it were given in a different context? What could have been done differently in order to make the message more persuasive?

4. Within recent years, there has been much debate around the issue of political correctness. Using *Infotrac College Edition,* search for articles that debate this issue as it relates to public communication. As you examine them, highlight the current debate on this topic and how it influences the messages we construct when we communicate in a large (and small) group context. More importantly, consider how these ideals are addressed within a racialized environment. (Are there some groups that are more sensitive to issues of political correctness than others? What role does this issue play in improving race relations between and among all racial groups?)

5. Recall an occasion when you attended a public presentation and were in the minority (e.g., the only Latina, only male). List the feelings you had about being in that situation, hearing the speech, and the speaker's (in)ability to connect with you as an audience member. On another list, write down suggestions for that speaker which would have made his or her speech more effective in a racialized environment.

RACE/ETHNICITY, INTERRACIAL COMMUNICATION, AND THE MASS MEDIA

THE IMPORTANCE OF THE MASS MEDIA

MASS MEDIA REPRESENTATIONS
OF RACIALIZED OTHERS

OTHER MASS MEDIA VENUES

RACIALIZED VIEWING HABITS:
FOCUS ON TELEVISION

IMPLICATIONS AND CONSEQUENCES
OF MEDIA IMAGES

CONCLUSION

OPPORTUNITIES FOR EXTENDED LEARNING

How often do you watch television, read the newspaper, listen to the radio, or use new technology to get information on a particular issue or topic of interest? All of us, in one way or another, rely on the media to help shape our opinions, attitudes, and beliefs on a variety of social issues that interest or affect us. Although using the media may seem very straightforward in terms of being informed or entertained, the consequences can be far reaching. The perceptions that we develop of ourselves, others, and the world are grounded in representations of reality vis-à-vis mass media images. This chapter begins by discussing the importance of the mass media and then follows with specific descriptions of how racial/ethnic groups are typically represented in various media outlets. Once this foundation has been established, we present the implications and consequences that these mass media images have in terms of interracial communication.

THE IMPORTANCE OF THE MASS MEDIA

Consider, for a moment, how our lives are inundated by media images. One hundred years ago most people in the United States were likely to get information about the world from only two sources: word of mouth and newspapers/newssheets.

Only a small number had immediate access to telephones. The early 1900s witnessed the growing importance of radio and newspapers for mass communication. Within the last 50 years, however, our communication has been transformed through technological advances. Some of you reading this text can not remember a world without a television, VCR, personal computer, cordless phone, pager, CNN, fax machine, or satellite TV. In concrete ways, the role that the media plays in our lives is central to our very existence.

As demonstrated throughout this book, many elements influence how we think about race/ethnicity in the United States. However, the pervasiveness of the media places it as a central influence on how we come to create, maintain, and/or transform our perceptions of race. In a society where formal racial barriers have been eradicated for several decades, a racial division continues to be perpetuated in the media. Whether it is in the newsroom, film, music television, situation comedies, or radio, the images of racial/ethnic groups (or lack thereof) presented in the media contribute to the ideologies that preserve the status quo of racism and discrimination in the United States. In addition, we must acknowledge how our interpersonal/interracial interactions are influenced by the media (Kellner, 1995; Omi, 1989). Because the media inform us about issues salient to our local, national, and international communities, our perceptions of each other are shaped and influenced by misinformation that only works to maintain the racial divide.

Let's be more explicit about the connection between the media and interracial communication. Mass media venues are used as primary sources of information for many people (Gray, 1995). Because we live in a largely segregated society, then, it is very likely that preliminary information received about those who are racially and ethnically different will come from some form of mass communication. The media may be used as an escape from or confirmation of reality. However, the images that we come to know through mass media exposure are often perceived as representative of certain racial, ethnic, or cultural groups (Gray, 1995). These (mis)representations can make interracial communication difficult because they may create false perceptions of others. In many cases, these media images can evolve into barriers and stereotypes (Entman, 1994) that hinder positive interracial interactions from occurring.

Studying mass communication is important to developing a deeper understanding of race relations in the United States. In addition to seeing the connection between mass media images and interracial interaction, several other points reflect why a mass media chapter is needed in a book about interracial communication. First, mass media images *reflect* societal values and ideas about race/ethnicity. Second, these images also *reinforce* widely shared ideals in terms of what is defined as normal. Increasing our critical awareness of these images, like those that appear in popular culture, enhance our understanding of how our society negotiates race

(Artz, 1998). Finally, it is important to understand how the media serves as gatekeepers to information about race/ethnicity. In other words, by selectively regulating what we see, the media influence how we ultimately come to understand issues related to race. Acknowledging these things allows us to see how the media influence everyday interracial communication.

MASS MEDIA REPRESENTATIONS OF RACIALIZED OTHERS

As indicated by the statistics provided in Chapter 1, the United States is becoming an increasingly diverse racial and ethnic society. In terms of mass media consumption, research reports that racial and ethnic microcultures (specifically, studies have focused on Latino/a and African Americans) watch more television and go to the movies more often than European Americans (Perkins, 1996; Tucker, 1997). Despite this reality, representations of "racialized others"—those racial/ethnic group members that are identified by their nondominant racial status in the United States—have a marginal presence in the U.S. media. People of color are largely underrepresented in all dominant mass media outlets; in some areas, some groups (e.g., Native Americans) are blatantly invisible. When images of microcultures do appear, more often than not they are placed in stereotypical roles. In order to clarify these statements for you, we review how each microculture has been represented in television and film. As you read through these descriptions, think about how each set of representations reflects general patterns of (1) invisibility, (2) underrepresentation, and (3) stereotypical depictions.

African Americans

Without question, images of African Americans in the mass media have attracted significantly more attention than those of other racial and ethnic U.S. minorities. While the majority of research has focused on images within television and film (e.g., Berry, 1992; Bogle, 1994; Evoleocha & Ugbah, 1989; Gray, 1989; MacDonald, 1992), mass media images of African Americans in a number of contexts have also been critiqued including those in cartoons (McLean, 1998), newspapers (Byrd, 1997; Martindale, 1997), magazine advertising (Seiter, 1990), and pornography (Mayall & Russell, 1997). Consistently these studies have revealed that African American images are largely confined to traditional stereotypes that have been associated with people of African descent in the United States for hundreds of years.

Mass-marketed images featuring racially charged humor can be traced to the late 1700s when stereotypical caricatures of African slaves appeared in theater presentations (Moore, 1980). European American performers, and later African

American ones as well, entertained the nation by wearing blackface, exaggerating African American behaviors, and subsequently creating racist stereotypes that continue to exist in the mass media (Bogle, 1994; MacDonald, 1992). These images permeate every aspect of the media and include representations of African American males as a sambo (lazy, jolly, content with life), coon (foolish, idiotic), Uncle Tom (quiet, respectful, goal is to please White man), and buck (strong, athletic, and sexually powerful). African American females portrayals include those of mammies (asexual, nurturing caregiver) or sapphires (sexually enticing). Both female and male pickaninnies (dirty, unkempt animal-like children) and mulattos (African Americans light enough to deceive European Americans to think they were White) are also prevalent.

According to Gandy and Matabane (1989), African Americans appeared on television in numbers representative of their general population during the 1980s. This was due to the increasing number of shows that appeared in the 1970s and continued—with new programs or reruns—well into the 1980s. Included in this large influx were shows like *Sanford & Son*, *Good Times*, *The Jeffersons*, *What's Happening*, *Different Strokes*, *227*, and *Amen*. Although these shows remained highly popular with African American audiences, they were continually criticized by researchers as simply reinventing traditional stereotypes in a contemporary context (MacDonald, 1992). In fact, some saw them as little more than characters with Black faces (or *in* blackface) paid to entertain European American audiences by exaggerating African American stereotypes.

This criticism leads to a significant trend in African American images in the mass media: They most often are relegated to comedic roles (Harris, 1997a; MacDonald, 1992; Narine, 1988). Rarely are African American female and male roles portrayed in venues that are primarily dramatic or romantic. A primary example of this marginalization is the critically acclaimed drama *Frank's Place* (1987–1988), which aired for a year on CBS. Network programmers failed to allow it to find its niche in a weekly time slot. After moving it to six different time slots on four different nights, it was difficult for viewers to give the show a chance. What is more disturbing, however, is that audiences were watching the program expecting it to be a traditional comedy (Campbell, 1999). Instead, the serious content centered around such issues as drugs, homelessness, and religion (Campbell, 1999). Unlike traditional representations of African Americans as "Black Minstrelsy" (MacDonald, 1992), *Frank's Place* did not provide a "safe or unthreatening context" to deal with the issues of class *and* race. This alternative format, coupled with few viewers, led to the demise of a promising drama that broke the expectation that racial/ethnic groups should be confined to sitcoms. Consider if this typecasting has continued: How many non–situation comedy shows featuring African Americans can you recall? If you were able to think of any, how many lasted more than a season or two?

Asian Americans

In reality the diverse group of U.S. citizens described within the umbrella term *Asian Americans* occupy diverse walks of life. However, you would never realize this diversity by relying on Asian American images that appear in movies and television. In early film portrayals, Asian women were typically seen as geishas, dragon ladies, whores, and exotic-erotics (Hagedom, 1997). Asian men were characterized as sinister, evil, buck-toothed subhuman villains, or passive detectives (Sing, 1989). Ironically, these stereotypical roles have been performed by Asian actors as well as by European Americans in "yellow face." Examples of the latter include such renowned actors as Katherine Hepburn (*Dragon Seed*, 1940s), Shirley MacLaine (*My Geisha* and *Gambit*, 1960s), Jerry Lewis (*Hardly Working*, 1981), and Joel Grey (*Remo Williams: The Adventures Begins*, 1985).

As television's popularity grew, the stereotypical images of Asian Americans traveled from the big screen into the homes of U.S. viewers. On television, the number of minority-lead series was greatest during the 1970s (Atkin, 1992). However, the majority of these shows featured African American actors. Like prior decades, images of Asian Americans remained largely invisible. One exception was the premiere of *Hong Kong*, which featured a number of Asian characters. However, representations of Asian American life were limited to Chinese intrigue, sexy women, smuggling, and drug peddling (Wilson & Gutierrez, 1985). Generally speaking, Asian Americans remained absent in leading roles. When they did appear on television, it was most often within the same stereotypical roles seen in film. One of the largest sources of Asian representation on U.S. television came with *Hawaii Five-O*, which aired from 1968 to 1980. At least three Asian actors fulfilled regular roles on the show, with more diverse but still stereotypical characters. After the mid-1980s, the number of Asian American roles increased and included less confining portrayals. Television shows such as *Gung Ho*, *After Mash*, *St. Elsewhere*, *Tour of Duty*, *21 Jumpstreet*, *Ohara* (which starred Pat Morita, the first Asian American actor to have a network series in prime time), *The Mystery Files of Shelby Woo*, *Marital Law*, and *Ally McBeal* included Asian American characters in a wide variety of less stereotypical and more complex roles (Sing, 1989).

Another significant program, in terms of Asian American representation on television, occurred in 1994 with the premiere of *All-American Girl*. This series, starring Korean American stand-up comedienne Margaret Cho, was the first prime-time series to feature a family of Asian Americans. Placed in a highly visible slot (immediately following top-rated *Roseanne*), the show regularly placed in the Top 20 programs. However, rating analyses indicated that the show did best in bigger cities on both coasts. This pattern revealed that the show was most popular in regions with significant Asian American populations, but struggled to find an audience outside of those areas (Dorsey, 1995). In terms of representations of Asian American culture, the show has been criticized by researchers as inauthentic of any one Asian culture, thereby reinforcing outgroup stereotypes that all Asian cultures are the same (Orbe, Seymour, & Kang, 1998).

Latino/a Americans

While mass media images of African Americans were increasing during the 1970s and 1980s, Latino/a representation in television and film lagged far behind (Gandy & Matabane, 1989). Like Asian Americans and Native Americans, Latino/as have been nearly absent in prime-time television (Lichter, Lichter, Rothman, & Amundson, 1987). The invisibility of this growing segment of the U.S. population is further maintained through non-Latino/a depictions of Latino/a culture (Hadley-Garcia, 1990) and the increasing number of Latino actors who are placed in "cross-over" roles (National Council of La Raza, 1998). For example, several Latino actors have recently portrayed characters whose appearance or behaviors present vague clues to their Latino culture. These include Dr. Philip Watters on *Chicago Hope* (played by Hector Elizondo) and Detective Bobby Simone of *NYPD Blue* (played by Jimmy Smits). Despite the actors' Latino identity, the racial/ethnic backgrounds of their characters remain ambiguous to viewers and invisible within the program's story line. Some see such "crossover appeal" as improvement within an industry that historically only hired Latinos in limiting stereotypical roles. However, others see it as a means to further extend the invisibility of Latino/a culture in mass media venues.

Traditionally when they do appear in television or in films, people of Latin descent are limited to stereotypical roles most always associated with lower-status occupations (Atkin, 1992). Latinos, for instance, are portrayed as inner-city criminals—usually Puerto Rican or Mexican American—who are violent and/or drug addicted (Rios, 1997; Siegel, 1995). Latina images have also been seen in equally limiting roles, including that of a virgin, whore, maid, or mother-saint (Rios, 1997). In this regard, Valdivia (1998) sees mass media images of Latinas as similar to African American women (e.g., welfare mother) but also different. Some of her work has analyzed the different roles that Rosie Perez has played in several films (e.g., *Do the Right Thing, Fearless, White Men Can't Jump*, and *It Could Happen to You*). Her conclusions are that Latinas are portrayed uniquely in terms of their stereotypical accents, loud personalities communicated both verbally and nonverbally (e.g., dress) and out-of-control sexuality (most often represented through sexually suggestive dancing). Valdivia's conclusions are made even more problematic given that most images of Latino/a culture are of men, further limiting the chance for a greater range of Latina images. In the 1980s, for instance, television portrayals of Latinos outnumbered Latinas 5 to 1 (Gandy & Matabane, 1989).

With such limited opportunities, it is nearly impossible for mass media images to capture the complexities of the diverse racial and ethnic groups that fall under the label of Latino/a. However, although still largely underrepresented on television, a mid-1990s analysis indicated that the number of negative portrayals of Latino/as has declined (National Council of La Raza, 1997). Some researchers (e.g., Delgado, 1998) see Latino/a mass media images following earlier patterns set by African Americans. For instance, some of the earliest nonstereotypical roles have been featured in police and espionage dramas where Latinos have been part of interracial partnerships (e.g., *New York Undercover*). In addition, opportunities for Latinos to play a more central role in the creation of mass media images have arisen within the comedy arena (e.g., *House of Buggin'* featuring John Leguizamo). Furthermore, the visibility of several movies (*Selena, Colors, Stand & Deliver, Extreme Prejudice*) has represented a move from Latino/a images as stereotyped "Other" into opportunities for self-representation (Delgado, 1998; Kellner, 1994). Like other racial and ethnic groups that continue to be under- and misrepresented in the mass media, self-representation will play a central role to more accurate, realistic portrayals.

Native Americans

Like Asian Americans, Native Americans have largely been invisible in terms of their representation in film and television. Check this statement with your life experiences. How many different Native American characters, in either films or on television, can you recall? Chances are you struggled to name very many, beyond stereotypical depictions of Native Americans in television programming that featured the U.S. frontier (e.g., *F-Troop*). This reality reflects the vast invisibility of Native culture in every aspect of the mass media. When Native American characters have appeared in film and television, like many of the other microcultures in the United States, they have been limited to roles that are largely stereotypical and marginal to the main plot.

Historically, Native American life has been portrayed negatively in the mass media. On television, Native Americans characters are typically depicted as vicious, cruel, lazy, and incompetent (in terms of keeping a job or surviving away from reservations) (Tan, Fujioka, & Lucht, 1997). In film, these portrayals have consistently involved characters who are bloodthirsty savages, barbaric drunkards, or uncivilized (free) spirits (Dwyer, 1993; Morris & Stuckey, 1998). In many instances, these characters were created and performed by non-Native people who knew little about Native culture outside of larger societal stereotypes. Because of this, many of the images of Native Americans that appeared in the mass media were actually outrageous *mis*representations of Native culture and language. *Taza, Son of Cochise*, for instance, was released in 1954. Throughout the film, the "Indian" characters do not

THEORY INTO PRACTICE

Within the past five to ten years, racial/ethnic marginalization in film, television programs, and awards ceremonies (e.g., the Oscars) has become an issue of great concern for many. As you consider the following tips, challenge yourself to think more critically about media marginalization.

- Be aware of myths and stereotypes perpetuated in the media about different racial/ethnic groups.
- Research how communities have actively made the media more conscious of and responsible for their stereotypic portrayals of racial/ethnic groups.
- Support television programs and networks (e.g., Warner Brothers [WB], Black Entertainment Television) that target urban audiences.
- Engage in open and honest dialogue with friends and peers from different racial/ethnic groups about racial/ethnic representation in the media.
- Be open to films, newspapers, music, and so on, targeted to racial/ethnic groups other than your own.
- Recognize that racial/ethnic stereotypes do exist and are often offensive to certain groups of people.
- Rethink the types of stereotypes you have about racial/ethnic groups.
- Rethink how you perceive racial/ethnic groups based on messages and images communicated in the media.
- Become more acquainted with magazines, films, and television programs targeted to certain racial/ethnic groups.

speak in any one of the many Native American languages. Instead, they speak gibberish. In a couple of scenes "Indian" characters actually are seen speaking Spanish (Dwyer, 1993)! Similar forms of misrepresentation appeared throughout the 1970s, including the film *Billy Two Hats* (1974). In this film, Native Americans were depicted by Israeli actors whose language and culture overshadowed any attempt to portray Native American life accurately (Dwyer, 1993).

In more recent years, however, some examples of more realistic media images of Native Americans have appeared on screen. In many instances, this is the result of including Native Americans in the creation and production of Native representations in different films (Sonny Skyhawk, founder of American Indians in Film, quoted in Dwyer, 1993). The result has been some positive depictions of Native American life. For instance, *Thunderheart* (1992) featured a story line that exposed the U.S. government's exploitation of Native people and their resources. *Dances With Wolves* (1990) and *Geronimo: An American Legend* (1993) helped show that Native people can be complex, multidimensional beings in terms of their human qualities (humor, fear, sensitivity, love). Some critics, however, see past stereotypes being substituted for new ones. Morris and Stuckey (1998) argue that new depictions romanticize Native Americans—and subsequently Native culture—as inherently gentle, peaceful, noble, and passive. These images reflect a "natural" connection to the environment, one which is contrasted with non-Native Americans who are more "civilized" and technologically advanced. Based within all these criticisms is one central idea: Accurate portrayals of Native Americans can not be reflected in the mass media until more developed characters appear in a variety of contexts. This improvement, coupled with more frequent contact with Native people (Tan et al., 1997), will begin a lengthy process to reduce the effects of negative media images. Only then will audiences be able to more fully understand the complexities of Native American culture and enhance their interracial communication effectiveness. This last point is an important one because of its general applicability to all microcultural mass media images.

OTHER MASS MEDIA VENUES

Our discussion of mass media representation of racialized others has focused thus far on television and film images for one simple reason: That is what is contained in most of the research. However, we must recognize the role that other mass media venues play in showcasing specific images of race relations in the United States. This section focuses on four mass media contexts (newspaper, advertising, comic strips, and the Internet) and explores research that describes how each represents microcultural images.

Newspapers

Although newspapers and other written communication have traditionally been targeted to general mass audiences, they did little in covering the news within different racial and ethnic groups outside of the mainstream. When microcultural groups did appear in these newspapers, they were reported as people who either *had* problems or *caused* problems for society (Wilson & Gutierrez, 1985). For instance, coverage of African Americans heavily emphasized stories about crime and did little to cover the everyday life activities of the African American community (Martindale, 1980). Similar patterns appeared for Latino communities; individual stories presented Latino/as as a threat or problem for the larger society (Gutierrez, 1980). Native Americans were largely ignored in the press except in times of conflict or when presented as exotic curiosities (Weston, 1992). In comparison, coverage of Asian Americans appeared to reinforce cultural stereotypes and reflect a clear racial hostility to various Asian American communities (Heuterman, 1987).

Ethnic Newspapers   As a result of the problematic nature of these limited stereotypical images, other newspapers written for and by specific racial/ethnic group members began to emerge (Campbell, 1999). These alternative forms of journalism were greatly needed because they presented views and issues affecting the everyday lives of many groups of color who could not get such information from mainstream newspapers. Can you imagine reading a newspaper where you are unable to relate to any of the articles or issues written by the journalists? Because mainstream newspapers have not been sensitive to the needs of various racial/ethnic groups, ethnic newspapers have historically filled a tremendous void for various microcultural communities in the United States (Shim, 1997). These have included publications geared toward new immigrants that were written in German, Yiddish, Russian, Spanish, and Polish and circulated throughout racial and ethnic communities (Campbell, 1999). Even as recently as the 1980s we have seen Cuban, Haitians, Pakistani, Laotian, Cambodian, and Chinese newspapers, some of which are still in existence today. Ethnic newspapers also include those designed for racial and ethnic groups whose histories in the United States extend that of "newcomer status." For instance, over 200 Spanish-language and 350 Native American newspapers have been documented (Campbell, 1998). Similar publications also exist within other racial and ethnic communities. In fact, during the mid-1800s over 40 African American newspapers were documented in the United States.

Improvements (?) in Racialized Images   In recent years, mainstream newspapers have worked to diversify their staff as a means to improve their coverage of different racial and ethnic communities. The result, according to some, has been a greater sensitivity in terms of negative portrayals and a conscious attempt to include positive images whenever possible. In light of these improvements, some scholars question the continued need for ethnic newspapers (e.g., Shim, 1997).

Recent studies have confirmed some improvement in how racial and ethnic minorities in the United States are represented in newspapers. Martindale (1997), for instance, reported that coverage on the African American community is "more, abundant, varied and balanced than ever before" (p. 90). However, she also notes that it still tends to focus on the negative aspects of African American life. In terms of other groups, it appears that mainstream newspaper coverage continues to be problematic. Analyses reveal age-old stereotypical images of Native Americans within the same old story lines (e.g., alcoholism, poverty, conflict). Latino/as were found to be depicted largely as foreign to the United States and its values. The same pattern emerged for the coverage of Asian Americans, who were consistently presented as foreigners in the United States regardless if they were fifth-generation citizen or newly arrived immigrant. Although these images retain some traditional stereotypes of Asian Americans, Wong (1997) notes that they are increasingly becoming more representative of the diversity within Asian American communities.

Dialogue on Responsible Journalism You might assume that the change in the faces reporting the news in mainstream newspapers would bring multiple viewpoints on newsworthy issues. Unfortunately, such is not always the case. First, the increased diversity among newspaper staff has been minimal. According to noted journalist Ellis Cose, there is a "skewed reality" because of unequal racial/ethnic representation within the ranks of news reporters (Hernandez, 1994a). Second, although some increases have been noted, critics report that they—absent of other major changes—have done very little to alter the mainstream attitudes and beliefs promoted in the papers. At the Unity '94 conference held in Atlanta, journalists from different U.S. racial and ethnic minority groups met to discuss concerns regarding representation and diversity in journalism. Issues addressed dealt with exploitation not only occurring in print but among the journalists as well. For example, Unity '94 spoke out against the use of Native American names and symbols used by athletic teams, yet chauffeured conference attendees around on a bus displaying the "tomahawk chop" (Hernandez, 1994b).

Bridge's (1994) essay articulates an important dilemma facing mainstream newspapers. By ignoring and omitting the opinions and concerns of racial/ethnic communities, the media are contributing to the racialized tensions in the United States (Fitzgerald & Hernandez, 1994). Individuals exposed to the purported truths about racial/ethnic groups and race relations are subject to perpetuating existing stereotypes. As a result, individuals are less likely to engage in healthy interracial interactions. As Bridge describes it, the use of a one-dimensional perspective in the newsroom fails to capture the richness of our racial/ethnic diversity. In essence, this tunnel vision is played out in the hiring practices of the industry and the thinking process involved in determining what is newsworthy and what is not (Bridge, 1994). One result of this process is a heightened tension in terms of race relations and a fear of being insensitive to others, or even possibly being labeled a racist. In her observations from the Unity '94 conference, Hernandez (1994b) reports that the personal fears of the journalists influence whether or not racial issues and news items are covered. When addressed, these same personal fears inform how the stories are researched, written, and edited. This point is confirmed by John Santos, director of program development at public television in New York. He points to how cultural baggage reporters bring to the newsroom has a direct influence in the ways that news is eventually reported.

The topic of racial and ethnic diversity continues to be an important issue for mainstream newspapers. In 1994, USA TODAY/CNN/Gallup Polls showed that approximately one third of African Americans, Asian Americans, and Latino/a Americans read their local newspapers regularly ("Polls Find Minorities Dissatisfied with Media," 1994). This is compared to more than one half of European Americans who do so. At least part of this trend can be attributed to how racial/ethnic group members perceive the coverage of their communities.

Advertising

Another area of the mass media in which race/ethnicity is problematic is in magazine and television advertising (Taylor, Lee, & Stern, 1995; Taylor & Stern, 1997). The goal of advertising has evolved to selling merchandise within a consumer-driven society (Campbell, 1999). By using persuasive techniques, advertisers are more likely to experience high sale volumes in a given market as long as the product is one that consumers will purchase. More likely than not, consumers will be drawn to those products and images they find appealing. In terms of representations of racial and ethnic minorities, advertising treatment of diversity is consistent with other mass media venues. Historically, the images of people of color in advertisements have appeared in significantly fewer numbers than that reflected in the U.S. population. More recently, advertisers have included greater racial/ethnic diversity as a means to obtain a more broad market appeal. However, people of color in ads largely continue to appear in stereotypical and complementary roles (Seiter, 1990). For instance, Bowen and Schmid (1997) report that the number of African American models used in magazine advertisements has increased. However, these persons were most often represented as athletes or musicians. Seiter (1990) sees this as an attempt by advertisers to "use" a single African American to visually represent "diversity" in general. In this regard, advertisers are criticized for aligning racial/ethnic diversity in simple "Black-White" terms.

Looking at current advertisements, magazine ads continue to feature images of underrepresented racial/ethnic groups sparingly (Taylor, Lee, & Stern, 1995; Taylor & Stern, 1997). By being excluded from mainstream magazines, racial/ethnic microcultural groups are more likely to fall victim to damaging stereotypical depictions when they are included in advertisements. Taylor et al. (1995) reviewed mainstream magazines and found stereotypical depictions of Latino/as, Asian Americans, and African Americans in magazine ads to be very powerful, with only a few stereotypes disappearing. Most of these ads are largely within a business context, which presents an interesting issue relative to representation. Although African Americans are presented more positively than they traditionally have been (professionals versus domestics), they are also in nontechnical categories, confirming the stereotype of being an uneducated group of people (Taylor et al., 1995). Asian Americans are portrayed as workaholics and appear in technical product categories, consistent with the stereotype of being hardworking, intelligent, and highly skilled in math and science (i.e., model minority). Latino/as are stereotyped as being family oriented and are placed in family settings instead of professional contexts. In general, Latino/as are severely underrepresented. They account for 9% of the U.S. population yet appear in only 4.7% of the sample ads in this study (Taylor et al., 1995). Overall, the findings indicate an unwelcome tokenism occurring in advertising (Taylor et al., 1995). The charge for advertisers is to deconstruct stereotypes by placing microcultural actors in major roles and in settings and relationships they are not stereotypically associated with.

In a later study, Taylor and Stern (1997) explored television advertising limited to the "model minority" stereotype ascribed to Asian Americans. The model minority stereotype refers to the notion that the work ethic of Asian Americans dispels any belief that racial/ethnic groups cannot achieve "the American Dream." Therefore, the economic success of Asian Americans is something that can be attained by all other racial/ethnic groups. Using prime-time television ads, the authors analyzed the content of approximately 1,300 commercials containing at least one Asian American character. Taylor and Stern (1997) found Asian Americans to be highly represented in background roles and in roles where greater emphasis was placed on work ethic (i.e., business settings) and business relationships. Despite increased representation on television, advertisements continue to perpetuate stereotypes of the "model minority" (Taylor & Stern, 1997). The authors again observe a form of tokenism occurring in advertising. Instead of being less accusatory in the diverse representations of each group's membership, advertisers are diversifying their models but maintaining the very stereotypes that need to be challenged.

As we can see in the research summarized here, the invisibility of diverse racial/ethnic images in advertising contributes to an overall social marginalization. When they do appear in ads, more than likely, people of color are regulated to limited stereotypical roles. These stereotypical representations can be obvious or more subtle, they reflect—and therefore reinforce—other negative images of diverse racial/ethnic groups in the media.

Comic Strips

Do you remember racing for the Sunday paper to get the full-page comic section before anyone else could? Most likely, it was the weekly or daily antics of *Garfield* the cat or the *Peanuts* gang that captured your interest and tickled your funny bone. As we have come to know them, cartoons as a visual culture (Whetmore, 1998) can be either humorous or serious (Campbell, 1998). They eventually included "social comics" (e.g., *Cathy*), adventure strips (e. g., *Superman*), and reality-based comics (e.g., *For Better or Worse*) that appealed to a cross section of readers. In reality-based comic strips in newspapers (e.g., Garry Trudeau's *Doonesbury* and newcomer Aaron McGruder's *Boondocks*) provide satirical commentaries on social and political events of the day. These comic strips challenge readers to think about the issue at hand—many of which are avoided by other forms of the media.

Historically, racial/ethnic members of underrepresented groups in the United States have appeared marginally in comic strips. Most often their images reflected either blatantly racist thinking or limited stereotypical roles (e.g., Latin lover, savage native, Black sambo or mammy) (McLean, 1998). Comic strips, like other mass media venues, have attempted to diversify their characters in order to better reflect the general public (and also attract wider readership). In many instances, these attempts have focused on incorporating a single minority character as a means to represent a commitment to diversity (e.g., Franklin in *Peanuts*). In other cases, comic strips introduced an array of racial/ethnic characters, only to have them assume marginal status in relation to the central European American characters (e.g., *Beetle Bailey*). Without exception, the only non–European American lead roles appear in more recent comic strips that feature predominate non-European American characters (e.g., *Curtis*, *Jump Start*, *Boondocks*). As a general rule, researchers have found that the more prominent the character in the comic strip, the less stereotypical the portrayal (McLean, 1998).

Editorial cartoonists were recently challenged to think about how intended and perceived meanings in comic strips further complicate race relations in the United States. This was in response to a study (News Watch: A Critical Look at Coverage of People of Color) produced by the Center for Integration and Improvement of Journalism at San Francisco State University (Stein, 1997). This comprehensive study was conducted in conjunction with the national organizations of Asian American, African American, Latino/a, and Native American journalists. In more recent times, editorial cartoonists have continued to discuss comic stereotypes and caricatures (Astor, 1996). At issue is what constitutes offensiveness in a comic strip. Although some cartoonists note that blatant stereotypes of racial/ethnic groups are no longer a part of cartoons, others point out the subtle ways in which stereotyping occurs. In the end, however, it is the reader's reaction to these images that truly determines what is offensive and what is not. Several recent examples illustrate this point, including images of a pipe-smoking Native American (*St. Paul Pioneer Press*), satirical images of Mexican men and women (*New Yorker*), and the use of derogatory words to describe people of color (*Sacramento Bee*) (Stein, 1997). As illustrated later, the impact of such images—even when they are intended to condemn racism—is questioned.

A recent comic satirizing a social tragedy reignited controversy over and interest in the moral responsibility and ethics of cartoonists. Cartoonist Kirk Walters of the *Toledo* (Ohio) *Blade* drew a cartoon condemning the Ku Klux Klan for their slurs against the June 6, 1998, dragging death of James Byrd, Jr., an African American man, by two European American men in Jasper, Texas (Noack, 1998). In the cartoon, Walters drew a hood-wearing Klan member "speaking out against" the crime, commenting that tying the man to the bumper "could hurt the resale value of the truck" (Noack, 1998, p. 10). In response to public outcries against the cartoon, co-publisher and executive vice president of the newspaper John Block proposed a more strict editorial cartoon review process, which would have ideally prevented this cartoon from reaching print. As for Walters, he was distressed by how people interpreted his cartoon. Reportedly, it was his intention to bring attention to the irony of the Klan's condemnation of this horrible act when they themselves have a history of lynching African Americans (Noack, 1998). Walters struggled over his cartoon and intentions, stating that he was now being accused of the very thing he was totally opposed to—racism. In the end, Block stated that the cartoon, whether intended or not, trivialized the Ku Klux Klan's legacy of terrorism and violence (Noack, 1998). Conversely, Paul Fell, an editorial cartoonist in Nebraska, felt that the cartoon was not done in bad taste. According to Fell, people were simply "misreading" the cartoon.

Internet

Because of space limitations we have not been able to discuss interracial communication within the context of every type of the mass media. However, the unique form of the Internet (or cyberspace) as a media text deserves some attention. The Internet was first introduced in the 1990s as a free and open system of information. In order to bring some semblance of order to this technology, the World Wide Web (WWW) was used by the Internet to standardize the information accessible to users across the world. One unique aspect of the Internet that distinguishes it from other media is that it allows users to engage in simulated interface exchanges. Instead of communicating with individuals face to face, people can become a part of a "virtual community" (Campbell, 1999). This cyberspace site allows users to transcend space and time and engage in on-screen conversations with people who share similar interests. Within this mass media venue, interracial communication can occur between individuals whose racial/ethnic identity is unknown. Some see one of the greatest benefits of cyberspace communication as its ability to nurture interactions that occur within a "color-blind" context.

11.1   *Hate Groups on the Internet*

In 1997, the Southern Poverty Law Center reported the existence of 474 hate groups in the United States (Estes, 1999). Within this number were different types of hate groups (as defined by the center) including Ku Klux Klan, neo-Nazi, skinhead, Christian Identity, and Black separatist groups. In 1998, the number of hate groups jumped to almost 550! Florida had the most hate groups (38), followed by California (36), Texas (31), Pennsylvania (27), and Alabama (25) (Estes, 1999). According to those who track the growth of hate groups in the United States, the Internet is the primary factor in this large increase.

Many hate groups use radio, magazine, newspaper, and telephone hot lines to support their movements. However, the Internet has provided these groups with a new way to communicate. As reported in a number of articles, the Internet has been used to promote an increased visibility and accessibility of hate groups. Between 1997 and 1998, for instance, there was a 60% increase in the number of White supremacist Web sites (Raspberry, 1999). According to Mark Potok, a researcher for the Southern Poverty Law Center, "The Internet is allowing the white supremacy movement to reach places it has never reached before" (quoted in Estes, 1999, p. 5). The heightened visibility on the Internet has also had another effect. Traditionally, individuals who believed in racial supremacy were typically isolated within their own communities, alone or with a few compatriots. However, the Internet has allowed these individuals to connect with another and obtain a sense of a national movement. The result is a drastic increase in organized hate groups in the United States.

At this point, not much research has been conducted on the nature of interracial communication on the Internet. However, Victoria Shannon, a reporter for the *Washington Post*, has written about some of the positive and negative experiences of African Americans who communicate on-line (Shannon, 1997). Like most U.S. American Internet users, African Americans on-line see the Internet as an invaluable resource for information and open interaction. Shannon (1997) explained its effect on open, honest communication:

> The anonymity of typed words on a computer screen encourages people to speak their minds. On-line chatting is unlike hallway conversations you have with your colleagues. . . .

> It's quick, it's often emotional, it's often without facts. . . . On racial issues, this anonymity can be positive. People truly communicate, bring up forbidden subjects and come away with a new understanding of one another. (p. 259)

However, cyberspace anonymity also can provide a forum where individuals with racist beliefs can make quality interracial communication difficult. According to Estes (1999), the presence of hate groups on the Internet is growing (see accompanying box) Some persons associated with these groups may engage in hostile and threatening interactions with people of color communicating on-line (even those in forums dedicated specifically to one microcultural racial/ethnic group). However, Shannon (1997) reported that African Americans experience a larger problem during interracial communication in cyberspace. During many on-line conversations, African Americans are confronted with postings from European Americans that reflect cultural ignorance and racist ideologies. The presence (and subsequent defense) of these anonymous messages may work to foster a disconnection between different racial and ethnic groups. In this regard, they act as a constant reminder to people of color in the United States that racist beliefs are still prevalent despite not always being apparent in face-to-face interactions.

Another related concern to the information gained through cyberspace is that the messages on Web sites are not always accurate (Campbell, 1999). Because few regulations prevent misinformation from being leaked to the masses, the Internet is not as accurate as other media (e.g., information via newspapers, magazines, television). An example of how difficult it is to regulate Internet access occurred on February 8, 1996, when Congress passed and President Clinton signed a law restricting children's access to obscene, indecent, or harassing material. However, the Communications Decency Act (CDA) was later ruled as violating First Amendment rights. The judge's position was that the law is too broad and goes against the very democratic nature of the Internet.

The Internet is a definite asset in society because it provides us with unlimited access to resources and information that may not be available in newspapers, magazines, or on television. This unlimited access, however, does not appear equally across the different racial and ethnic groups in the United States. Research consistently reports that Asian Americans and European Americans have much greater access to the information superhighway than others. Although some reports indicate this gap is closing ("Blacks Closing Gaps," 1999), others point to the growing disparity between specific groups. For instance, a study found that 47% of European Americans own computers, but fewer than half as many African Americans do. Only about 25% of Latino/as Americans own computers. However, over 55% of Asian Americans have one, and 36% have Internet access—the highest of all racial/ethnic groups ("NAACP, AT&T Work to Narrow 'Digital Divide,'" 1999). Most troubling is that these differences are not solely based on income disparities.

Children in lower-income European American families are three times more likely to have Internet access as children in a comparable African American family and four times more likely than those in a Latino/a American household. Consider one specific study that looked at families earning between $15,000 and $35,000 ("Report: Online Gap Grows for Blacks," 1999). More than 33% of European Americans owned computers, but only 19% of African Americans did—a gap that *has widened nearly 62%* since 1994 despite more affordable computer prices.

11.2 *Personal Reflection*

I was recently using the Internet to find current research on interracial dating. I wanted to find personal narratives or stories that would provide a real-life perspective on what it is like to be involved in an interracial romantic relationship. After skimming over a few Web sites, I accidentally came across a chat room. People were involved in an ongoing and heated debate on this very topic. Apparently, this cyberspace discussion had been going on for several weeks, and people were continuing to respond to comments and opinions shared by others.

At first, the comments were innocent enough. However, as I began to click onto different sites, I was horrified to see peoples' opinions about interracial dating. Insulting comments involved references to African Americans as beasts, Asian Americans as "White wanna-be's," and the European American race as superior to all others. I was sickened by these ignorant comments and began to wonder if any cyberspace police were monitoring this kind of racism on the Internet.

After calming down, I was faced with the reality of cyberspace. The information highway has its benefits, which include the freedom of speech. However, should this freedom in cyberspace allow people to promote their racist ideologies in a public forum? Because the United States is a democratic society, people do have the right to exercise their First Amendment rights, even on the Internet. If people's negative attitudes toward race are going to change, there should be more sites accenting positive experiences with interracial communication. What's more important is that accusatory and attacking tactics should not be used to improve race relations. Instead, we should use the Internet as a platform for honest dialogue and interchanges on how interracial communication *is possible.*—TMH

As illustrated through this section, the introduction of the Internet to the worldwide community has been both a blessing and a curse in terms of interracial communication and race relations in the United States. The Internet offers people the freedom to share ideas and opinions with others across the globe yet runs the risk of communicating inaccurate and potentially damaging information to users. As a medium still in its early stages of evolution, the issue of democracy, equity, and globalized freedom of speech will remain at the center of the debate circling the use of the Internet for years to come.

RACIALIZED VIEWING HABITS: FOCUS ON TELEVISION

As we described in the opening paragraphs of this chapter, television plays a tremendous role in the lives of most U.S. Americans. We have presented some information about the representation of racial/ethnic images on television. However, we turn now to another television phenomenon worth some attention: the viewing habits of different racial/ethnic groups.

In terms of television viewing, two clear patterns emerge when comparing different racial/ethnic groups. First, Latino/a and African Americans watch considerably more television than their European American counterparts (Perkins, 1996; Tucker, 1997). Although this behavior may be more reflective of socioeconomic differences rather than simply race/ethnicity, the differences are noteworthy. For instance, in a study conducted from October 1993 to January 1994, African Americans were found to watch television 74.9 hours a week compared to 49.9 hours for non–African Americans (Perkins, 1996). The largest differences occurred during late night programming when African Americans were found to watch 90% more TV!

The second pattern, regarding racialized television viewing habits includes the specific types of programs that attract specific racial groups. Like most other research on race, studies found glaring differences in European American and African American viewing habits. (We would suggest that differences among other racial/ethnic group comparisons exist; however they are not as notable as the gaps between "Blacks" and "Whites"; therefore they have not received as much attention from researchers.) For instance, three studies completed at different times throughout the 1990s reveal the weak correlations between the Top 10 prime-time shows when comparing African American and European American viewers. For the 1993–1994 season, not one show appeared on both lists ("African-Americans' Viewing Habits," 1994). *Home Improvement*, the top-rated program among European Americans, barely made the Top 30 list for African Americans. Other popular shows for European American viewers, like *Seinfeld* (no.3) and *Frasier* (no. 6), did not even crack the Top 90 most watched shows for African American viewers.

Living Single, the top-rated show among African Americans, ranked 69th among all audiences (Farhi, 1992). This trend was repeated in a study conducted on the 1996–1997 season. One show, ABC's *Monday Night Football*, managed to appear in the Top 10 programs for both European American and African American viewers' list (Dorsey, 1997). However, the differences between racialized viewing habits remained apparent. Ten of the fifteen most watched programs for African American households had predominately African American casts. Overall, their top three shows—*Living Single*, *New York Undercover*, and *Martin* (all which appeared on Fox)—had dismal numbers among European American viewers (ranking numbers 103, 105, and 100, respectively). The most recent data available at the time of publication echoes these patterns. Not one show ranked in the Top 10 list for both groups in 1998 (Hass, 1998). The number 1 and 2 shows among European American viewers, *ER* and *Seinfeld* (NBC), ranked 18 and 52 for African American viewers. The top-rated show for African Americans, *Between Brothers* (Fox), was the 107th most watched show among European Americans.

As you read through our descriptions comparing the viewing habits of European Americans and African Americans, you have probably been considering your own personal choices when it comes to prime-time programming. How would your Top 10 programs compare to others within your own racial/ethnic group? If recent research is correct, your age may play as an important role as race/ethnicity in your viewing habits. Consider the following conclusion drawn from audience analysis research (Farhi, 1994; Hass, 1998): The racial/ethnic divisions among television viewing is most apparent among middle-aged adults. When focusing on younger viewers (ages 12–17), research indicates that they are much more likely to watch shows on either Top 10 lists. The same goes for viewers over the age of 50. Both African American and European households in this age group watched 13 of the same 20 shows (Dorsey, 1997). These findings are consistent with a central theme of our book (see Chapter 5 in particular): Focusing on race/ethnicity is helpful in understanding behaviors, but not as useful as analyzing intersections of race, ethnicity, and other cultural elements like age. Take some time to reflect on your television viewing habits. In addition to your race/ethnicity and age, what are some other elements of your cultural identity (socioeconomic status, spirituality, gender, etc.) that influence them?

TV Sitcoms

The situation comedy is currently the only genre to appear in the Top 10 programs every year since 1949 (Campbell, 1999). It has also emerged as most responsible for addressing controversial issues with humor (Whetmore, 1998). It was through the show *All in the Family* that producer Norman Lear was able to present realistic commentary addressing racial and ethnic issues. With the development of other shows such as *The Jeffersons*, *Maude*, and *Good Times*, Lear was able to bring some diversity to television programming. Lear's programs were also unique because he took a risk and centered his sitcoms around controversial racial and social issues that other networks and programs avoided. Although Lear is to be recognized and commended for his attempts to include racial/ethnic issues in television, it appears that representations of microcultural groups with any success with viewers have been relegated to sitcoms (e.g., *The Cosby Show*, *A Different World*, *Living Single*) and not television dramas (e.g., *Frank's Place*, or *Under One Roof*). Such disparity reinforces the stereotype that people of color cannot be taken seriously. Instead, the use of humor and stereotypes may potentially reinforce bigotry (Harris & Hill, 1998) targeted toward different racial/ethnic groups.

Hass (1998) describes prime-time comedy shows as "one of the last bastions of public segregation" (p. D3). As described earlier, the increasing racial divide behind audience-viewing patterns is relatively new, however. This is because, until the early to mid 1990s, there were not enough shows with microcultural casts (predominately Latino, African American, etc.) to fragment the audience. An increased awareness of the large numbers of African American and Latino viewers in a highly competitive market prompted new networks (Fox, WB, and UPN) to establish an audience base by offering shows featuring predominately African American (and a few Latino/a) casts (*In Living Color*, *Buggin' Out*, *South Central*, *The Parent Hood*, *Martin*, *Living Single*, *Between Brothers*). Although considerably successful with viewers of color, as well as young European Americans, these shows seemingly follow a similar network life: They are abandoned for more traditional shows (with more mainstream appeal) once they have helped secure an audience viewer base for the network. The logic of the network executives is that although these shows are popular with some segments of the population, they can never achieve "true success" because European American viewers will not watch programs with predominately microcultural casts. Various sources of media research support their reasoning.

One of the only exceptions that was able to transcend the racial (and generational) divide of viewer habits was *The Cosby Show*, which aired on NBC from 1984 to 1992. Like many of the shows in the 1980s (*227*, *Amen*, *Benson*), this situation comedy featured representations of a successful African American middle class—one that had greater universal appeal (Merritt, 1991). In fact, *The Cosby Show* has been recognized as paving the way for other shows featuring African Americans because it was a "real life example of a previously unrecognized class of Black Americans who are making it in American society" (Tucker, 1997, p. 103). Both adult characters on the show (Claire and Cliff Huxtable) were accomplished professionals (lawyer, doctor) and supportive parents to five children (all of which were in—or on their way to—various stages of higher education). Ranking as the number-one watched show by both African American and European American viewers, the crossover appeal of *The Cosby Show* was unprecedented for modern-day television. In fact, it was the first situation comedy with a predominately African American cast to accomplish the feat of being the number-one watched program. According to research, African American viewers appreciated the positive cultural images presented on the show, and European Americans enjoyed the universal appeal of the show (Jhally & Lewis, 1992). Although his ratings have not been as impressive, Bill Cosby's most recent sitcom, *Cosby*, has also enjoyed similar crossover appeal (Hass, 1998).

IMPLICATIONS AND CONSEQUENCES OF MEDIA IMAGES

If media images had no effect on how we communicate within our everyday lives, there would be little need for concern. However, research clearly demonstrates that the racial/ethnic images which appear in the media work to reinforce societal stereotypes of others (Omi, 1989). According to Kellner (1995), mass media images are a central beginning in how "many people construct their sense of 'us' and 'them'" (p. 1). Therefore, they play a central role in all of our everyday lives (Brooks & Jacobs, 1996)—especially whenever "we" come into contact with "them" (however those categories are created along racial/ethnic boundaries). As indicated throughout this chapter, mass media images of underrepresented group members are especially powerful given the quality and quantity of portrayals. The power of these mostly negative images has not gone unnoticed by people of color in the United States. For instance, think about the comments of Henry Louis Gates (1992):

> Historically blacks have always worried aloud about the image that white Americans harbor of us, first because we have never had control of those images and, second, because the greater number of those images have been negative. And given television's immediacy and its capacity to reach so many viewers so quickly, blacks . . . have been especially concerned with our images on screen.

Clearly, one effect that mass media images have had on interracial communication can be seen in how they have reinforced existing racial/ethnic stereotypes. However, an equally important effect is related to how the mass media has presented examples of interracial communication. According to some scholars (e.g., Gray, 1995), most media texts create separate worlds for different racial/ethnic groups. For instance, the vast majority of television programs and films feature casts of one racial or ethnic group. And although some may include one or two token representations of outgroup members, their presence is marginal to the overall plot. When interracial communication does occur, it is done with little, or no, attention to any sort of racial/ethnic barriers. These depictions are too simplistic to model any concrete strategies for effective interracial communication for viewers. Some scholars, as explained in the next section, even see how these more positive images of race/ethnicity contribute to a new form of racism.

11.3   *Case Study: Lifetime's* Any Day Now

In 1998, *Any Day Now*, an original series created by Lifetime Television, premiered to a responsive audience. The series revolves around the interracial friendship between two women, one African American and the other European American. Throughout each episode, viewers are presented with flashbacks of how their friendship developed within the context of a small Alabama town during the height of the civil rights movement. However, the show focuses on how these two friends reunite decades later only to find themselves leading different lives. Viewers for Quality Television gave the show its highest rating for any new drama on basic cable (Petrozzello, 1998).

Any Day Now builds on a number of themes familiar to Lifetime viewers (women's roles, friendship, marriage, family). However, it also deals honestly and openly with issues of racial equality, discrimination, and the history of the U.S. civil rights movement. For instance, many of the episodes contain story lines that feature different challenges and rewards that come with interracial friendships. In addition, a balance is maintained in the show so that viewers come to understand the complexities of each woman's perspective. In this regard, the friendship between the two main characters represents something largely absent from television images: a model of effective interracial communication that features how individuals can work through racial/ethnic differences. Unlike other shows that tend to only include race relations in superficial ways, *Any Day Now* presents an example of effective interracial communication on a more personal level. Ideally viewers can use some of these images to enhance their own interracial effectiveness within their everyday lives.

Are you aware of other mass media images that help viewers understand the complexity of race relations in the United States? If so, where do they appear (in mainstream or other alternative media formats)? Think about how these images extend beyond traditional stereotypes. Do they also model examples of effective interracial communication? How so?

Fostering an "Enlightened Racism"

As described earlier, one of the most positive images of race/ethnicity on television was *The Cosby Show*. In terms of its representation of race relations in the United States, however, the success of the show was called into question by several media scholars (Jhally & Lewis, 1992; Tucker, 1997). Their primary criticism focused on how the show presented a candy-coated snapshot of the African American family that ignored the devastating social conditions of many African Americans in the United States. The show, according to Jhally and Lewis (1992), never offered viewers even the slightest glimpse of the economic disadvantages and deep-rooted discrimination that pervade the lives of most African Americans. Instead, the show was criticized for featuring African American characters with the values of European American middle-class culture (Tucker, 1997). The Huxtables, then, were proof that issues related to family had universal appeal among all viewers—as long as certain areas of African American life (e.g., racism) were made invisible.

According to Jhally and Lewis (1992), the Huxtables' accomplishments in their personal, family, and professional lives worked to perpetuate the myth of the "American Dream:" We live in a just world where hard work and perseverance are rewarded and racial barriers no longer exist. In other words, the Huxtables proved that Black people can succeed. However, in doing so, they also promoted the perception that when African Americans do not succeed (like the Huxtables) they only have themselves to blame (Tucker, 1997). In this regard, the show cultivated the perception, particularly for European Americans, that racism is no longer a significant problem in the United States. The reason why most African Americans do not succeed, according to this line of thinking, is because they use racism as a crutch. Within these perceptions is the development of a new form of "enlightened racism" (Jhally & Lewis, 1992). This perspective of racial relations acknowledges the historical significance of racism in the United States. However, it sees the 21st century as a time when the effects of racism have been greatly reduced to the point that the American Dream is now available for all those who are willing to work to achieve it.

Television is not the only mass medium where a new form of enlightened racism has been promoted. Other researchers (e.g., Artz, 1998; Bogle, 1994) have demonstrated how the growing number of "interracial buddy films" have also perpetuated the idea of individual equality while ignoring realities of race relations in the United States. A number of well-publicized and highly popular movies depict (mostly, but not exclusively) European American–African American partnerships: *Silver Streak*, *48 Hours*, *Beverly Hills Cops*, *The Last Boy Scout*, *Die Hard*, *Lethal Weapon*, *The Money Train*, *Men in Black*, *Rush Hour*, and *Wild, Wild West*. Beyond their attraction as action-adventure-comedy pictures, these films use the name recognition of stars (e.g., Bruce Willis, Eddie Murphy, Mel Gibson, Danny Glover, Tommy Lee Jones, and Will Smith) within their respective communities to draw diverse audiences to the box office. According to Artz (1998), however, different segments of the audience are attracted to interracial buddy films for different reasons. African Americans enjoy seeing African American actors in roles that exhibit strength, dignity, and intelligence. They are also drawn to these movies because African American culture is recognizable and portrayed in positive ways. European Americans are attracted to these films because they represent the fantasy of interracial cooperation. Artz (1998) argues that what is most appealing is that these partnerships exist without challenging the status quo. For instance, he notes that in most interracial buddy films two things exist: (1) European American authorities are ultimately in charge, and (2) the lone African American hero is separated from his community.

So how do these films, like *The Cosby Show*, perpetuate an enlightened racism among media consumers? Critics argue that interracial buddy films, like most other mass media representations of interracial communication, portray the positive aspects of interracial partnerships with no substantial attention to the real-life problems that plague such relationships. Bogle (1994) describes them as "wish-fulfillment fantasies for a nation that has repeatedly hoped to simplify its racial tensions" (pp. 271–272). Like what media critics have said about *The Cosby Show*, these fictitious depictions of interracial cooperation bring the focus of U.S. race relations to the personal (individual) level while ignoring the larger societal context in which they exist.

CONCLUSION

This chapter described the crucial role that the mass media plays in our perceptions of race relations in the United States. Specifically, we discussed how different racial and ethnic groups are portrayed in the media. In addition, by examining specific areas of the media we focused our attention on media use and its influence on viewers' attitudes and beliefs. We hope that the material shared throughout the chapter enhanced your understanding of the key role that mass media images play in terms of everyday life interactions.

Although many may think that reading the newspaper, watching television, and using the Internet are activities that do not directly involve issues of racial/ethnic representation, we now know such is not the case. All media images—whether ignoring, stereotyping, or advancing racial and ethnic diversity—play some role in shaping how people come to understand race relations in the United States. In terms of mass media images of underrepresented group members, this means the presence or absence of each portrayal either "advances or retards the struggle" toward interracial understanding (Elise & Umoja, 1992, p. 83). Because the media plays such a central role in how persons come to understand self and others, we must rethink how we use and interpret messages communicated via mass communication channels. Additionally, we must think critically about the media's role in contributing to perceptions that hinder effective interracial communication.

You might be thinking to yourself, "Is it really the *media's* responsibility to improve race relations?" To some degree, it is. The media should restructure their messages to reflect and not distort the news, entertainment, and the real world in which we live. Because we greatly rely on the media to inform us on political and social issues, it is even more important that we recognize how this communication process perpetuates our resistance to address the significance of race in the 21st century. However, we should not stop with the media. As mass media consumers, we also have some responsibility.

First, we can become active participants in decision-making processes that ultimately affect mass media images of underrepresented group members. Wilkinson (1996) suggests that viewers can increase their power in this struggle over representation by (1) participating in the Nielsen Media Research surveys when the opportunity arises; (2) orchestrating letter-writing campaigns; (3) advocating quality programming; (4) supporting the ownership and employment of underrepresented group members in the media industry; and (5) becoming familiar with the communication laws of the FCC. An example of viewer activism occurred in the spring of 1997 when fans of *Living Single* instigated a letter-writing, phone-calling, and e-mail campaign petitioning Fox TV to bring the sitcom back (Jet, 1997, p. 58). Second, on a more personal level, we can use a number of approaches to think critically about mass media representations of race/ethnicity. For instance, we can examine the *types* (e.g., friendship, family, professional) and *quality* of interactions (e.g., affirming, hostile, devaluing) occurring between the persons in the media. Just as important is to maintain an increased awareness of the obvious—and not so obvious—ways that visibility, marginalization, and stereotyping occur within various mass media texts.

As you read the newspaper, see an ad, watch television, or laugh at a cartoon, ask yourself several questions. What is being communicated here—explicitly or implicitly—about race/ethnicity? Am I being entertained, informed, or both? How are these images consistent with, or different than, what mainstream media typically portrays? Is there anything here that I or others might find offensive? What alternative images are present? By becoming more critical about our own use of the media, we can gain a better understanding of how influential the media are in shaping our attitudes, beliefs, and perceptions of self and others. If change does not start within ourselves, we will continue to be what we are: a society living in fear of difference and diversity.

OPPORTUNITIES FOR EXTENDED LEARNING

1. Explore one area of the mass media that we were not able to include in this chapter—music. Specifically, use your *InfoTrac College Edition* to learn more about the "Latino explosion" that gained significant media coverage in recent years (keywords: *Latin-American music, Ricky Martin, Jennifer Lopez*). As you read through the media's account of this phenomenon, think about how it reflects on the issues of invisibility, stereotyping, and marginalization.

2. In order to understand the impact of television in framing our attitudes about race and crime, watch your national and local news for a two-week period. Make note of the kinds of criminal activities being reported. As a class, answer the following questions: Is the news coverage fair in describing perpetrators of these crimes? Are certain racial/ethnic groups presented more positively or negatively than others? When are racial/ethnic identities mentioned? How pertinent is race to the report? Is a distinction made between types of crimes (e.g., "white" collar and violent crimes)? How are these distinctions related to race/ethnicity issues?

 3. Have you ever seen Aaron McGruder's new comic strip *Boondocks*? After being launched nationally in April 1999, the strip has gained a significant amount of attention for its images of racism, race, and racial/ethnic identity. Some accuse McGruder of inciting racial conflict; others appreciate his satire. Use your *InfoTrac College Edition* to come to understand people's perceptions of this new comic strip (using keyword *Boondocks*). You can also visit McGruder's Web site (www.theboondocks.net).

4. Go to your library and complete a search for magazines targeted to a racial/ethnic group other than your own. After reading through at least three issues from different magazines, think about how these publications differ from those geared toward your own racial/ethnic group. Are the stories covered in each the same? What are some key similarities and differences?

 5. In 1999, the National Association for the Advancement of Colored People (NAACP) contemplated actions against the top four television networks for the lack of diversity in the upcoming season (Shepard, 1999). The civil rights organization's criticism was based on the fact that none of the 27 new comedies and dramas premiering in the fall of 1999 had any lead, and few supporting, microcultural cast members. Consider how this reflects on the historical trend of racial/ethnic representation on TV. Use your *InfoTrac College Edition* to

review the most recent programming lineups for each network. Then determine if these new programs continue marginalizing certain groups or create greater opportunities for a more balanced representation.

6. Locate a specific media text (e.g., film, music video, book, television program, etc.) that portrays realistic, positive images of effective interracial communication. Then share this source with others and discuss why you chose that particular mass media image. During this exchange, try and reach consensus in terms of how "realistic" and "positive" should be defined. What types of images were selected? How were they similar and/or different?

MOVING FROM THE THEORETICAL TO THE PRACTICAL

IDENTIFYING POTENTIAL BARRIERS TO
INTERRACIAL COMMUNICATION

SETTING THE STAGE FOR EFFECTIVE
INTERRACIAL COMMUNICATION

FOSTERING INTERRACIAL DIALOGUE

CONCLUSION

OPPORTUNITIES FOR EXTENDED LEARNING

As the previous chapters have demonstrated, the issue of race has become incredibly complex. Although some may argue that race relations have improved, personal testimonies, research, and other resources tell us that such is not the case. Instead, racism, prejudice, and stereotyping remain a staple in the diet of many U.S. Americans.

Earlier we described theories that analyze the complexities associated with race and communication. In this chapter, we present some practical approaches to effective interracial communication. We hope that you will continue to apply concepts and new knowledge gathered from previous chapters to the issues here. We begin by identifying potential barriers to interracial communication, which includes discussion of unproductive assumptions and problematic communication approaches that perpetuate a cycle of ineffective interracial communication. From there, we explore communication strategies observed by some as most effective within an interracial context. The concept of dialogue is described as it relates to communication in the 21st century. The summary challenges you to extend your knowledge from the classroom into your real-world experiences.

IDENTIFYING POTENTIAL BARRIERS TO
INTERRACIAL COMMUNICATION

As with any communication process, interracial communication may be hindered by potential barriers that prevent interactants from communicating effectively with each other. It is most often our prejudices, racist attitudes, stereotypes, and uncertainty that create these barriers, and their mere presence or existence within the individual and society as a whole may complicate an otherwise natural communicative exchange. As we discussed earlier, interracial communication is so critical to the social and political success of our nation that President Clinton initiated a federally funded grant designed to assess the short-and long-term effects of racism on racial/ethnic groups living within the United States. People continue to assert that race relations have greatly improved over the past few decades; however, hate crimes, church burnings, murders, and contemporary forms of lynching (e.g., the 1998 dragging death of an African American man in Texas by three male self-described White supremacists) demonstrate the reality of racism in the United States. With the influx of racially diverse individuals entering many of our public and private institutions, we must examine the barriers to effective and positive interracial communication. Pettigrew (1981) collected survey data to better understand European Americans' attitudes toward and beliefs about the state of race relations in the United States. Twenty percent of the participants opposed racist propositions, 20% supported racist propositions, and 60% reportedly had no opinion. Although it may be encouraging to see a small percentage of people in support of a racist ideology, Bowser and Hunt (1996) assert that this 50-year trend of racism and apathy has remained constant over time. In other words, "the more things change, the more they stay the same."

Six Orders of Contact

As you think about your interracial interactions, how have you been socialized to communicate (or not) with other racial/ethnic group members? Has your family or society socialized you to believe that such interactions are healthy and normal, or were you discouraged from having any type of interracial contact at all? Whatever your experience has been, it is our hope that you have become sensitized to how cultural group membership (e.g., dominant culture, U.S. nationality) influences our attitudes toward and beliefs about interracial contact.

Banton (1967) developed six orders of interracial contact to describe how two racial/ethnic groups positively or negatively manage this unique communicative experience. As you will see, four of these orders discourage, and two orders encourage, an appreciation of racial/ethnic difference in varying degrees.

The four orders fostering negative or no interracial contact include peripheral contact, institutionalized contact, pluralism, and assimilation. *Peripheral contact* refers to a minimal amount of contact between racial/ethnic groups that is transient (e.g., in classrooms, grocery shopping, riding the bus). In this framework, limited interracial interaction is expected and maintained by individuals.

Institutionalized contact refers to contact occurring between independent nations. As we noted in previous chapters, this type of contact is manifested through colonialism (subordination) or paternalism (sharply defined roles and status). More importantly, the dominant group maintains social distance through regulation (e.g., antimiscegenation laws) and repeated demonstrations of power. *Pluralism* occurs when racial/ethnic differences reflect variations in expected behavior and there is minimum social interaction. In general, racial/ethnic groups are coexisting without much effort put into interracial contact, which could potentially be mutually beneficial. The final order that fails to value racial/ethnic difference is *assimilation* or amalgamation. Banton describes this order as an unavoidable consequence resulting from integration via interracial marriage. Others have operationalized assimilation as a people adopting the dominant group's attitudes and beliefs while forsaking those of their primary racial/ethnic group. For the purposes of this text, the latter definition is used to describe the tensions associated with interracial contact.

The two orders that foster more positive interracial contact are *acculturation* and *integration* (Banton, 1967). These two processes are more effective in resolving tensions related to interracial contact by valuing difference and accommodating for this difference in one way or another. Acculturation occurs when racial/ethnic group members learn about a culture (dominant group) that is different from the one they are born into (racial/ethnic group). In this case, people learn to live in both worlds while maintaining their racial/ethnic heritage and identity. In the case of integration, however, racial distinctions are given minor consideration and interracial interactions are maximized. More importantly, friendships and social relationships are fostered which provide individuals with choices that allow them to move across racial/ethnic lines. Ideally, both orders of interracial contact would greatly contribute to effective interracial communication. Unfortunately, various barriers prevent this utopic state of race relations from occurring. In order to achieve this complex, yet attainable, goal of positive interracial communication, we must first consider what barriers prevent this process from occurring.

Barriers and Unproductive Assumptions

According to Blubaugh and Pennington (1976), a racial assumption "is a consciously or unconsciously held premise that is considered to be true regarding a race or ethnic group and that is acted on as though it were true" (p. 45). Racial assumptions are held with no supporting evidence or they are based on hearsay, or generalizations. Stereotyping is one of the most natural cognitive behaviors we as humans engage in (see Tables 12.1 and 12.2). This process involves efforts to categorize information in an effort to make sense of information to which we are exposed. Although this behavior brings order to chaos, the process of stereotyping becomes even more complex when it relates to racial/ethnic and sexual identities (among others). These stereotypes make interracial interactions problematic on three distinct levels. Stereotypes that affect our interracial interactions on an interpersonal level are often referred to as individual racism (Bowser & Hunt, 1996). It is on this level that stereotypes impede one of the most effective means for improving race relations.

Consider one of your interracial friendships as an example. More likely than not, both you and your friend had preexisting stereotypes of each other based on race or even personality. As your relationship developed and you got to know each other on a more intimate level, those stereotypes were probably challenged in some way. In your opinion, was this friendship more effective in diminishing racist thoughts and beliefs than hearing the news, reading the newspaper, or reading a journal article? The potency of any of the mass mediums varies from person to person; however, research indicates that interpersonal interaction is quite effective in improving race relations on a more humanistic level. Individuals are now able to place a face on the reality of racism. Institutionalized racism is different from individual racism in that group communication perpetuates racist ideologies in a much larger context. It is at this level that individual racist beliefs are reinforced by a larger body of like-minded people (Bowser & Hunt, 1996). Historically, people in positions of power have preserved racism by preventing various racial/ethnic groups

TABLE 12.1   TWELVE COMMUNICATION TRAITS MOST FREQUENTLY ASSIGNED TO OTHER ETHNIC GROUPS BY WHITE STUDENTS

Black Americans	%	Mexican Americans	%	Japanese Americans	%
1. Argumentative	40	1. Emotional	53	1. Intelligent	73
2. Emotional	35	2. Argumentative	32	2. Courteous	60
3. Aggressive	32	3. Sensitive	25	3. Industrious	48
4. Straightforward	26	4. Straightforward	19	4. Quiet	42
5. Critical	23	5. Talkative	19	5. Soft-spoken	36
6. Sensitive	19	6. Intelligent	16	6. Reserved	31
7. Ostentatious	17	7. Persistent	15	7. Sensitive	25
8. Defiant	17	8. Loud	15	8. Efficient	25
9. Hostile	17	9. Courteous	14	9. Practical	23
10. Open	17	10. Hesitant	13	10. Alert	21
11. Responsive	17	11. Open	13	11. Humble	19
12. Intelligent	17	12. Critical	12	12. Conservative	15

Blubaugh & Pennington, 1976

members equal access to institutions and organizations to which *all* people should have access (see Turner, Singleton, & Musick, 1984). In an attempt to resolve these economic and social inequities, "[c]ontemporary institutional leaders are caught in a dilemma of redressing historical group disadvantage (thereby disadvantaging others) or disregard[ing] racial group membership and treat[ing] all persons "equally" which may perpetuate this disadvantage" (Bowser & Hunt, 1996, p. 17). Social and political institutions (e.g., colleges, businesses, government, political parties) are used as a means for preserving the resources that appear to threaten the existing class and racial hierarchy (see Vargas, 1996).

Cultural racism is much like ethnocentrism in that people present their own racial/ethnic group's cultural preferences and values as superior to those of other groups (Bowser & Hunt, 1996). The consequence of this type of thinking is that all aspects of one culture and heritage are deemed culturally acceptable, thus negating the value of all other racial/ethnic groups. Although this ideology may appear antiquated, current events indicate otherwise. The rising number of hate groups on the Internet and society at large are a testament to the pervasiveness of racism in contemporary society. Although such groups use the First Amendment to support these extremist beliefs, their culture breathes life into a racist ideology that potentially leads to violence and, in some cases, death.

These forms of racism provide a context for understanding how people can individually and collectively adopt ideologies that have short-and long-term consequences. In any event, race relations and interracial contact are hindered in the process. These barriers ultimately make our communicative interactions problematic. Next explore the effects of racism on our communicative processes.

TABLE 12.2 **TWELVE COMMUNICATION TRAITS MOST FREQUENTLY ASSIGNED TO OTHER ETHNIC GROUPS BY BLACK GHETTO RESIDENTS**

White Americans	%	Japanese Americans	%	Mexican Americans	%
1. Evasive	41	1. Intelligent	47	1. Emotional	52
2. Critical	26	2. Industrious	40	2. Radical	25
3. Conservative	24	3. Soft-spoken	37	3. Talkative	23
4. Ignorant	24	4. Reserved	36	4. Argumentative	22
5. Boastful	23	5. Nonmilitant	33	5. Loud	22
6. Aggressive	22	6. Quiet	30	6. Aggressive	22
7. Arrogant	21	7. Courteous	26	7. Sensitive	19
8. Ostentatious	21	8. Humble	20	8. Critical	16
9. Concealing	19	9. Submissive	19	9. Defiant	15
10. Emotional	18	10. Uninvolved	18	10. Straightforward	15
11. Individualistic	15	11. Sensitive	18	11. Rude	14
12. Nonmilitant	15	12. Passive	18	12. Ostentatious	13
		13. Efficient	18		

Rich, 1974

Problematic Communication Approaches

As we have emphasized throughout this text, very little has happened to improve interracial communication nationally and/or globally. Interracial communication is problematic for a variety of reasons, one of them being "a serious mismatch in racial perception[s] of change" (Patterson, 1995, p. 26). Patterson asserts that middle-class European Americans believe race relations and attitudes toward African Americans have improved, and African Americans believe and experience racism, which has led to feelings that the state of race relations has either not changed or gotten worse (see also Turner, Singleton, & Musick, 1984). Although perceptual difference is illustrative of European American–African American race relations, such beliefs are applicable to other interracial relations as well.

Researchers have asserted that interpersonal interactions contribute to improved race relations; however, this same relational context has the potential to increase ethnocentrism (Neuliep & McCroskey, 1997a). The racial difference between inter-actants becomes maximized and prevents them from evaluating their preconceived beliefs and attitudes toward their respective racial/ethnic groups. The following quotation is from a business manager discussing the need for organizations and society as a whole to acknowledge the existing barriers to interracial communication and their effect on the organizational climate:

> When you have a racial difference the assumption is driven by the stereotype and perceived prejudice. When you get into those cases, we usually find out that [the problem] is just good old-fashioned failure to communicate or a reluctance to interact in an open way for fear of being misinterpreted. So race does create a barrier but it's not a racism type barrier. It's an uncertainty, a lack of comfort or a lack of familiarity barrier and not wanting to be perceived as having difficulty working with a white person, a black person, or an Asian. (Laabs, 1993, p. 35)

If effective interracial communication is to occur, members of society must have some level of consciousness and, ultimately, responsibility for engaging in dialogue about race and race issues. McIntosh (1995b) asserts that acknowledgment of "white privilege" makes European Americans accountable for deconstructing the racial hierarchy pervasive in Western society. This observation is quite striking in that McIntosh herself is a European American woman who has committed to raising our daily consciousness about the advantages of being White (or whiter) skinned (see Table 12.3). Although it is not our intention to place blame on all European Americans for the sins of their ancestors, it is critical that European Americans, particularly those in positions of power, understand their role in racism. Similarly, we should all examine our own roles in improving race relations. As the saying goes, "if you are not a part of the solution, you must be a part of the problem." In order for systematic change to occur, we must all make it our responsibility to deconstruct the existing racial hierarchy and create a democracy that provides opportunities and access to all citizens regardless of racial/ethnic identity.

Blatant forms of racism within the context of interpersonal relationships have changed since the 1950s and 1960s. Nevertheless, racist attitudes and beliefs are manifested in various ways and contexts. As we have already mentioned, people oftentimes experience uncertainty when they are interacting with a person from a different racial/ethnic or cultural group. This apprehension may stem from limited interracial contact, preconceived notions, stereotypes, prejudices, or general communicator apprehension (e.g., fear of losing face). Although there is not one clear answer to why people are uncertain about interracial/interethnic interactions, Neuliep and McCroskey (1997b) believe that this apprehension is essentially "the fear associated with either real or anticipated interaction with people from different groups, especially different cultural and ethnic groups" (p. 152). In other words, the idea and/or reality of contact and communication with a person from a racial/ethnic group different from your own increases your level of anxiety. Have these thoughts gone through your mind? Have you ever been apprehensive about working with someone who is European American, Latino/a American, or Native American? If we examine the hows, whys, and whens of this uncertainty, we will then be able to deal with racist ideologies.

TABLE 12.3	PRIVILEGED CHECKLIST

Here are a few sample statements (from McIntosh's original list of 26) designed to challenge European Americans to recognize and acknowledge how they potentially benefit from their social and racial positions in the United States.

1. I can if I wish arrange to be in the company of people my race most of the time.

2. If I should need to move, I can be pretty sure of renting or purchasing housing in an area which I can afford and in which I would want to live.

3. I can go shopping alone most of the time, pretty well assured that I will not be followed.

4. I can turn on the television or open to the front page of the paper and see people of my race widely represented.

5. When I am told about our national heritage or about "civilization," I am shown that people of my color made it what it is.

6. I can be sure that my children will be given curricular materials that testify to the existence of their race.

7. If I want to, I can be pretty sure of finding a publisher for this piece on white privilege.

8. I can go into a music shop and count on finding the music of my race represented, into a supermarket and find the staple foods which fit with my cultural traditions, into a hairdresser's shop and find someone who can cut my hair.

McIntosh, 1995b

Currently, few scales in research are designed to assess the degree to which our (dis)comfort level with interracial communication is manifested in our interpersonal behaviors. In other words, what communication strategies or behaviors are used or experienced that complicate the communicative process between people from different racial/ethnic groups? Can you recall times when you were interacting with someone from another racial/ethnic group and he or she appeared somewhat uncomfortable talking with you? What verbal or nonverbal cues did you observe that communicated discomfort? To what did you attribute this behavior? For people who continually struggle with racial identity and racism, they more likely have a higher level of consciousness to these cues within an interracial context. (This does not mean, however, that individuals sensitized to issues of race are not attuned to the significance of verbal and nonverbal cues.)

Neuliep and McCroskey's (1997b) Personal Report of Interethnic Communication Apprehension Scale (PRECA) explores one underlying dimension of this tension that sometimes arises in interracial/interethnic communication. This scale is a modified version of the Personal Report of Intercultural Communication Apprehension (PRICA), which explores the importance of culture in interpersonal interactions. PRECA is a very important tool used in research. The reality of racism in the United States is reflected in the reliability of this scale. The reliability of these scales has been tested, and, if we examine the content items, or statements to which participants respond, we are able to better understand how communication behaviors can potentially become problematic within an interracial exchange.

President Clinton's initiative on race relations must remain at the forefront of our national agenda. Coupled with self-examination of our communication behaviors and an understanding of the motivations guiding these behaviors (e.g., racism, uncertainty, personality), our interpersonal interactions provide an excellent context for identifying problematic communication approaches. According to the scale, factors used to assess apprehension and perceptions of communication competence are dislike, comfort level, tension, nervousness, calmness, relaxation, fear, and confidence. Neuliep and McCroskey (1997b) emphasize that racial, ethnic, and cultural diversity on college campuses and within organizations throughout the nation are in need of such measures that will educate students, faculty, employers, and employees alike about the important role of communication in our interracial interactions.

More importantly, studies designed with the organizational community in mind may have far-reaching implications. They describe this observation as follows: "Within multinational organizations, the scales could be administered to managers and employees to predict potential problems in culturally, ethnically, and/or racially diverse work settings" (Neuliep & McCroskey, 1997b, p. 154).

THEORY INTO PRACTICE

By definition, a hate crime involves any unlawful act that is motivated by bias. According to Carrier (1999), a hate crime is committed in the United States every hour, over half of which are motivated by racial bias. Many people feel powerless to confront hate crimes when they occur on campus, in their neighborhoods, or larger communities. Here are several guidelines provided by the Southern Poverty Law Center to respond effectively to hate crimes.

1. *Do something.* Lack of action will be interpreted as apathy or acceptance. Speak up and use your First Amendment rights too!
2. *Unite.* Call friends, colleagues, or neighbors. Organize diverse coalitions that can come together for a larger cause. Elicit the support of community leaders and public officials.
3. *Support the victims.* They may feel especially vulnerable, fearful, and alone; let them know that they are not facing this battle by themselves.
4. *Do your homework.* Obtain accurate information about the missions, agendas, and symbols of hate groups. Learn about how they use their legal rights, informal networks, and the media to promote their ideas.
5. *Commit yourself to teaching tolerance.* Racial/ethnic bias is learned early; however, these attitudes can also be unlearned through long-term programs and curricula. Never stop trying to make a difference.
6. *Dig deeper.* Press beyond the surface issues related to hate crimes. Develop more complex understandings of how other issues beyond race divide us. Continue to learn about self and others.

SETTING THE STAGE FOR EFFECTIVE INTERRACIAL COMMUNICATION

Now that we have explored theories, concepts, and case studies to assist us in our understanding of interracial communication, we must challenge ourselves to set the stage for effective race relations. Let's use the theater as a metaphor to illustrate this point. Imagine you are an actor working with an improvisational ensemble with other actors who are equally committed to the production you are scheduled to perform. On the first day of the improvisation, you are given the theme comic-tragedy which you are to perform that evening for an anxious audience. Because the performance is improvisational, no script guides the show and the team must work together to perform this comic-tragedy successfully. Of course, the cast must negotiate to determine what will work best for the night's performance. However, it is through trial and error that they learn what best achieves the designated goal of this particular play. Well, the same applies to those individuals committed to improving race relations on both the micro and macro levels.

No one methodology is most effective in fostering positive interracial communication. Therefore, individuals and organizations alike must employ multiple methods before they find the most appropriate and effective way to create the desired communication context. More importantly, people from historically oppressed racial and ethnic groups should not carry this burden alone. As McIntosh (1995b) has already suggested, European Americans must join in this fight against racist ideologies embedded within the psyche of Western culture. Crenshaw (1997) provides further support for this need in the following statement: "Whiteness functions ideologically when people employ it consciously or unconsciously, as a framework to categorize people and understand their social locations. Within this framework, whiteness as a social position has value and has been treated legally as property" (p. 255). Therefore, those who are not privileged have been oppressed in a society that places more value on skin color than character.

Racial/ethnic diversity is inevitable as we begin the 21st century. We must learn about approaches that facilitate effective interracial communication and increase knowledge and understanding about the reality of racism. The next section provides a variety of approaches and communication strategies that have been used by communication scholars and consultants trained in the area of race relations and diversity. With each approach and strategy we suggest how we can employ these into our daily lives and interactions with others from diverse racial/ethnic groups.

Productive Approaches and Strategies

When it comes to the topic of racial reconciliation, some may wonder, "What for? Things are no longer 'separate but equal,' so there's no need to fight for change." As the rise in hate crimes indicates, a great wall of resistance to the goal of improving race relations remains. For those people who embrace a separatist and/or supremacist ideology, these efforts may appear futile. However, for those of us committed to this goal or interested in doing our part but do not know how, we must become aware of the approaches and communication strategies we can use to increase our interracial communication competence. You might be asking yourself, "How do these approaches come about? I'm sure they don't just appear." Through trial and error, people are able to determine ultimately what method is most effective in resolving the problem at hand.

For some researchers, applied research is the most appropriate means for achieving this goal. Applied communication research has three benefits: (1) to help people solve socially relevant problems, (2) to provide support for the "predictive validity of communication theory" based on the success of a real-world test (generalizability), and (3) to make clear the practicality of the communication discipline (Kreps, Frey, & O'Hair, 1991). These benefits are appropriate for all forms of communication, and they become imperative when we examine interracial communication. If we as a society cannot engage in public discourse regarding the pervasiveness of racism, are we able to communicate in private? Better yet, are we willing to leave our racial comfort zones and discuss race relations in racially mixed company? The following approaches and strategies address this tension directly by providing guidelines that will educate us about these very issues.

Race Relations Training

In Chapter 9, we discussed the importance of organizational communication and the far reaching effect of race on the culture and the process of communication in this context. Now we must turn our attention to specific strategies that people have used to improve race relations on both the micro and macro levels. Again, we emphasize that one approach is not better than another. You must use discretion as you choose the tactic you deem most appropriate and effective in decreasing the tension levels associated with race.

When discussing the topic of race relations, many people think immediately of interpersonal conflict between racially/ethnically different people. However, this is not always the case. Oftentimes, ethnocentric thinking creates a site for conflict that prevents positive race relations from materializing. If a person believes her or his race is superior to all others, it is very likely that she or he will be very defensive when interacting with people from different racial/ethnic groups. This way of thinking is problematic for a variety of reasons.

First, ethnocentrism fosters an ingroup bias that allows those individuals to perceive (and believe) their racial/ethnic group possesses moral traits (e.g., trustworthiness, honesty, pacifism, virtue, obedience) that are lacking in all other groups (Deutsch, 1994). Thus, when the two (or more) groups interact, they compete for the same resources (e.g., jobs, housing, college education). This competition is natural because the resources may be limited. Nevertheless, the division along racial/ethnic lines only perpetuates racism and the unequal distribution of and/or access to those resources.

Second, this ethnocentric thinking prevents individuals from having interracial interactions. Therefore, interactions with ingroup members only magnify the perceived attitudes held of outgroup members. In other words, ingroup members' intragroup interactions discourage interracial contact. Even when they do occur, preconceived perceptions are reinforced (Deutsch, 1994).

The final factor that creates this adversarial climate is the pyramidal segmentary, where a societal organization is perceived as actively promoting ingroup ethnocentrism, which in turn creates intergroup strife on a macro level (Deutsch, 1994). In other words, micro- and microculture group members are expected to accept the dominant culture (within that organization) as part of their sole identity. For those individuals who maintain a high level of ethnocentrism, it is very difficult for training to facilitate significant change in behavior unless greater emphasis is placed on the importance of skills. Additionally, individuals should be trained on how to transfer these learned skills from the training session to real-life situations.

You may be thinking that people who are ethnocentric would not choose to attend a race relations training session. This may be true, but what happens when they are part of an organizational culture that is becoming racially/ethnically diverse? More likely than not, they will be working directly with people who are different from them and, as a result of their beliefs they may be hostile, confrontational, or even ignore the very existence of those organizational members. In any event, it is very likely that the CEO or a human resources representative will require a race relations training session of all the employees. By acknowledging the crucial role of ethnocentrism within traditionally hegemonic cultures, proactive approaches to race relations training can work toward resolving "racial" conflict and changing intergroup prejudices, stereotyping, and discriminatory behaviors (Deutsch, 1994).

Training Models   Foeman (1997) suggests five interpersonal behavioral objectives of race relations training: (1) discuss race-related issues (demystification), (2) articulate, (3) examine, and (4) find validity in the other groups' perspectives, and (5) utilize others' perspectives in order to work together effectively while striving toward common goals. During a race relations workshop or training session, information sharing and open discussion are frequently most effective (see Laabs, 1993). These processes are successful because they increase sensitivity among people who, for whatever reason, were not attuned to the significance of race prior to the workshop. By sharing their experiences and perceptions of racism, participants/co-workers have a better understanding of how racial/ethnic identity locates them in society as well as in the organizational context.

There are three training models (didactic, experiential training, and groupwork) that achieve the objectives just described and are designed to change the behaviors of macrocultural and microcultural group members. No matter which model is used to train people about race relations, all three have similar goals. The models vary in their approach to race relations. However, each provides information bases and social context designed to train participants, increase cross-racial dialogues, and encourage participants to apply this knowledge to their interpersonal interracial interactions and the larger social system (Foeman, 1997).

The *didactic model* is one of the most common forms of race relations training. The teaching mechanism used in this model is lecture, in which the trainer presents facts and information to participants. This linear, or one-way, approach confronts the macrocultural group members by making an information-based appeal. However, this style is very ineffective in bringing about change. First, the interpersonal goals of participants are not always met because they are not able to interact and exchange ideas and information. Second, macrocultural group members may perceive this approach as "defensive re-education," which may indicate an inability to personalize and internalize information gained from the social experiences of the "others" (Foeman, 1997).

The *experiential training model* centers on the assumption that interaction among race relations training participants is necessary. Unlike the didactic model, the experiential training model depends heavily on the personal experiences of individuals from various racial/ethnic groups. All persons are expected to share their racialized realities with fellow participants in an effort to reduce prejudice through personal contact, which may in turn facilitate change. One primary drawback of this model is that people of color take on the role of spokespersons for all members of their respective racial/ethnic groups. For example, in sharing her experiences with the group, a Filipina woman is then perceived as representative of all other Filipino/as. This can be harmful in that other participants may take this one perspective and generalize it to all other racial/ethnic minorities, which then can feed into the vicious cycle of stereotyping. As a result, the people of color participating in the training receive fewer benefits from the experience and have the additional stress of being a representative for all other racial/ethnic group members.

The *groupwork model* strikes a good medium between the didactic and experiential models in that trainers incorporate information and experience into the learning process. Doing so assists participants in discerning in what social contexts interracial contact will occur, which ultimately expands each person's frame of reference and their understanding of and responses to cross-race issues (Foeman, 1997). Because they are dealing with a variety of people who have different learning styles, trainers use film, discussion, and role play, among others, to encourage learner participation. The most appealing aspect of this model is that it promotes dialogue (see next section) among and between participants, particularly microcultural group members. It is hoped that participants will act on the information they are provided. Bowser and Hunt (1996) describe this newfound social consciousness as follows:

> European Americans are not one-dimensional in their racial identities and there is an important psychological connection, conditioned by historic culture, between racial identity and where one stands on the racism to antiracism continuum. By better understanding their own historic backgrounds, EA's growth in racial identity is possible along with progression from individual racism to individual antiracism. (p. 250)

By becoming aware of their privileged location in the racial hierarchy, European Americans ideally are more educated about the reality of racism as experienced by their co-workers and colleagues. After participating in race relations training and developing some level of consciousness, they are then morally responsible (McIntosh, 1995b) for resolving racial tensions at a level they are most comfortable with. We must also acknowledge that racial/ethnic group members bear responsibility for this problem as well. If a Latino male is participating in a workshop with his European American colleagues, he must not directly blame them individually and/or collectively for his racist experiences with other European Americans. Although he has experienced cumulative racism (a series of racist experiences over a long period of time), the Latino male must recognize his role in this process of awareness. By educating his colleagues about racism and directing his anger at the racial hierarchy (society) and the perpetrators of racism, he is becoming a part of the solution to remedying unproductive interracial communication in the workplace.

Ideally, the use of any of these models will achieve the goal of sensitizing people to the reality of racism. Unfortunately, the possibility remains that not everyone will reach the same level of consciousness after completing one of the training sessions. Some European Americans, may remain blinded or unconvinced by the evidence presented by the trainer and/or participants from other racial/ethnic groups. The accounts of racism may be perceived as atypical or unimportant, which only works to problematize race relations on a more complex level. Even though they are hearing the experiences about oppression from the oppressed, some individuals may choose to remain in denial about the saliency of racism in the United States.

Conflict Resolution

Firth (1991) provides a proactive approach to conflict resolution that can be applied to interracial communication. Although the source of tensions in the workplace and society may not be solely attributed to race, it is very important that we remain focused on the goal(s) of that organization. Organization and society members should remain committed to their purpose, and the introduction of race into a hegemonic environment can be a difficult transition for all involved. In order to adjust to this restructuring, we can remind ourselves of seven key strategies that minimize the potential for conflict. Overall, there should be a *vision* that is shared by all and provides a framework for achieving a long-term goal.

In order to fulfill that vision, the organization should have *goals* that are simple and specific and manifested within the everyday work activities. In other words, the daily activities of organizational members should contribute to the vision. The most important strategy in this process is *communication*. "You must create a system of open communication in your organization. It deals with sensitive issues responsibly without laying blame or creating feelings of guilt in an employee" (Firth, 1991, p. 4). In order to maintain some semblance of order, there must be *leadership*, which involves one or more individuals taking initiative in leading the group toward its vision through the various goals that have been outlined. *Education* is equally important, requiring employees to be educated about organizational roles (as individuals and group members), which can lead to empowerment and organizational commitment. If this commitment is going to be maintained and members are to feel valued, leaders must *key in to morale* by observing employees in their work environment. Are they excited about being there? Are they excelling in job performance? Finally, *feedback* is an ongoing dimension of this process, wherein employees receive encouragement and constructive criticism relative to job performance.

These strategies are very important in contexts where a group of people is working together for a common goal. Whether it is in the workplace, the community, or in a professional (or student) organization, the social collectivity of people involved in this process must be aware of those strategies that are essential to achieving the overarching goal of the body. These strategies become even more important when the organization becomes increasingly diverse.

Consider this scenario: A European American male is a part of the Student Government Association (SGA) at his university, which is predominately Native American. He attends the first meeting of the school year and indicates interest in becoming an active member of the organization. Several months later, the body is meeting to discuss activities for Ethnic Heritage Week. The European American student speaks up and suggests a day celebrating European culture. Various members are very covert in expressing their opposition, which leaves the student puzzled when no one comments one way or the other when his suggestion is "tabled for later discussion." Throughout the remainder of the meeting, he feels isolated and angry but does not really know any members in whom he can confide his frustrations. When the meeting is adjourned, he quietly exits the student center and proceeds to walk to his car. All the while, he berates himself, "You are so stupid! How did you ever think you could belong on this campus? Your friends and family *told* you this would never work!" His thoughts are interrupted when he feels a tap on his shoulder. He turns around to find himself facing the president who tabled his suggestion. Anger and frustration fill him as he waits to hear what the president has to say. The president first apologizes for any misunderstanding that may have developed as a result of the tabling decision. He begins to explain that this action was not a personal attack against him; instead, the student body was shocked by this suggestion because they never had to deal with an outgroup member taking an active role in the organization. After a long discussion about the miscommunication, the new member now has a better understanding of how his race/ethnicity affected the organizational and communicative dynamic of the group. He realizes that through honest communication and continued dialogue with other students about the organization's mission, the SGA is able to reach its goals and vision while educating its members through feedback, education, and morale building.

As we have reiterated throughout the text, interpersonal contact and communication are critical to race relations if racism is to become a part of our past. Therefore, it is reasonable that approaches created to change intergroup prejudices, stereotyping, and discriminatory behaviors would promote intergroup contact (Deutsch, 1994). We must acknowledge that intergroup contact is influenced by context, power dynamics, time, status, individuality, and acquaintance potential. By receiving information, education, sensitivity training, and problem-solving workshops, all members of society can become more skilled in their approaches to interracial communication. Although it is very likely that personal relationships beyond the workplace may not "naturally" develop in most contexts, these skills and knowledge are necessary as we enter the 21st century. The increasing racial/ethnic diversity will affect all areas of life in society—colleges, public schools, churches, restaurants, government, corporate American, among others. Therefore, we must be proactive in our efforts to educate ourselves and others about the importance we have placed on racial and ethnic identity. Not only should we acknowledge the saliency of our racial/ethnic identities in a society consumed by race, we should make a conscious effort to combat racism in the public and private areas of our lives.

FOSTERING INTERRACIAL DIALOGUE

We believe, as do Johannesen (1971) and Tanno (1997, 1998), that dialogue is best viewed as attitude or an orientation. Compare this approach to dialogue with popular myths that describe dialogue as simple, relatively effortless, and easy to maintain. Within this more common perspective, dialogue is seen as a strategy or technique—consciously achieved with little or no preparation. But our use of the concept of dialogue, is different than "honest expression," "frank conversation, "or "good communication." To foster an environment where dialogue can emerge, community members must work hard to promote a supportive (caring) climate in which genuineness, empathic understanding, unconditional positive regard, and mutual equality are maintained (Johannesen, 1971). Setting the stage for dialogue also includes addressing existing power differentials from which speech is enacted and utilizing tactics to empower those persons who enter a specific situational context with less social, organizational, and/or personal power than others (Cooks & Hale, 1992).

According to Tanno (1997, 1998), six elements are crucial to the promotion of dialogue. The first involves recognition that our past, present, and future are inextricably tied together (*connection*). As a way to prepare for dialogue, community members must come to understand how their shared history (sometimes at odds, sometimes together) informs, to a certain extent, current interactions. Connection also involves simultaneously recognizing both similarities and differences.

The second element is a *commitment* over time. "Dialogue does not, or should not, have a discernible beginning and end" (Tanno, 1998, p.2). One of the defining characteristics of dialogue is that it represents a process, one in which all parties are actively involved and committed In other words, dialogue can *only* emerge through commitment and time.

Another key element to dialogue is a developed *realness/closeness*, both in terms of physical and psychological distance. Genuineness, honest, and candor—even that which initially may be potentially offensive—all are central to the emergence of dialogue (Johannesen, 1971). A central element of dialogue is the desire, ability, and commitment to "keep it real" even when such an endeavor may initiate tension or hostility.

As it relates to freedom of expression, a fourth element of dialogue is the *creation/maintenance* of space where everyone's *voice* is valued. This includes the recognition and an appreciation that each person may speak for a variety of voices (professional, personal, cultural).

The fifth element of dialogue includes an *engagement of mind, heart, and soul*. The mind may be where logic and reasoning are located, however, the heart and soul is where emotion, commitment, accountability, and responsibility reside (Tanno, 1998). Attempts to isolate some aspects (fact, logic, reason) with no or little consideration of others (emotions, experiences, institution) does not contribute to a healthy communication environment. Instead, it creates a traditional, hostile climate where certain voices are privileged over others.

The final element that is crucial in setting the stage for dialogue is *self-reflection*. According to Tanno (1998), all of the other elements previously described depend on each person's resolution to engage in self-reflection that is critical, constructive, and continuous. Such a process of self-examination can be initially difficult, and ultimately painful, especially when dealing with such issues as cultural oppression, societal power, and privilege. However, the process by which persons situate themselves—professionally, culturally, and personally—within the context of a healthy communication environment is crucial to establishing a readiness for dialogue. Through self-reflection, an understanding can emerge where individuals begin to recognize the relevance of their lived experiences in perceptions of self and others. In this regard, "objective" positions stemming from a "neutral standpoint" are acknowledged as problematic. So, as we work to discuss the saliency of interracial communication, we must continue to engage in self-reflexivity. Through this process, we are encouraged to recognize that neutralization (apathy) only perpetuates the problem of racism. Strategic efforts must be made that challenge our socially conditioned behaviors. Instead of accepting racism, oppression, and discrimination as an inherent part of our social reality, we must become a collective body committed to changing the way we think, talk, and feel about race as we enter the 21st century.

CONCLUSION

It is our hope that this text has challenged you to think critically about interracial communication and your place on the "racism–antiracism continuum." Most people are either not challenged to think about race (European Americans) or are forced to think about it continually (microcultural racial/ethnic groups). Although this does not mean European Americans are not sensitized to issues of race and racism in the United States, racial/ethnic microcultural groups must deal with racism, stereotyping, prejudice, and discrimination more frequently than we care to admit.

On February 25, 1999, California "shock jock" Doug Tracht was on the air commenting about the Grammy (music) awards that had aired the previous night on television. African American R&B artist Lauryn Hill was awarded with five Grammys for her work in 1998 (*The Miseducation of Lauryn Hill*). In reaction to her awards, Tracht retorted, "Well, I guess that's why they drag them on the back of trucks" (referring to the tragic dragging death of an African American man by three self-proclaimed White supremacists). Public outrage over his insensitivity to Hill and, more importantly, to the surviving family members of victim James Byrd led to the suspension and ultimate firing of the shock jock. A few days later, Tracht publicly apologized to the family, Hill, and the United States for his incredibly insensitive remark. In an interview with ABC News television anchor Ted Koppel (*Nightline*, March 4, 1999), Tracht expressed chagrin about his behavior and puzzlement over where he is on the racism–antiracism continuum. Although he does not consider himself a racist, Tracht is willing to do whatever it takes, specifically undergoing counseling, to understand the origins of his subconscious racism. More importantly, Tracht spoke about veteran coach John Thompson's (who is African American) lecture to him about his socially conditioned behavior:

> John Thompson gave me the biggest, most well-spoken reaming I've ever had in my life. He just looked at me and went one end down the other. "Have you ever had therapy?," he said to me. "Have you ever seen a doctor? Are you stupid?" No. "Are you a racist?"

No. "Then why did you say that? There must be something wrong in your brain. . . . You need a check-up from the neck up," is what he told me. He said, "You're offering to do things, would you do that?" I said, "I never thought about doing that. I never thought I was nuts." He said, "I would do it. I would do it." I challenged him, he threw the challenge. I will do it. I'm going to do it . . . I'll seek counseling, and say . . . here's what I said: "Is that an indication that while I don't think I'm a racist that somewhere inside me a crumb of some behavior that I've tolerated and people listening to me have tolerated over the years until finally out came this horrible thing and people said "We will stand no more!" I also noticed, in his eyes, compassion, and I've noticed that a lot these past several days . . . to be honest with you, this has been a devastating week.

This media frenzy is a sad commentary on the state of race relations as we know it. It is unfortunate that this man felt a need to shock people with his public display of inhumanity and insensitivity. But a positive outcome is public and private dialogue addressing the cross section of race, racism, and public rhetoric. It is only through dialogue and communication that we can deconstruct the racist ideology that remains a pervasive part of Western culture.

OPPORTUNITIES FOR EXTENDED LEARNING

1. Speak to five friends outside of class and ask them to write on a piece of paper as many traits they feel describe Japanese Americans, Mexican Americans, European Americans, and African Americans. Compile these different lists into one master list and during one class session. In groups, compare the lists to those included in Andrea Rich's 1974 list of communication traits (Table 12.2). Discuss the differences and similarities between the lists. Also address how time has influenced (or not) the types of the stereotypes ascribed to each group.

2. Using Andrea Rich's list of communication traits associated with four different racial/ethnic groups, you will be provided with four groups of 12 traits. (Instructor: Be sure there are no identifiers on each list.) Breaking into small groups, each group will discuss what racial/ethnic group they feel the grouped terms represent. After the discussion, the groups should share their findings with the class. Once each group has contributed to the discussion, the instructor will guide the class in a discussion designed to compare the class list to Rich's list. Students should also discuss the origins of these traits/stereotypes and how time has or has not influenced our perceptions of each other.

3. For this activity, students should be paired off. Each pair will conduct informal interviews with members of different organizations in the community. A total of four interviews will be conducted, two with European Americans (one male and one female) and two with people from other racial/ethnic groups. Interviewees will be asked to share their opinions about the state

of race relations in the workplace and whether or not race relations (cultural diversity) training is still a necessary in the 21st century. After the project is completed, each pair will share their findings with their class.

4. During the first 10 minutes of class, the class will think to themselves about the statements in Peggy McIntosh's privilege list (see Table 12.3). As a whole the class will discuss if and how important it is to address privilege and its role in perpetuating racism in the United States. More importantly, the class should engage in honest discussion about feelings of guilt that privileged individuals may experience once they become cognizant of their social location in the racial hierarchy.

5. Neuliep and McCroskey's PRECA (1997b) is promoted as an effective measure of communicator apprehension and its effect on interracial/ interethnic interactions. As a class, discuss the appropriateness of this scale. Would study participants be sensitized to the purpose of the study? Would their responses be accurate, or would they be hesitant to complete the questionnaire for fear of appearing racist or ethnocentric? What could the researchers do differently, if anything, to improve how we gather data on attitudes relative to race? If you were to complete this questionnaire, how would you respond to the manner in which the questions are presented? If you were asked to create your own scale, what would you do differently?

6. Using *InfoTrac College Edition*, search for articles and essays that examine racial conflict (keyword: *racial conflict*). What role does geography play in how the conflict originates and is resolved? Are certain racial/ethnic groups in conflict more than others? Is race a factor in the conflict, or is the conflict over a nonrace issue? Address whether race and/or racial/ethnic difference appears to contribute to the conflict. Compare and contrast those situations in which solutions are and are not utilized within those specific contexts. Consider the effectiveness of each strategy and, more importantly, apply strategies from this text that could resolve these racial conflicts effectively.

References

Aamidor, A. (1994, February 27). The last word on PC. *Indianapolis (IN) Star*, pp. J1–2.

Acuna, R. (1988). *Occupied America: A history of Chicanos*. New York: Harper & Row.

Adler, J. (1990, December 24). Taking offense. *Newsweek*, pp. 48–55.

Adler, J. (1991, September 23). African dreams. *Newsweek*, pp. 42–45.

African-Americans' viewing habits on the rise. (1994, March 26). *TV Guide*, p. 36

Alba, R. D., & Chamlin, M. B. (1983). A preliminary examination of ethnic identification among whites. *American Sociological Review, 48*, 240–247.

Alba, R. D., & Golden, R. N. (1986). Patterns of ethnic marriage in the United States. *Social Forces, 65*, 202–223.

Alexander, L. (1998, November) Created equal: The principles of racial reconciliation. *Policy Review, 92*, 18–21.

Alexander, S. (1994). Vietnamese Amerasians: Dilemmas of individual identity and family cohesion. In E. P. Salett & D. R. Koslow (Eds.), *Race, ethnicity and self: Identity in multicultural perspective* (pp. 198–216). Washington, DC: MultiCultural Institute.

Allen, B. J. (1996). Feminist standpoint theory: A Black woman's (re)view of organizational socialization. *Communication Studies, 47*(4), 257–271.

Allen, B. J. (1997). Sapphire and Sappho: Allies in authenticity. In A. Gonzalez, M. Houston, & V. Chen (Eds.), *Our voices: Essays in culture, ethnicity, and communication* (pp. 143–148). Los Angeles: Roxbury.

Allen, B. J. (1998). Black womanhood and feminist standpoints. *Management Communication Quarterly, 11*, 575–586.

Allen, P. G. (1986). *The sacred hoop: Recovering the feminism in American Indian traditions*. Boston: Beacon Press.

Allport, G. W. (1958). *The nature of prejudice*. Garden City, NY: Doubleday.

Alperstein, N. (1994). Memories, anticipation, and self-talk: A cultural study of the inward experience of television advertising. *Journal of Popular Culture, 28*(1), 209–221.

American Psychological Association. (1996). *Publication manual of the American Psychological Association* (4th ed.). Washington, DC : Author.

Andersen, P. A. (1998). Researching sex differences within sex similarities: The evolutionary consequences of reproductive differences. In D. J. Canary & K. Dindia (Eds.), *Sex differences and similarities in communication: Critical essays and empirical investigations of sex and gender in interaction.* (pp. 83–100). Mahwah, NJ: Erlbaum.

Anzaldua, G. (1987). *Borderlands: La Frontera.* San Francisco: Aunt Lute.

Artz, B. L. (1998). Hegemony in Black and White: Interracial buddy films and the new racism. In Y. R. Kamalipour & T. Carilli (Eds.), *Cultural diversity in the U.S. media* (pp. 67–78). Albany: SUNY Press.

Asante, M. K. (1988). *Afrocentricity.* Trenton, NJ: Africa World Press.

Asante, M. K. (1991). The Afrocentric idea in education. *Journal of Negro Education, 60*(2), 170–180.

Asante, M. K. (1998a). *The Afrocentric idea.* Philadelphia: Temple University Press.

Asante, M. K. (1998b). Identifying racist language, linguistic acts, and signs. In M. L. Hecht (Ed.), *Communicating prejudice* (pp. 87–98). Thousand Oaks, CA: Sage.

Astor, D. (1996, June 22). Laughs and gripes about stereotypes. *Editor & Publisher, pp.* 46–47.

Atkin, D. (1992). An analysis of television series with minority-lead characters. *Critical Studies in Mass Communication, 9,* 337–349.

Ayres, J. (1996). Speech preparation and speech apprehension. *Communication Education, 45*(3), 228–235.

Ayres, J., Hopf, T., Brown, K., & Suck, J. M. (1994). The impact of communication apprehension, gender, and time on turn-taking behavior in initial interactions. *Southern Communication Journal, 59*(2), 142–152.

Ayres, J., Keereetaweep, T., Chen, P. E., & Edwards, P. (1998). Communication apprehension and employment interviews. *Communication Education, 47*(1), 1–17.

Ayers, K. (1994, April). *Life transitions: Exploring how retirement affects interpersonal communication.* Paper presented at the annual Women's Studies Conference, Indiana University at Kokomo.

Baker, J. R. (1974). *Race.* New York: Oxford University Press.

Baldwin, J. (1990). Quoted in Introduction: A way of images. In J. L. Dates and W. Barlow (Eds.), *Split image* (pp. 1–21). Washington, DC: Howard University Press.

Banaji, M. R., Hardin, C., & Rothman, A. J. (1993). Implicit stereotyping in person judgement. *Journal of Personality and Social Psychology, 65*(2), 272–281.

Banks, J. A. (1976). The emerging stages of ethnicity: Implications for staff development. *Educational Leadership, 34*(3), 190–193.

Banks, S. P. (1987). Achieving "unmarkedness" in organization discourse: A praxis perspective on ethnolinguistic identity. *Journal of Language and Social Psychology, 6,* 171–189.

Banton, M. (1967). *Race relations.* London: Tavistock.

Basso, K. H. (1979). *Portraits of "The Whiteman."* Cambridge: Cambridge University Press.

Bawer, B. (1994, October 18). Confusion reigns. *The Advocate,* p. 80.

Baxter, L. A., & Goldsmith, D. (1990). Cultural terms for communication events among some American high school adolescents. *Western Journal of Speech Communication, 54,* 377–394.

Beebe, S. A., & Beebe, S. J. (1991). *Public speaking: An audience-centered approach.* Englewood Cliffs, NJ: Prentice Hall.

Beech, H. (1996, April 8). 'Don't you dare list them as other.' *U.S. News & World Report,* p. 56.

Begley, S. (1995, February 13). Three is not enough. *Newsweek*, pp. 67–69.

Bell, D. (1992). *Faces at the bottom of the well: The permanence of racism.* New York: Basic.

Bell, D. (1992, July). Organizational communication techniques for managers. *Public Management, 79*(7), 24–25.

Bell, K., Orbe, M., Drummond, D. K., & Camara, S. K. (in press). Accepting the challenge of centralizing without essentializing: Black feminist thought and African American women's communicative experiences. *Women's Studies in Communication.*

Berger, C. R., & Douglas, W. (1981). Studies in interpersonal epistemology III: Anticipated interaction, self-monitoring, and observational context selection. *Communication Monographs, 48,* 183–196.

Berry, J. W., & Sam, D. L. (1997). *Acculturation and adaptation.* Needham Heights, MA: Allyn & Bacon.

Berry, V. T. (1992). From *Good Times* to *The Cosby Show*: Perceptions of changing televised images among Black fathers and sons. In S. Craig (Ed.), *Men, masculinity, and the media* (pp. 111–123). Newbury Park, CA: Sage.

Besherov & Smith (1996). Cited in Holmes, S. A. Study finds number of interracial couples is increasing sharply. *Louisville (KY) Courier-Journal,* p. A4.

Birdwhistell, R. (1970). *Kinesics and context.* Philadelphia: University of Pennsylvania Press.

Blacks closing gap in use of technology. (1999, March 11). *Kalamazoo (MI) Gazette,* p. A11.

Blau, P., Blum, T. C., & Schwartz, J. E. (1982). Heterogeneity and intermarriage. *American Sociological Review, 47,* 45–62.

Blubaugh, J. A., & Pennington, D. L. (1976). *Crossing difference . . . Interracial communication.* Columbus, OH: Charles E. Merrill.

Blumenbach, J. F. (1973). *The anthropological treatises of Johann Friedrich Blumenback.* Boston: Milford House. (Original work published 1865)

Blumer, H. (1969). *Symbolic interactionism: Perspective and method.* Englewood Cliffs, NJ: Prentice-Hall.

Bogle, D. (1994). *Toms, coons, mulattoes. mammies, and bucks: An interpretive history of Blacks in American films.* New York: Viking Press.

Boswell, J. (1994). *Same-sex unions in premodern Europe.* New York: Villard.

Botan, C., & Smitherman, G. (1991). Black English in the integrated workplace. *Journal of Black Studies, 22,* 168–185.

Bourhis, R. Y., & Giles, H. (1977). The language of intergroup distinctiveness. In H. Giles & R. St. Clair (Eds.), *Language, ethnicity, and intergroup relations* (pp. 119–135). London: Academic Press.

Bourhis, R. Y. (1979). Language in ethnic interaction: A social psychological approach. In H. Giles & B. Saint-Jacques (Eds.), *Language and ethnic relations* (pp. 117–141). Oxford: Pergamon.

Bower, L., & Schmid, J. (1997). Minority presence and portrayal in mainstream magazine advertising: An update. *Journalism and Mass Communication Quarterly, 74,* 134–146.

Bowser, B. P. (1995). *Racism and anti-racism in world perspective.* (Vol. 13). Thousand Oaks, CA: Sage.

Bowser, B. P., & Hunt, R. G. (1996). *Impacts of racism on White Americans.* Thousand Oaks, CA: Sage.

Braithwaite, C. (1990). Communicative silence: A cross cultural study of Basso's hypothesis. In D. Carbaugh (Ed.), *Cultural communication and intercultural contact* (pp. 321–327). Hillsdale, NJ: Erlbaum.

Braithwaite, D. O. (1990). From majority to minority: An analysis of cultural change from able-bodied to disabled. *International Journal of Intercultural Relations, 14,* 465–483.

Braithwaite, D. O. (1991). Just how much did that wheelchair cost?: Management of privacy boundaries by persons with disabilities. *Western Journal of Speech Communication, 55,* 254–274.

Braithwaite, D. O., & Braithwaite, C. A. (1997). Understanding communication of persons with disabilities as cultural communication. In L. A. Samovar & R. E. Porter (Eds.), *Intercultural communication: A reader* (pp. 154–163). Belmont, CA: Wadsworth.

Braithwaite, D. O., & Thompson, T. L. (Eds.). (in press). *Handbook of communication and people with disabilities: Research and application.* Mahwah, NJ: Erlbaum.

Branch, S. (1998, July 6). What blacks think of corporate America. *Fortune,* pp. 140–143.

Brewer, M., & Campbell, D. T. (1976). *Ethnocentrism and intergroup attitudes.* New York: Wiley.

Bridge, J. (1994, April). Media mirror: Distorted reflections—distorted treatment. *The Quill,* pp.16–18.

Brilhart, J. K., & Galanes, G. J. (1995). *Effective group discussion* (8th ed.). Dubuque, IA: WCB Brown & Benchmark.

Brooks, D. E., & Jacobs, W. R. (1996). Black men in the margins: Space Traders and the interpositional strategy against b(l)acklash. *Communication Studies, 47,* 289–302.

Brown, J. C. (1993, June). In defense of the N word. *Essence,* p. 138.

Brown, P., & Levinson, S. (1978). Universals in language use: Politeness phenomena. In E. Goody (Ed.), *Questions and politeness* (pp. 56–289). London: Cambridge University Press.

Brummett, B. (1992, November). *Forget rhetoric, study "R" instead.* Paper presented at the annual meeting of the Speech Communication Association, Chicago.

Brummett, B. (1994). *Rhetoric in popular culture.* New York: St. Martin's Press.

Burke, P. J., & Franzoi, S. L. (1988). Studying situations and identities using experiential sampling methodology. *American Sociological Review, 53,* 559–568.

Burke, P. J., & Tully, J. (1977). The measurement of role/identity. *Social Forces, 55,* 881–897.

Burke, P. J., & Reitzes, D. C. (1981). The link between identity and role performance. *Social Psychology Quarterly, 44,* 83–92.

Byers, L. A., & Hart, R. D. (1996, May). *I had my own identity for the first time in my life: The relational dialectics between self and society.* Paper presented at the annual meeting of the International Communication Association, Chicago.

Byers, P. Y. (1997). *Organizational communication: Theory and behavior.* Boston: Allyn & Bacon.

Byrd, J. (1997). Blacks, whites in news pictures. In S. Biagi & M. Kem-Foxworth (Eds.), *Facing difference: Race, gender. and mass media* (pp. 95–97). Thousand Oaks, CA: Pine Forge Press.

Byrne, D. (1971). *The Attraction Paradigm.* New York: Academic.

Calvert, C. (1997). Hate speech and its harms: A communication theory perspective. *Journal of Communication, 47*(l), 4–19.

Campbell, R. (1999). Media and culture: *An introduction to mass communication.* New York: St. Martin's Press.

Canary, D., & Dindia, K. (Eds.). (1998). *Sex differences and similarities in communication: Critical essays and empirical investigations of sex and gender in interaction.* Mahwah, NJ: Erlbaum.

Carbaugh, D. (1987). Communication rules in Donahue discourse. *Research on Language and Social Interaction, 21,* 31–61.

Carbaugh, D. (1989). *Talking American: Cultural discourses on Donahue.* Norwood, NJ: Ablex.

Carbaugh, D. (1990). Intercultural communication. In D. Carbaugh (Ed.), *Cultural communication and intercultural contact* (pp. 151–176). Hillsdale, NJ: Erlbaum.

Carbaugh, D. (1995). The ethnographic communication theory of Philipsen and associates. In D. Cushman & B. Kovacic (Eds.), *Watershed research traditions in communication theory* (pp. 241–265). Albany: SUNY Press.

Carbaugh, D. (1998). "I can't do that! but I can actually see around the corners": American Indian students and the study of public communication. In J. N. Martin, T. K. Nakayama, & L. A. Flores (Eds.), *Reading in cultural contexts* (pp. 160–171). Mountain View, CA: Mayfield.

Cargile, A. C., & Giles, H. (1996). Intercultural communication training: Review, critique, and a new theoretical framework. In B. R. Burleson (Ed.), *Communication Yearbook, 19* (pp. 385–423). Thousand Oaks, CA: Sage.

Carrasco, R. (1996, January 8). Pivotal minority movements strive for racial unity. *Christianity Today,* p. 70.

Carrier, J. (1999). *Ten ways to fight hate: A community response guide.* Montgomery, AL: Southern Poverty Law Center.

Carroll, J. B. (1992). Anthropological linguistics: An overview. In W. Bright (Ed.), *International encyclopedia of linguistics* (pp. 33–49). New York: Oxford University Press.

Carson, C. (1981). *In struggle: SNCC and the Black awakening of the 1960s.* Cambridge, MA: Harvard University Press.

Carter, R. A. (1995, December). Improving minority relations. *FBI Law Enforcement Bulletin* pp. 14–17.

Carter, R. T. (1990). The relationship between racism and racial identity among White Americans: An exploratory investigation. *Journal of Counseling and Development, 69,* 46–50.

Case, C. E., & Greeley, A. M. (1990). Attitudes toward racial equality. *Humboldt Journal of Social Relations, 16*(1), 67–94.

Casmir, F. L., & Asuncion-Lande, N. C. (1989). Intercultural communication revisited: Conceptualization, paradigm building, and methodological approaches. *Communication Yearbook, 12,* 278–309.

Casmir, F. L. (1993). Third-culture building: A paradigm shift for international and intercultural communication. *Communication Yearbook, 16,* 107–124.

Chan, S. (1989). You're short, besides! In Asian Women United of California (Eds.), *Making waves: An anthology of writings by and about Asian American women* (pp. 265–272). Boston: Beacon Press.

Chapa, J. (1998, June). Conquering the recruitment challenge. *Hispanic,* p. 62.

Chen, G. M., & Starosta, W. J. (1998). *Foundations of intercultural communication.* Boston: Allyn & Bacon.

Chen, V. (1997). (De)hyphenated identity: The double voice in *The Woman Warrior.* In A. Gonzalez, M. Houston, & V. Chen (Eds.), *Our voices: Essays in culture, ethnicity, and communication* (pp. 3–13). Los Angeles: Roxbury.

Chism, N. V. N., & Border, L. L. B. (Eds.). (1992). *Teaching for diversity*. San Francisco, CA: Jossey-Bass.

Cho, S. K. (1995). Korean Americans vs. African Americans: Conflict and construction. In M. L. Andersen & P. H. Collins (Eds.), *Race, class, and gender: An anthology* (pp. 461–469). Belmont, CA: Wadsworth.

Clark, K., & Diggs, R. C. (in press). Connected or separated?: Towards a dialectical view of interethnic relationships. In T. A. McDonald, M. Orbe, & T. Ford-Ahmed (Eds.), *Building diverse communities: Applications of communication research*. Cresskill, NJ: Hampton Press.

Clayton, O., Jr. (1995, Winter). The churches and social change: Accommodation, moderation, or protest. *Daedulus*, pp. 101–117.

Clifton, J. A. (Ed.). (1989). *Being and becoming Indian: Biographical studies of North American frontiers*. Homewood, IL: Dorsey.

Close, E. (1997, January 13). Why Ebonics is irrelevant. *Newsweek*, p. 80.

Cohen, G., & Faulkner, D. (1986). Does "elderspeak" work? The effect of intonation and stress on comprehension and recall of spoken discourse in old age. *Language and Communication, 6*, 91–98.

Cole, J. B. (1995). Commonalities and differences. In M. L. Andersen & P. H. Collins (Eds.), *Race, class, and gender: An anthology* (pp. 148–154). Belmont, CA: Wadsworth.

Coleman, L. M., & DePaulo, B. M. (1991). Uncovering the human spirit: Moving beyond disability and 'missed' communications. In N. Coupland, H. Giles, & J. M. Wiemann (Eds.), *Miscommunication and problematic talk* (pp. 61–84). Newbury Park, CA: Sage.

Collier, M. J. (1988). A comparison of intracultural and intercultural communication among acquaintances: How intra-and intercultural competencies vary. *Communication Quarterly, 36*, 122–144.

Collier, M. J. (1991). Conflict competence within African, Mexican, Anglo American friendships. In S. Ting-Toomey & F. Korzenny (Eds.), *Cross-cultural interpersonal communication* (pp. 132–154). Newbury Park, CA: Sage.

Collier, M. J. (1997). Cultural identity and intercultural communication. In L. A. Samovar & R. E. Porter (Eds.), *Intercultural communication: A reader* (pp. 36–44). Belmont, CA: Wadsworth.

Collier, M. J. (1998). Intercultural friendships as interpersonal alliances. In J. N. Martin, T. K. Nakayama, & L. A. Flores (Eds.), *Readings in cultural contexts* (pp. 370–378). Mountain View, CA: Mayfield.

Collier, M.J., & Bowker, J. (1994, November). *U.S. American women in intercultural friendships*. Paper presented at the Speech Communication Association conference, New Orleans.

Collier, M. J., Ribeau, S. A., & Hecht, M. L. (1986). Intracultural communication rules and outcomes within three domestic cultures. *International Journal of Intercultural Relations, 10*, 439–457.

Collier, M. J., & Thomas, M. (1988). Cultural identity: An interpretive perspective. In Y. Y. Kim & W. B. Gudykunst (Eds.), *Theories in intercultural communication* (pp. 99–120). Newbury Park, CA: Sage.

Collier, M. J., Thompson, J., & Weber, D. (1996, November). *Identity problematics among U.S. ethnics*. Paper presented at the annual meeting of the Speech Communication Association, San Diego.

Collins, P. H. (1986). Learning from the outsider within: The sociological significance of black feminist thought. *Social Problems, 33*(6), S14–S23.

Collins, P. H. (1990). *Black feminist thought: Knowledge, consciousness, and the politics of empowerment.* Boston: Unwin Hyman.

Collins, P. H. (1995). Pornography and Black women's bodies. In G. Dines & J. M. Humez (Eds.), *Gender. race and class in media* (pp. 279–286). Thousand Oaks, CA: Sage.

Collins, P. H. (1998). *Fighting words: Black women and the search for justice.* Minneapolis: University of Minnesota Press.

Condit, C. M., & Lucaites, J. (1993). *Crafting equality: America's Anglo African word.* Chicago: University of Chicago Press.

Cooks, L. M., & Hale, C. L. (1992). A feminist approach to the empowerment of women mediators. *Discourse & Society, 3*(3), 277–300.

Coombes, W. T., & Holladay, S. T. (1995). The emerging political power of the elderly. In N. F. Nussbaum & J. Coupland (Eds.), *Handbook of communication and aging research* (pp. 317–343). Mahwah, NJ: Erlbaum.

Cooper, M. (1990). Rejecting "femininity": Some research notes on gender identity development in lesbians. *Deviant Behavior, 11,* 371–380.

Cordova, F. (1973). The Filipino-American: There's always an identity crisis. In S. Sue & N. Wagner (Eds.), *Asian Americans: Psychological perspectives.* Palo Alto, CA: Science & Behavior Books.

Cornwell, N. C., Orbe, M., & Warren, K. (1999, May). *Hate speech/free speech: Using feminist perspectives to foster on-campus dialogue.* Paper presented at the annual meeting of the International Communication Association, San Francisco.

Cosby, B. (1995, November). 50 years of blacks on TV. *Ebony,* pp. 215–218.

Coward, J. M. (1993, August). *'The sculking Indian enemy': Colonial newspapers' portrayal of Native Americans.* Paper printed at the annual meeting of the Association for Education in Journalism and Mass Communication, Kansas City, MO.

Crawley, R. L. (1995, January). *Communicating about diverse people: An experiential workshop.* Presentation to the students at Indiana University Southeast, New Albany.

Crenshaw, C. (1997). Resisting whiteness' rhetorical silence. *Western Journal of Communication, 61*(3), 253–278.

Crenshaw, K., Gotanda, N., Peller, G., & Thomas, K. (Eds.). (1995). *Critical race theory: The key writings that formed the movement.* New York: New Press.

Crompton, R. (1993). *Class and stratification: An introduction to current debates.* Cambridge, UK: Polity.

Cross, W. E. (1971). The Negro-to-Black conversion experience: Toward a psychology of Black liberation. *Black World, 20,* 13–27.

Cross, W. E. (1978). The Thomas and Cross models of psychological nigrescence: A review. *Journal of Black Psychology, 5*(1), 13–31.

Cummings, M. C. (1988). The changing image of the Black family on television. *Journal of Popular Culture, 22*(2), 75–85.

Cupach, W. R., & Imahori, T. T. (1993). Identity management theory: Communication competence in intercultural episodes and relationships. *International and Intercultural Communication Annual, 17,* 112–131.

Dace, K. L. (1994). Dissonance in European-American and African-American communication. *Western Journal of Black Studies, 18,* 18–26.

Dace, K. L., & McPhail, M. L. (1998). Crossing the color line: From empathy to implicature in intercultural communication. In J. N. Martin, T. K. Nakayama, & L. A. Flores (Eds.), *Readings in cultural contexts* (pp. 434–441). Mountain View, CA: Mayfield.

Dalton, T. A. (1997). Reporting on race: A tale of two cities. *Columbia Journalism Review, 36*(3), 54–58.

Daly, J. A., Vangelisti, A. L., & Weber, D. J. (1995). Speech anxiety affects how people prepare speeches: A protocol analysis of the preparation processes of speakers. *Communication Monographs, 62*(4), 383–398.

Davidson, J. R., & Schneider, L. J. (1992). Acceptance of Black-White interracial marriage. *Journal of Intergroup Relations, 24*(3), 47–52.

Davis, F. J. (1991). *Who is Black: One nation's definition.* University Park: Pennsylvania State University Press.

Davis, R. A. (1997). *The myth of Black ethnicity: Monophylety, diversity, and the dilemma of identity.* Greenwich, CT: Ablex.

Day, A. G. (1960). *Hawaii and its people.* New York: Duell, Sloan & Pearce.

Degler, C. N. (1971). *Neither Black nor White: Slavery and race relations in Brazil and the United States.* New York: Macmillan.

De La Torre, W. (1997). Multiculturalism: A redefinition of citizenship and community. *Urban Education, 31*(3), 314–345.

Delgado, F. (1998). Moving beyond the screen: Hollywood and Mexican American stereotypes. In Y. R. Kamalipour & T. Carilli (Eds.), *Cultural diversity in the U.S. media* (pp. 169–182). Albany: SUNY Press.

Delgado, F. P. (1998). When the silenced speak: The textualization and complications of Latino/a identity. *Western Journal of Communication, 62,* 420–438.

Delgado, R. (Ed.). (1995). *Critical race theory: The cutting edge.* Philadelphia: Temple University Press.

Deloria, V. (1985). *Behind the trail of broken treaties: An Indian declaration of independence.* Austin: University of Texas Press.

Deutsch, M. (1994). Constructive conflict resolution: Principles, training, and research. *Journal of Social Issues, 50*(1), 13–32.

DeVito, J. (1998). *The interpersonal communication book* (8th ed.). New York: Longman.

DeVos, G. A. (1982). Ethnic pluralism: Conflict and accommodation. In G. A. DeVos & L. Romanucci-Ross (Eds.), *Ethnic identity: Cultural continuities and change* (pp. 5–41). Chicago: University of Chicago Press.

Diamond, J. (1994, November). Race without color. *Discover,* pp. 83–89.

Dodd, C. H., & Baldwin, J. R. (1998). The role of family and macrocultures in intercultural relationships. In J. N. Martin, T. K. Nakayama, & L. A. Flores (Eds.), *Readings in cultural contexts* (pp. 335–344). Mountain View, CA: Mayfield.

Dorsey, T. (1995, June 20). Many of the season's losers didn't deserve to be canceled. *Louisville (KY) Courier-Journal,* p. C3.

Dorsey, T. (1997, March). Blacks' viewing habits assessed. *Louisville (KY) Courier-Journal,* p. E2.

Doughtery, D. S. (1999). Dialogue through standpoint: Understanding women's and men's standpoints of sexual harassment. *Management Communication Quarterly, 12,* 436–468.

Drummond, D. K. (1997, November). *An exploration of multiple identity negotiation over the Internet.* Paper presented at the annual meeting of the National Communication Association, Chicago.

Du Bois, W. E. B. (1982). *The souls of Black folks.* New York: Signet. (Original work published 1903)

Duckitt, J., & du Toit, L. (1989). Personality profiles of homosexual men and women. *Journal of Psychology, 123*, 497–505.

Dwyer, E. (1993, December 10-12). The story behind 'Geronimo.' *USA Weekend*, p. 10.

Eddings, J. (1996, October 23). The covert color war: A persistent stealth racism is poisoning black-white relations. *U.S. News & World Report*, pp. 40–42.

Eddings, J. (1997, July 14). Counting a 'new' type of American. *U.S. News & World Report*, pp. 22–23.

Ehrenreich, B. (1989). *Fear of falling: The inner life of the middle class.* New York: HarperCollins.

Ehrenreich, B. (1990). Are you middle class? In M. L. Andersen & P. H. Collins (Eds.), *Race, class, and gender: An anthology* (pp. 100–109). Belmont, CA: Wadsworth.

Elise, S., & Umoja, A. (1992). Spike Lee constructs the new Black man: Mo' better. *Western Journal of Black Studies, 6*, 82–89.

Ellison, G. C., & Powers, D. A. (1994). The contact hypothesis and racial attitudes among Black Americans. *Social Science Quarterly, 75*(2), 385–400.

El Nasser, H. (1997, May 9). Millions in America claim a varied racial heritage. *Louisville (KY) Courier-Journal*, p. A7.

Ely, J. H. (1998). If at first you don't succeed, ignore the question next time? Group harm in *Brown v. Board of Education* and *Loving v. Virginia. Constitutional Commentary, 15*(2), 215–223.

Emry, R., & Wiseman, R. L. (1987). An intercultural understanding of ablebodied and disabled persons communication. *International Journal of Intercultural Relations, 11*, 7–27.

Entman, R. (1994). Representation and reality in the portrayal of blacks on network television shows. *Journalism Quarterly, 71*(1), 509–520.

Erikson, E. H. (1963). *Childhood and society* (2nd ed.). New York: Norton.

Erikson, E. H. (1968). *Identity: Youth and crisis.* New York: Norton.

Essed, P. (1991). *Understanding everyday racism: An interdisciplinary theory.* Newbury Park, CA: Sage.

Estes, A. (1999, February 25). Internet reported as major factor in hate speech group growth. *Western Michigan University Herald*, p. 5.

Ethridge, R. (1991, September 26). Politically correct speech. *Black Issues in Higher Education*, pp. B1–2.

Etzioni, A. (1996, September). From melting pot to mosaic: America's community of communities. *Current, 385*, pp. 8–13.

Evans, D. (1993, March 1). The wrong examples. *Newsweek*, p. 10.

Evoleocha, S. U., & Ugbah, S. D. (1989). Stereotypes, counter-stereotypes, and Black television images in the 1990s. *Western Journal of Black Studies, 12*, 197–205.

Ezekiel, R. S. (1997). *The racist mind: Portraits of American neo-Nazis and Klansmen.* New York: Penguin.

Fairchild, H. H. (1985). Black, Negro, or Afro-American? The difference are crucial! *Journal of Black Studies, 16*(1), 47–55.

"Families of many colors." (1998, February 9). *Scholastic Update*, pp. 12–21.

Farhi, P. (1997). A television trend: Audiences in black and white. In S. Biagi & M. Kem-Foxworth (Eds.), *Facing difference: Race, gender, and mass media* (pp. 202–204). Thousand Oaks, CA: Pine Forge Press.

Fayol, H. (1916). *General and Industrial Management*. London: Pitman.

Feagin, J. (1992). The continuing significance of racism: Discrimination against black students in white colleges. *Journal of Black Studies, 22*(4), 546–578.

Feagin, J., & Feagin, C. B. (1996). *Racial and ethnic relations* (5th ed). Englewood Cliffs, NJ: Prentice Hall.

Ferguson, R., Gever, M., Trinh, T. M., & West, C. (Eds.). (1990). *Out there: Marginalization and contemporary cultures*. Cambridge, MA: MIT Press.

Fernandez, C. A. (1992). La Raza and the melting pot: A comparative look at multiethnicity. In M. P. P. Root (Ed.), *Racially mixed in America* (pp. 126–143). Newbury Park, CA: Sage.

Field, D., & Travisano, R. (1984). Social history and American preoccupation with identity. *Free Inquiry in Creative Sociology, 12*, 51–56.

Fink, B., & Wild, K.-P. (1995). Similarities in leisure interests: Effects of selection and isolation in friendships. *Journal of Social Psychology, 135*(4), 471–483.

Firth, J. (1991, November). A proactive approach to conflict resolution. *Supervisory Management*, pp. 3–4.

Fitch, N. E. (1992). Multiculturalism and diversity, or business as usual in the 20th century? *Diversity: A Journal of Multicultural Issues, 1*, 43–64.

Fitzpatrick, K. M., & Hwang, S. S. (1992). The effects of community structure on opportunities for interracial contact: Extending Blau's macrostructural theory. *Sociological Forum, 7*(3), 517–536.

Fitzgerald, M., & Hernandez, D. G. (1994, August 27). Diversity diversions: Entries from reporters' logs at the unity '94 conference. *Editor & Publisher*, pp. 26–28.

Flores, L. A. (1996). Creating discursive space through a rhetoric of difference: Chicana feminists craft a homeland. *Quarterly Journal of Speech, 82*, 142–156.

Flynn, G. (1998a). Experts explain the evolution of diversity programs. *Workforce, 77*(12), 32.

Flynn, G. (1998b). The harsh reality of diversity programs. *Workforce, 77*(12), 26–31.

Foeman, A. K. (1997, July). Managing multiracial institutions: Goals and approaches for race-relations training. *Communication Education, 40*(3), 255–265.

Foeman, A. K., & Nance, T. (1999). From miscegenation to multiculturalism: Perceptions and stages of interracial relationship development. *Journal of Black Studies, 29*(4), 540–557.

Folb, E. A. (1997). Who's got room at the top?: Issues of dominance and nondominance in intracultural communication. In L. A. Samovar & R. E. Porter (Eds.), *Intercultural communication: A reader* (pp. 138–146). Belmont, CA: Wadsworth.

Fong, M. (1997). The crossroads of language and culture. In L. A. Samovar & R. E. Porter (Eds.), *Intercultural communication: A reader* (pp. 207–212). Belmont, CA: Wadsworth.

Ford-Ahmed, T., & Orbe, M. (1992, November). *African American graduate students, their majority host institution and ethnic prejudice: A bright side?* Paper presented at the annual meeting of the Speech Communication Association, Chicago.

Foster-Fishman, P. G., & Keys, C. B. (1997). The person/environment dynamics of employee empowerment: An organizational culture analysis. *American Journal of Community Psychology, 25*(3), 345–369.

Fox, S. A., & Giles, H. (1997). "Let the wheelchair through!" In W. P. Robinson (Ed.), *Social psychology and social identity: Festschrift in honor of Henri Tajfel*. Amsterdam: Elsevier.

Fox, S. A., Giles, H., Bourhis, R. Y., & Orbe, M. (in press). Communication between people with and without disabilities: A review, critique, and expansion of interability communication theories. In D. O. Braithwaite & T. L. Thompson (Eds.), *Handbook of communication and people with disabilities: Research and application*. Mahwah, NJ: Erlbaum.

Frankenberg, R. (1993). *White women, race matters: The social construction of Whiteness*. Minneapolis: University of Minnesota Press.

Fredrickson, G. M. (1971). *The Black image in the White mind*. New York: Harper & Row.

Fujino, D. C. (1997). The rates, patterns, and reasons for forming heterosexual interracial dating relationships among Asian Americans. *Journal of Social and Personal Relationships, 14*(6), 809–828.

Funderburg, L. (1993). *Black, White, other: Biracial Americans talk about race and identity*. New York: Morrow.

Funderburg, L. (1998, December 14). Loving thy neighborhood. *Nation*, pp. 23–26.

Gaines, S. O., Jr. (1997). Communalism and the reciprocity of affection and respect among interethnic married couples. *Journal of Black Studies, 27*(3), 352–364.

Galen, M. (1994, January 31). White, male, and worried. *Business Week*, pp. 50–55.

Gallagher, C. A. (1994). White construction in the university. *Socialist Review, 1/2*, 167–187.

Gallois, C., Giles, H., Jones, E., Cargile, A. C., & Ota, H. (1995). Accommodating intercultural encounters: Elaborations and extensions. In R. Wiseman (Ed.), *Intercultural communication theory* (pp. 115–147). Thousand Oaks, CA: Sage.

Gandy, O. H., & Matabane, P. W. (1989). Television and social perceptions among African Americans and Hispanics. In M. K. Asante & W. B. Gudykunst (Eds.), *Handbook of international and intercultural communication* (pp. 318–350). Newbury Park, CA: Sage.

Gangotena, M. (1997). The rhetoric of La Familia among Mexican Americans. In A. Gonzalez, M. Houston, & V. Chen (Eds.), *Our voices: Essays in culture, ethnicity, and communication* (pp. 70–83). Los Angeles: Roxbury.

Garofalo, R. (1997). *Rockin' out: Popular music in the USA*. Boston: Allyn & Bacon.

Garner, T. (1994). Oral rhetorical practice in African American culture. In A. Gonzalez, M. Houston, & V. Chen (Eds.), *Our voices: Essays in culture, ethnicity, and communication* (pp. 81–91). Los Angeles: Roxbury.

Garza, R. T., & Herringer, L. G. (1987). Social identity: A multidimensional approach. *Journal of Social Psychology, 127*, 299–308.

Gates, H. L. (1992). TV's Black world turns—but stays unreal. In M. L. Andersen & P. H. Collins (Eds.), *Race. class, and gender: An anthology* (pp. 310–316). Belmont, CA: Wadsworth.

Gates, H. L., Jr., (1994). War of words: Critical race theory and the first amendment. In Griffin, A. P., Lively, D. E., Post, R. C., Rubenstein, W. B. & Strossen, N. (Eds.), *Speaking of race, speaking of sex: Hate speech, civil rights, and civil liberties*, (pp. 17–58). New York: New York University Press.

Geertz, C. (1976). From the native's point of view: On the nature of anthropological understanding. In P. Rabinow & W. M. Sullivan (Eds.), *Interpretive social science* (pp. 225–241). Berkeley: University of California Press.

Gergen, K. J. (1991). *The saturated self: Dilemmas of identity in contemporary life.* New York: Basic.

Giaridina, J. C. (1998). A program to celebrate human diversity. *Education Digest, 63*(7), 9–14.

Gibbs, J. T. (1987). Identity and marginality: Issues in the treatment of biracial adolescents. *American Journal of Orthopsychiatry, 57,* 265–278.

Giles, H. (1973). Accent mobility: A model and some data. *Anthropological Linguistics, 15,* 87–109.

Giles, H. (1977). Social psychology and applied linguistics. *ITL: Review of Applied Linguistics, 33,* 27–42.

Giles, H., Bourhis, R. Y., & Taylor, D. M. (1977). Towards a theory of language in ethnic group relations. In H. Giles (Ed.), *Language and intergroup relations* (pp. 307–348). London: Academic Press.

Giles, H., & Coupland, N. (1991). *Language: Contexts and consequences.* Pacific Grove, CA: Brooks/Cole.

Giles, H., Coupland, N., Coupland, J., Williams, A., & Nussbaum, J. (1992). Intergenerational talk and communication with older people. *International Journal of Aging and Human Development, 34,* 271–297.

Giles, H., & Hewstone, M. (1982). Cognitive structures, speech and social situations: Two integrative models. *Language Sciences, 4,* 187–219.

Giles, H., Mulac, A., Bradac, J. J., & Johnson, P. (1987). Speech accommodation theory: The first decade and beyond. *Communication Yearbook, 10,* 13–48.

Giles, H., & Noels, K. A. (1998). Communication accommodation in intercultural encounters. In J. N. Martin, T. K. Nakayama, & L. A. Flores (Eds.), *Readings in cultural contexts* (pp. 139–149). Mountain View, CA: Mayfield.

Giles, H., Taylor, D. M., & Bourhis, R. Y. (1973). Towards a theory of interpersonal accommodation through language: Some Canadian data. *Language in Society, 2,* 177–192.

Gitlin, T. (1991). On the virtues of a loose canon. *New Perspectives Quarterly, 8,* 53–55.

Gladwell, M. (1996, April/May). Black like them. *The New Yorker,* pp. 74–80.

Goffman, E. (1967). *Interaction ritual: Essays on face–to–face behavior.* Garden City, NY: Anchor.

Gong, G. (1997). When Mississippi Chinese talk. In A. Gonzalez, M. Houston, & V. Chen (Eds.), *Our voices: Essays in culture, ethnicity, and communication* (pp. 84–93). Los Angeles: Roxbury.

Gonzalez, A., Houston, M., & Chen, V. (Eds.). (1997). *Our voices: Essays in culture, ethnicity, and communication.* Los Angeles: Roxbury.

Gonzalez, M. C. (1998). Painting the White face red: Intercultural contact presented through poetic ethnography. In J. N. Martin, T. K. Nakayama, & L. A. Flores (Eds.), *Readings in cultural contexts* (pp. 485–496). Mountain View, CA: Mayfield.

Gordon, M. M. (1964). *Assimilation in American life,* New York: Oxford University Press.

Gordon, M. M. (1978). *Human nature, class, and ethnicity.* New York: Oxford University Press.

Gose, B. (1996, May 10). Public debate over a private choice. *Chronicle of Higher Education,* pp. A45–A47.

Gosset, T. F. (1963). *Race: The history of an idea in America.* New York: Schocken.

Gould, S. J. (1994, November). The geometer of race. *Discover,* pp. 65–69.

Graham, J. A., & Cohen, R. (1997). Race and sex factors in children's sociometric ratings and friendship choices. *Social Development, 6*(3), 355–372.

Grant, M. (1970). *The passing of the great race.* New York: Arno. (Original work published 1918)

Gray, H. (1989). Television, Black Americans, and the American dream. *Critical Studies in Mass Communication, 6,* 376–386.

Gray, H. (1995). *Watching race: Television and the struggle for "Blackness."* Minneapolis: University of Minnesota Press.

Gray, J. (1992). *Men are from Mars, women are from Venus.* New York: HarperCollins.

Greene, C. (1996). "In the best interest of the total community"?: Women–in–action and the problems of building interracial, cross-class alliances in Durham, North Carolina, 1968-1975. *Frontiers, 16*(2–3), 190–218.

Gudykunst, W. B. (1985). A model of uncertainty reduction in intercultural encounters. *Journal of Language and Social Psychology, 4,* 79–98.

Gudykunst, W. B. (1988). Uncertainty and anxiety. In Y. Y. Kim & W. B. Gudykunst (Eds.), *Theories in intercultural communication* (pp. 125–128). Newbury Park, CA: Sage.

Gudykunst, W. B. (1993). Toward a theory of effective interpersonal and intergroup communication: An anxiety/uncertainty management (AUM) perspective. In R. L. Wiseman & J. Koester (Eds.), *Intercultural communication competence* (pp. 33–71) Newbury Park, CA: Sage.

Gudykunst, W. B. (1995). Anxiety/uncertainty management (AUM) theory: Current status. In R. L. Wiseman (Ed.), *Intercultural communication theory* (pp. 8–58). Newbury Park, CA: Sage.

Gudykunst, W. B., & Hammer, M. (1988). The influence of social identity and intimacy of interethnic relationships on uncertainty reduction processes. *Human Communication Research, 14,* 569–601.

Gudykunst, W. B., & Kim, Y. Y. (1992). *Communicating with strangers.* New York: McGraw-Hill.

Gumperz, J. J., & Cook-Gumperz, J. (1982). Introduction: Language and the communication of social identity. In J. J. Gumperz (Ed.), *Language and social identity* (pp. 1–21). New York: Cambridge University Press.

Guthrie, P. (1995). The impact of perceptions on interpersonal interactions in an African American/Asian American housing project. *Journal of Black Studies, 25*(30), 377–395.

Gutierrez, F. (1980, May). *Latinos and the media in the United States: An overview.* Paper presented at the annual meeting of the International Communication Association, Acapulco, Mexico.

Hacker, A. (1992). *Two nations: African American and White, separate, hostile, unequal.* New York: Ballantine.

Hadley-Garcia, G. (1990). *Hispanic Hollywood: The Latins in motion pictures.* New York: Citadel Press.

Hagedom, J. (1997). Asian women in film: No joy, no luck. In S. Biagi & M. Kem-Foxworth (Eds.), *Facing difference: Race, gender, and mass media* (pp. 32–37). Thousand Oaks, CA: Pine Forge Press.

Hale–Bensen, J. E. (1986). *Black children: Their roots, culture, and learning styles.* Baltimore, MD: Johns Hopkins University Press.

Hall, C.C.I. (1980). *The ethnic identity of racially mixed people: A study of Black–Japanese.* Unpublished manuscript.

Hall, E. T. (1959).*The silent language.* New York: Doubleday.

Hall, E. T. (1966). *The hidden dimension.* New York: Doubleday.

Hallinan, M. T., & Williams, R. A. (1987). The stability of students interracial friendships. *American Sociological Review, 52,* 653–664.

Hallinan, M. T., & Williams, R. A. (1989). Interracial friendship choices in secondary schools. *American Sociological Review, 54,* 67–78.

Hamlet, J. D. (1997). Understanding traditional African American preaching. In A. Gonzalez, M. Houston, & V. Chen (Eds.), *Our voices: Essays in culture, ethnicity, and communication* (pp. 94–98). Los Angeles: Roxbury.

Halualani, R. T. (1998). Seeing through the screen: "A struggle of culture." In J. N. Martin, T. K. Nakayama, & L. A. Flores (Eds.), *Readings in cultural contexts* (pp. 264–274). Mountain View, CA: Mayfield.

Haraway, D. (1988). Situated knowledges: The science question in feminism and the privilege of partial perspective. *Signs, 14,* 575–599.

Hardiman, R. (1994). White racial identity development in the United States: In E. P. Salett & D. R. Koslow (Eds.), *Race, ethnicity, and self: Identity in multicultural perspective* (pp. 117–142). Washington, DC: National Multicultural Institute.

Harding, S. (Ed.). (1987). *Feminism & methodology.* Bloomington: Indiana University Press.

Harding, S. (1991). *Whose science? Whose knowledge? Thinking from women's lives.* Ithaca, NY: Cornell University Press.

Harris, M. (1964). *Patterns of race in the Americas.* New York: Norton.

Harris, T. M. (1997a). *Black sitcoms of the 1990's: Friend or foe?* Paper presented at the "Situating the Comedy: Celebrating 50 Years of American Television Situation Comedy, 1947–1997," Conference, Bowling Green, OH.

Harris, T. M. (1997b). "I know it was the blood": Defining the biracial self in a Euro-American society. In A. Gonzalez, M. Houston, & V. Chen (Eds.), *Our voices: Essays in culture, ethnicity, and communication* (pp. 149–156). Los Angeles: Roxbury.

Harris, T. M., & Hill, P. S. (1998). "Waiting to Exhale" or "Breath{ing}": A search for identity, empowerment, and love in the 1990s. *Women & Language, 11*(2), 9–20.

Hartsock, N. C. M. (1983). The feminist standpoint: Developing the ground for a specifically feminist historical materialism. In S. Harding & M. D. Hintikka (Eds.), *Discovering reality: Feminist perspectives on epistemology, metaphysics, methodology, and philosophy of science* (pp. 283–310). Boston: D. Reidel.

Hasian, M., & Delgado, F. (1998). The trials and tribulations of racialized critical rhetorical theory: Understanding the rhetorical ambiguities of Proposition 187. *Communication Theory, 8*(3), 245–270.

Hass, N. (1998, March 12). Black and white. *Kalamazoo (MI) Gazette,* pp. D1, D3.

Hawkins, P. (1997, April). Organizational culture: Sailing between evangelism and complexity. *Human Relations, 50*(4), 417–440.

Hayman, R. L., Jr., & Levit, N. (1997). The constitutional ghetto. In R. Delgado & J. Stefancie (Eds.), *Critical White studies: Looking behind the mirror* (pp. 239–247). Philadelphia: Temple University Press.

Heaton, T. B., & Albrecht, S. L. (1996). The changing pattern of interracial marriage. *Social Biology, 43*(3–4), 203–217.

Hecht, M. L., Collier, M. J., & Ribeau, S. A. (1993). *African American communication: Ethnic identity and cultural interpretation.* Newbury Park, CA: Sage.

Hecht, M. L., & Ribeau, S. A. (1984). Ethnic communication: A comparative analysis of satisfying communication. *International Journal of Intercultural Relations, 8,* 135–151.

Hecht, M. L., Ribeau, S. A., & Alberts, J. K. (1989). An Afro-American perspective on interethnic communication. *Communication Monographs, 56,* 385–410.

Hecht, M. L., Ribeau, S. A., & Sedano, M. V. (1990). A Mexican American perspective on interethnic communication. *International Journal of Intercultural Relations, 14,* 31–55.

Heidegger, M. (1962). *Being and time* (J. Macquarrie & E. Robinson, Trans.). New York: Harper.

Hegde, R. S. (1998). Swinging the Trapeze: The negotiation of identity among Asian Indian immigrant women in the United States. In D. V. Tanno & A. Gonzalez (Eds.), *Communication and identity across cultures* (pp. 34–55). Thousand Oaks, CA: Sage.

Heller, S. (1991, November 27). Frame-up of multicultural movement dissected by scholars and journalists. *Chronicle of Higher Education,* pp. A15–A16.

Helms, J. E. (1990). *Black and White racial identity: Theory, research, and practice.* Greenwich, CT: Greenwood Press.

Helms, J. E. (1994). *A race is a nice thing to have: A guide to being a White person or understanding the White persons in your life.* Topeka, KS: Content Communications.

Hernandez, D. G. (1994b, August 24). Diversity diversions: Entries from reporters' logs at the unity '94 conference. *Editor & Publisher,* pp. 26–28.

Hernandez, D. G. (1994a, August 20). The race quotient: Unity panelists see race playing a hand in the news. *Editor & Publisher,* pp. 12–14.

Herring, R. D. (1994). Native American Indian identity: A people of many peoples. In E. P. Salett & D. R. Koslow (Eds.), *Race, ethnicity, and self: Identity in multicultural perspective* (pp. 170–197). Washington, DC: MultiCultural Institute.

Herrnstein, R. J., & Murray, C. (1994). *The bell curve: Intelligence and class structure in American life.* New York: Free Press.

Heuterman, T. (1987). "We have the same rights as other citizens": Coverage of Yakima Valley Japanese Americans in the "missing decades" of the 1920s and 1930s. *Journalism History, 14,* 94–102.

Hewstone, M., & Giles, H. (1986). Social groups and social stereotypes in intergroup communication: Review and model of intergroup communication breakdown. In W. B. Gudykunst (Ed.), *Intergroup communication* (pp. 10–26). London: Edward Arnold.

Hildebrandt, N., & Giles, H. (1984). The Japanese as subordinate group: Ethnolinguistics identity theory in a foreign language context. *Anthropological Linguistics, 25,* 436–466.

Hocker, J. L., & Wilmont, W. W. (1995). *Interpersonal conflict.* Dubuque, IA: Wm C. Brown.

Hodge, J. L. (1989). Domination and the will in Western thought and culture. In C.E. Jackson & E. J. Tolbert (Eds.), *Race and culture in America: Readings in racial and ethnic relations* (pp. 27–48). Edina, MN: Burgess.

Hoetink, H. (1967). *Caribbean race relations: A study of two variants.* New York: Oxford University Press.

Hofman, J. E. (1985). Arabs and Jews, Black and Whites: Identity and group relations. *Journal of Multilingual and Multicultural Development, 6,* 217–237.

Hoijer, H. (1994). The Sapir-Whorf hypothesis. In L. A. Samovar & R. E. Porter (Eds.), *Intercultural communication: A reader* (7th ed.) (pp. 194–200). Belmont, CA: Wadsworth.

Holloway, J. E. (Ed.). (1990). *Africanisms in American culture.* Bloomington: Indiana University Press.

Holmes, S. A. (1996, July 5). Study finds number of interracial couples is increasing sharply. *Louisville (KY) Courier-Journal,* p. A4.

Homans, G. C. (1961). *Social behavior: Its elementary forms.* New York: Harcourt Brace.

hooks, b. (1992). *Black looks: Race and representation.* Boston: South End Press.

Horno–Delgado, A., Ortega, E., Scott, N. M., & Stembach, M. C. (Eds.). (1989). *Breaking boundaries: Latina writing and critical readiness.* Amherst: University of Massachusetts Press.

Houston, M., & Wood, J. T. (1996). Difficult dialogues, expanded horizons: Communicating across race and class. In J. T. Wood (Ed.), *Gendered relationships* (pp. 39–56). Mountain View, CA: Mayfield.

Houston, M. (1997). When Black women talk with White women: Why dialogues are difficult. In A. Gonzalez, M. Houston, & V. Chen (Eds.), *Our voices: Essays in culture, ethnicity, and communication* (pp. 187–194). Los Angeles: Roxbury.

Hout, M., & Goldstein, J. (1994). How 4.5 million Irish immigrants became 40 million Irish Americans: Demographic and subjective aspects of the ethnic composition of White Americans. *American Sociological Review, 59,* 64–82.

Howard, A. (1980). Hawaiians. In S. Thernstorm (Ed.), *Harvard encyclopedia of American ethnic groups* (pp. 449–452). Cambridge, MA: Harvard University Press.

Howell, W. S. (1982). *The empathic communicator.* Belmont, CA: Wadsworth.

Hummert, M. L., Wiemann, J. M., & Nussbaum, J. F. (1994). *Interpersonal communication in older adulthood: Interdisciplinary theory and research.* Newbury Park, CA: Sage.

Hurtado, S. (1992). The campus racial climate. *Journal of Higher Education, 63*(5), 539–566.

Hymes, D. (1974). *Foundations in sociolinguistics: An ethnographic approach.* Philadelphia: University of Pennsylvania Press.

Infante, D. A., Rancer, A. S., & Womack, D. F. (1990). *Building communication theory.* Prospect Heights, IL.: Waveland Press.

Inniss, L. B., & Feagin, J. (1995). *The Cosby Show:* The view from the Black middle class. *Journal of Black Studies, 25*(6), 692–711.

Jackson, B. W., & Hardiman, R. (1983). Racial identity development. *The NTL Managers' Handbook, 13*(2), 107–119.

Jackson, C. E., & Tolbert, E. J. (Eds.). (1989). *Race and culture in America: Readings in racial and ethnic relations.* Edina, MN: Burgess.

Jackson, L. A., Sullivan, L. A., & Hodge, C. N. (1993). Stereotype effects on attributions, predictions, and evaluations: No two social judgements. *Journal of Personality and Social Psychology, 65*(1), 69–84.

Jacobs, J. H. (1992). Identity development in biracial children. In M. P. P. Root (Ed.), *Racially mixed people in America* (pp. 190–206). Newbury Park, CA: Sage.

Jacobs, J. J., & Furstenberg, F. F. (1986). Changing places, conjugal careers, and women's marital mobility. *Social Forces, 64,* 714–732.

Jahn, J. (1979). *Muntu: The new African culture*. New York: Grove Press.

James, N. C. (1997a). When Miss America was always White. In A. Gonzalez, M. Houston, & V. Chen (Eds.), *Our voices: Essays in culture, ethnicity, and communication* (pp. 46–51). Los Angeles: Roxbury.

James, N. C. (1997b). Classroom climate and teaching (about) racism: Notes from the trenches. In A. Arseneau Jones & S. P. Morreate (Eds.) *Proceedings of the National Communication Association Summer Conference on Racial and Ethnic Diversity in the 21st Century*, (pp. 195–201). Annandale, VA: National Communication Association.

Jeanquart–Barone, S. (1993). Trust differences between supervisors and subordinates: Examining the role of race and gender. *Sex Roles, 29*(1–2), 1–11.

JET Magazine (1997). Popular demand brings 'living single' back for fifth season. 92(17), Sept., 58–61.

Jeter, K. (1982). Analytic essay: Intercultural and interracial marriage. *Marriage and Family Review, 5*, 105–111.

Jhally, S., & Lewis, J. (1992). *Enlightened racism:* The Cosby Show, *audiences, and the myth of the American dream*. San Francisco: Westview Press.

Jiobu, R. M. (1988). *Ethnicity and assimilation*. Albany: SUNY Press.

Johannesen, R. L. (1971). The emerging concept of communication as dialogue. *Quarterly Journal of Speech, 57*, 373–382.

Johnson, P. C. (1999). Reflections on critical White(ness) studies. In T. K. Nakayama & J. N. Martin (Eds.), *Whiteness: The communication of social identity* (pp. 1–12). Thousand Oaks, CA: Sage.

Johnson, R.A. (1980). *Religious assortative marriage in the United States*. New York: Academic Press.

Jones, J. M. (1972). *Prejudice and racism*. Reading, MA: Addison-Wesley.

Jordan, K. (1998). Diversity training in the workplace today: A status report. *Journal of Career Planning and Employment, 59*(1), 46–51.

Jordan, W. D. (1969). *White over Black*. Baltimore: Penguin.

Kalish, R. (1979). The new ageism and the failure models: A polemic. The *Gerontologist, 19*, 398–402.

Kalmijn, M. (1991a). Shifting boundaries: Trends in religious and educational homogamy. *American Sociological Review, 56*, 786–800.

Kalmijn, M. (1991b). Status homogamy in the United States. *American Journal of Sociology, 97*, 496–523.

Kalmijn M. (1993). Trends in Black/White in intermarriage. *Social Forces, 72*, 119–146.

Kalmijn, M. (1998). Intermarriage and homogamy: Causes, patterns, trends. *Annual Review of Sociology, 24*, 395–421.

Kamalipour, R., & Carilli, T. (Eds.). (1998). *Cultural diversity in the U.S. media*. Albany: SUNY Press.

Kathman, J. M., & Kathman, M. D. (1998). What difference does diversity make in managing student employees? *College & Research Libraries, 59*(4), 378–389.

Kautzer, K. (1986). Growing numbers, growing force: Older women organize. In R. Lefkowitz & A. Withorn (Eds.), *For crying out loud: Women and poverty in the United States* (pp. 89–98). Cleveland: Pilgrim Press.

Kay, P., & Kempton, W. (1984). What is the Sapir-Whorf hypothesis? *American Anthropologist, 86,* 65–73.

Kearney, P., & Plax, T. G. (1999). Public speaking in a diverse society (2nd ed.). Mountain View, CA: Mayfield.

Kellner, D. (1995). *Media culture.* New York: Routledge.

Kellner, O. D. (1994). *Hispanics and United States film: An overview and handbook.* Tempe, AZ: Bilingual Review/Press.

Kelly, H. H. (1973). The process of causal attribution. *American Psychologist, 28,* 107–128.

Kennedy, R. J. R. (1944). Single or triple melting pot? Intermarriage trends in New Haven, 1870–1940. *American Journal of Sociology, 49,* 331–339.

Kich, G. K. (1992). The developmental process of asserting a biracial, bicultural identity. In M. P. P. Root (Ed.), *Racially mixed people in America* (pp. 304–317). Newbury Park, CA: Sage.

Kim, Y. Y. (1988). *Communication and cross–cultural adaptation.* Philadelphia: Multilingual Matters LTD.

Kim, Y. Y. (1993, May). *Synchrony and intercultural communication competence.* Paper presented at the annual meeting of the International Communication Association, Washington, DC.

Kim, Y. Y. (1995). Cross-cultural adaptation: An integrative theory. In R. L. Wiseman (Ed.), *Intercultural communication theory* (pp. 170–193). Thousand Oaks, CA: Sage.

Kim, Y. Y. (1998). Cross-cultural adaption: An integrative theory. In J. N. Martin, T. K. Nakayama, & L. A. Flores (Eds.). *Readings in cultural contexts* (pp. 295–303). Mountain View, CA: Mayfield.

King, J. C. (1981). *The biology of race.* Berkeley: University of California Press.

Kitano, H. H. L. (1991). *Race relations.* Englewood Cliffs, NJ: Prentice Hall.

Knapp, M. (1973). Dyadic relationship development: In J. Wiemann & R. Harrison (Eds.), *Nonverbal interaction* (pp. 102–118). Beverly Hills, CA: Sage.

Kouri, K. M., & Lasswell, M. (1993). Black–White marriages: Social change and intergenerational mobility. *Marriage and Family Review, 19*(3–4), 241–255.

Kramarae, C. (1981). *Women and men speaking.* Rowley, MA: Newbury.

Kreps, G. L., Frey, L., & O'Hair, D. (1991). Applied communication research: Scholarship that can make a difference. *Journal of Applied Communication Research, 19* (1, 2), 71–87.

Krupansky, J. (1995, July/August). Clips. *Out,* p. 20.

Kuhn, M. H., & McPartland, T. S. (1954). An empirical investigation of self-attitudes. *American Sociological Review, 19,* 68–76.

Laabs, J. J. (1993, December). Employees manage conflict and diversity. *Personnel Journal,* pp. 30–33.

Labov, W. (1972). *Sociolinguistics patterns.* Philadelphia: University of Pennsylvania Press.

Lacayo, R. (1995, October 9). An ugly end to it all. *Time,* pp. 30–35.

La Greca, A. M., & Lopez, N. (1998). Social anxiety among adolescents: Linkages with peer relations and friendships. *Journal of Abnormal Child Psychology, 26*(2), 83–95.

Lahiry, S. (1994). Building commitment through organizational culture. *Training and Development, 48*(4), 50–52.

Langston, D. (1995). Tired of playing monopoly? In M. L. Andersen & P. H. Collins (Eds.), *Race, class, and gender: An anthology* (pp. 100–109). Belmont, CA: Wadsworth.

Larkey, L. K., Hecht, M. L., & Martin, J. N. (1993). What's in a name?: African American ethnic identity terms and self–determination. *Journal of Language and Social Psychology, 12,* 302–317.

Lasker, G. W., & Tyzzer, R. N. (1982). *Physical anthropology.* New York: Holt.

Lawhon, T. (1997, Summer). Encouraging friendships among children. *Childhood Education, 73* (4), 228–231.

Lazerwitz, B. (1995). Jewish-Christian marriages and conversions, 1971 and 1990. *Sociology of Religion, 56,* 433–443.

LeCroy, C. (1988). Parent-adolescent intimacy: Impact on adolescent functioning. *Adolescence, 23*(89), 137–147.

Lee, S. M., & Fernandez, M. (1998). Trends in Asian American racial/ethnic intermarriage: A comparison of 1980 and 1990 census data. *Sociological Perspectives, 41*(2), 323–343.

Lee, W. S. (1993). Social scientists as ideological critics. *Western Journal of Communication, 57,* 221–232.

Leff, A., & Penn, Z. (1994, April 29). Puncturing political correctness. *USA Weekend Magazine,* p. 16.

Leigh, P. R. (1997). Segregation by gerrymander: The creation of the Lincoln Heights (Ohio) school district. *Journal of Negro Education, 66*(2), 121–136.

Leonard, R., & Locke, D. C. (1993). Communication stereotypes: Is interracial communication possible? *Journal of Black Studies, 22*(3), 332–343.

Leslie, K. B., & Orbe, M. (1997, November). *"Medical crisis" and "miracle?": A phenomenological inquiry of transplant recipient communication.* Paper presented at the annual meeting of the National Communication Association, Chicago.

Leveen, L. (1996). Only when I laugh: Textual dynamics of ethnic humor. *Melus, 21*(4), 29–55.

Levin, J., & Levin, W. C. (1980). *Ageism: Prejudice and discrimination against the elderly.* Belmont, CA: Wadsworth.

Lewis, B. (1998). Diversity training should focus on appreciating different perspectives. *InfoWorld, 20*(20), 110.

Lian, K. F. (1982). Identity in minority group relations. *Ethnic and Racial Studies, 5,* 42–52.

Lichter, S. R., Lichter, L. S., Rothman, S., & Amundson, D. (1987, July/August). Prime–time prejudice: TV's images of blacks and Hispanics. *Public Opinion,* pp. 13–16.

Lieberson, S. (1963). *Ethnic patterns in American cities.* New York: Free Press of Glencoe.

Lind, A. H. (1980). *Hawaii's people* (4th ed.). Honolulu: University Press of Hawaii.

Lopez, I. F. H. (1997). *White by law: The legal construction of race.* New York: New York University Press.

Lorde, A. (1984). *Sister outsider.* Freedom, CA: Crossing Press.

Lozano, E. (1997). The cultural experience of space and body: A reading of Latin American and Anglo American comportment in public. In A. Gonzalez, M. Houston, & V. Chen (Eds.), *Our voices: Essays in culture, ethnicity, and communication* (pp. 195–202). Los Angeles: Roxbury.

Luna, A. (1989). Gay racism. In M. S. Kimmel and M. A. Messner (Eds.), *Men's lives* (pp. 440–447). New York: Macmillan.

Lundy, B., Field, T., McBride, C., Field, T., & Largie, S. (1998). Same-sex and opposite–sex best friend interactions among high school juniors and seniors. *Adolescence, 33*(130), 279–290.

MacDonald, J. F. (1992). *Black and white TV: Afro-Americans in television since 1948*. Chicago: Nelson-Hall.

MacIntyre, P. D., & MacDonald, J. R. (1998). Public speaking anxiety: Perceived competence and audience congeniality. *Communication Education, 47*(4), 359–365.

Mackenzie, G. (1991, September 4). Fallacies of PC. *Chronicle of Higher Education*, pp. B1–2.

Maltz, D., & Borker, R. (1982). A cultural approach to male-female miscommunication. In J. J. Gumperz (Ed.), *Language and social identity* (pp. 196–216). Cambridge: Cambridge University Press.

Mandelbaum, D. G. (Ed.). (1949). *Selected writings of Edward Sapir*. Los Angeles: University of California Press.

Marable, M. (1997, March 6). What's in a name: African American or multiracial? *Black Issues in Higher Education*, p. 112.

Marrow, L. (1995, October 9). O. J. and race: Will the verdict split America? *Time*, p. 28.

Martin, J. N., Krizek, R. L., Nakayama, T. K., & Bradford, L. (1996). Exploring Whiteness: A study of self labels for White Americans. *Communication Quarterly, 44*, 125–144.

Martin, J. N., & Nakayama, T. K. (1997). *Intercultural communication in contexts*. Mountain View, CA: Mayfield.

Martindale, C. (1980). *The White press and Black America*. Westport, CT: Greenwood Press.

Martindale, C. (1997). Only in glimpses: Portrayal of America's largest minority groups by *The New York Times*, 1934-1994. In S. Biagi & M. Kem-Foxworth (Eds.), *Facing difference: Race, gender, and mass media* (pp. 89–94). Thousand Oaks, CA: Pine Forge Press.

Matsuda, M. J., Lawrence, C. R., Delgado, R., & Crenshaw, K. W. (Eds.). (1993). *Words that wound: Critical race theory, assaultive speech, and the First Amendment*. San Francisco: Westview Press.

Mayall, A., & Russell, D. E. H. (1995). Racism in pornography. In G. Dines & J. M. Humez (Eds.), *Gender, race and class in media* (pp. 287–297). Thousand Oaks, CA: Sage.

McCaa, R. (1993). Ethnic intermarriage and gender in New York City. *Journal of Interdisciplinary History, 24*(2), 207–231.

McCall, G. J., & Simmons, J. L. (1978). *Identities and interaction* (rev. ed.). New York: Free Press.

McClenahan, C., Cairns, E., Dunn, S., & Morgan, V. (1996). Intergroup friendships: Integrated and desegregated schools in northern Ireland. *Journal of Social Psychology, 136*(5), 549–558.

McCutcheon, A. L. (1988). Denominations and religious intermarriage: Trends among White Americans in the twentieth century. *Review of Religion Research, 29*, 213–227.

McGreevy, J. T. (1996). *Parish boundaries: The Catholic encounter with race in the twentieth century urban North*. Chicago: University of Chicago Press.

McIntosh, P. (1992). White privilege and male privilege. In A. L. Andersen & P. H. Collins (Eds.), *Race, class, and gender: An anthology* (pp. 65–69). Belmont, CA: Wadsworth.

McIntosh, P. (1995a). White privilege and male privilege: A personal account of coming to see correspondences through work in women's studies. In M. L. Andersen & P. H. Collins (Eds.), *Race, class, and gender: An anthology* (pp. 78–86). Belmont, CA: Wadsworth.

McIntosh, P. (1995b). White privilege: Unpacking the invisible backpack. In A. Kesselman, L. D. McNair, & N. Schneidewind (Eds.), *Women, images, and realities: A multicultural anthology.* Mountain View, CA: Mayfield.

McKay, V. C. (1997). Understanding the co-culture of the elderly. In L. A. Samovar & R. E. Porter (Eds.), *Intercultural communication: A reader* (pp. 174–182). Belmont, CA: Wadsworth.

McKissack, F., Jr. (1997). The problem with black T.V. *Progressive, 61*(2), 38–40.

McLean, S. (1998). Minority representation and portrayal in modem newsprint cartoons. In Y. R. Kamalipour & T. Carilli (Eds.), *Cultural diversity in the U.S. media* (pp. 23–38). Albany: SUNY Press.

McMahon, E. (1995). *What parish are you from? A Chicago Irish community and race relations.* Lexington: University Press of Kentucky.

McPhail, M. L. (1998). From complicity to coherence: Rereading the rhetoric of Afrocentricity. *Western Journal of Communication, 62,* 114–140.

Mead, G. H. (1934). *Mind, self, and society.* Chicago: University of Chicago Press.

Mehrabian, A. (1982). *Silent messages: Implicit communication of emotion and attitudes* (2nd ed.). Belmont, CA: Wadsworth.

Meltzer, B. N., & Petras, J. W. (1970). The Chicago and Iowa Schools of symbolic interactionism. In T. Shibutani (Ed.), *Human nature and collective behavior* (pp. 74–92). Englewood Cliffs, NJ: Prentice–Hall.

Melville, M. B. (1988). Hispanics: Race, class, or ethnicity? *Journal of Ethnic Studies, 16*(1), 67–84.

Merritt, B. (1991). Bill Cosby: TV auteur? *Journal of Popular Culture, 24*(4), 89–102.

Merton, R. K. (1941). Intermarriage and the social structure. *Psychiatry, 4,* 361–374.

Messner, M. (1989). Sports and the politics of inequality. In M. S. Kimmel & M. A. Messner (Eds.), *Men's lives* (pp. 187–190). New York: Macmillan.

Miller, K. (1999). (Eds.). *Organizational communication: Approaches and processes.* Belmont, CA: Wadsworth.

Miller, R. L., & Rotheram–Borus, M. J. (1994). Growing up biracial in the United States. In E. P. Salett & D. R. Koslow (Eds.), *Race, ethnicity and self: Identity in multicultural perspective* (pp. 143–169). Washington, DC: Multicultural Institute.

Mills, J. K., Daly, J., Longmore, A., & Kilbride, G. (1995). A note on family acceptance involving interracial friendships and romantic relationships. *Journal of Psychology, 129*(3), 349–351.

Miner, S., & Tolnay, S. (1998). Barriers to voluntary organizations membership: An examination of race and cohort differences. *Journals of Gerontology, 53B*(5), S241–S248.

Mirande, A., & Enriquez, E. (1979). *La Chicano: The Mexican American woman.* Chicago: University of Chicago Press.

Monahan, T. P. (1976). An overview of statistics on interracial marriage in the United States, with data on its extent from 1963–1970. *Journal of Marriage and the Family, 38,* 223–231.

Montagu, A. (1964). *The concept of race.* New York: Free Press of Glencoe.

Montagu, A. (1972). *Statement on race: An annotated elaboration and exposition of the four statements on race issued by the United Nations educational, scientific, and cultural organization.* New York: Oxford University Press.

Montagu, A. (1997). *Man's most dangerous myth: The fallacy of race* (6th ed.). Walnut Creek, CA: AltaMira Press.

Moody, L. (1993, December 26). Politically correct dictionary updated. *Louisville (KY) Courier-Journal*, p. A8.

Moon, D. G. (1998). Performed identities: "Passing"as an inter/cultural discourse. In J. N. Martin, T. K. Nakayama, & L. A. Flores (Eds.), *Readings in cultural contexts* (pp. 322–330). Mountain View, CA: Mayfield.

Moon, D. G., & Rolison, G. L. (1998). Communication of classism. In M. L. Hecht (Ed.), *Communicating prejudice* (pp. 122–135). Thousand Oaks, CA: Sage.

Moore, M. M. (1980). *Small voices & great trumpets: Minorities & the media.* New York: Praeger.

Moore, Q. (1993/1994). A "whole new world of diversity." *Journal of Intergroup Relations, 20*(4), 28–40.

Moran, R., & Harris, P. (Eds.). (1982). *Managing cultural synergy.* Houston, TX: Gulf.

Morganthau, T. (1995, February 13). What color is Black? *Newsweek*, pp. 63–65.

Morris, R., & Stuckey, M. E. (1998). Destroying the past to save the present: Pastoral voice and native identity. In Y. R. Kamalipour & T. Carilli (Eds.), *Cultural diversity in the U.S. media* (pp. 137–148). Albany: SUNY Press.

Morrison, T. (1991). *Playing in the dark: Whiteness and the literary imagination.* Cambridge, MA: Harvard University Press.

Munoz, C. (1989). *Youth, identity, power: The Chicano movement.* London: Verso.

Murstein, B., Merigihi, J. R., & Malloy, T. E. (1989). Physical attractiveness and exchange theory in interracial dating. *Journal of Social Psychology, 129*(3), 325–334.

Muwakkil, S. (1998). Real minority, media majority. *In These Times, 22*(15), 18–19.

Myra, H. (1994, March 7). Love in black and white. *Christianity Today*, pp. 18–19.

NAACP, AT&T work to narrow "digital divide." (1999, July 13). *Kalamazoo (MI) Gazette*, p. A9.

Nakane, C. (1984). The social system reflected in the interpersonal communication. In J. Condon & M. Saito (Eds.), *Intercultural encounters with Japan.* Tokyo: Simul Press.

Nakashima, C. (1992). Blood quantum: Native American mixed bloods. In M. P. P. Root (Ed.), *Racially mixed people in America* (pp. 162–180). Newbury Park, CA: Sage.

Nakayama, T. (1997). Dis/orienting identities. In A. Gonzalez, M. Houston, & V. Chen (Eds.), *Our voices: Essays in culture, ethnicity, and communication* (pp. 14–20). Los Angeles: Roxbury.

Nakayama, T. (1998). Communication of heterosexism. In M. L. Hecht (Ed.), *Communicating prejudice* (pp. 112–121). Thousand Oaks, CA: Sage.

Nakayama, T. K., & Martin, J. N. (Eds.). (1999). *Whiteness: The communication of social identity.* Thousand Oaks, CA: Sage.

Nance, T., & Foeman, A. K. (1993). Rethinking the basic public speaking course for African American students and other students of color. *Journal of Negro Education, 67*(4), 448–458.

Nance, T. A., & Foeman, A. K. (1998). On being biracial in the United States. In J. N. Martin, T. K. Nakayama, & L. A. Flores (Eds.), *Reading in cultural contexts* (pp. 53–61). Mountain View, CA: Mayfield.

Narine, D. (1988, March). Black TV and movie scriptwriters: The write stuff. *Ebony,* pp. 92–98.

National Council of La Raza. (1997). Don't blink: Hispanics in television entertainment. In S. Biagi & M. Kem–Foxworth (Eds.), *Facing difference: Race, gender, and mass media* (pp. 29–31). Thousand Oaks, CA: Pine Forge Press.

Nero, C. I. (1997). Black queer identity, imaginative rationality, and the language of home. In A. Gonzalez, M. Houston, & V. Chen (Eds.), *Our voices: Essays in culture, ethnicity, and communication* (pp. 61–69). Los Angeles: Roxbury.

Neuliep, J. W., & McCroskey, J. (1997a). The development of the U.S. and generalized ethnocentrism scale. *Communication Research Reports, 14*(4), 385–398.

Neuliep, J. W., & McCroskey, J. (1997b). The development of intercultural and interethnic communication apprehension scales. *Communication Research Reports, 14*(2), 145–156.

Neuliep, J. W., & Ryan, D. J. (1998). The influence of intercultural communication apprehension and socio–communicative orientation on uncertainty reduction during initial cross-cultural interaction. *Communication Quarterly, 46*(1), 88–99.

Nguyen, L. T. (1998). To date or not to date a Vietnamese: Perceptions and expectations of Vietnamese American college students. *Amerasia Journal, 24*(1), 143–169.

Noack, D. (1998, July 11). Racism or satire? Cartoon sparks outrage. *Editor & Publisher,* pp. 10–11.

No place for mankind. (1989, September 4). *Newsweek*, p. 17.

Norment, L. (1994, November). Black men, white women: What's behind the new furor? *Ebony*, pp. 44–50.

Nuessel, F. (1982). The language of ageism. *The Gerontologist, 22*, 273–276.

Nwanko, R. L. (1979). Intercultural communication: A critical review. *Quarterly Journal of Speech, 65*, 324–346.

Oguntoyinbo, L. (1997, September 14). The way we live: Black women, White men: More African-American women are marrying outside their race. *Detroit Free Press*, pp. 1,4, sec F.

Omi, M. (1989). In living color: Race and American culture. In I. Angus & S. Jhally (Eds.) *Cultural politics in contemporary America* (pp. 111–122). New York: Oxford University Press.

Orbe, M. (1994). "Remember, it's always Whites' ball": Descriptions of American American male communication. *Communication Quarterly, 42*(3), 287–300.

Orbe, M. (1995a). African American communication research: Toward a deeper understanding of interethnic communication. *Western Journal of Communication, 59*(1), 61–78.

Orbe, M. (1995b). Intergroup relations in the classroom: Strategies for cultivating a sense of true community. *Journal of Intergroup Relations, 22*, 28–38.

Orbe, M. (1996). Laying the foundation for co–cultural communication theory: An inductive approach to studying "non–dominant"communication strategies and the factors that influence them. *Communication Studies, 47*, 157–176.

Orbe, M. (1997). A co-cultural communication approach to intergroup relations. *Journal of Intergroup Relations, 24*, 36–49.

Orbe, M. (1998a). Constructions of reality on MTV's "The Real World": An analysis of the restrictive coding of Black masculinity. *Southern Communication Journal, 64*, 32–47.

Orbe, M. (1998b). *Constructing co-cultural theory: An explication of culture, power, and communication*. Thousand Oaks, CA: Sage.

Orbe, M. (1998c). From the standpoint(s) of traditionally muted groups: Explicating a co–cultural communication theoretical model. *Communication Theory, 8,* 1–26.

Orbe, M. (1998d). An outsider within perspective to organizational communication: Explicating the communicative practices of co–cultural group members. *Management Communication Quarterly, 12,* 230–279.

Orbe, M. (1998e, November). *African Americans in corporate America: Everyday lived experiences as points of negotiation.* Paper presented at the annual meeting of the National Communication Association, New York.

Orbe, M. (1999). Communicating about "race" in interracial families. In T. Socha & R. Diggs (Eds.), *Communication, race, and family: Exploring communication in black, white, and biracial families* (pp. 167–180). Mahwah, NJ: Erlbaum.

Orbe, M., Drummond, D. K., & Camara, S. K. (1998, November). *Black feminist thought, Black feminist talk.* Paper presented at the annual meeting of the National Communication Association, New York.

Orbe, M., & Knox, R. J. (1994, September). *Building community among diverse peoples: Strategies in the classroom and larger global community.* Paper presented at the annual Enhancing Minority Attainment Conference, Kokomo, IN.

Orbe, M., Seymour, R., & Kang, M. E. (1998). Ethnic humor and ingroup/outgroup positioning: Explicating viewer perceptions of *All-American Girl.* In Y. R. Kamalipour & T. Carilli (Eds.), *Cultural diversity in the U.S. media* (pp. 125–136). Albany: SUNY Press.

Owen, M. (1998, August 14). A desegregation success story in the making in Louisiana. *Chronicle of Higher Education,* pp. A27–A28.

Pacheco, G. K. (1990). On native Hawaiians: Lost in the shuffle? *Focus, 4,* 6–7.

Padden, C., & Humphries, T. (1988). *Deaf in America: Voices from a culture.* Cambridge, MA: Harvard University Press.

Page, C. (1994, January 5). Uneasy journey to political correctness. *Louisville (KY) Courier–Journal,* p. A19.

Pagnini, D.L., and Morgan, S.P. (1990). Intermarriage and social distance among U.S. immigrants at the turn of the century. *American Journal of Sociology, 96,* 405–432.

Palmer, P. J. (1993). *To know as we are known: Education as a spiritual journey.* San Francisco, CA: Harper.

Palmore, E. B. (1990). *Ageism: Negative and positive.* New York: Springer.

Parham, T. A., & Helms, J. E. (1985). Relation of racial identity attitudes to self–actualization and affective states in Black students. *Journal of Counseling Psychology, 32,* 431–440.

Parham, T. A., & Williams, P. T. (1993). The relationship of demographic and background factors to racial identity attitudes. *Journal of Black Psychology, 19,* 17–24.

Parrillo, V. N. (1996). *Diversity in America.* Thousand Oaks, CA: Pine Forge Press.

Pascoe, P. (1996). Miscegenation law, court cases, and ideologies of "race" in twentieth–century America. *Journal of American History, 83*(10), 44–69.

Paset, P. S., & Taylor, R. (1991). Black and white women's attitudes toward interracial marriage. *Psychological Reports, 69,* 753–754.

Patterson, O. (1995, November 6). The paradox of integration. *The New Republic,* pp. 24–27.

Patton, P. L. (1998). The gangstas in our mids. *Urban Review, 30*(1), 49–76.

Pearlman, J. (1997). Multiracial, intermarriage, ethnicity. *Society, 34*(60), 20–24.

Pearson, J. C., & Davilla, R. A. (1993). The gender construct. In L.P. Arliess & D. J. Borisoff (Eds.), *Women and men communicating: Challenges and changes* (pp. 1–14). New York: Harcourt Brace.

Peart, K. N. (1994, May 6). Where do you stand: Race relations. *Scholastic Update*, pp. 6–9.

Peck, M. S. (1987). *The different drum: Community making and peace.* New York: Simon & Schuster.

Peck, M. S. (1992). The true meaning of community. In W. B. Gudykunst & Y. Y. Kim (Eds.), *Readings in communicating with strangers* (pp. 435–444). New York: McGraw-Hill.

Pennington, D. L. (1979). Black–white communication: An assessment of research. In M. K. Asante, E. Newark, & C. A. Blake (Eds.), *Handbook of intercultural communication* (pp. 383–402). Beverly Hills, CA: Sage.

Perkins, K. R. (1996). The influence of television images on black females' self-perceptions of physical attractiveness. *Journal of Black Psychology, 22*(4), 453–469.

Peterson, M. S. (1998). Personnel interviewers' perceptions of the importance and adequacy of applicants' communication skills. *Communication Education, 46*(4), 287–291.

Petrie, P. (1991, August). Afrocentrism in a multicultural democracy. *American Visions*, pp. 20–26.

Petronio, S., Ellemers, N., Giles, H., & Gallois, C. (1998). (Mis)communicating across boundaries: Interpersonal and intergroup considerations. *Communication Research, 25*(6), 571–595.

Petrozzello, D. (1998, October 26). Civil rights and more: "Any Day Now." *Broadcasting & Cable*, p. 52.

Pettigrew, T. F. (1998). Intergroup contact theory. *Annual Review of Psychology, 49*, 65–76.

Pettigrew, T. F., Fredrickson, G. M., Knoble, D. T., Glazer, N., & Ueda, R. (1982). *Prejudice: Dimensions of ethnicity.* Massachusetts: Belknap Press of Harvard University Press.

Philipsen, G. (1975). Speaking "like a man" in Teamsterville: Culture patterns of role enactment in an urban neighborhood. *Quarterly Journal of Speech, 61*, 13–22.

Philipsen, G. (1976). Places for speaking in Teamsterville. *Quarterly Journal of Speech, 62*, 15–25.

Philipsen, G. (1992). *Speaking culturally: Explorations in social communication.* Albany: SUNY Press.

Philipsen, G. (1996). A theory of speech codes. In G. Philipsen and T. Albrecht (Eds.), *Developing communication theory* (pp. 119–156). Albany: SUNY Press.

Philipsen, G. (1997). A theory of speech codes. In G. Philipsen & T. Albrecht (Eds.), *Developing communication theory* (pp. 119–156). Albany: SUNY Press.

Phillips, N. (1993). Afrocentricity "purposeful." *Black Issues in Higher Education, 9*, 10.

Phinney, J. S. (1993). A three-stage model of ethnic identity development in adolescence. In M. E. Bernal & G. P. Knight (Eds.), *Ethnic identity: Formation and transmission among Hispanics and other immigrants* (pp. 61–79). Albany: SUNY Press.

Phinney, J. S., & Rotherham, J. J. (Eds.). (1987). *Children's ethnic socialization: Pluralism and development.* Newbury Park, CA: Sage.

Pino, F. (1980). The "great" cultural tradition of Hispanics. *Agenda, 10*(3), 38–42.

Polls find minorities dissatisfied with media. (1994, July 26). *Louisville (KY) Courier-Journal*, p. C4.

Ponterotto, J. G. (1989). Expanding directions for racial identity research. *The Counseling Psychologist, 17*, 264–272.

Ponterotto, J. G., & Pedersen, P. B. (1993). *Preventing prejudice: A guide for counselors and educators*. Newbury Park, CA: Sage.

Pope-Davis, D. H., & Ottavi, T. M. (1994). The relationship between racism and racial identity among White Americans: A replication and extension. *Journal of Counseling and Development, 72*, 293–297.

Porterfield, E. (1982). Black American intermarriage in the United States. *Marriage and the Family Review, 5*, 14–34.

Poston, W. S. C. (1990). The biracial identity development model: A needed addition. *Journal of Counseling and Development, 69*, 152–155.

Poussaint, A. (1988, October). The Huxtables: Fact or fantasy? *Ebony*, pp. 72–74.

Powell, D. (1996). Group communication. *Communication of the ACM, 39*(4), 50–53.

Powell, R., & Collier, M. J. 1990). Public speaking instruction and cultural bias. *American Behavioral Scientist, 34*(2), 240–250.

Power, J. G., Murphy, S., & Coover, G. (1996). Priming prejudice: How stereotypes and counter–stereotypes influence attribution of responsibility and credibility among ingroups and outgroups. *Human Communication Research, 23*(1), 36–58.

Powers, D. A., & Ellison, C. (1995). Interracial contact and black racial attitudes: The contact hypothesis and selectivity bias. *Social Forces, 74*(1), 205–226.

Praeger, R. (1995). A world worth living in. In M. L. Andersen & P. H. Collins (Eds.), *Race, class, and gender: An anthology* (pp. 523–531). Belmont, CA: Wadsworth.

Pratt, S. B. (1998). Razzing: Ritualized uses of humor as a form of identification among American Indians. In D. V. Tanno & A. Gonzalez (Eds.), *Communication and identity across cultures* (pp. 80–99). Thousand Oaks, CA: Sage.

Price, D. (1998). Civil rites: Arguments against same-sex marriage mirror those that kept the races apart. www.ftm.org/loving/civil-rites.html.

Provine, W. B. (1973). Geneticists and the biology of race crossing. *Science, 182*, 790–796.

Qian, Z. (1998). Changes in assortative mating: The impact of age and education, 1970–1990. *Demography, 35*(3), 279–292.

Radford, A. J. (1987). Ageism: Public prejudice and private preconceptions. *Australian Journal on Ageing, 6*, 4–9.

Ramsey, S. (1981). The kinesics of femininity in Japanese women. *Language Sciences, 3*(11), 104–123.

Randolph, L. B. (1994, May). Life after the Cosby show: Activist-actor celebrates 30 years of wedded bliss, continues fight against stereotypes on TV. *Ebony*, pp. 100–104.

Raspberry, W. (1989, January 4). When "Black" becomes "African American." *Washington Post*, p. A19.

Raspberry, W. (1999, March 2). Is racism getting better or worse? *Kalamazoo (MI) Gazette*, p. A8.

Reardon, K . K. (1996). The crossroads of organizational communication: Definition or dichotomy. *Management Communication Quarterly, 10*(1), 106–111.

Remar, P. (1991, November). *Should college and universities prohibit 'hate speech' on campus?* Paper presented at the annual meeting of the Speech Communication Association, Atlanta, GA.

Report: Online gap grows for blacks. (1999, July 8). *Kalamazoo (MI) Gazette*, p. A14.

Rhea, J. T. (1997). *Race pride and the American identity*. Cambridge, MA: Harvard University Press.

Ribeau, S. A. (1997). How I came to know in self-realization there is truth. In A. Gonzalez, M. Houston, & V. Chen (Eds.), *Our voices: Essays in culture, ethnicity, and communication* (pp. 21–27). Los Angeles: Roxbury.

Ribeau, S. A., Baldwin, J. R., & Hecht, M. L. (1997). An African-American communication perspective. In L. A. Samovar & R. E. Porter (Eds.), *Intercultural communication: A reader* (pp. 147–154). Belmont, CA: Wadsworth.

Rich, A. (1974). *Interracial communication*. New York: Harper & Row.

Rich, A. L., & Ogawa, D. M. (1972). Intercultural and interracial communication: An analytical approach. In L. A. Samovar & R. E. Porter (Eds.), *Intercultural communication: A reader* (pp. 22–29). Belmont, CA: Wadsworth.

Rios, D. I. (1997). Mexican American cultural experiences with mass-mediated communication. In A. Gonzalez, M. Houston, & V. Chen (Eds.), *Our voices: Essays in culture, ethnicity, and communication* (pp. 105–112). Los Angeles: Roxbury.

Roberts, G., & Orbe, M. (1996, May). *'Creating that safe place': Descriptions of intergenerational gay male communication*. Paper presented at the annual meeting of the International Communication Association, Chicago.

Rodriguez, D. (1998). Diversity training brings staff closer. *Education Digest, 64*(1), 28–31.

Roediger, D. R. (1994). *Towards the abolition of whiteness*. New York: Verso.

Romano, L., & Trescott, J. (1992, February). Love in black and white. *Redbook*, pp. 88–94.

Root, M. P. P. (1992). Within, between, and beyond race. In M. P. P. Root (Ed.), *Racially mixed people in America* (pp. 3–11). Newbury Park, CA: Sage.

Root, M. P. P. (Ed.). (1996). *The multiracial experience: Racial borders as the new frontier*. Thousand Oaks, CA: Sage.

Rosenthal, D. A. (1987). Ethnic identity development in adolescents. In J. S. Phinney & M. J. Rotheram (Eds.), *Children's ethnic socialization: Pluralism and development* (pp. 156–179). Newbury Park, CA: Sage.

Ross, C. (1996, March). Blacks drawn to indy TV, cable. *Advertising Age*, pp. 4, 8.

Rothenberg, P. S. (1992). *Race, class, and gender in the United States: An integrated study*. New York: St. Martin's Press.

Rowan, K. E. (1995). A new pedagogy for explanatory public speaking: Why arrangement should not substitute for invention. *Communication Education, 44*(3), 236–250.

Rubin, D., & Hampton, S. (1998). National performance standards for oral communication K–12: New standards and speaking/listening/viewing. *Communication Education, 47*(2), 183–193.

Ryan, E. B. (1979). Why do low-prestige language varieties persist? In H. Giles & R. St. Clair (Eds.), *Language and social psychology* (pp. 145–175). Oxford: Blackwell.

Sachdev, I., & Bourhis, R. Y. (1990). Language and social identification. In D. Abrams & M. A. Hogg (Eds.), *Social identity theory: Constructive and critical advances* (pp. 211–229). New York: Harvester Wheatsheaf.

Saenz, R., Sean-Shong, H., Aguirre, B. E., & Anderson, R. N. (1995). Persistence and change in Asian identity among children of intermarried couples. *Sociological Perspectives, 38*(2), 175–195.

Sailer, S. (1997). Is love colorblind? *National Review, 49*(13), 30–33.

Samovar, L., & Mills, J. (1998). *Oral communication: Speaking across cultures* (10th ed.). San Francisco: McGraw-Hill.

Sarup, M. (1996). *Identity, culture and the postmodern world*. Athens: University of Georgia Press.

Schaefer, R. T. (1993). *Racial and ethnic groups*. New York: HarperCollins.

Schein, E. H. (1985). *Organizational culture and leadership*. San Francisco: Jossey-Bass.

Schmid, R. E. (1997, July 9). "Multiracial" category for census rejected. *Louisville (KY) Courier-Journal*, p. A5.

Schoen R., & Wooldredge, J. (1989). Marriage choices in North Carolina and Virginia, 1969–71 and 1979–81. *Journal of Marriage and the Family, 51*, 465–481.

Schupack, A. (1996, October 30). Students debate interracial dating. *Brown Daily Herald*. www.theherald.org/issues/103096/forum.f.html.

Scott, K. D. (1996, June). *Style switching as ideological position in Black women's talk*. Paper presented at the annual meeting of the Speech Communication Association's Black Caucus/African American Communication and Culture Division Summer Conference, Frankfort, KY.

Sebring, D. L. (1985). Considerations in counseling interracial children. *The Personnel and Guidance Journal, 13*, 3–9.

Seeger, M. (1992). Responsibility in organizational communication: Individual, organizational, and environmental accounts. In J. Jaska (Ed.), Proceedings of the 1992 National Communication Ethics Conference (pp. 172–183). Annandale, VA: Speech Communication Association.

Seiter, E. (1990). Different children, different dreams: Racial representation in advertising. *Journal of Communication Inquiry, 14*, 31–47.

Seymour, H. N., & Seymour, C. M. (1979). The symbolism of Ebonics: I'd rather switch than fight. *Journal of Black Studies, 9*, 397–410.

Shannon, V. (1997). Networking: When race meets life on–line, there's a disconnection. In S. Biagi & M. Kem–Foxworth (Eds.), *Facing difference: Race, gender, and mass media* (pp. 258–260). Thousand Oaks, CA: Pine Forge Press.

Shaver, L. D. (1998). The cultural deprivation of an Oklahoma Cherokee family. In D. V. Tanno & A. Gonzalez (Eds.), *Communication and identity across cultures* (pp. 100–121). Thousand Oaks, CA: Sage.

Shea, C. (1997, May 2). Intermarriage rates found to be on the rise. *Chronicle of Higher Education*, p. A14.

Shepard, P. (1999, July 13). NAACP to fight TV's "whitewash," too many guns. *Kalamazoo (MI) Gazette*, p. D4.

Shibutani, T., & Kwan, K. (1965). *Ethnic stratification: A comparative approach*. New York: Macmillan.

Shim, J. C. (1997). The importance of ethnic newspapers to U.S. newcomers. In S. Biagi & M. Kem–Foxworth (Eds.), *Facing difference: Race, gender, and mass media* (pp. 250–255). Thousand Oaks, CA: Pine Forge Press.

Shotter, J., & Gergen, K. J. (Eds.). (1989). *Tests of identity*. London: Sage.

Shreeve, J. (1994, November). Terms of estrangement. *Discover*, pp. 57–63.

Shuter, R. (1993). On third-culture building. *Communication Yearbook, 16*, 407–428.

Siegel, G. (1995, May). Familia values. *Los Angeles Times*, p. 21.

Sigelman, L., Bledsoe, T., & Combs, M. (1996). Making contact? Black-white social interaction in an urban setting. *American Journal of Sociology, 101*(5), 1306–1332.

Sigelman, L., & Welch, S. (1993). The contact hypothesis revisited: Black-White interaction and positive racial attitudes. *Social Forces, 71*(3), 781–795.

Sing, B. (1989). *Asian Pacific Americans: A handbook on how to cover and portray our nation's fastest growing minority group*. Los Angeles: National Conference of Christians and Jews.

Smalls, J. (1998). Visualizing race: A lifelong process and training. *Art Journal, 57*(3), 2–3.

Smith, A. (1973). *Transracial communication*. Englewood Cliffs, NJ: Prentice-Hall.

Smith, B. (1983). Homophobia: Why bring it up? *Interracial Books for Children Bulletin, 14*, 112–113.

Smith, C. E. (1966). Negro-White intermarriage: Forbidden sexual union. *Journal of Sex Research, 2*, 169–177.

Smith, D. E. (1987). *The everyday world as problematic: A feminist sociology of knowledge*. Boston: Northeastern University Press.

Smith, D. E. (1992). Sociology from women's experiences: A reaffirmation. *Sociological Theory, 10*, 1–12.

Smith, A. & Ahuja, S. (1999). *Intergroup relations in the United States: Seven promising practices*. New York: The National Conference for Community and Justice.

Smitherman, G. (1995). Students' right to their own language: A retrospective. *English Journal, 84*(1), 21–27.

Snipp, C. M. (1986). Who are the American Indians: Some perils and pitfalls for data for race and ethnicity. *Population Research and Policy Review, 5*, 237–252.

Snowden, F. (1970). *Blacks in antiquity: Ethiopians in Greco-Roman experience*. Cambridge, MA: Belknap Press of Harvard University Press.

Sodowsky, R. G., Kwan, K. L. K., & Pannu, R. (1995). Ethnic identity of Asians in the United States. In J. Ponterotto, J. M. Casas, L. A. Suzuki, & C. M. Alexander (Eds.), *Handbook of multicultural counseling* (pp. 123–154). Thousand Oaks, CA: Sage.

Solomon, M. R., Ashmore, R. D., & Longo, L. C. (1992). The beauty match-up hypothesis: Congruence between types of beauty and product images in advertising. *Journal of Advertising, 21*(4), 23–34.

Spaights, E., & Dixon, H. (1984). Socio-psychological dynamics in pathological Black-White romantic alliances. *Journal of Instructional Psychology, 11*(3), 133–138.

Spickard, P.R. (1989). *Mixed blood: Intermarriage and ethnic identity in twentieth-century America*. Madison: University of Wisconsin Press.

Spickard, P. R. (1992). The illogic of American racial categories. In M. P. P. Root (Ed.), *Racially mixed people in America* (pp. 12–23). Newbury Park, CA: Sage.

Spielberg, B. J. (1980). The "little" cultural tradition of Hispanics. *Agenda, 10*(3), 30–36.

Spradlin, A. L. (1995, November). *The price of "passing": A lesbian perspective on authenticity in organizations*. Paper presented at the annual meeting of the Speech Communication Association, San Antonio, TX.

Stanton, M. (1971). A remnant Indian community: The Houma of southern Louisiana. In J. K. Moorland (Ed.), *The not so solid South: Anthropological studies in a regional subculture* (pp. 82–92). Athens: University of Georgia Press.

Starosta, W. J., & Olorunnisola, A. A. (1993, November). *A meta-model for third culture development*. Paper presented at the annual meeting of the International Communication Association, Sydney, Australia.

Stateline: Not color blind yet (1996). *State Legislatures, 22*(3), 13.

Stein, M. L. (1997). Racial stereotyping and the media. In S. Biagi & M. Kern-Foxworth (Eds.), *Facing difference: Race, gender, and mass media* (pp. 125–128). Thousand Oaks, CA: Pine Forge Press.

Stevens, G., Owens, D., & Schaefer, E. C. (1990). Education and attractiveness in marriage choices. *Social Psychology Quarterly, 53*, 62–70.

St. Jean, Y. (1998). Let people speak for themselves: Interracial unions and the general social survey. *Journal of Black Studies, 28*(3), 398–414.

Stone, E. (1996). Family ground rules. In K. M. Galvin & P. Cooper (Eds.), *Making connections* (pp. 59–67). Los Angeles, CA: Roxbury.

Stonequist, E. V. (1937). *The marginal man: A study in personality and culture conflict*. New York: Russell & Russell.

Stowe, D. W. (1996, September/October). Uncolored people: The rise of Whiteness studies. *Lingua Franca*, pp. 68–72, 74–77.

Stroman, C. A. (1991). Television's role in the socialization of African American children and adolescents. *Journal of Negro Education, 60*, 314–327.

Stryker, S., & Statham, A. (1984). Symbolic interaction and role theory. In G. Lindzey & E. Aronson (Eds.), *Handbook of social psychology* (pp. 311–378). Reading, MA: Addison-Wesley.

Sung, B. L. (1990). Chinese American intermarriage. *Journal of Comparative Family Studies, 21*(3), 337–352.

Swigonski, M. E. (1994). The logic of feminist standpoint theory for social work research. *Social Work, 39*(4), 387–393.

Taifa, N. (1996). Racism in the criminal justice system. *Christian Social Action, 9*(6), 15–16, 25.

Tajfel, H. (1974). Social identity and intergroup behavior. *Social Science Information, 13*, 65–93.

Tajfel, H. (1978). Social categorization, social identity, and social comparison. In H. Tajfel (Ed.), *Differentiation between social groups* (pp. 61–76). London: Academic Press.

Tajfel, H., & Turner, J. C. (1979). An integrative theory of intergroup conflict. In W. Austin & S. Worchel (Eds.). *The social psychology of intergroup relations* (pp. 33–47). Pacific Grove, CA: Brooks/Cole.

Tajfel, H. (1981). *Human categories and social groups*. Cambridge: Cambridge University Press.

Tan, A., Fujioka, Y., & Lucht, N. (1997). Native American stereotypes, TV portrayals, and personal contact. *Journalism and Mass Communication Quarterly, 74*, 265–284.

Tannen, D. (1990). *You just don't understand: Women and men in conversation*. New York: Morrow.

Tanno, D. V. (1997). Names, narratives, and the evolution of ethnic identity. In A. Gonzalez, M. Houston, & V. Chen (Eds.), *Our voices: Essays in culture, ethnicity, and communication* (pp. 28–34). Los Angeles: Roxbury.

Tanno, D. V., & Gonzalez, A. (1998). Sites of identity in communication and culture. In D. V. Tanno & A. Gonzalez (Eds.), *Communication and identity across cultures* (pp. 3–10). Thousand Oaks, CA: Sage.

Tarricone, S. (1996, February 9). "Wall of shame" provokes look at interracial dating. *Brown Daily Herald*. www.netspace.org/herald/issues/020996/dating.f.html.

Tatum, B. D. (1992). Talking about race, learning about racism: The application of racial identity development theory in the classroom. *Harvard Educational Review, 62*(1), 1–24.

Taylor, C. (1992). *Multiculturalism and the politics of recognition.* Princeton, NJ: Princeton University Press.

Taylor, C. R., Lee, J. Y., & Stern, B. (1995). Portrayals of African, Hispanic, and Asian Americans in magazine advertising. *American Behavioral Scientist, 38*(4), 608–622.

Taylor, C. R., & Stern, B. (1997). Asian-Americans: Television advertising and the "model minority" stereotype, *Journal of Advertising, 26*(2), 47–62.

Taylor, F. W. (1911). *The principles of scientific management.* New York: Harper Row.

Taylor, J. (1991, January 21). Thought police on campus. *Reader's Digest,* pp. 99–104.

Thibaut, J. W., & Kelley, H. H. (1959). *The social psychology of groups.* New York: Wiley.

Thomas, D. A. (1993, July). Black, white, or other? *Essence,* p. 118.

Todd, J., McKinney, J. L., Harris, R., Chadderton, R., & Small, L. (1992). Attitudes toward interracial dating: Effects of age, sex, and race. *Journal of Multicultural Counseling and Development, 20,* 202–208.

Tolbert, E. J. (1989). General introduction. In C. E. Jackson & E. J. Tolbert (Eds.), *Race and culture in America: Readings in racial and ethnic relations* (pp. 1–21). Edina, MN: Burgess.

Toynbee, A. J. (1939). *A study of history* (Vol. 1). London: Oxford University Press.

Tracy, M. (1997, October 28). Forum examines interracial dating. *Brown Daily Herald.* www.theherald.org/issues/102897/dating.f.html.

Tucker, L. R. (1997). Was the revolution televised?: Professional criticism about "The Cosby Show" and the essentialization of black cultural expression. *Journal of Broadcasting and Electronic Media, 41*(1), 90–108.

Tucker, M. B., & Mitchell-Kernan, C. (1995). Social structural and psychological correlates of interethnic dating. *Journal of Social and Personal Relationships, 12*(3), 341–361.

Turner, J. C. (1987). *Rediscovering the social group.* London: Basil Blackwell.

Turner, J. H., Singleton, R., & Musick, D. (1984). *Oppression: A sociohistory of Black-White relations in America.* Chicago: Nelson-Hall.

Turner, R. (1990, June). Interracial couples in the South. *Ebony,* pp. 41–49.

TV roles for minorities declining. (1999, May 11). *Kalamazoo (MI) Gazette,* p. D7.

U.S. Bureau of the Census (1993). Washington, DC: Government Printing Office.

U.S. Office of Management and Budget. (1997, October 30). Revisions to the standards for the classification of federal data on race and ethnicity. *Federal Register,* pp. 58782–58790.

Uunk, W. (1996). *Who marries whom? The role of social origins, education and high culture in mate selection of industrial societies during the twentieth century.* Unpublished doctoral dissertation. Nijmegen University, Netherlands.

Valdivia, A. N. (1998). Big hair and bigger hoops: Rosie Perez goes to Hollywood. In J. N. Martin, T. K. Nakayama, & L. A. Flores (Eds.), *Readings in cultural contexts* (pp. 243–249). Mountain View, CA: Mayfield.

Valentine, G. (1995, Spring). Shades of gray: The conundrum of color categories. *Teaching Tolerance*, p. 47.

Van Buren, H. J., III (1997). Ending the culture of corporate discrimination. *Business & Society Review, 98*, 20–23.

Van den Berghe, P. L. (1960). Hypergamy, hypergenation and miscegenation. *Human Relations, 13*, 83–91.

van Maanen, M. (1990). *Researching lived experience: Human science for action sensitive pedagogy*. Ontario, Canada: SUNY Press.

Vargas, L. (1996). *When the "other" is the teacher: Teaching as a transcultural practice within systems of inequality*. Paper presented at the Eastern Communication Association Conference, New York.

Vox pop. (1994, April 4). *Time*, p. 12.

Waldron, V.R., & Di Mare, L. (1998). Gender as a culturally determined construct: Communication styles in Japan and the United States. In D. J. Canary & K. Dindia (Eds.). *Sex differences and similarities in communication: Critical essays and empirical investigations of sex and gender in interaction* (pp. 179–202). Mahwah; NJ: Erlbaum.

Wander, P.C., Martin, J. N., & Nakayama, T. (1999). Whiteness and beyond: Sociohistorical foundations of Whiteness and contemporary challenges. In T. K. Nakaywna & J. N. Martin (Eds.), *Whiteness: The communication of social identity* (pp. 13–26). Thousand Oaks, CA: Sage.

Wardle, F. (1987, January). Are you sensitive to interracial children's special identity needs? *Young Children*, pp. 53–59.

Weber, M. (1947). *The theory of social and economic organization* (A. M. Henderson & T. Parsons, Trans.). New York: Oxford University Press.

Weedon, C. (1987). *Feminist practice and poststructuralist theory*. New York: Basil Blackwell.

Wei, W. (1993). *The Asian American movement*. Philadelphia: Temple University Press.

Weick, K. (1979). *The social psychology of organizing*. New York: Random House.

Weinberger, A. D. (1966). Interracial intimacy. *Journal of Sex Research, 2*, 157–168.

Wells, L., Jr. (1998) Consulting to Black-White relations in predominantly White organizations. *Journal of Applied Behavioral Science, 34*(4), 392–396.

West, C. (1993). *Race matters*. Boston: Beacon Press.

West, C. (1982). *Prophecy deliverance: An Afro-American revolutionary Christianity*. Philadelphia: Westminster Press.

Weston, M. A. (1992, August). *Native Americans in the news: Symbol, stereotype, or substance?* Paper presented at the annual meeting of the Association for Education in Journalism and Mass Communication, Montreal, Canada.

Whelan, S. A., Murphy, D., Tsumura, E., & Kline, S. F. (1998). Member perceptions of internal group dynamics and productivity. *Small Group Research, 29*(31), 371–393.

Whetmore, E. (1998). *Mediamerica, mediaworld: Form, content, and consequence of mass communication* (5th ed.). Belmont, CA: Wadsworth.

Whetstone, M. L. (1996, October). The '96 TV season: Cosby is back, but Black oriented shows decline. *Ebony*, pp. 54–58.

Why interracial marriages are increasing. (1996, September 15). *Jet Magazine,* pp. 12–15.

Why more Black women are dating White men. (1997, October 20). *Jet Magazine,* pp. 12–16.

Wilkinson, D. M. (1996). Power beyond the remote control. *Black Enterprise, 27*(5), 75–82.

Williams, A., & Giles, H. (1998). Communication of ageism. In M. L. Hecht (Ed.), *Communicating prejudice* (pp. 136–162). Thousand Oaks, CA: Sage.

Wilson, C. C., & Gutierrez, F. (1985). *Minorities and media: Diversity and the end of mass communication.* Beverly Hills, CA: Sage.

Wilson, D., & Lavelle, S. (1990). Interracial friendship in a Zimbabwean primary school. *Journal of Social Psychology, 130*(1), 111–113.

Wilson, M., & Russell, K. (1996). *Divided sisters: Bridging the gap between Black women and White women.* New York: Anchor.

Wilson, T. P. (1992). Blood quantum: Native American mixed bloods. In M. P. P. Root (Ed.), *Racially mixed people in America* (pp. 108–125). Newbury Park, CA: Sage.

Winker, K. J. (1994, May 11). The significance of race. *Chronicle of Higher Education,* pp. A10–A11.

Winn, P. (1995). *Americas: The changing face of Latin America and the Caribbean.* New York: Pantheon.

Woman who changed laws that prevented mixed marriages tells what it was like then. (1992, November 9). *Jet Magazine,* pp. 12–15.

Wong (Lau), K. (1998). Migration across generations: Whose identity is authentic? In J. N. Martin, T. K. Nakayama, & L. A. Flores (Eds.), *Reading in cultural contexts* (pp. 127–134). Mountain View, CA: Mayfield.

Wong, P., Manvi, M., & Wong, T. H. (1995). Asiacentrism and Asian American Studies? *Amerasia Journal, 12,* 137–147.

Wong, W. (1997). Covering the invisible "model minority." In S. Biagi & M. Kern-Foxworth (Eds.), *Facing difference: Race, gender, and mass media* (pp. 97–101). Thousand Oaks, CA: Pine Forge Press.

Woods, J. D. (1993). *The corporate closet: The professional lives of gay men in America.* New York: Free Press.

Wood, J. T. (1992). Gender and moral voice: Moving from women's nature to standpoint epistemology. *Women's Studies in Communication, 15*(1), 1–24.

Wood, J. T. (1993). Diversity and commonality: Sustaining tension in communication courses. *Western Journal of Communication, 57,* 367–380.

Wood, J. T. (Ed.). (1996). *Gendered relationships.* Mountain View, CA: Mayfield.

Wood, J. T. (1997b). *Communication theories in action: An introduction.* Belmont, CA: Wadsworth.

Wood, J. T. (1997b). Gender, communication, and culture. In L. A. Samovar & R. E. Porter (Eds.), *Intercultural communication: A reader* (pp. 164–173). Belmont, CA: Wadsworth.

Wood, J. T., & Dindia, K. (1998). What's the difference? A dialogue about differences and similarities between women and men. In D. J. Canary & K. Dindia (Eds.), *Sex differences and similarities in communication: Critical essays and empirical investigations of sex and gender in interaction.* (pp. 19–40). Mahwah, NJ: Erlbaum.

Woodward, K. L. (1993, June 12). The rites of Americans. *Newsweek*, pp. 80–82.

Woodyard, J. L. (1995). Locating Asante: Making use of the Afrocentric idea. In D. Ziegler (Ed.), *Molefi Kete Asante and Afrocentricity: In praise and criticism* (pp. 27–43). Nashville: James C. Winston.

Wright, L. (1994, July 25). One drop of blood. *The New Yorker*, pp. 46–55.

Xie, Y., & Goyette, K. (1997). The racial identification of biracial children with one Asian parent: Evidence from the 1990 census. *Social Forces, 76*(2), 547–571.

Yang, J. (1994, October 4). Anything but the girl. *Village Voice*, p. 47.

Yep, G. A. (1998). Navigating the multicultural identity landscape. In J. N. Martin, T. K. Nakayama, & L. A. Flores (Eds.), *Readings in cultural contexts* (pp. 79–84). Mountain View, CA: Mayfield.

Zaharna, R. (1989). Self–shock: The double–binding challenges of identity. *International Journal of Intercultural Relations, 13*(4), 501–525.

Zarefsky, D. (1998). *Public speaking: Strategies for success* (2nd ed.). Boston: Allyn & Bacon.

Zinsmeister, K. (1998). When black and white turn gray. *American Enterprise, 9*(6), 4–7.

Zook, K. B. (1995, January 17). Warner brothas. *Village Voice*, pp. 36–37.

Author Index

Subject Index